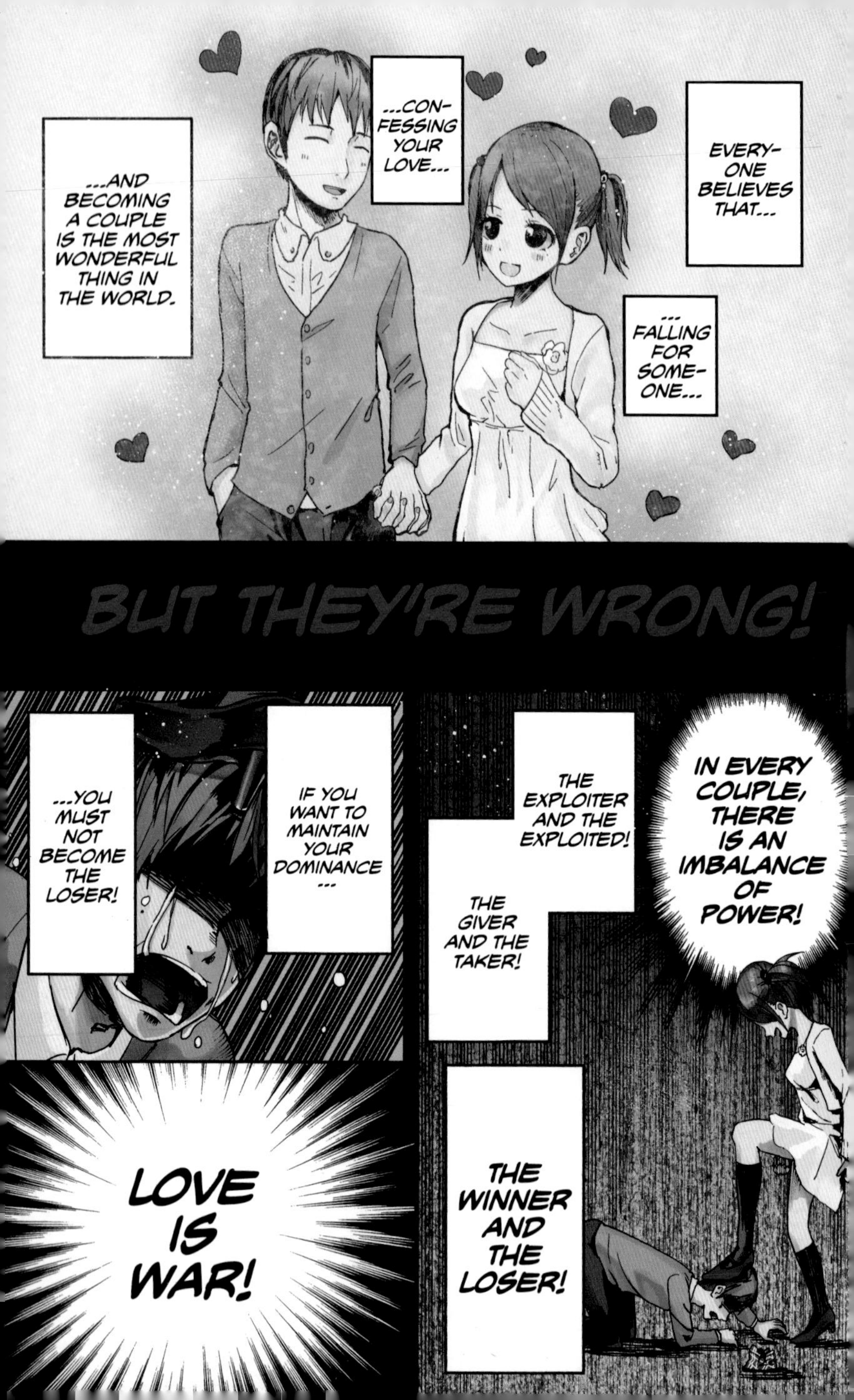
EVERYONE BELIEVES THAT...
...FALLING FOR SOMEONE...
...CONFESSING YOUR LOVE...
...AND BECOMING A COUPLE IS THE MOST WONDERFUL THING IN THE WORLD.
BUT THEY'RE WRONG!
IN EVERY COUPLE, THERE IS AN IMBALANCE OF POWER!
THE EXPLOITER AND THE EXPLOITED!
THE GIVER AND THE TAKER!
THE WINNER AND THE LOSER!
IF YOU WANT TO MAINTAIN YOUR DOMINANCE...
...YOU MUST NOT BECOME THE LOSER!
LOVE IS WAR!

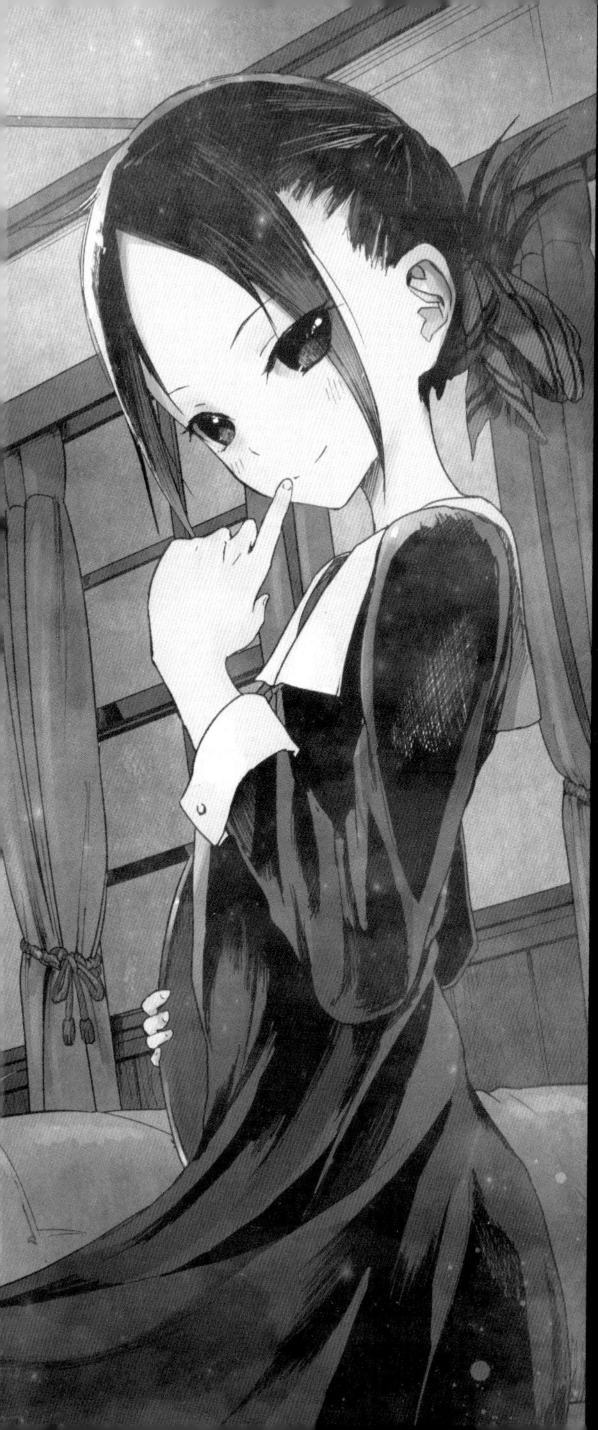

THE ONE WHO CON-FESSES THEIR LOVE FIRST LOSES!

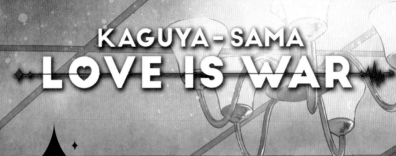

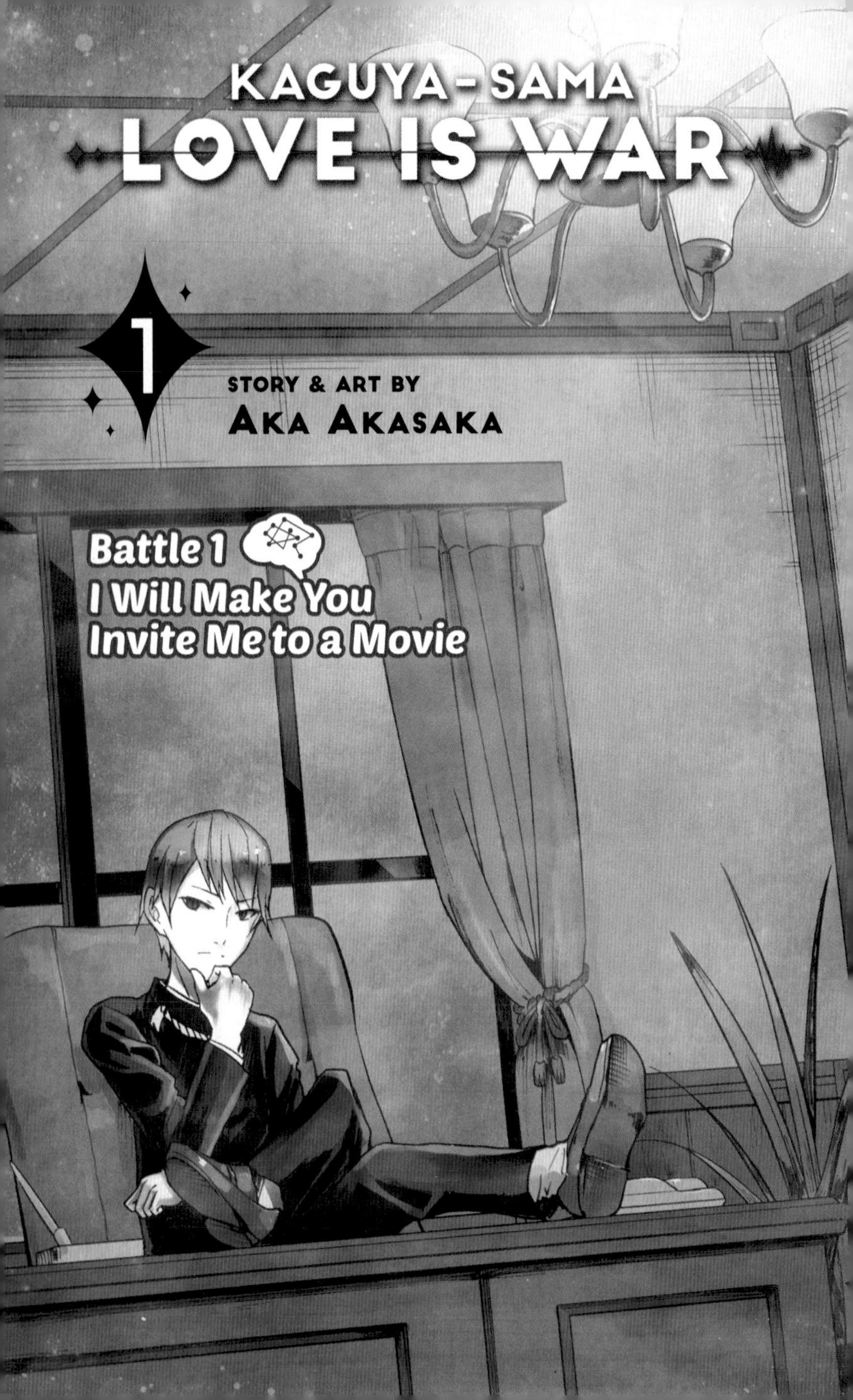

KAGUYA-SAMA LOVE IS WAR

1

STORY & ART BY
AKA AKASAKA

Battle 1
I Will Make You
Invite Me to a Movie

KAGUYA-SAMA LOVE IS WAR

1

BATTLE CAMPAIGNS

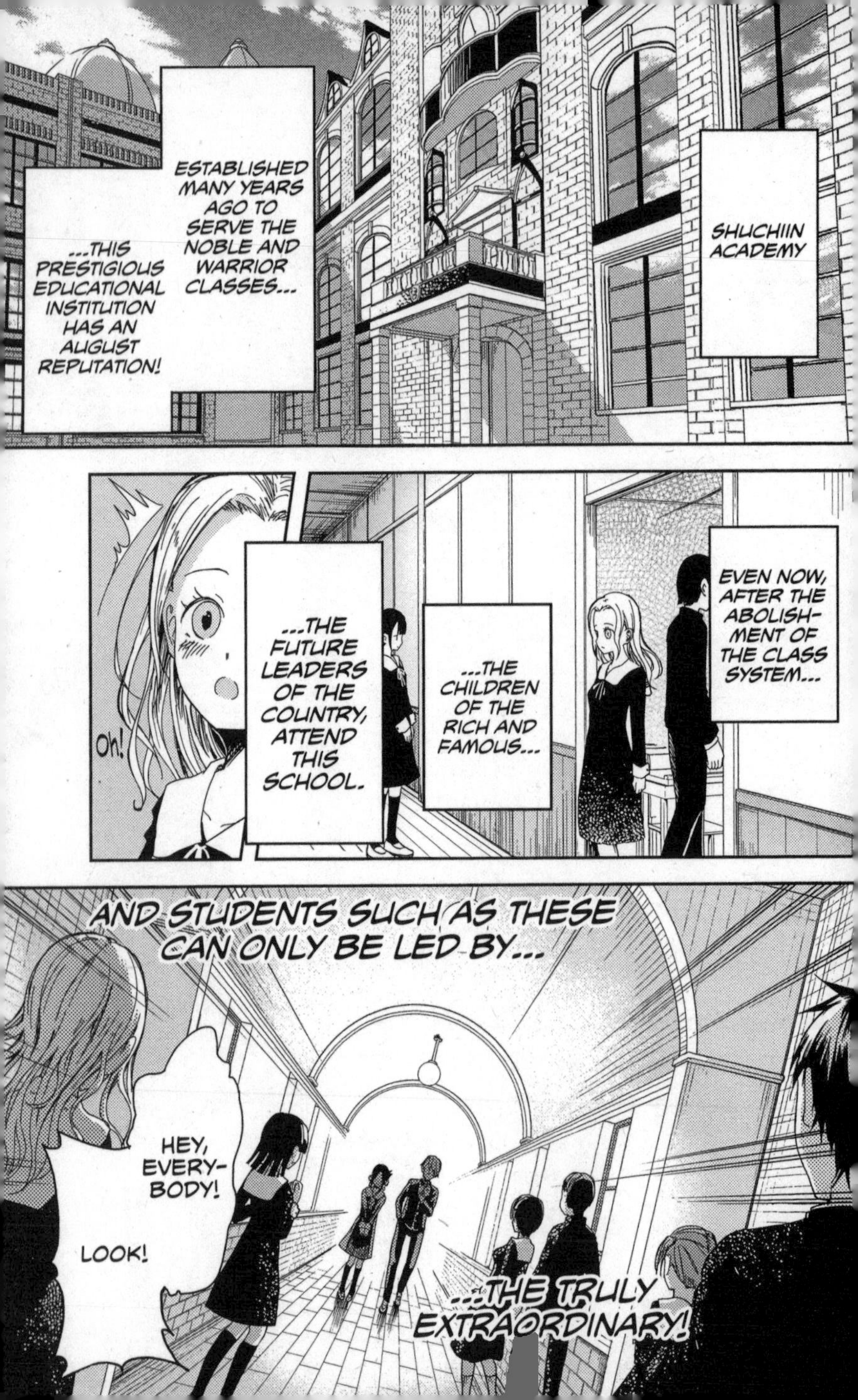
SHUCHIIN ACADEMY
ESTABLISHED MANY YEARS AGO TO SERVE THE NOBLE AND WARRIOR CLASSES...
...THIS PRESTIGIOUS EDUCATIONAL INSTITUTION HAS AN AUGUST REPUTATION!
EVEN NOW, AFTER THE ABOLISHMENT OF THE CLASS SYSTEM...
...THE CHILDREN OF THE RICH AND FAMOUS...
...THE FUTURE LEADERS OF THE COUNTRY, ATTEND THIS SCHOOL.
Oh!
AND STUDENTS SUCH AS THESE CAN ONLY BE LED BY...
HEY, EVERYBODY!
LOOK!
...THE TRULY EXTRAORDINARY!

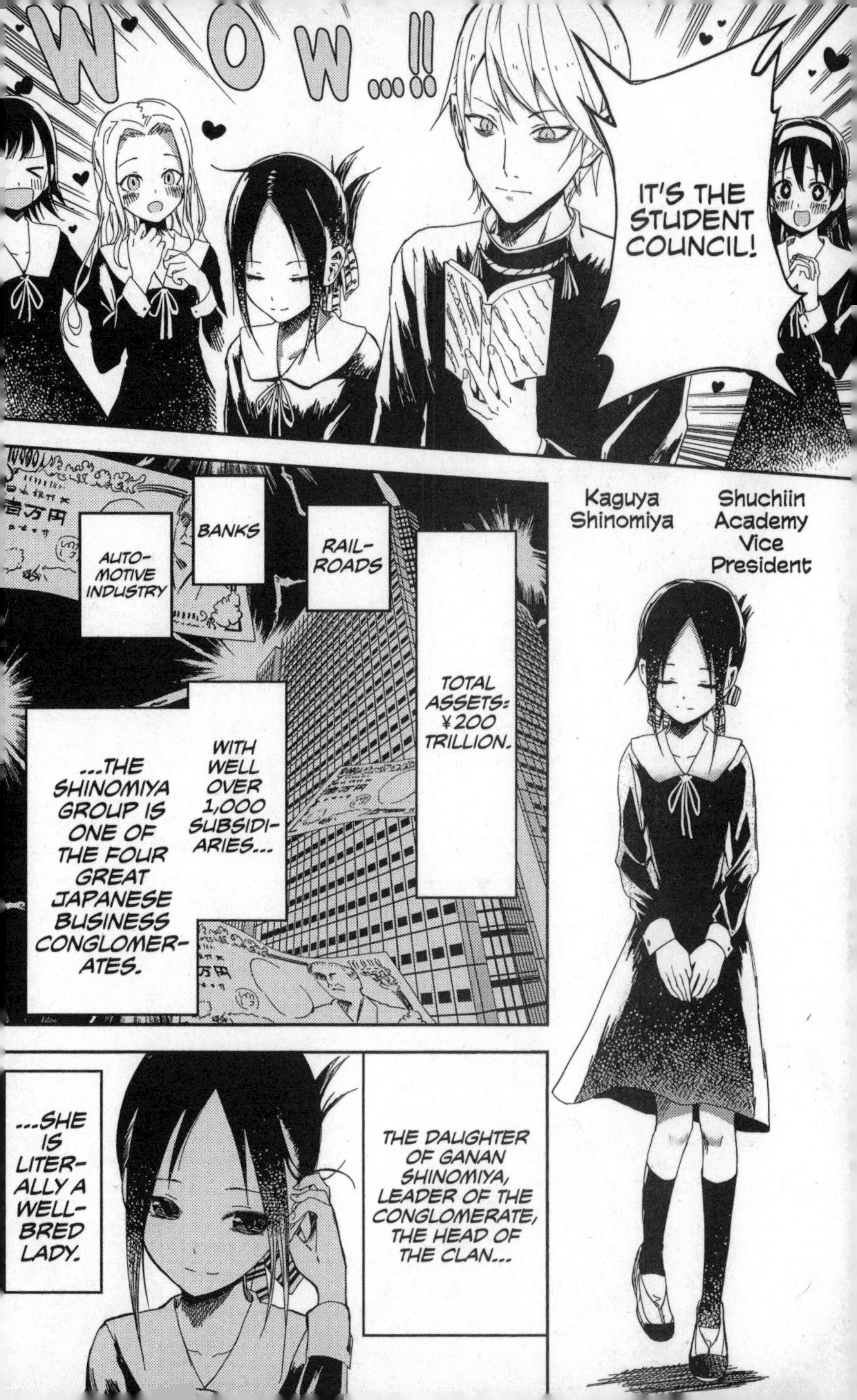
W O W...!!
IT'S THE STUDENT COUNCIL!
Shuchiin Academy Vice President
Kaguya Shinomiya
TOTAL ASSETS: ¥200 TRILLION.
RAIL-ROADS
BANKS
AUTO-MOTIVE INDUSTRY
WITH WELL OVER 1,000 SUBSIDI-ARIES...
...THE SHINOMIYA GROUP IS ONE OF THE FOUR GREAT JAPANESE BUSINESS CONGLOMER-ATES.
THE DAUGHTER OF GANAN SHINOMIYA, LEADER OF THE CONGLOMERATE, THE HEAD OF THE CLAN...
...SHE IS LITER-ALLY A WELL-BRED LADY.

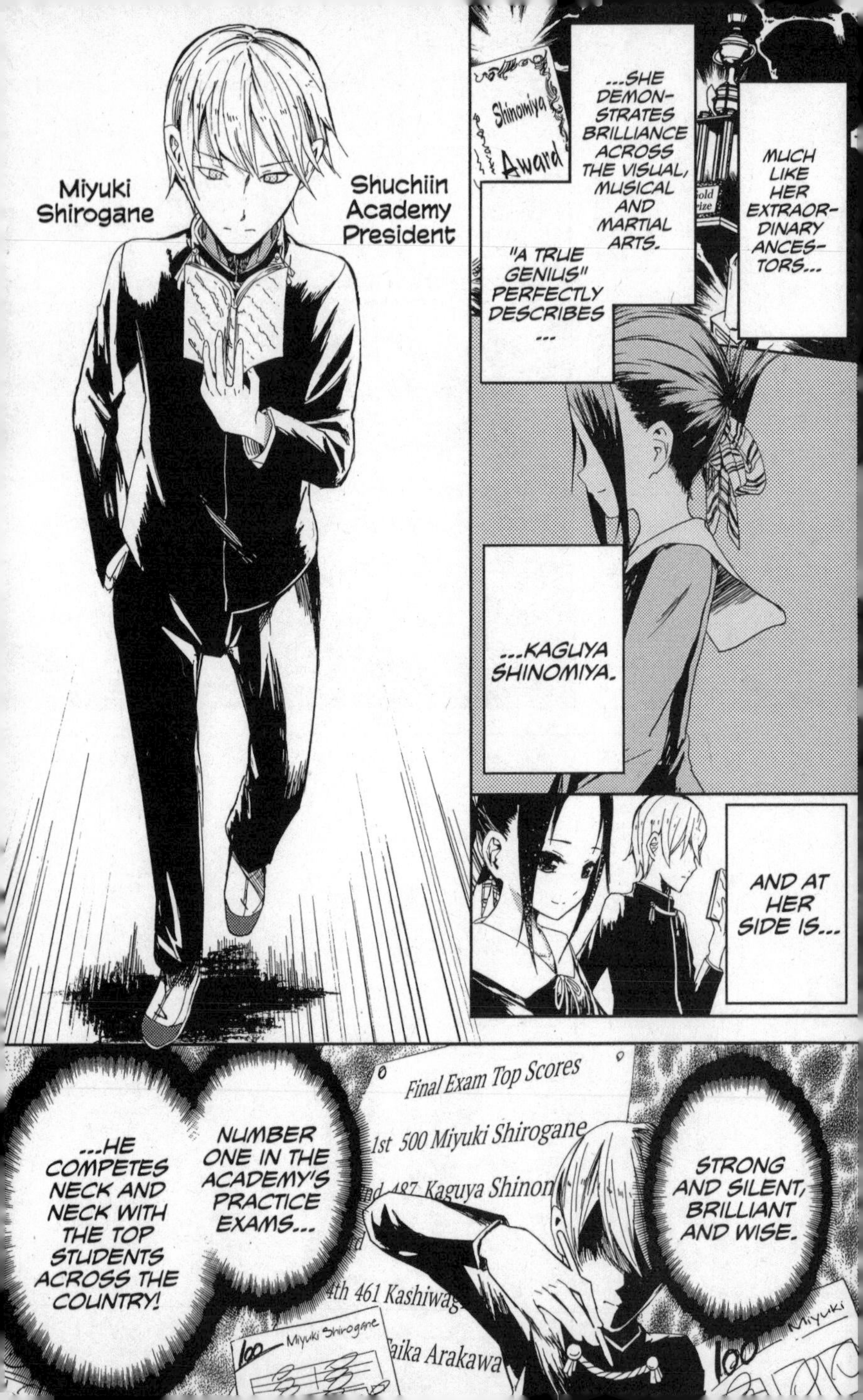
Shinomiya Award
MUCH LIKE HER EXTRAORDINARY ANCESTORS...
...SHE DEMONSTRATES BRILLIANCE ACROSS THE VISUAL, MUSICAL AND MARTIAL ARTS.
"A TRUE GENIUS" PERFECTLY DESCRIBES...
...KAGUYA SHINOMIYA.
AND AT HER SIDE IS...
Shuchiin Academy President
Miyuki Shirogane
Final Exam Top Scores
1st 500 Miyuki Shirogane
STRONG AND SILENT, BRILLIANT AND WISE.
NUMBER ONE IN THE ACADEMY'S PRACTICE EXAMS...
...HE COMPETES NECK AND NECK WITH THE TOP STUDENTS ACROSS THE COUNTRY!

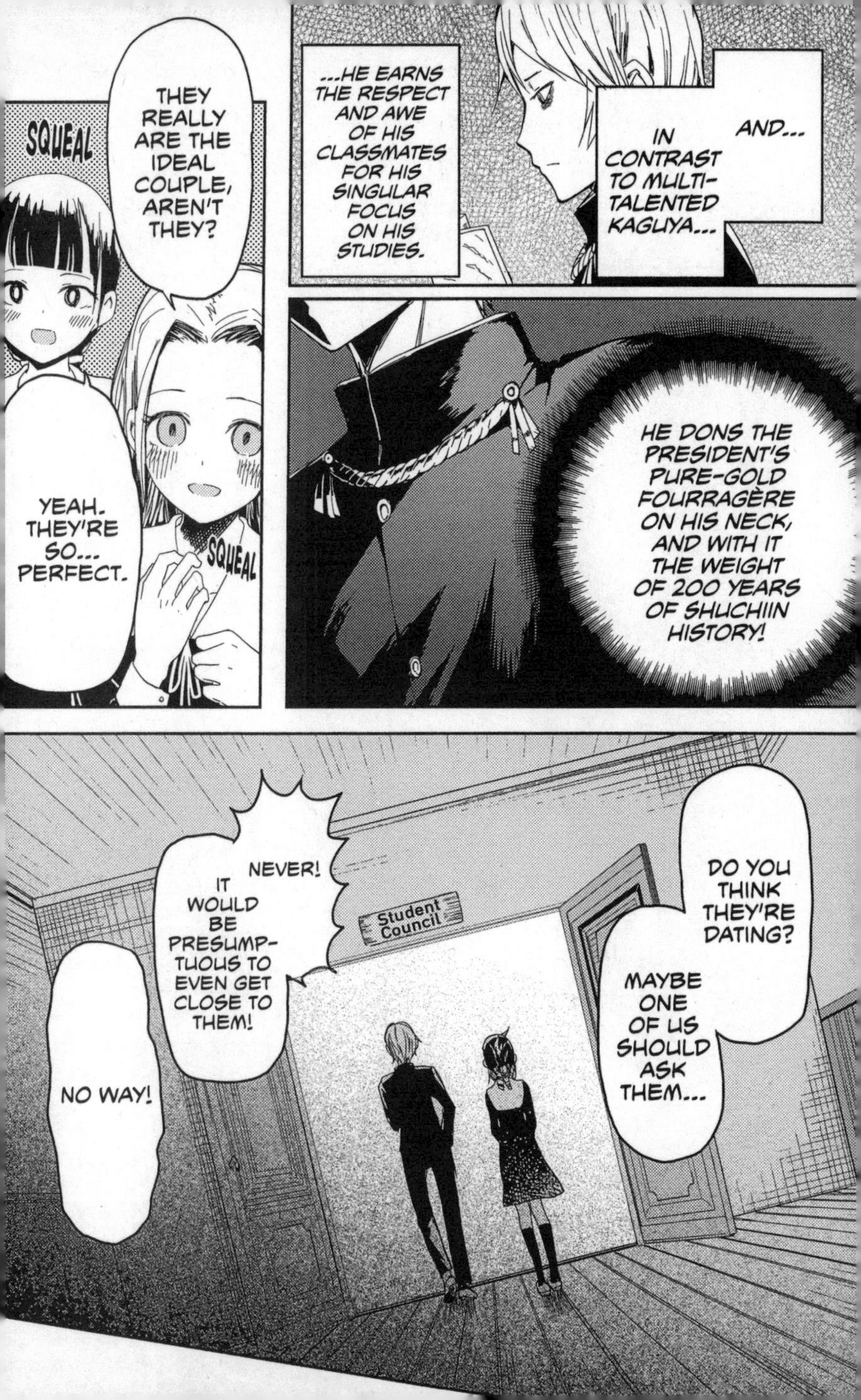
AND...
IN CONTRAST TO MULTI-TALENTED KAGUYA...
...HE EARNS THE RESPECT AND AWE OF HIS CLASSMATES FOR HIS SINGULAR FOCUS ON HIS STUDIES.
HE DONS THE PRESIDENT'S PURE-GOLD FOURRAGÈRE ON HIS NECK, AND WITH IT THE WEIGHT OF 200 YEARS OF SHUCHIIN HISTORY!
THEY REALLY ARE THE IDEAL COUPLE, AREN'T THEY?
SQUEAL
YEAH. THEY'RE SO... PERFECT.
SQUEAL
DO YOU THINK THEY'RE DATING?
MAYBE ONE OF US SHOULD ASK THEM...
NEVER! IT WOULD BE PRESUMPTUOUS TO EVEN GET CLOSE TO THEM!
Student Council
NO WAY!

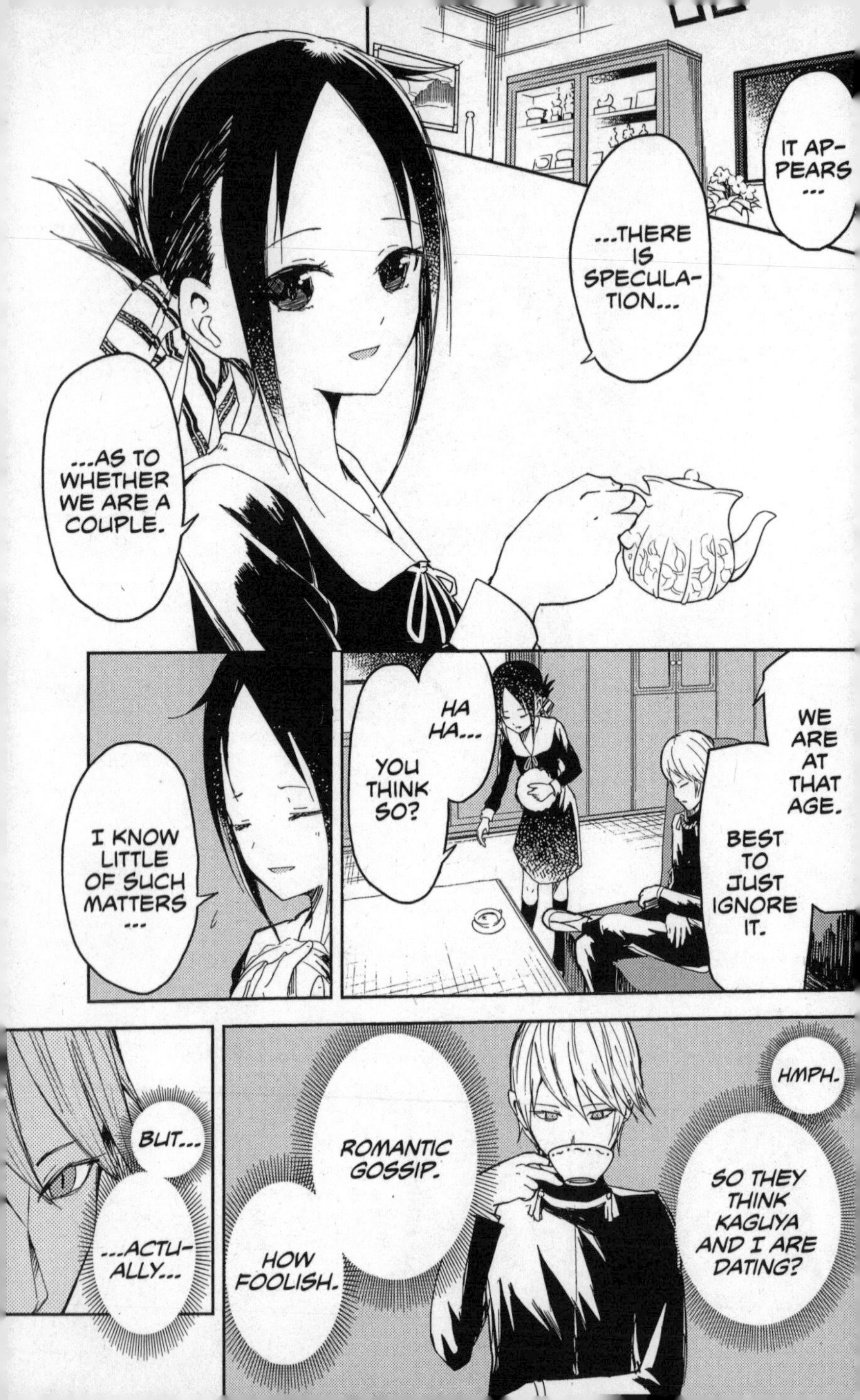
IT AP-PEARS...
...THERE IS SPECULA-TION...
...AS TO WHETHER WE ARE A COUPLE.
WE ARE AT THAT AGE.
BEST TO JUST IGNORE IT.
HA HA...
YOU THINK SO?
I KNOW LITTLE OF SUCH MATTERS...
HMPH.
SO THEY THINK KAGUYA AND I ARE DATING?
ROMANTIC GOSSIP.
HOW FOOLISH.
BUT...
...ACTU-ALLY...

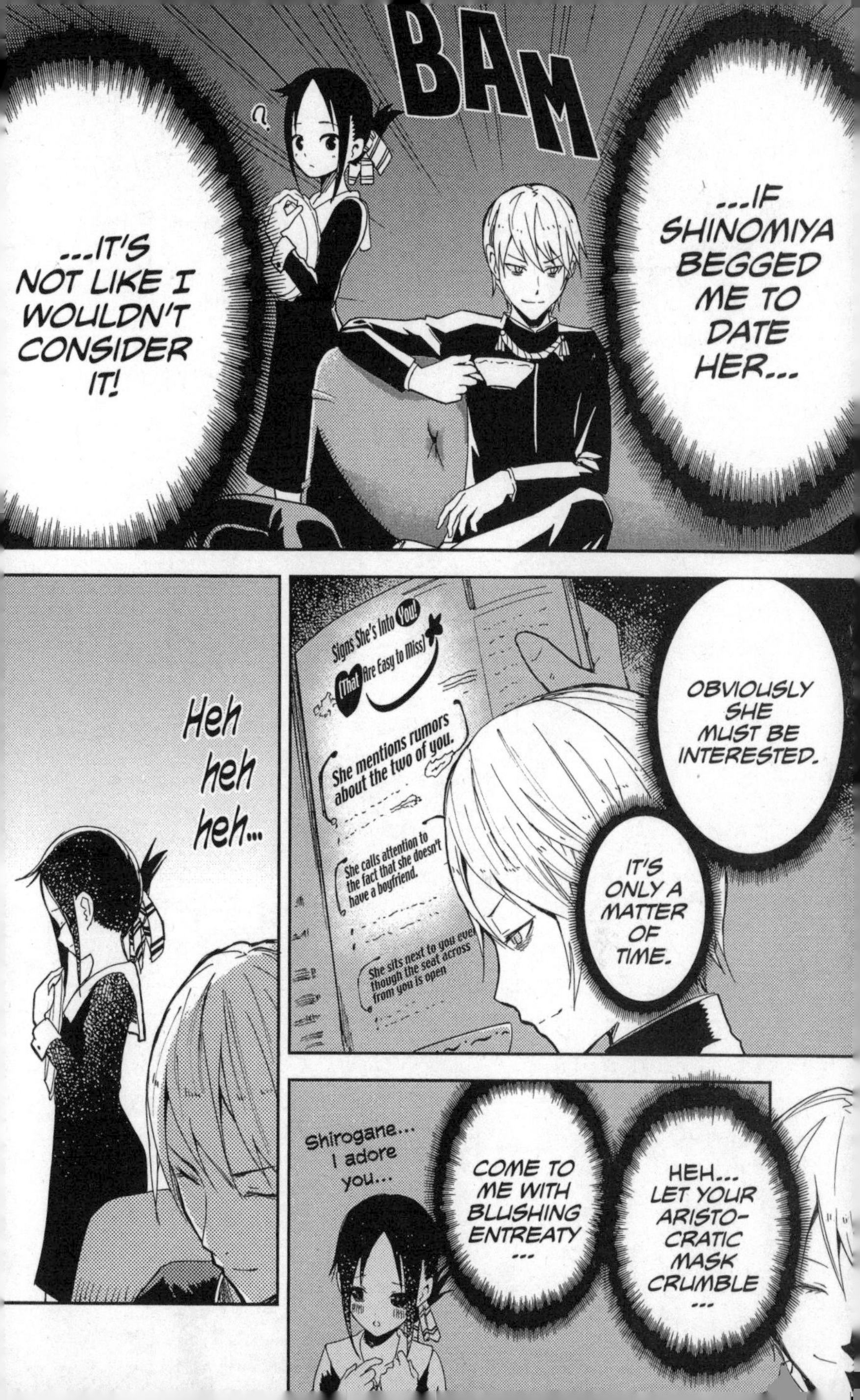
...IF SHINOMIYA BEGGED ME TO DATE HER...
BAM
...IT'S NOT LIKE I WOULDN'T CONSIDER IT!
OBVIOUSLY SHE MUST BE INTERESTED.
IT'S ONLY A MATTER OF TIME.
Signs She's Into You! (That Are Easy to Miss)
She mentions rumors about the two of you.
She calls attention to the fact that she doesn't have a boyfriend.
She sits next to you even though the seat across from you is open
HEH... LET YOUR ARISTO-CRATIC MASK CRUMBLE...
COME TO ME WITH BLUSHING ENTREATY...
Shirogane... I adore you...
Heh heh heh...

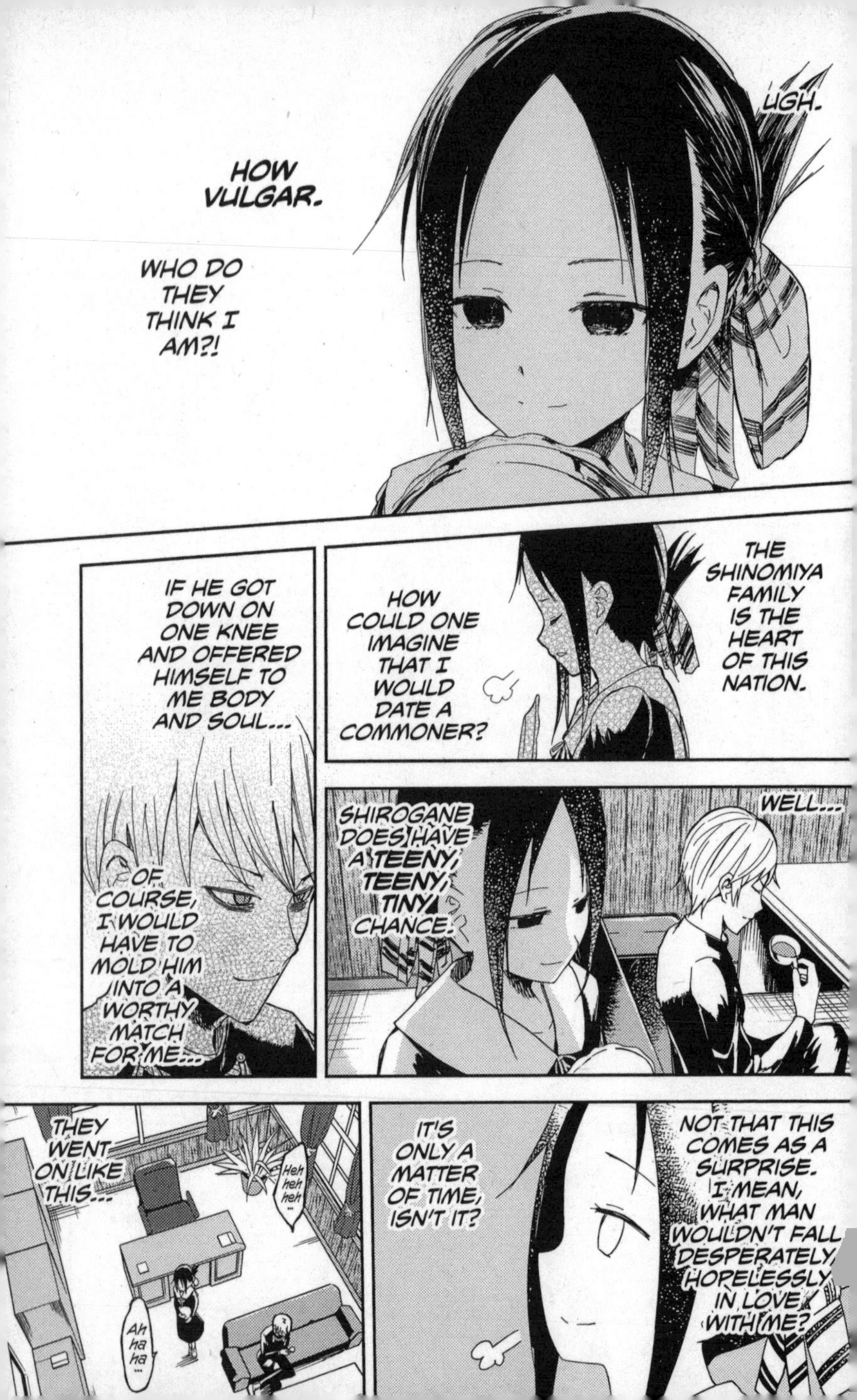
UGH.
HOW VULGAR.
WHO DO THEY THINK I AM?!
THE SHINOMIYA FAMILY IS THE HEART OF THIS NATION.
HOW COULD ONE IMAGINE THAT I WOULD DATE A COMMONER?
WELL...
SHIROGANE DOES HAVE A TEENY, TEENY, TINY CHANCE.
IF HE GOT DOWN ON ONE KNEE AND OFFERED HIMSELF TO ME BODY AND SOUL...
OF COURSE, I WOULD HAVE TO MOLD HIM INTO A WORTHY MATCH FOR ME...
NOT THAT THIS COMES AS A SURPRISE. I MEAN, WHAT MAN WOULDN'T FALL DESPERATELY, HOPELESSLY IN LOVE WITH ME?
IT'S ONLY A MATTER OF TIME, ISN'T IT?
THEY WENT ON LIKE THIS...
Heh heh heh...
Ah ha ha...

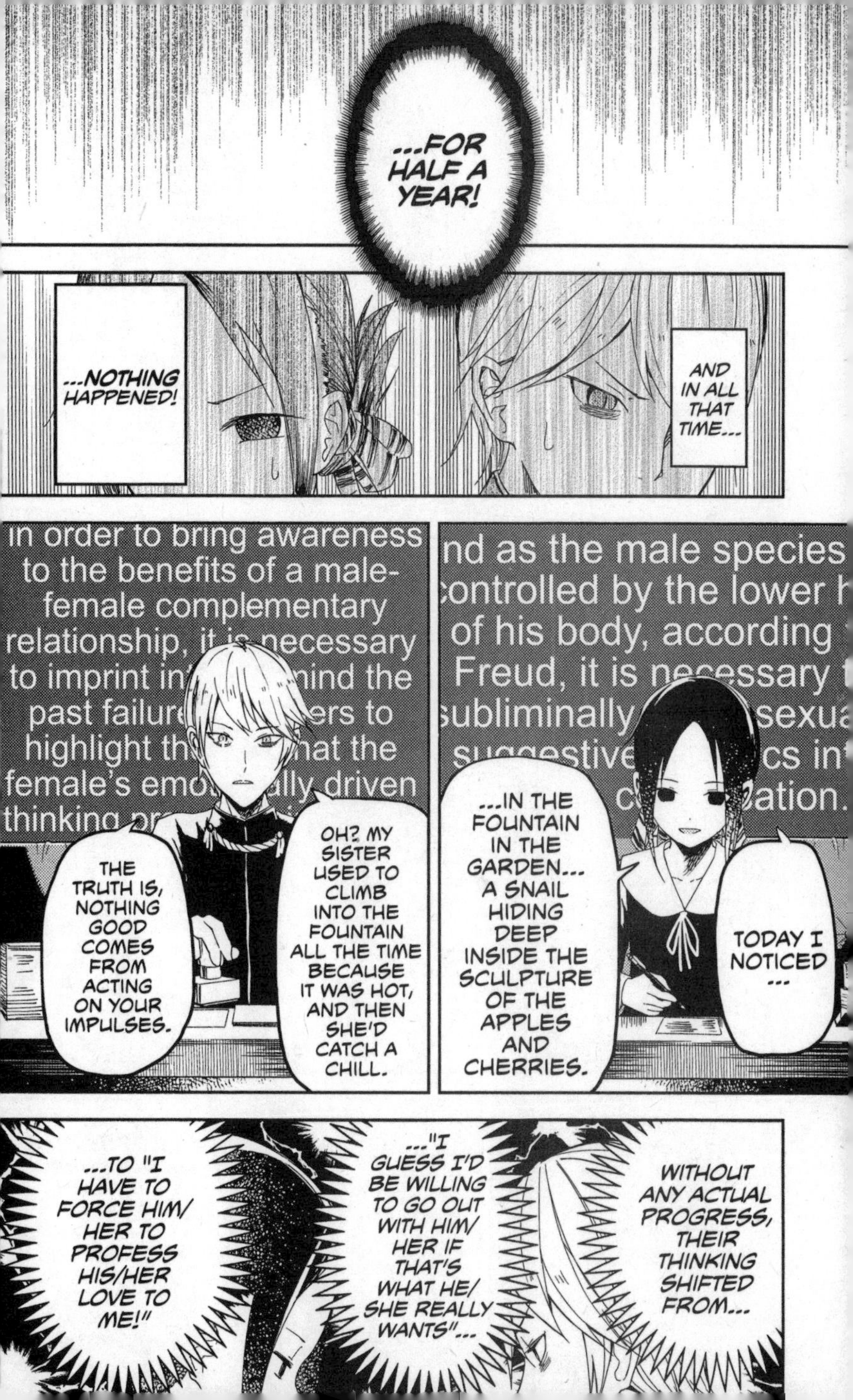
...FOR HALF A YEAR!
AND IN ALL THAT TIME...
...NOTHING HAPPENED!
nd as the male species
controlled by the lower
of his body, according
Freud, it is necessary
subliminally
suggestive
ation.
TODAY I NOTICED ...
...IN THE FOUNTAIN IN THE GARDEN... A SNAIL HIDING DEEP INSIDE THE SCULPTURE OF THE APPLES AND CHERRIES.
in order to bring awareness
to the benefits of a male-
female complementary
relationship, it is necessary
to imprint in mind the
past failure ers to
highlight th hat the
female's emo ally driven
thinking
OH? MY SISTER USED TO CLIMB INTO THE FOUNTAIN ALL THE TIME BECAUSE IT WAS HOT, AND THEN SHE'D CATCH A CHILL.
THE TRUTH IS, NOTHING GOOD COMES FROM ACTING ON YOUR IMPULSES.
WITHOUT ANY ACTUAL PROGRESS, THEIR THINKING SHIFTED FROM...
..."I GUESS I'D BE WILLING TO GO OUT WITH HIM/HER IF THAT'S WHAT HE/SHE REALLY WANTS"...
...TO "I HAVE TO FORCE HIM/HER TO PROFESS HIS/HER LOVE TO ME!"

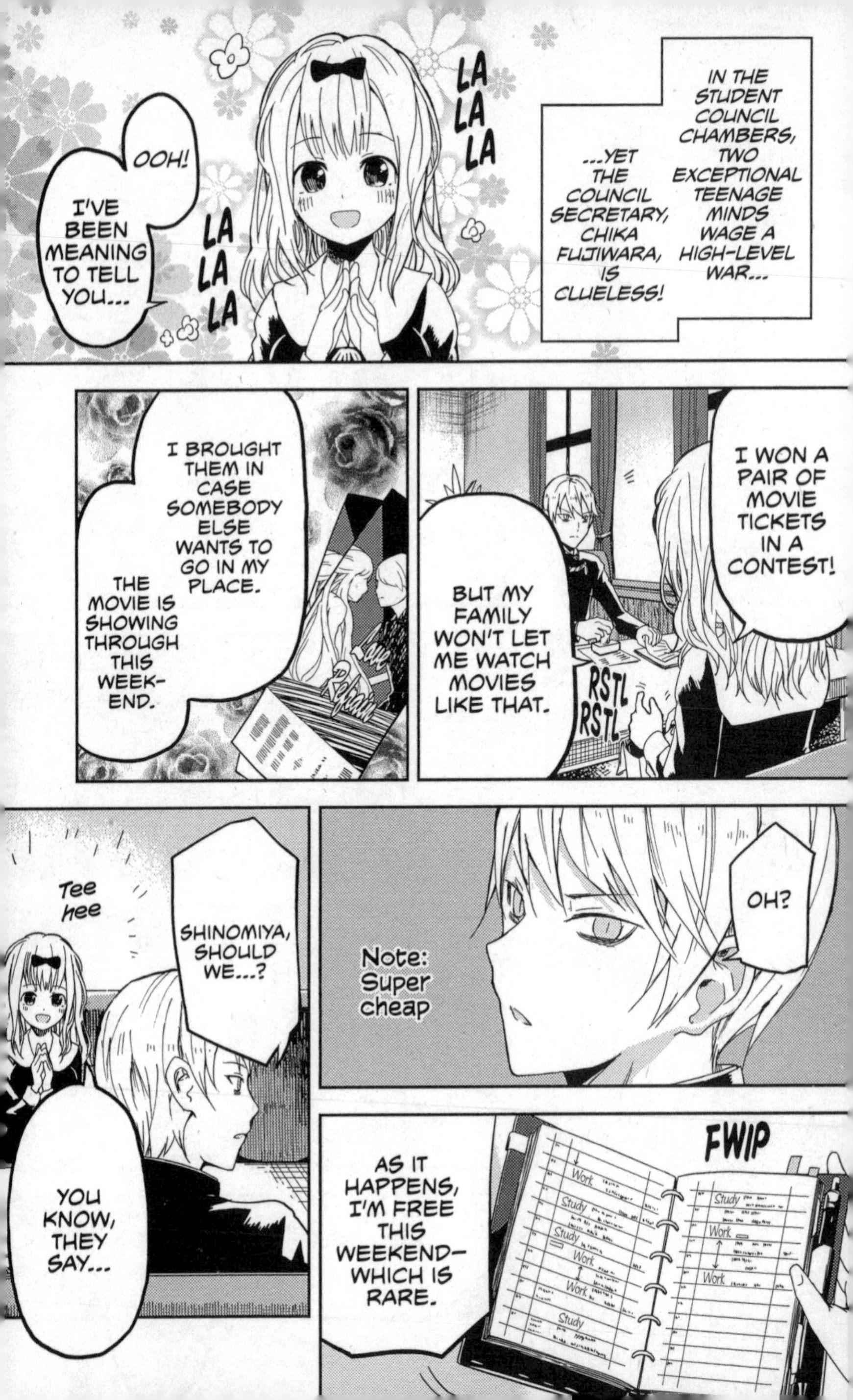
IN THE STUDENT COUNCIL CHAMBERS, TWO EXCEPTIONAL TEENAGE MINDS WAGE A HIGH-LEVEL WAR...
...YET THE COUNCIL SECRETARY, CHIKA FUJIWARA, IS CLUELESS!
LA LA LA
LA LA LA
OOH!
I'VE BEEN MEANING TO TELL YOU...
I WON A PAIR OF MOVIE TICKETS IN A CONTEST!
RSTL RSTL
BUT MY FAMILY WON'T LET ME WATCH MOVIES LIKE THAT.
I BROUGHT THEM IN CASE SOMEBODY ELSE WANTS TO GO IN MY PLACE.
THE MOVIE IS SHOWING THROUGH THIS WEEK-END.
OH?
Note: Super cheap
FWIP
AS IT HAPPENS, I'M FREE THIS WEEKEND—WHICH IS RARE.
Tee hee
SHINOMIYA, SHOULD WE...?
YOU KNOW, THEY SAY...

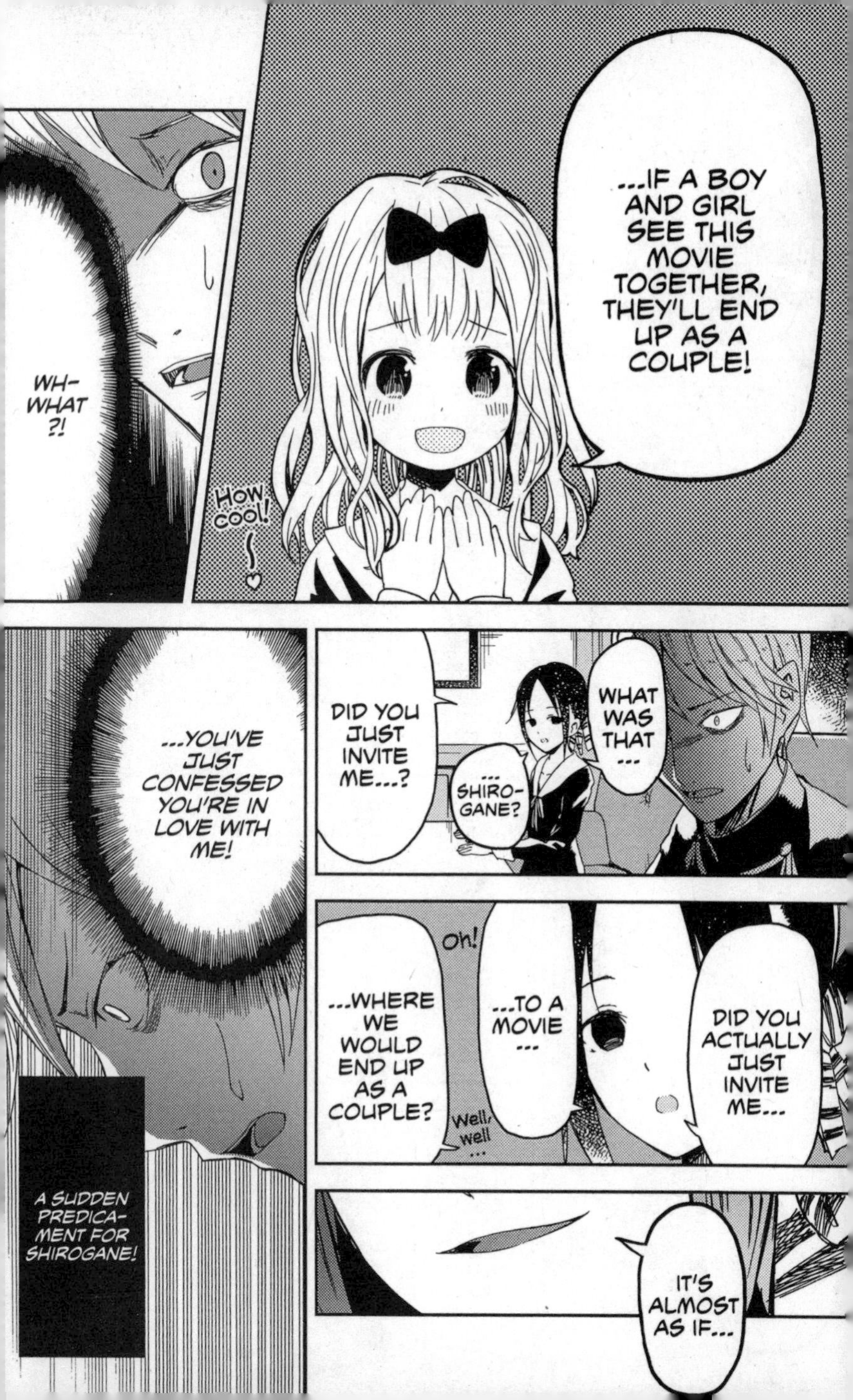
...IF A BOY AND GIRL SEE THIS MOVIE TOGETHER, THEY'LL END UP AS A COUPLE!
HOW COOL! ♡
WH- WHAT ?!
WHAT WAS THAT ...
... SHIROGANE?
DID YOU JUST INVITE ME...?
DID YOU ACTUALLY JUST INVITE ME...
...TO A MOVIE ...
Oh!
...WHERE WE WOULD END UP AS A COUPLE?
Well, well ...
IT'S ALMOST AS IF...
...YOU'VE JUST CONFESSED YOU'RE IN LOVE WITH ME!
A SUDDEN PREDICA- MENT FOR SHIROGANE!

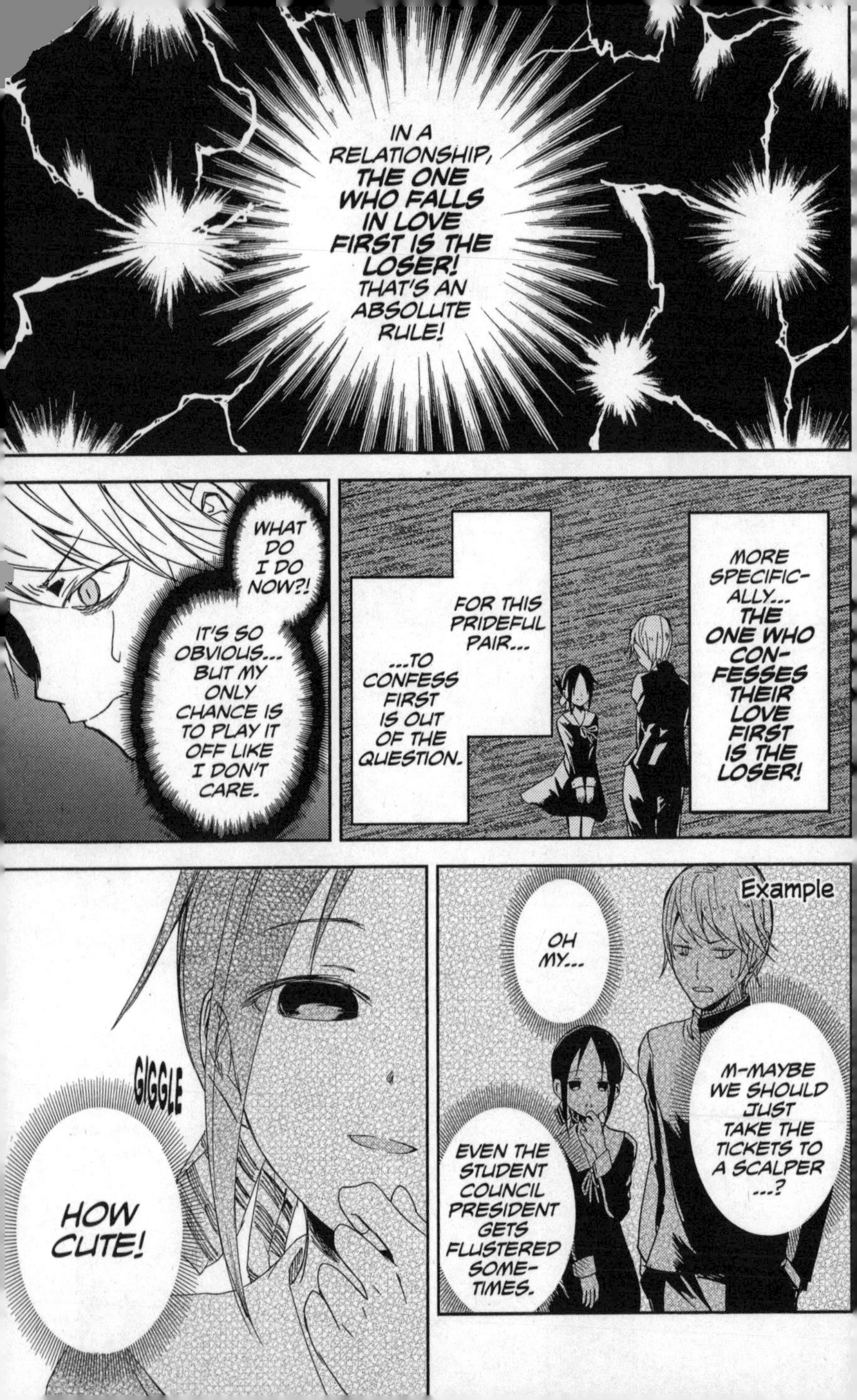

IN A RELATIONSHIP, THE ONE WHO FALLS IN LOVE FIRST IS THE LOSER! THAT'S AN ABSOLUTE RULE!
MORE SPECIFICALLY... THE ONE WHO CONFESSES THEIR LOVE FIRST IS THE LOSER!
FOR THIS PRIDEFUL PAIR...
...TO CONFESS FIRST IS OUT OF THE QUESTION.
WHAT DO I DO NOW?!
IT'S SO OBVIOUS... BUT MY ONLY CHANCE IS TO PLAY IT OFF LIKE I DON'T CARE.
Example
OH MY...
M-MAYBE WE SHOULD JUST TAKE THE TICKETS TO A SCALPER ...?
EVEN THE STUDENT COUNCIL PRESIDENT GETS FLUSTERED SOMETIMES.
GIGGLE
HOW CUTE!

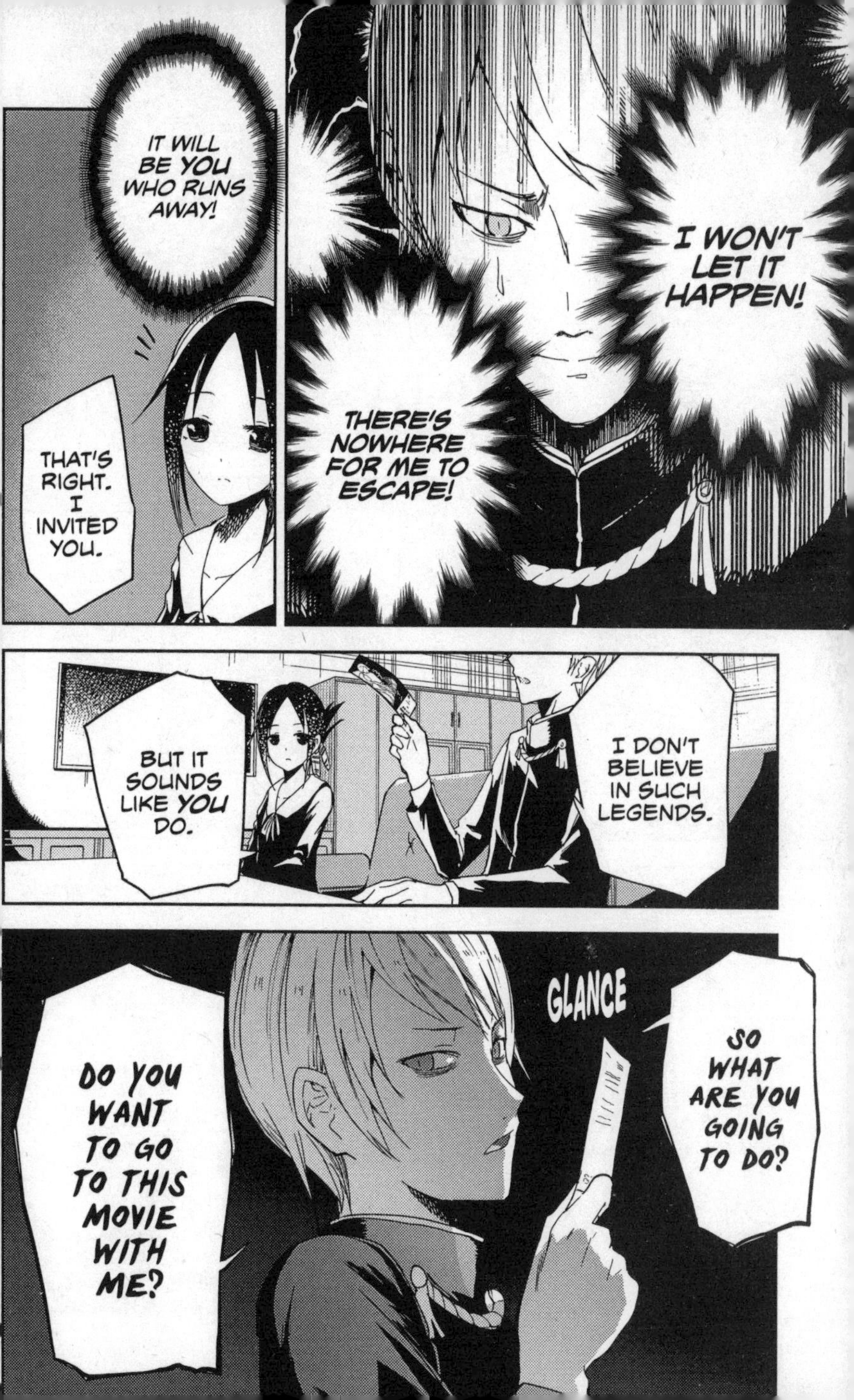
I WON'T LET IT HAPPEN!
THERE'S NOWHERE FOR ME TO ESCAPE!
IT WILL BE YOU WHO RUNS AWAY!
THAT'S RIGHT. I INVITED YOU.
I DON'T BELIEVE IN SUCH LEGENDS.
BUT IT SOUNDS LIKE YOU DO.
SO WHAT ARE YOU GOING TO DO?
GLANCE
DO YOU WANT TO GO TO THIS MOVIE WITH ME?

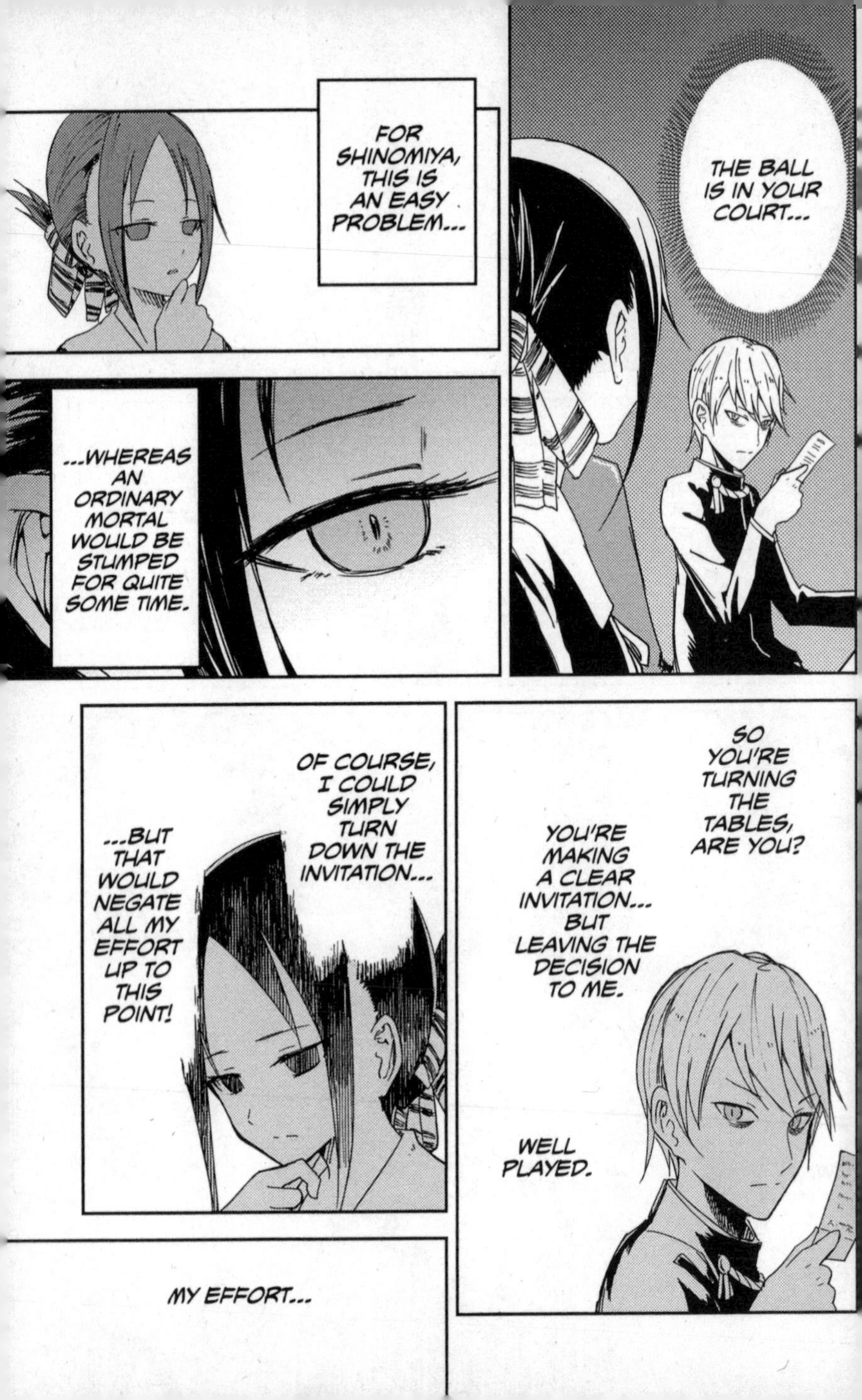
THE BALL IS IN YOUR COURT...
FOR SHINOMIYA, THIS IS AN EASY PROBLEM...
...WHEREAS AN ORDINARY MORTAL WOULD BE STUMPED FOR QUITE SOME TIME.
SO YOU'RE TURNING THE TABLES, ARE YOU?
YOU'RE MAKING A CLEAR INVITATION... BUT LEAVING THE DECISION TO ME.
WELL PLAYED.
OF COURSE, I COULD SIMPLY TURN DOWN THE INVITATION...
...BUT THAT WOULD NEGATE ALL MY EFFORT UP TO THIS POINT!
MY EFFORT...

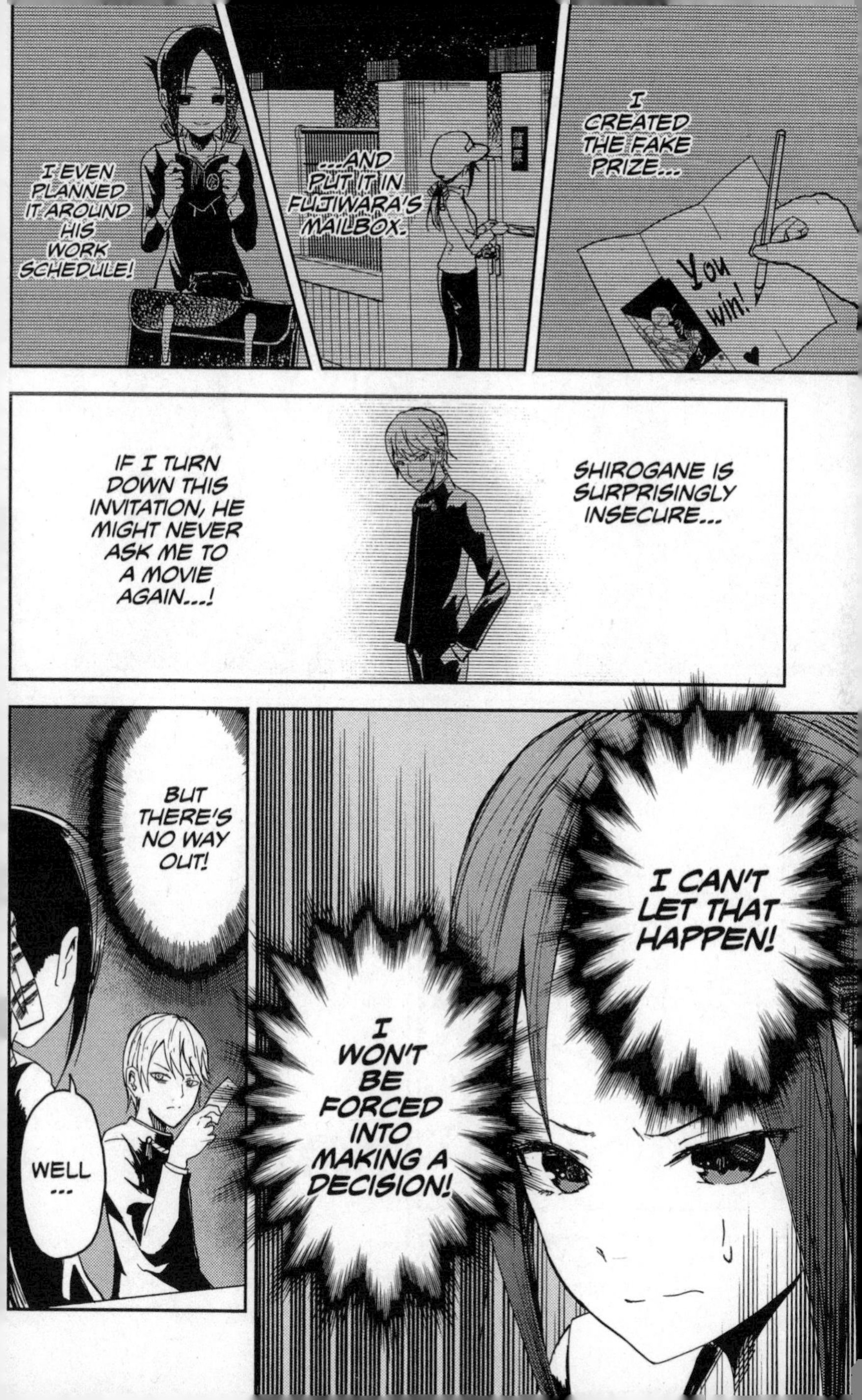

I CREATED THE FAKE PRIZE...
You win!
...AND PUT IT IN FUJIWARA'S MAILBOX.
I EVEN PLANNED IT AROUND HIS WORK SCHEDULE!
SHIROGANE IS SURPRISINGLY INSECURE...
IF I TURN DOWN THIS INVITATION, HE MIGHT NEVER ASK ME TO A MOVIE AGAIN...!
I CAN'T LET THAT HAPPEN!
I WON'T BE FORCED INTO MAKING A DECISION!
BUT THERE'S NO WAY OUT!
WELL...

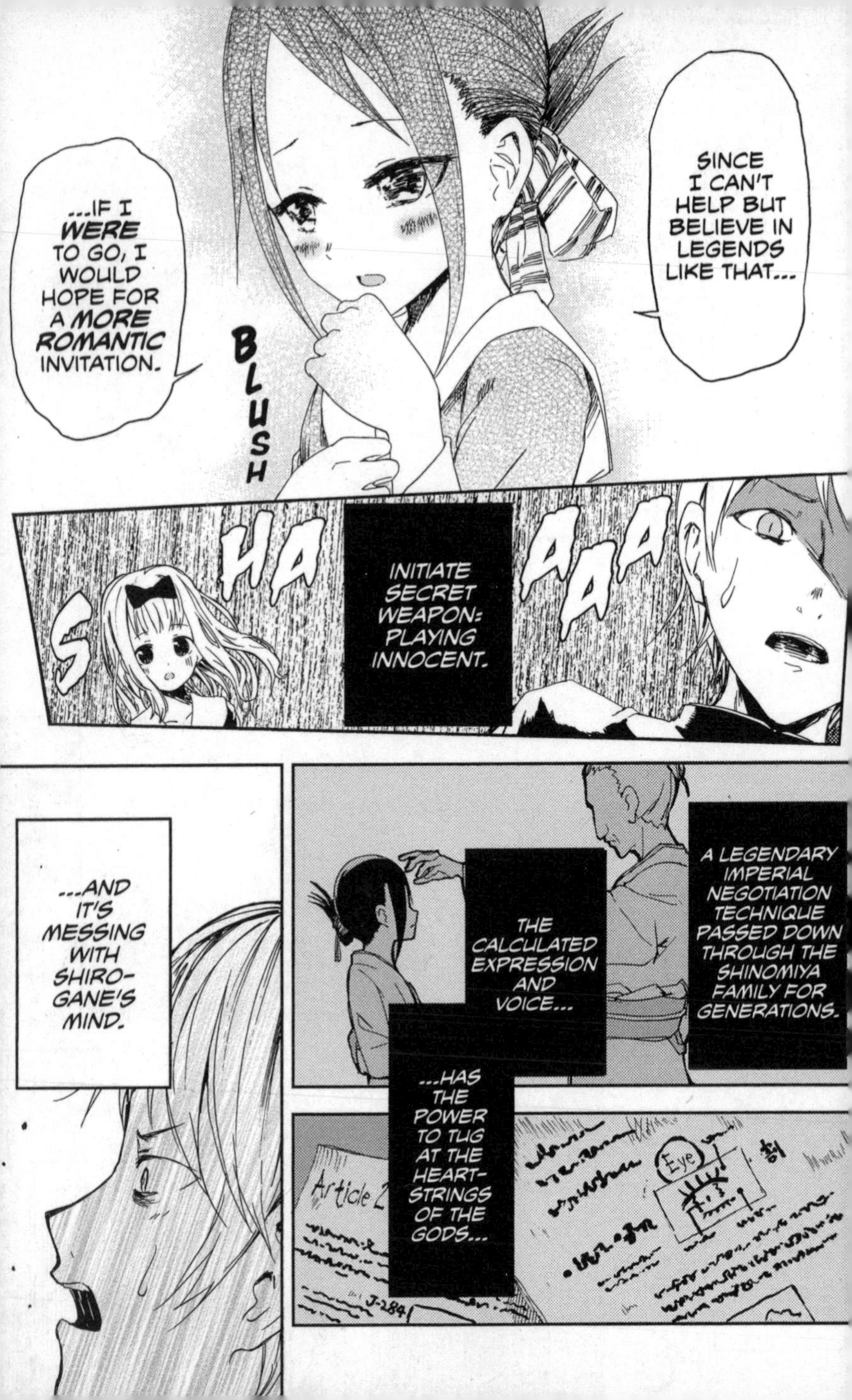
SINCE I CAN'T HELP BUT BELIEVE IN LEGENDS LIKE THAT...
...IF I *WERE* TO GO, I WOULD HOPE FOR A *MORE ROMANTIC* INVITATION.
BLUSH
SHAAAAA
INITIATE SECRET WEAPON: PLAYING INNOCENT.
A LEGENDARY IMPERIAL NEGOTIATION TECHNIQUE PASSED DOWN THROUGH THE SHINOMIYA FAMILY FOR GENERATIONS.
THE CALCULATED EXPRESSION AND VOICE...
...HAS THE POWER TO TUG AT THE HEART-STRINGS OF THE GODS...
Article 2
Eye
J-284
...AND IT'S MESSING WITH SHIRO-GANE'S MIND.

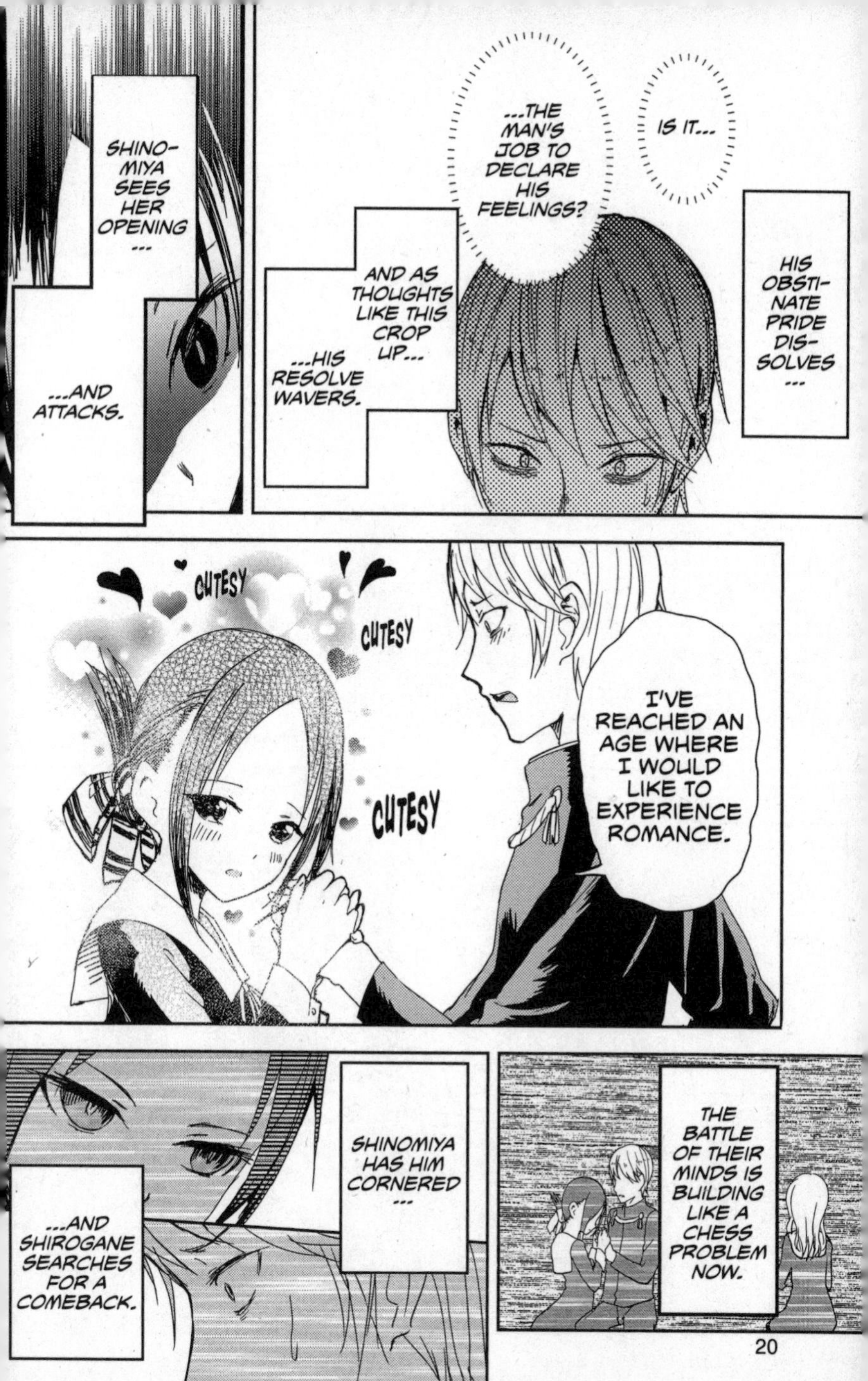
IS IT...
...THE MAN'S JOB TO DECLARE HIS FEELINGS?
HIS OBSTINATE PRIDE DISSOLVES...
AND AS THOUGHTS LIKE THIS CROP UP...
...HIS RESOLVE WAVERS.
SHINOMIYA SEES HER OPENING...
...AND ATTACKS.
I'VE REACHED AN AGE WHERE I WOULD LIKE TO EXPERIENCE ROMANCE.
CUTESY
CUTESY
CUTESY
THE BATTLE OF THEIR MINDS IS BUILDING LIKE A CHESS PROBLEM NOW.
SHINOMIYA HAS HIM CORNERED...
...AND SHIROGANE SEARCHES FOR A COMEBACK.

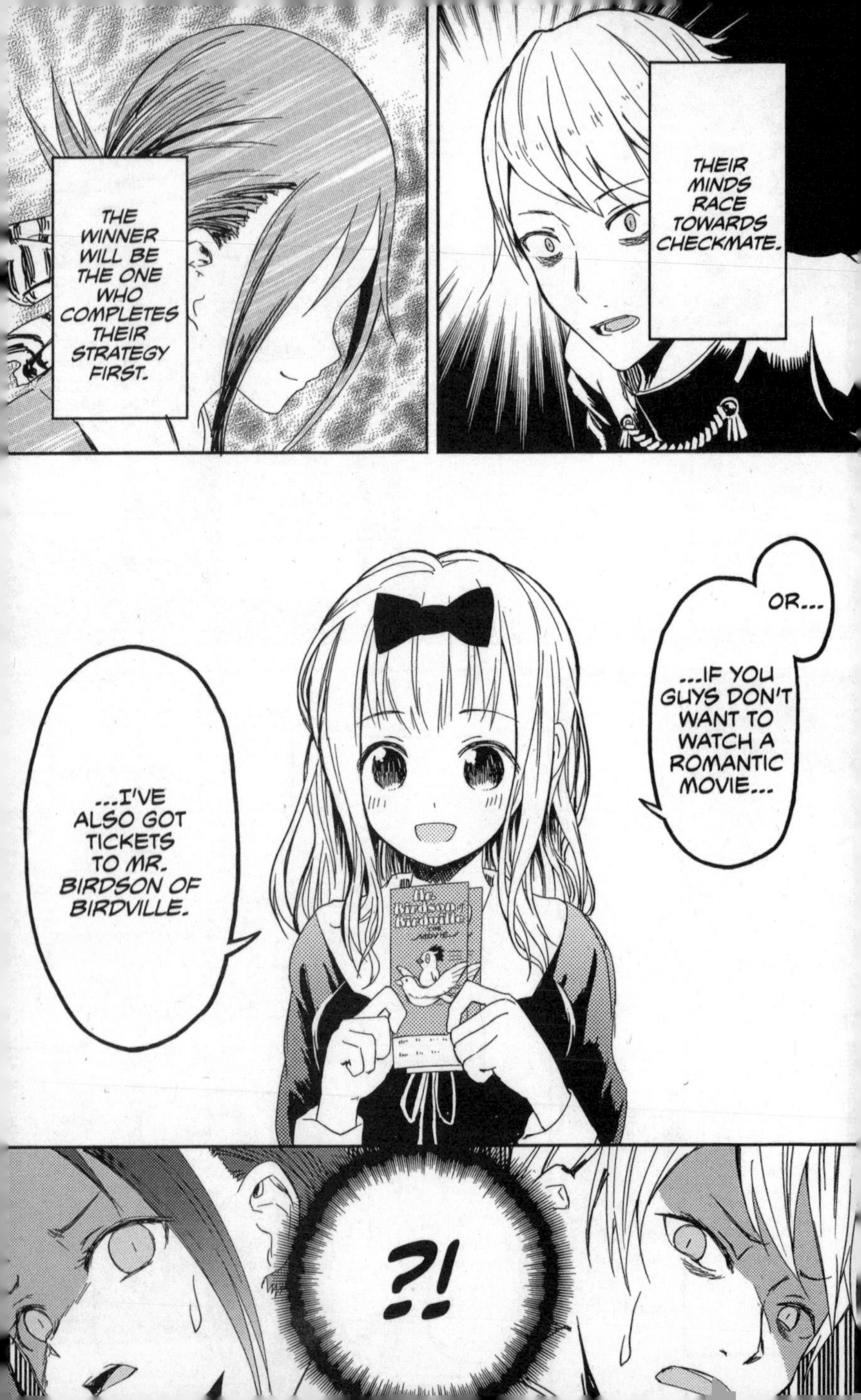
THEIR MINDS RACE TOWARDS CHECKMATE.
THE WINNER WILL BE THE ONE WHO COMPLETES THEIR STRATEGY FIRST.
OR...
...IF YOU GUYS DON'T WANT TO WATCH A ROMANTIC MOVIE...
...I'VE ALSO GOT TICKETS TO MR. BIRDSON OF BIRDVILLE.
?!

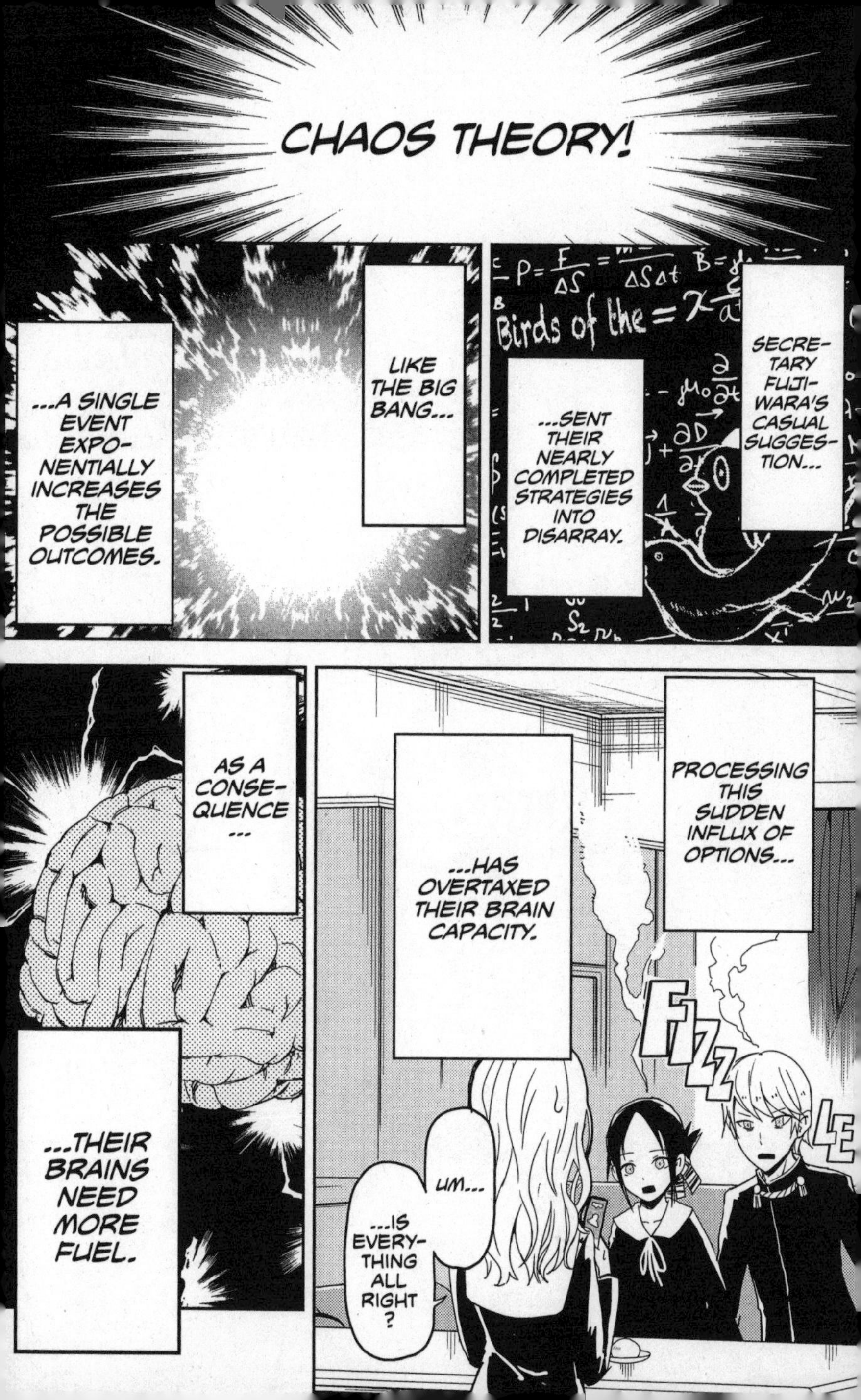
CHAOS THEORY!
SECRETARY FUJIWARA'S CASUAL SUGGESTION...
...SENT THEIR NEARLY COMPLETED STRATEGIES INTO DISARRAY.
Birds of the
LIKE THE BIG BANG...
...A SINGLE EVENT EXPONENTIALLY INCREASES THE POSSIBLE OUTCOMES.
PROCESSING THIS SUDDEN INFLUX OF OPTIONS...
...HAS OVERTAXED THEIR BRAIN CAPACITY.
FIZZLE
UM...
...IS EVERYTHING ALL RIGHT?
AS A CONSEQUENCE...
...THEIR BRAINS NEED MORE FUEL.

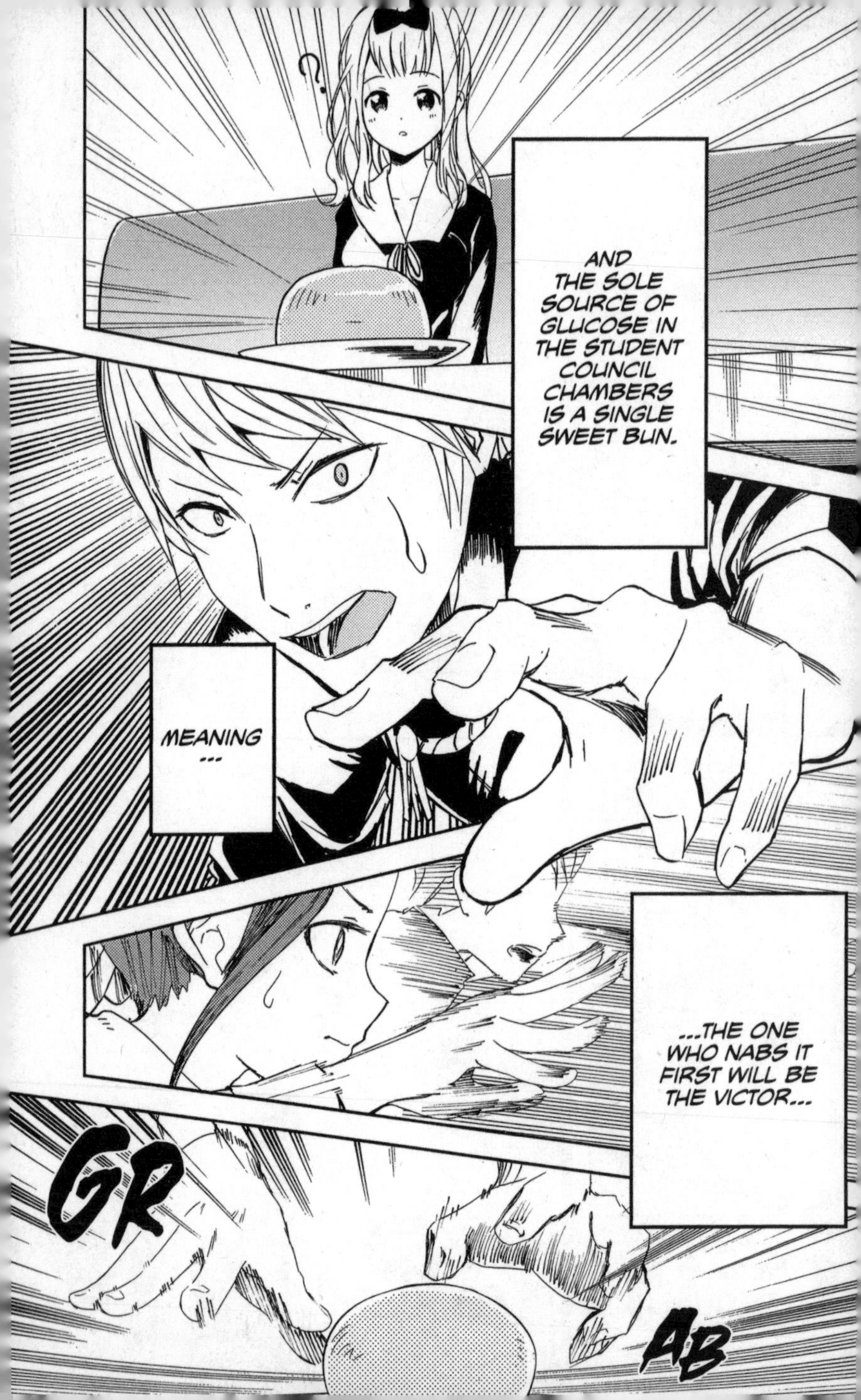
AND THE SOLE SOURCE OF GLUCOSE IN THE STUDENT COUNCIL CHAMBERS IS A SINGLE SWEET BUN.
MEANING ...
...THE ONE WHO NABS IT FIRST WILL BE THE VICTOR...
GR
AB

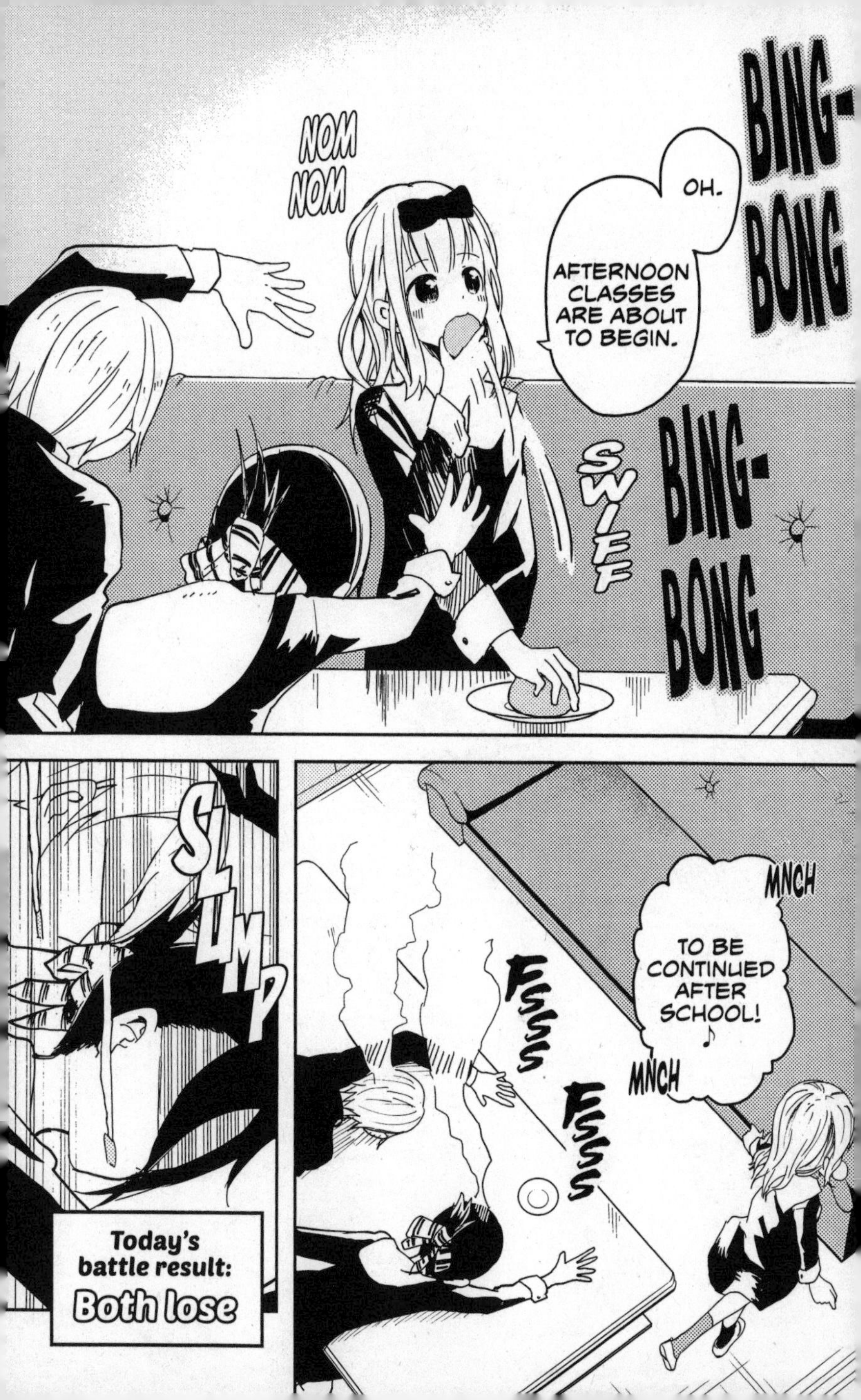
BING-BONG
OH.
AFTERNOON CLASSES ARE ABOUT TO BEGIN.
BING-BONG
SWIFF
NOM NOM
MNCH
TO BE CONTINUED AFTER SCHOOL! ♪
MNCH
FSSS
FSSS
SLUMP
Today's battle result:
Both lose

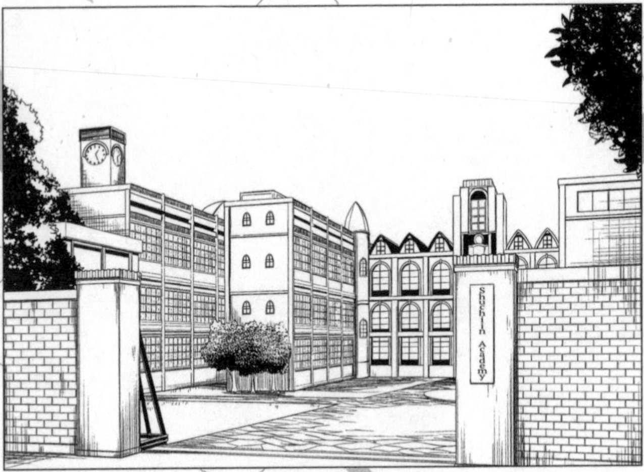
Shuchiin Academy

Shuchiin Academy

Located in Tokyo's Minato Ward, the school goes from preschool through university, but transfer students are accepted. The high school's standard test score ranking hovers at 77.

The school was established by the Edo shogunate government in the 18th century in response to the rising influence of Dutch scholars. Many private educational institutions were founded during this period, and the school grew as it merged with others. In 1849, the school was granted an imperial plaque from the emperor recognizing it as a place of great learning. Many parents from the nobility and samurai classes sent their children there, and their enrollment became a mark of status. At the time, students were also able to get in through bribery and other backdoor strategies.

After the war, with the liberalization of social classes, enrollment from the commoner class grew. Shuchiin began to offer entrance examinations to the general public. However, due to high tuition fees and expectations of large donations and bribes, enrollment continued to be limited to the elite, with only a few exceptions to maintain the appearance of fairness and diversity.

As its reputation for preferential treatment towards aristocrats and elite families grew, along with accusations of bribery and nepotism through the old boys' network, some intellectuals began to cry foul. For example, a hierarchy developed in which students who had enrolled at the earliest levels were considered "pure," whereas those who transferred at the junior high school level were considered "impure." When one "impure" student was elected to the office of student council president, he was expelled from the school before he could serve out his term. Subsequently, the number of "impure" students running for student council greatly decreased, and, to date, only three "impure" students have served as student council president.

KAGUYA-SAMA
LOVE IS WAR

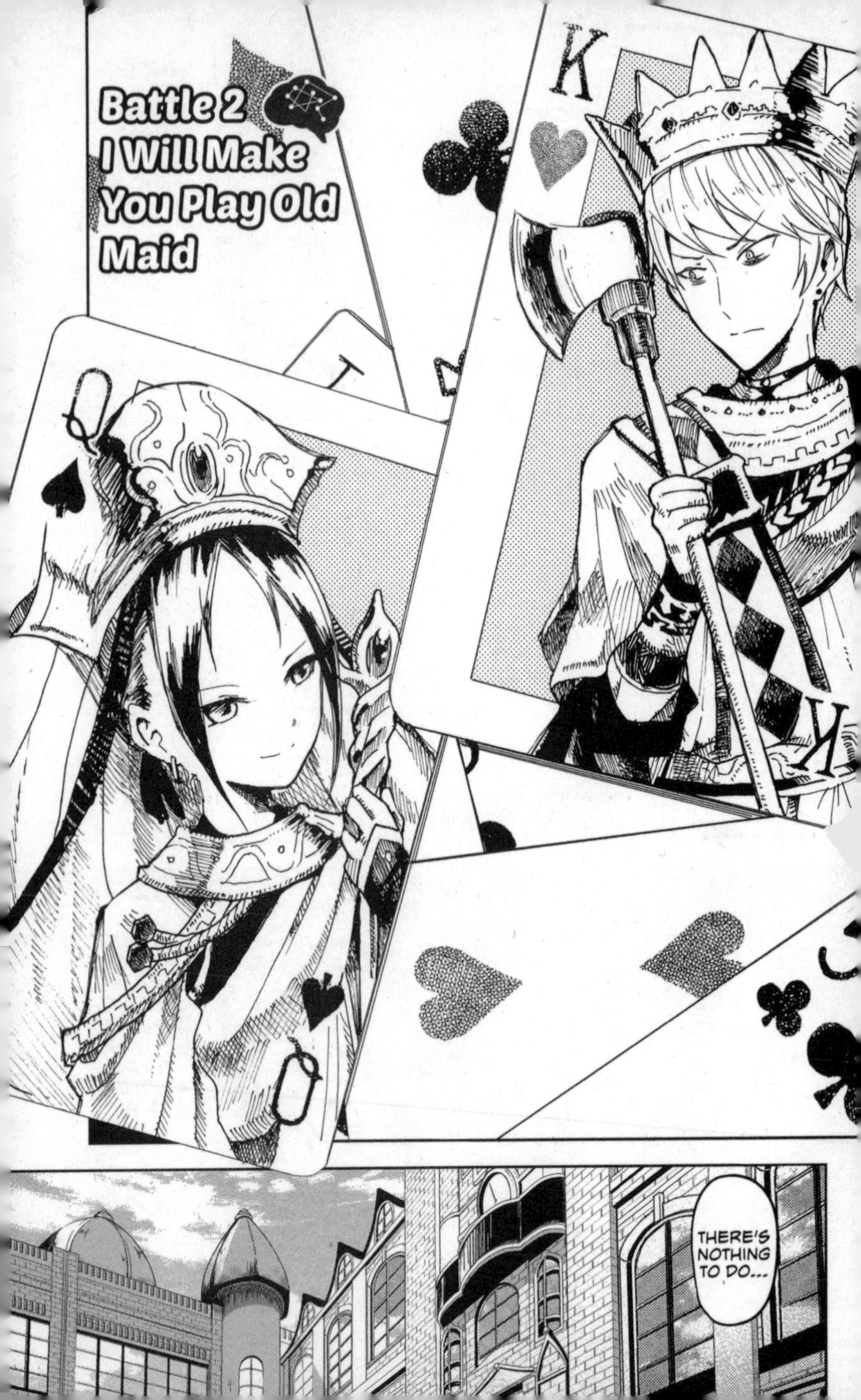
Battle 2
I Will Make You Play Old Maid
THERE'S NOTHING TO DO...

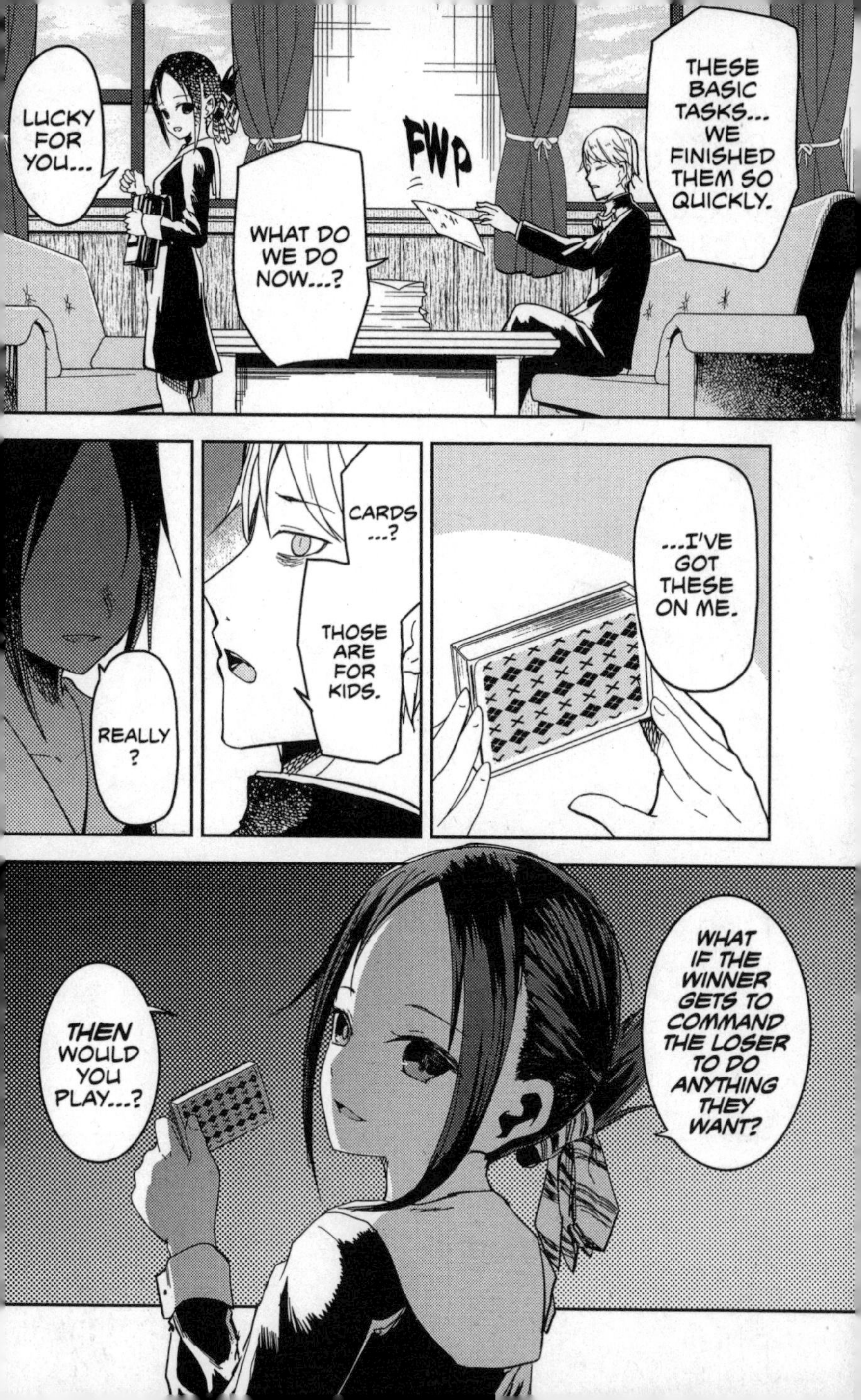
THESE BASIC TASKS... WE FINISHED THEM SO QUICKLY.
FWP
WHAT DO WE DO NOW...?
LUCKY FOR YOU...
...I'VE GOT THESE ON ME.
CARDS ...?
THOSE ARE FOR KIDS.
REALLY ?
WHAT IF THE WINNER GETS TO COMMAND THE LOSER TO DO ANYTHING THEY WANT?
THEN WOULD YOU PLAY...?

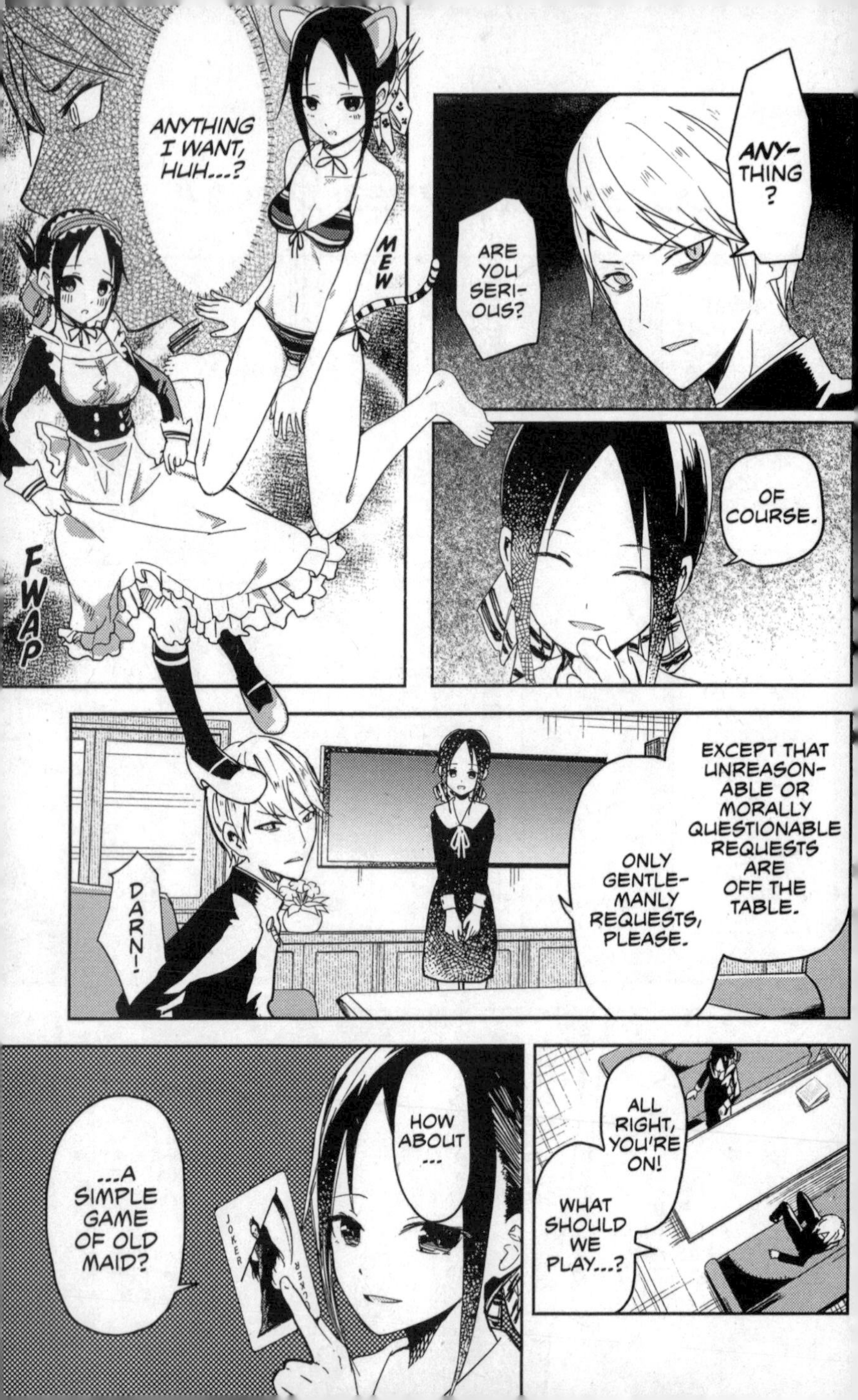
ANYTHING?
ARE YOU SERIOUS?
OF COURSE.
ANYTHING I WANT, HUH...?
MEW
FWAP
EXCEPT THAT UNREASONABLE OR MORALLY QUESTIONABLE REQUESTS ARE OFF THE TABLE.
ONLY GENTLEMANLY REQUESTS, PLEASE.
DARN!
ALL RIGHT, YOU'RE ON!
WHAT SHOULD WE PLAY...?
HOW ABOUT...
...A SIMPLE GAME OF OLD MAID?
JOKER

OLD MAID SUDDEN DEATH!

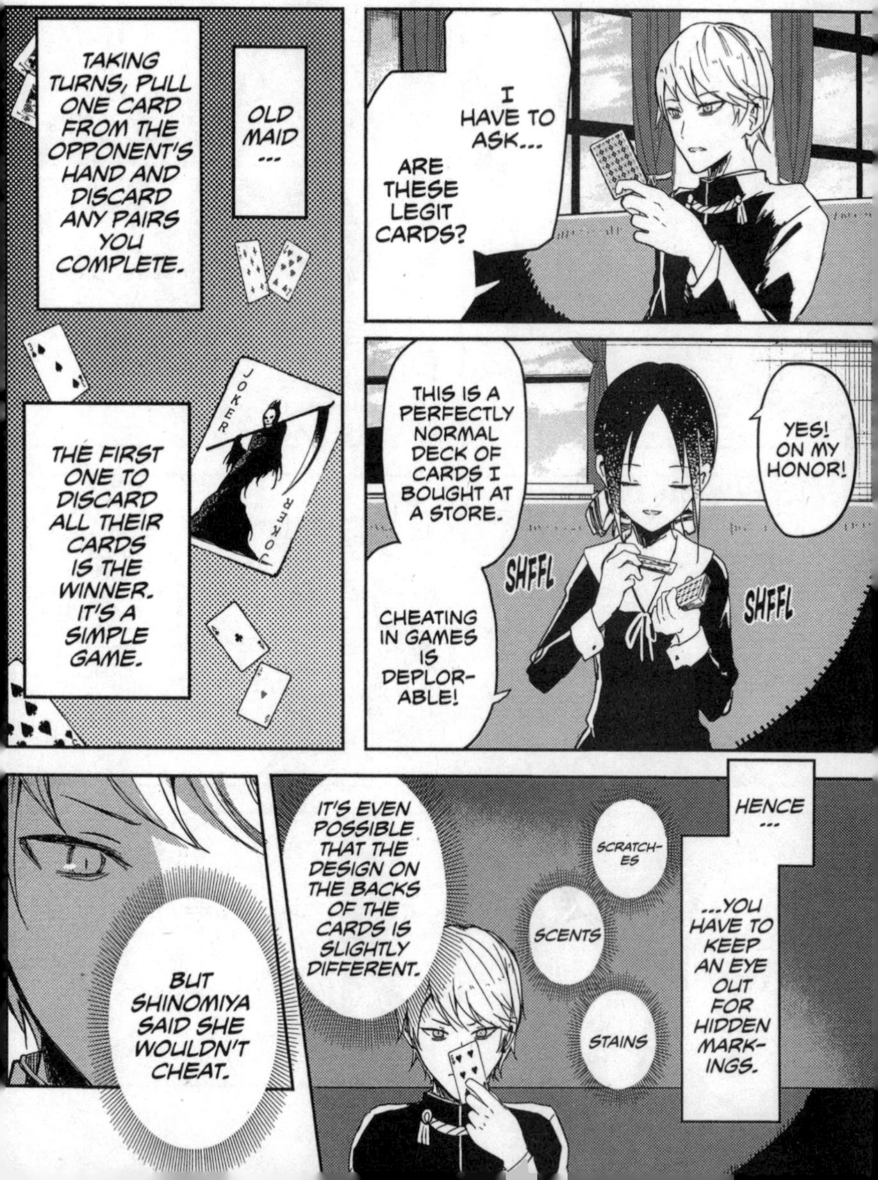
I HAVE TO ASK...
ARE THESE LEGIT CARDS?
YES! ON MY HONOR!
THIS IS A PERFECTLY NORMAL DECK OF CARDS I BOUGHT AT A STORE.
SHFFL
SHFFL
CHEATING IN GAMES IS DEPLORABLE!
OLD MAID...
TAKING TURNS, PULL ONE CARD FROM THE OPPONENT'S HAND AND DISCARD ANY PAIRS YOU COMPLETE.
JOKER
JOKER
THE FIRST ONE TO DISCARD ALL THEIR CARDS IS THE WINNER. IT'S A SIMPLE GAME.
HENCE...
...YOU HAVE TO KEEP AN EYE OUT FOR HIDDEN MARKINGS.
SCRATCHES
SCENTS
STAINS
IT'S EVEN POSSIBLE THAT THE DESIGN ON THE BACKS OF THE CARDS IS SLIGHTLY DIFFERENT.
BUT SHINOMIYA SAID SHE WOULDN'T CHEAT.

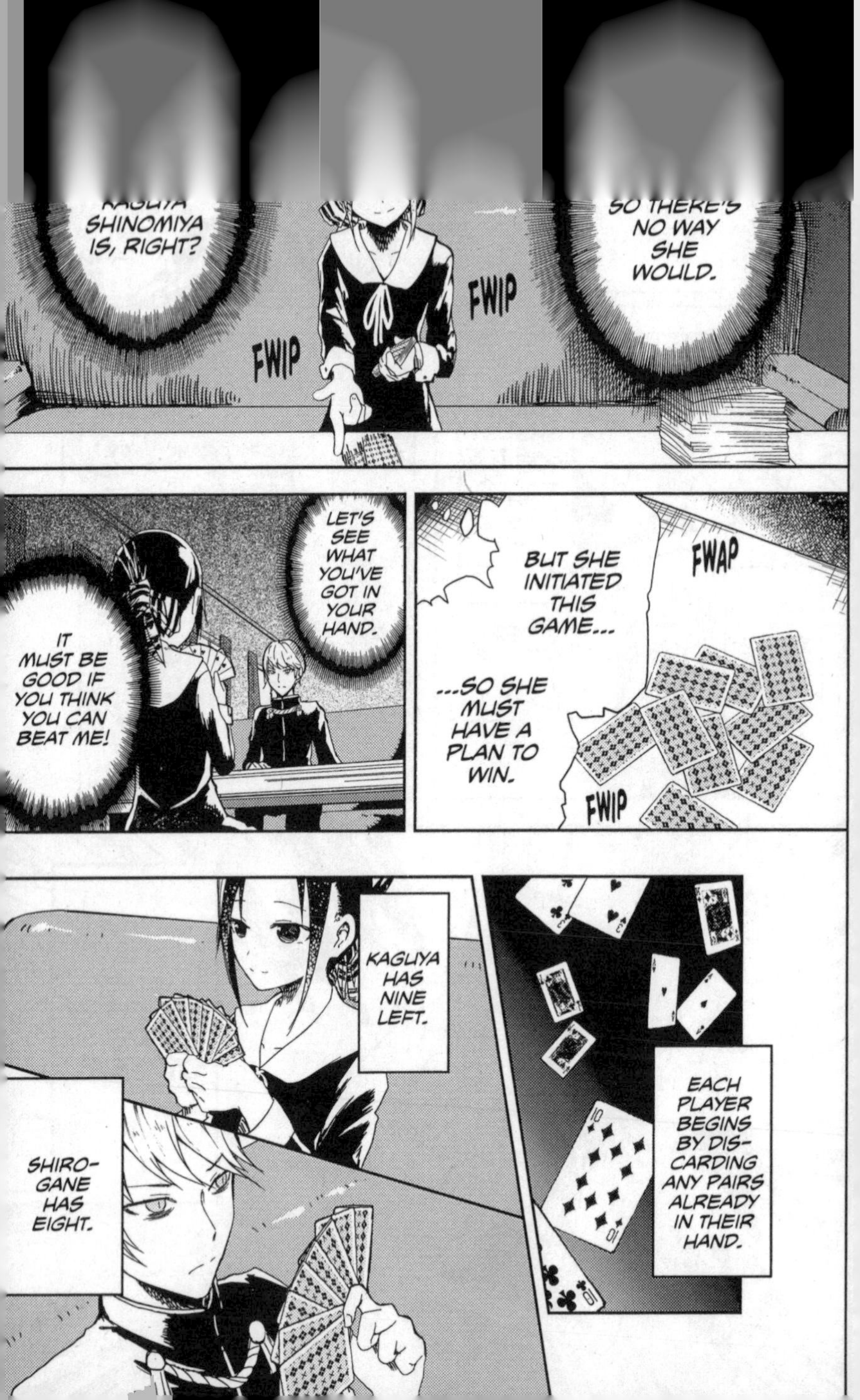
SO THERE'S NO WAY SHE WOULD.
FWIP
FWIP
SHINOMIYA IS, RIGHT?
BUT SHE INITIATED THIS GAME...
FWAP
...SO SHE MUST HAVE A PLAN TO WIN.
FWIP
LET'S SEE WHAT YOU'VE GOT IN YOUR HAND.
IT MUST BE GOOD IF YOU THINK YOU CAN BEAT ME!
EACH PLAYER BEGINS BY DIS-CARDING ANY PAIRS ALREADY IN THEIR HAND.
KAGUYA HAS NINE LEFT.
SHIRO-GANE HAS EIGHT.

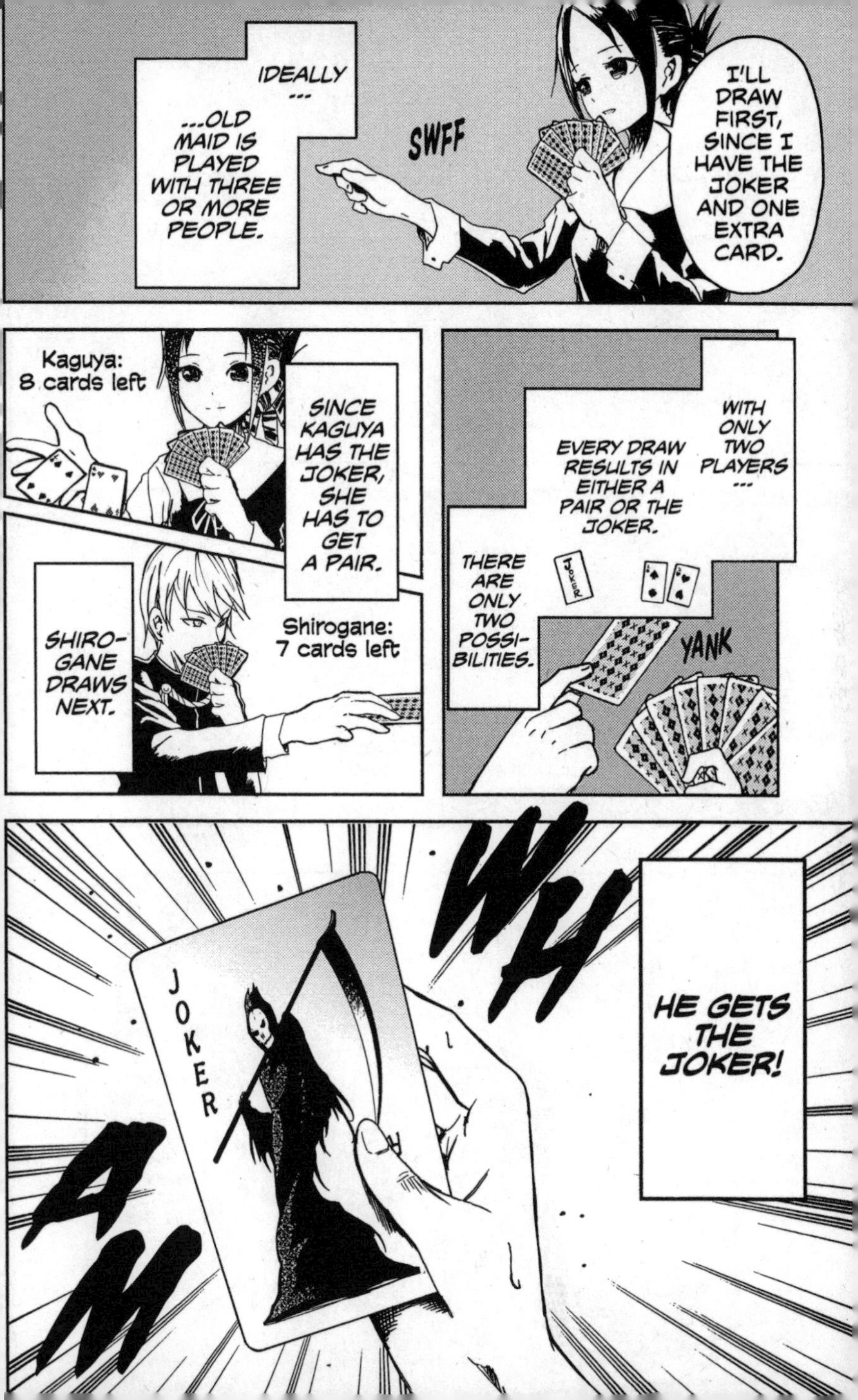
I'LL DRAW FIRST, SINCE I HAVE THE JOKER AND ONE EXTRA CARD.
SWFF
IDEALLY --- ...OLD MAID IS PLAYED WITH THREE OR MORE PEOPLE.
WITH ONLY TWO PLAYERS ---
EVERY DRAW RESULTS IN EITHER A PAIR OR THE JOKER.
THERE ARE ONLY TWO POSSIBILITIES.
JOKER
YANK
SINCE KAGUYA HAS THE JOKER, SHE HAS TO GET A PAIR.
Kaguya: 8 cards left
Shirogane: 7 cards left
SHIROGANE DRAWS NEXT.
HE GETS THE JOKER!
WHAM
JOKER

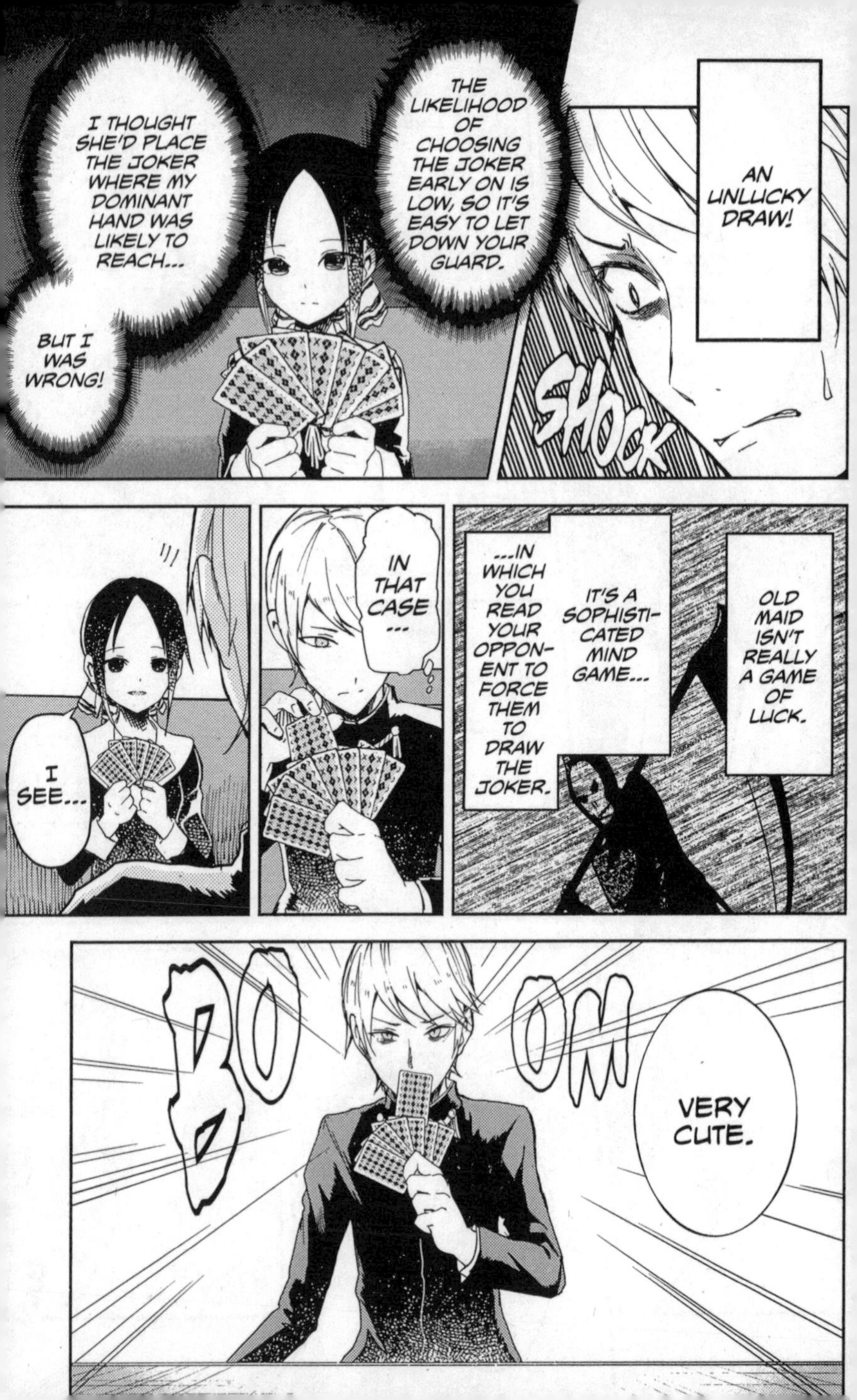
AN UNLUCKY DRAW!
SHOCK
THE LIKELIHOOD OF CHOOSING THE JOKER EARLY ON IS LOW, SO IT'S EASY TO LET DOWN YOUR GUARD.
I THOUGHT SHE'D PLACE THE JOKER WHERE MY DOMINANT HAND WAS LIKELY TO REACH...
BUT I WAS WRONG!
OLD MAID ISN'T REALLY A GAME OF LUCK.
IT'S A SOPHISTICATED MIND GAME...
...IN WHICH YOU READ YOUR OPPONENT TO FORCE THEM TO DRAW THE JOKER.
IN THAT CASE...
I SEE...
BOOM
VERY CUTE.

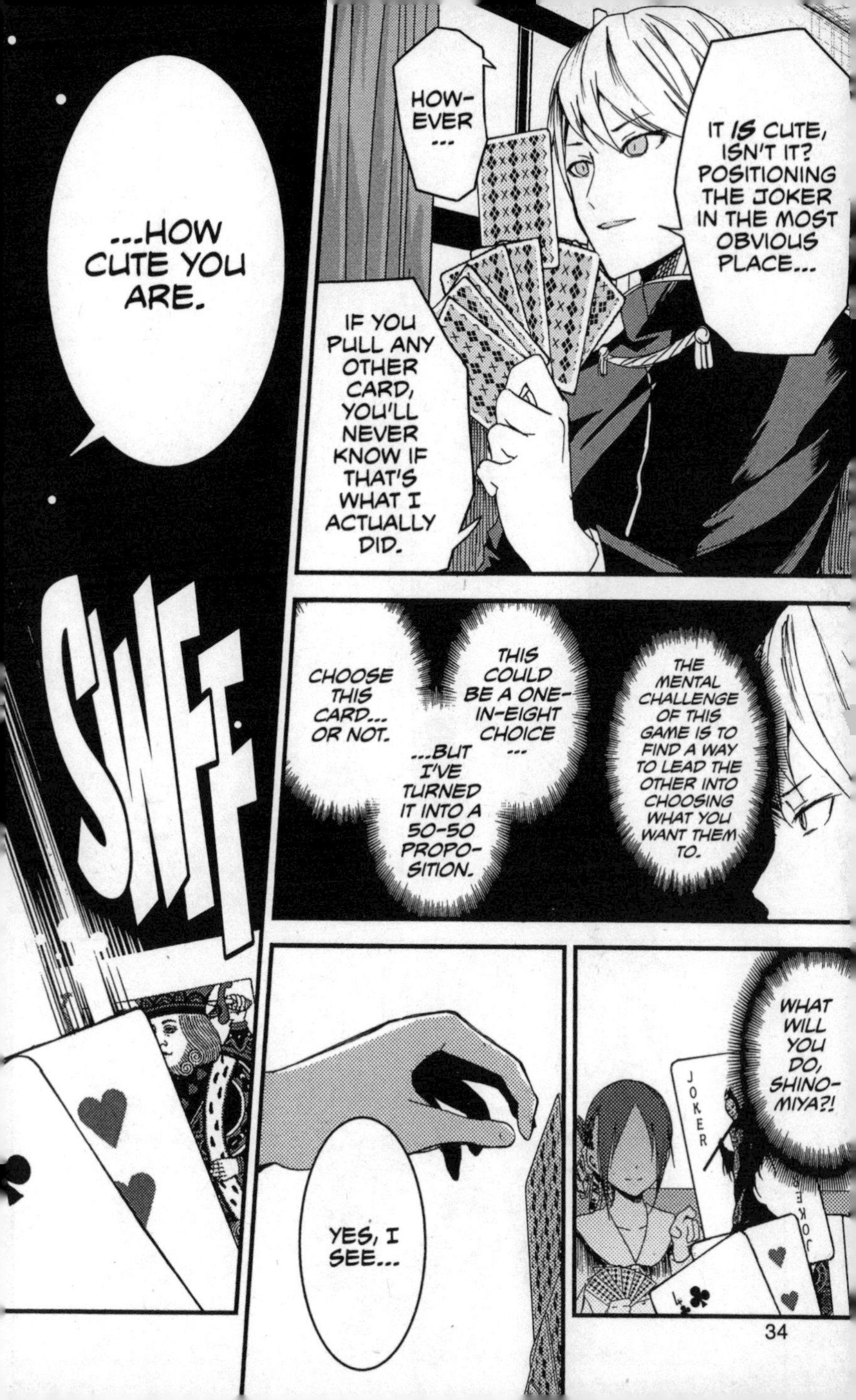
IT *IS* CUTE, ISN'T IT? POSITIONING THE JOKER IN THE MOST OBVIOUS PLACE...
HOW-EVER...
IF YOU PULL ANY OTHER CARD, YOU'LL NEVER KNOW IF THAT'S WHAT I ACTUALLY DID.
THE MENTAL CHALLENGE OF THIS GAME IS TO FIND A WAY TO LEAD THE OTHER INTO CHOOSING WHAT YOU WANT THEM TO.
THIS COULD BE A ONE-IN-EIGHT CHOICE...
...BUT I'VE TURNED IT INTO A 50-50 PROPOSITION.
CHOOSE THIS CARD... OR NOT.
WHAT WILL YOU DO, SHINOMIYA?!
JOKER
YES, I SEE...
...HOW CUTE YOU ARE.
SNIFF

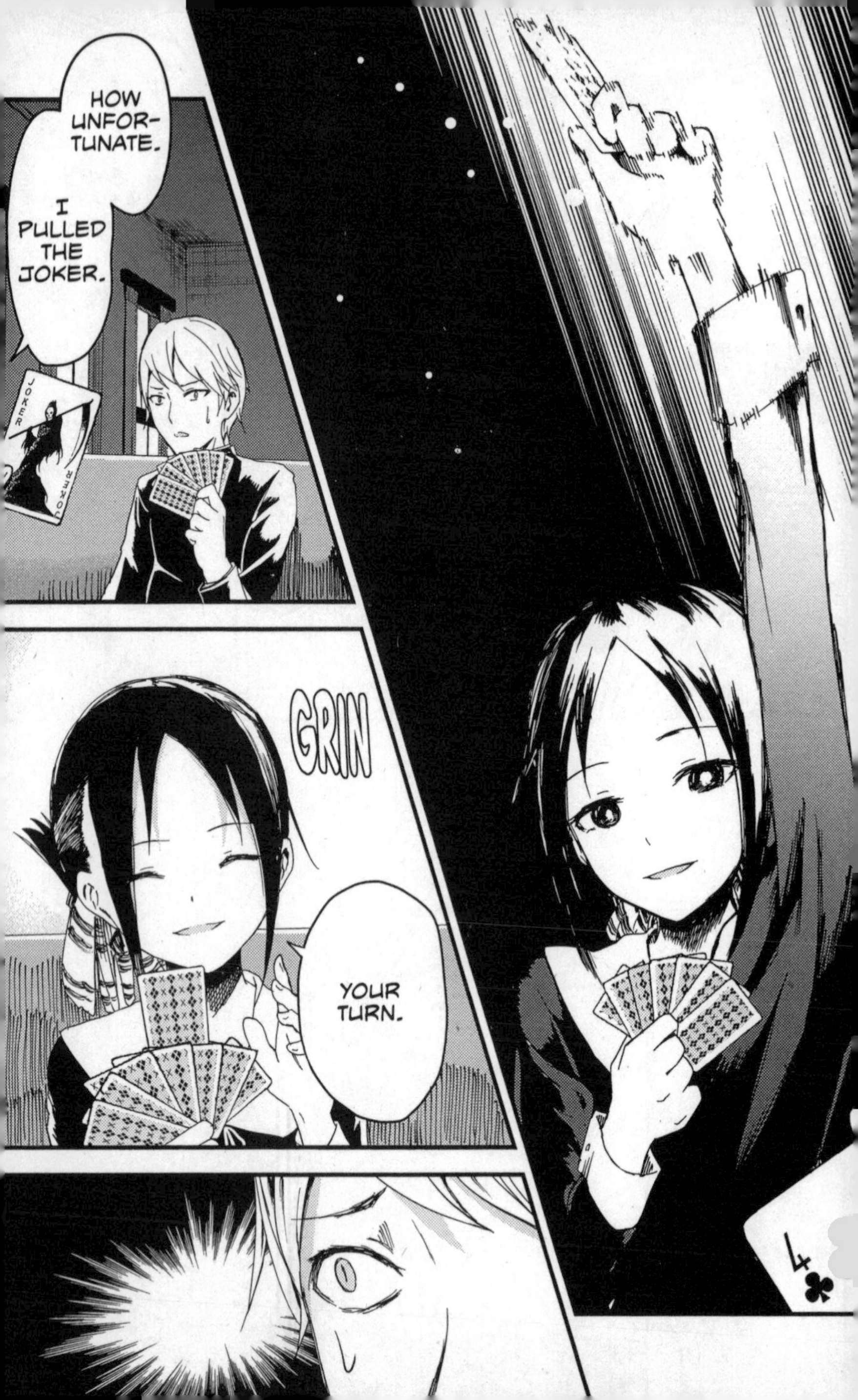
HOW UNFORTUNATE.
I PULLED THE JOKER.
JOKER
GRIN
YOUR TURN.

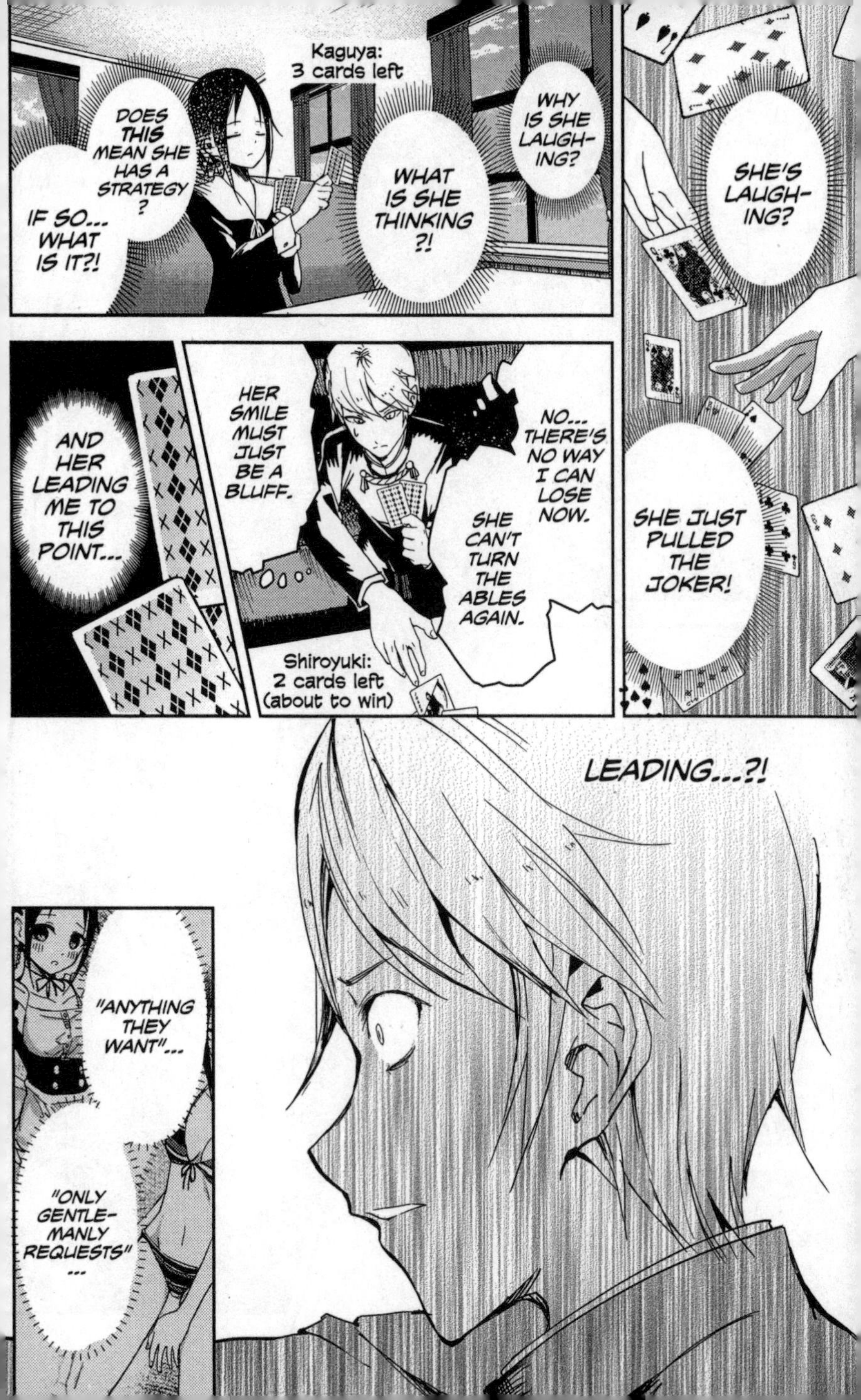
SHE'S LAUGHING?
SHE JUST PULLED THE JOKER!
WHY IS SHE LAUGHING?
WHAT IS SHE THINKING?!
Kaguya: 3 cards left
DOES THIS MEAN SHE HAS A STRATEGY?
IF SO... WHAT IS IT?!
NO... THERE'S NO WAY I CAN LOSE NOW.
SHE CAN'T TURN THE ABLES AGAIN.
HER SMILE MUST JUST BE A BLUFF.
Shiroyuki: 2 cards left (about to win)
AND HER LEADING ME TO THIS POINT...
LEADING...?!
"ANYTHING THEY WANT"...
"ONLY GENTLEMANLY REQUESTS"...

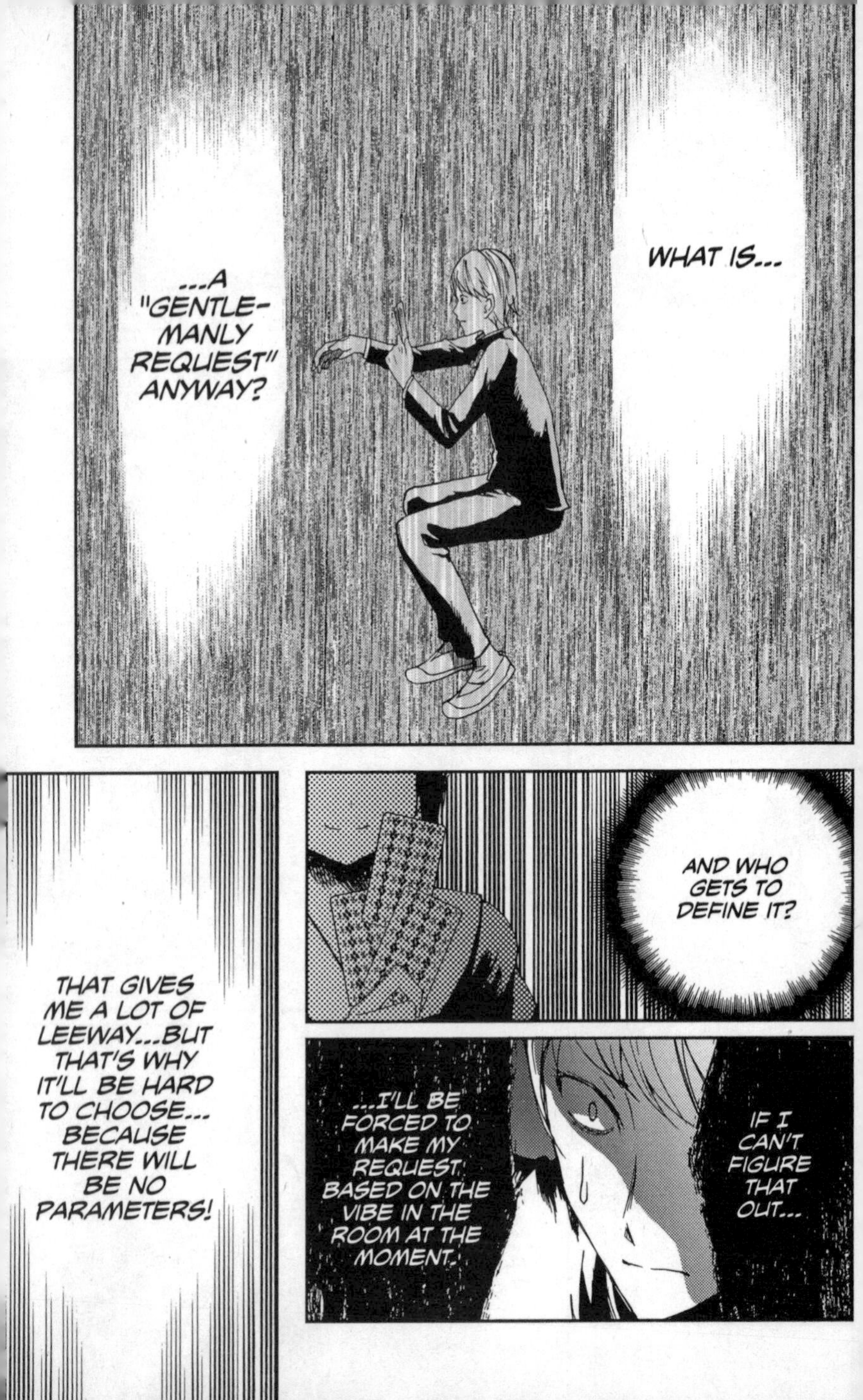
WHAT IS...
...A "GENTLE-MANLY REQUEST" ANYWAY?
AND WHO GETS TO DEFINE IT?
IF I CAN'T FIGURE THAT OUT...
...I'LL BE FORCED TO MAKE MY REQUEST BASED ON THE VIBE IN THE ROOM AT THE MOMENT.
THAT GIVES ME A LOT OF LEEWAY...BUT THAT'S WHY IT'LL BE HARD TO CHOOSE... BECAUSE THERE WILL BE NO PARAMETERS!

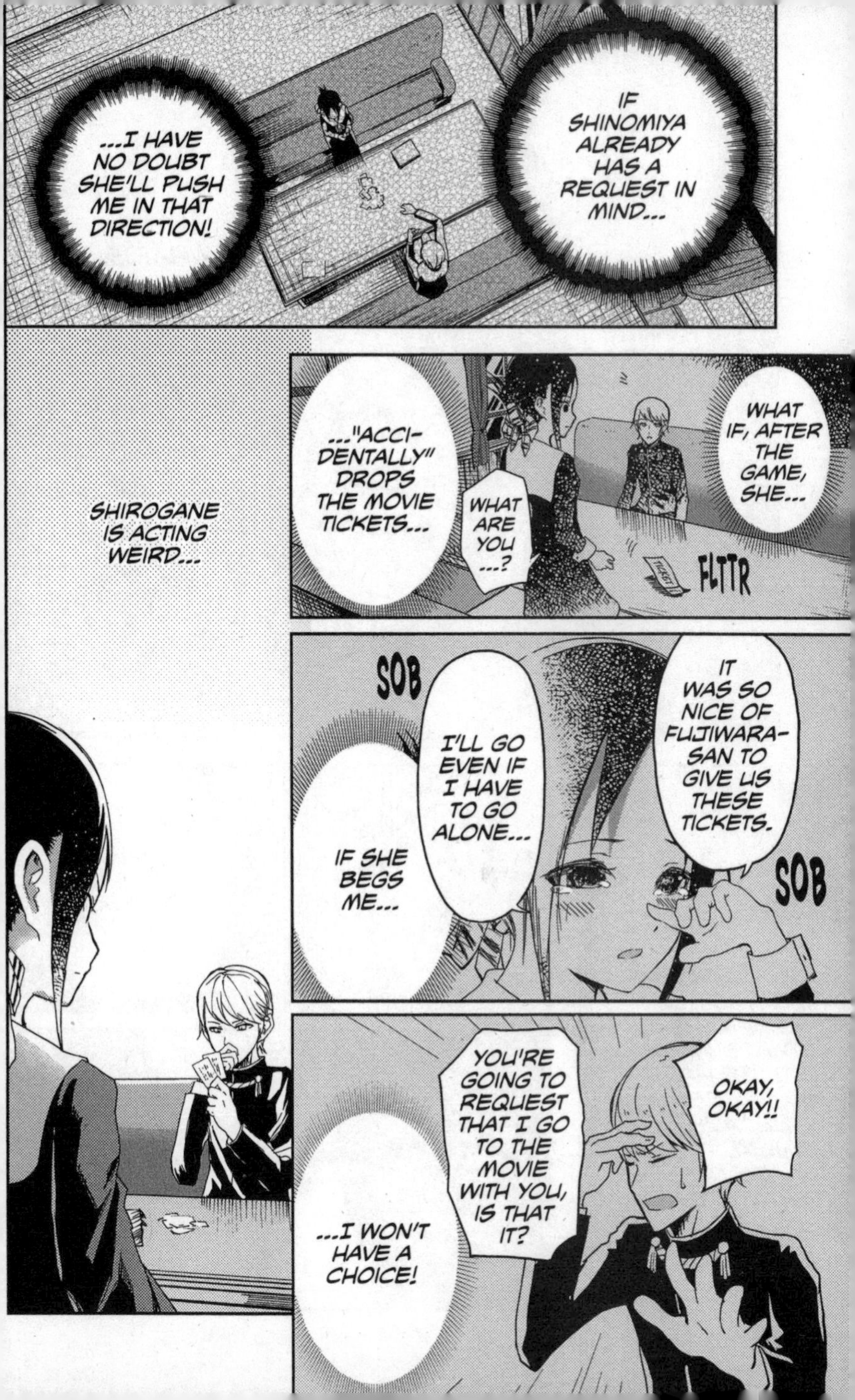
IF SHINOMIYA ALREADY HAS A REQUEST IN MIND...
...I HAVE NO DOUBT SHE'LL PUSH ME IN THAT DIRECTION!
WHAT IF, AFTER THE GAME, SHE...
FLTTR
WHAT ARE YOU ...?
..."ACCIDENTALLY" DROPS THE MOVIE TICKETS...
IT WAS SO NICE OF FUJIWARA-SAN TO GIVE US THESE TICKETS.
SOB
SOB
I'LL GO EVEN IF I HAVE TO GO ALONE...
IF SHE BEGS ME...
OKAY, OKAY!!
YOU'RE GOING TO REQUEST THAT I GO TO THE MOVIE WITH YOU, IS THAT IT?
...I WON'T HAVE A CHOICE!
SHIROGANE IS ACTING WEIRD...

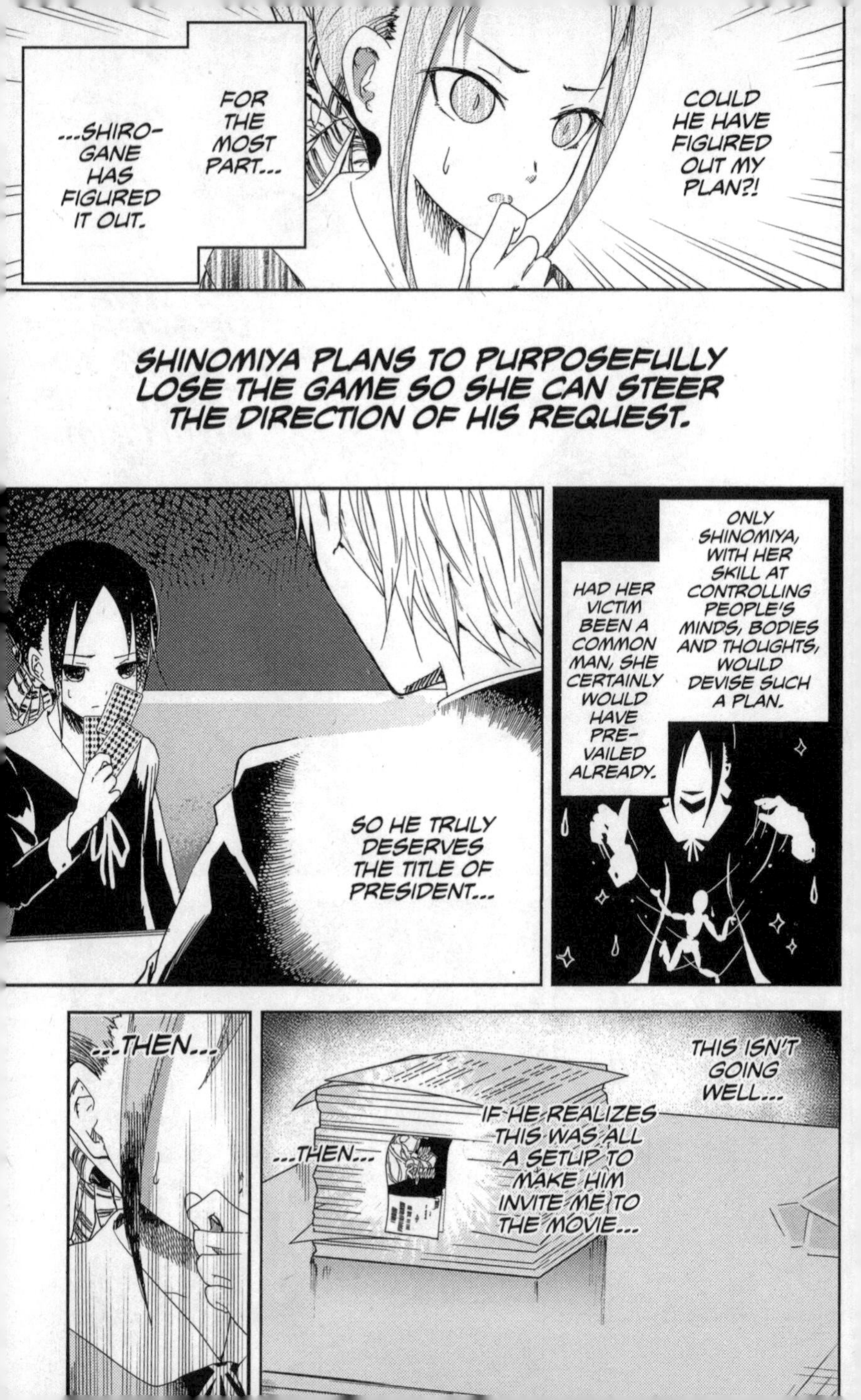
COULD HE HAVE FIGURED OUT MY PLAN?!
FOR THE MOST PART...
...SHIRO-GANE HAS FIGURED IT OUT.
SHINOMIYA PLANS TO PURPOSEFULLY LOSE THE GAME SO SHE CAN STEER THE DIRECTION OF HIS REQUEST.
ONLY SHINOMIYA, WITH HER SKILL AT CONTROLLING PEOPLE'S MINDS, BODIES AND THOUGHTS, WOULD DEVISE SUCH A PLAN.
HAD HER VICTIM BEEN A COMMON MAN, SHE CERTAINLY WOULD HAVE PRE-VAILED ALREADY.
SO HE TRULY DESERVES THE TITLE OF PRESIDENT...
THIS ISN'T GOING WELL...
IF HE REALIZES THIS WAS ALL A SETUP TO MAKE HIM INVITE ME TO THE MOVIE...
...THEN...
...THEN...

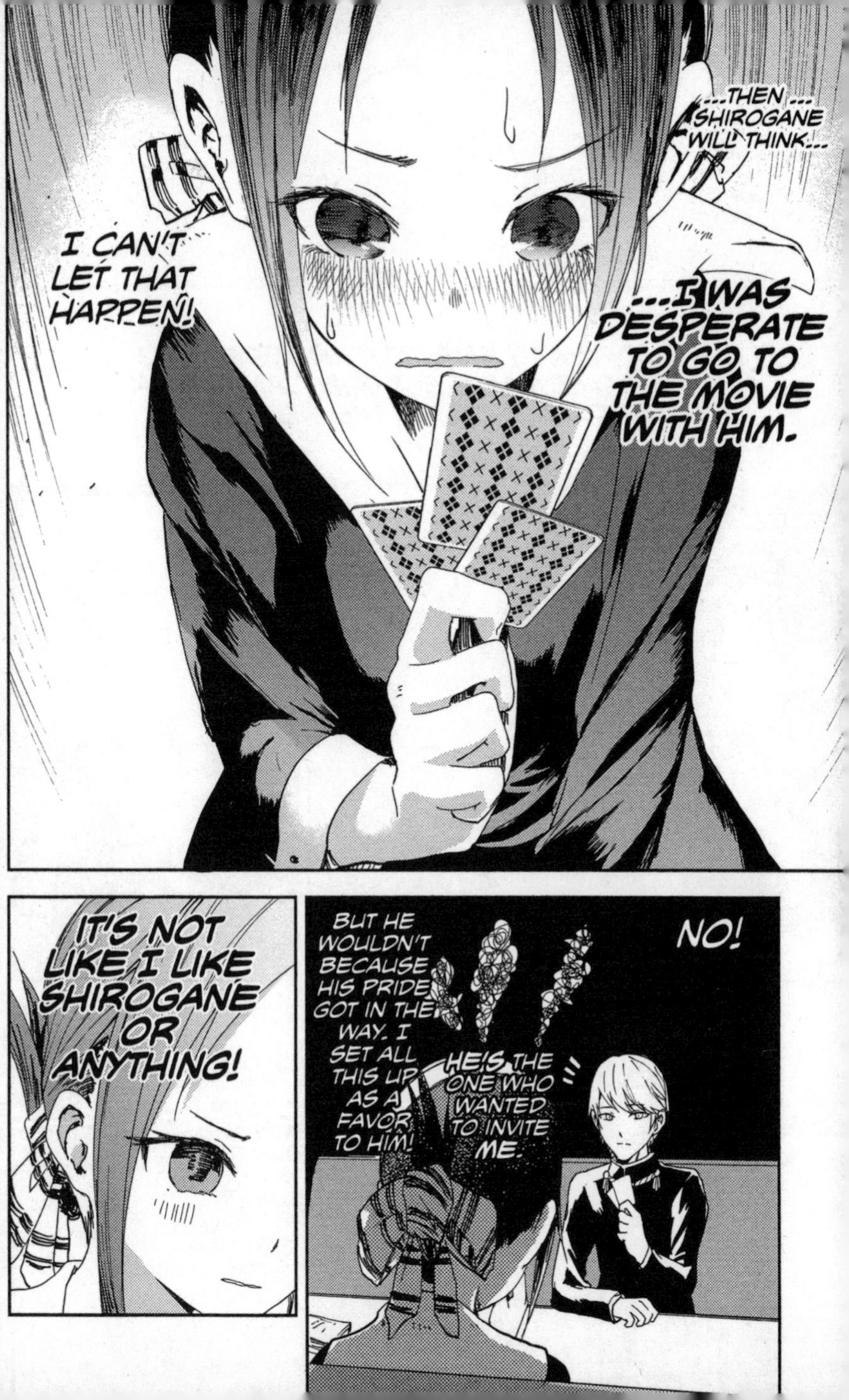
...THEN ... SHIROGANE WILL THINK...
...I WAS DESPERATE TO GO TO THE MOVIE WITH HIM.
I CAN'T LET THAT HAPPEN!
NO!
HE'S THE ONE WHO WANTED TO INVITE ME.
BUT HE WOULDN'T BECAUSE HIS PRIDE GOT IN THE WAY. I SET ALL THIS UP AS A FAVOR TO HIM!
IT'S NOT LIKE I LIKE SHIROGANE OR ANYTHING!

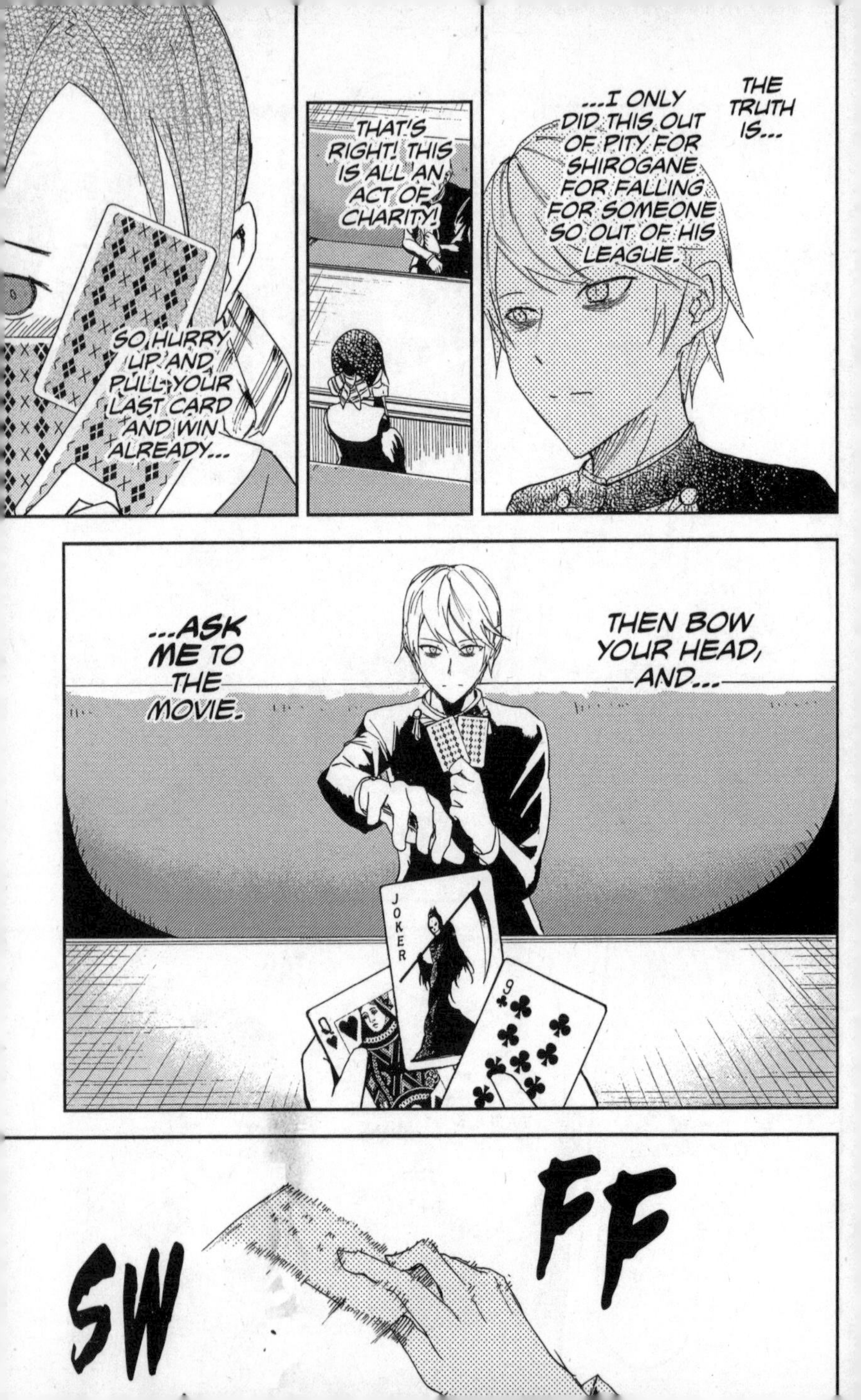
THE TRUTH IS...
...I ONLY DID THIS OUT OF PITY FOR SHIROGANE FOR FALLING FOR SOMEONE SO OUT OF HIS LEAGUE.
THAT'S RIGHT! THIS IS ALL AN ACT OF CHARITY!
SO HURRY UP AND PULL YOUR LAST CARD AND WIN ALREADY...
THEN BOW YOUR HEAD, AND...
...ASK ME TO THE MOVIE.
JOKER
SW FF

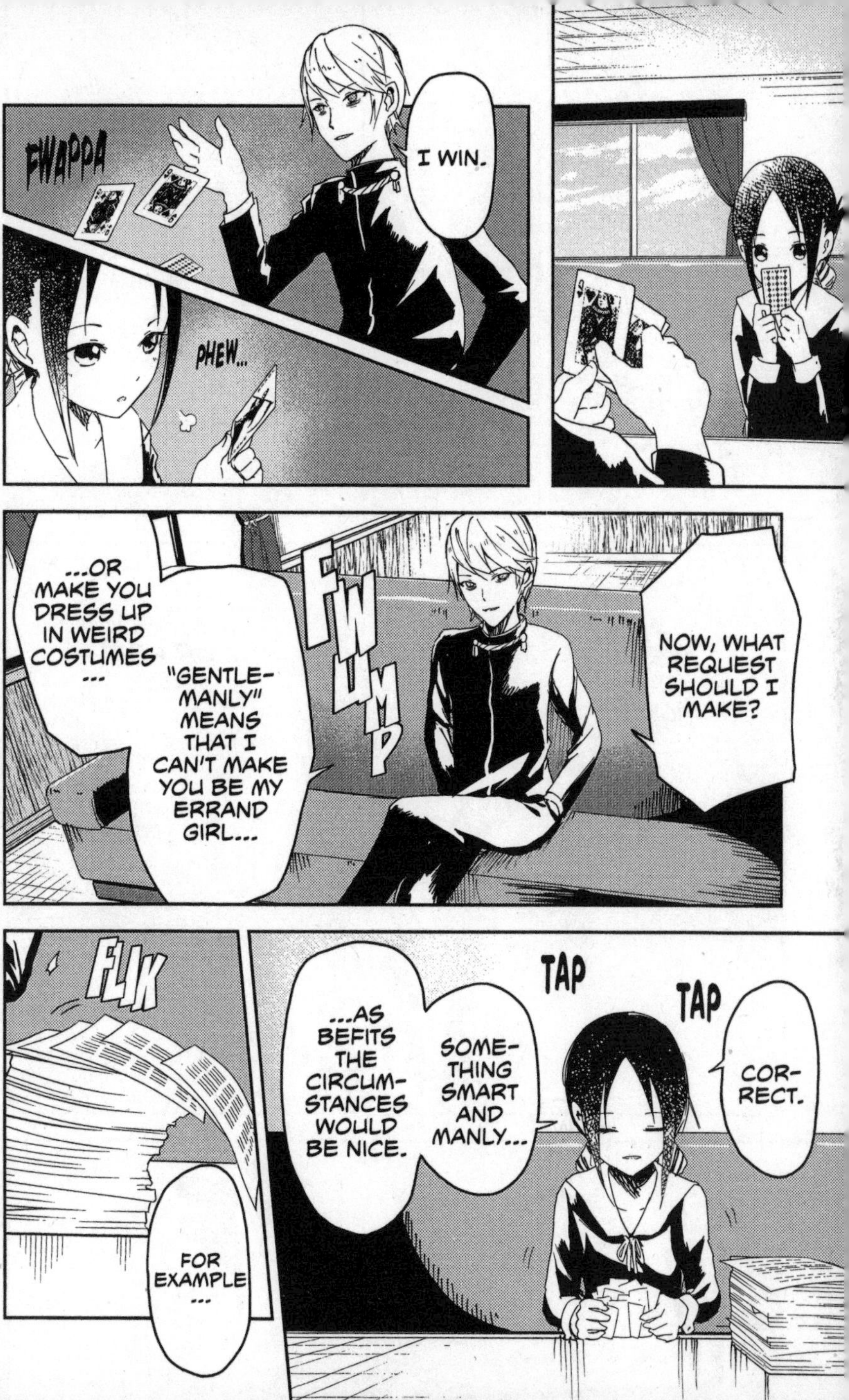
I WIN.
FWAPPA
PHEW...
NOW, WHAT REQUEST SHOULD I MAKE?
FWUMP
"GENTLE-MANLY" MEANS THAT I CAN'T MAKE YOU BE MY ERRAND GIRL...
...OR MAKE YOU DRESS UP IN WEIRD COSTUMES...
TAP
TAP
COR-RECT.
SOME-THING SMART AND MANLY...
...AS BEFITS THE CIRCUM-STANCES WOULD BE NICE.
FLIK
FOR EXAMPLE...

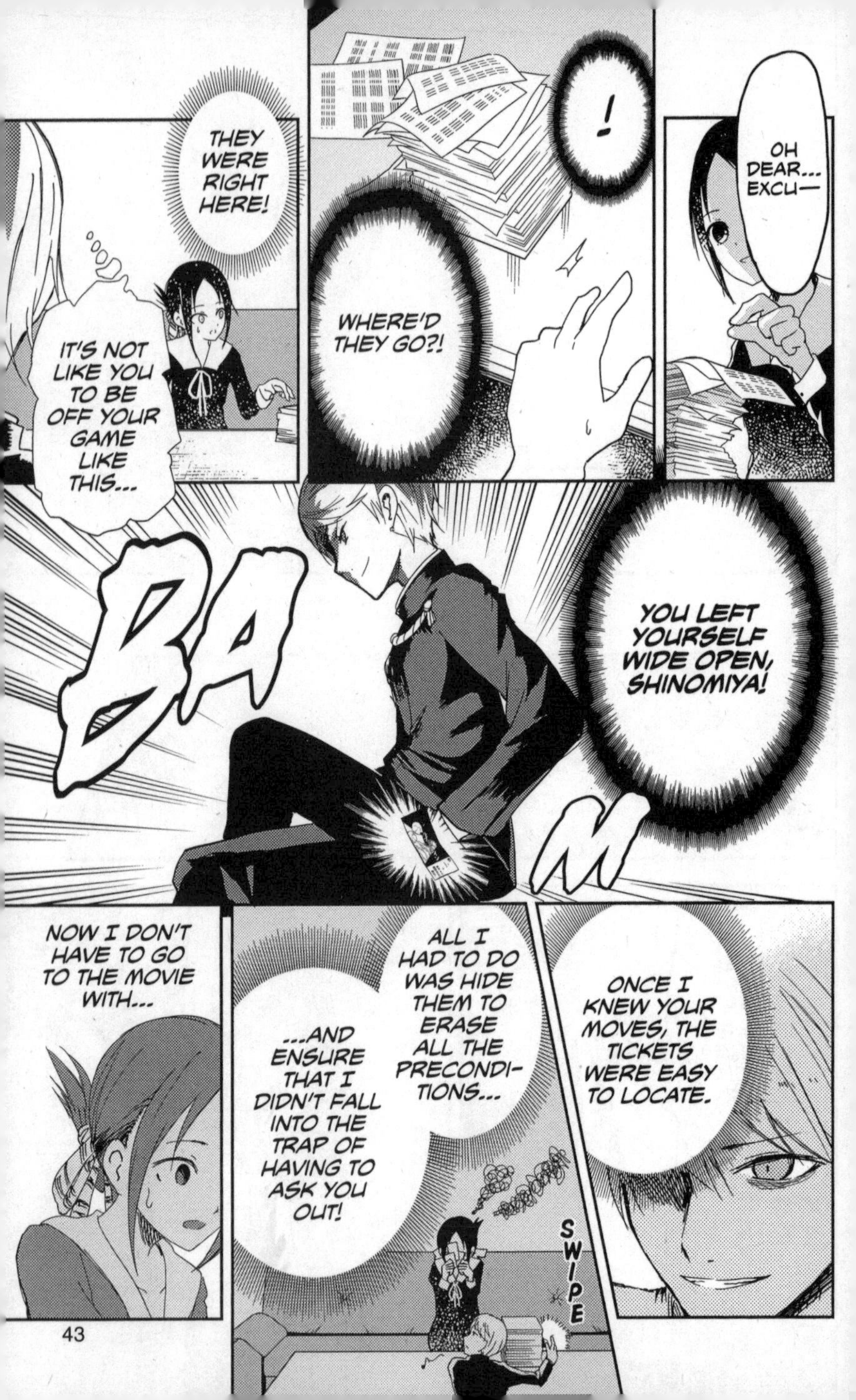
OH DEAR... EXCU—
!
WHERE'D THEY GO?!
THEY WERE RIGHT HERE!
IT'S NOT LIKE YOU TO BE OFF YOUR GAME LIKE THIS...
YOU LEFT YOURSELF WIDE OPEN, SHINOMIYA!
BAM
ONCE I KNEW YOUR MOVES, THE TICKETS WERE EASY TO LOCATE.
ALL I HAD TO DO WAS HIDE THEM TO ERASE ALL THE PRECONDI-TIONS...
...AND ENSURE THAT I DIDN'T FALL INTO THE TRAP OF HAVING TO ASK YOU OUT!
SWIPE
NOW I DON'T HAVE TO GO TO THE MOVIE WITH...

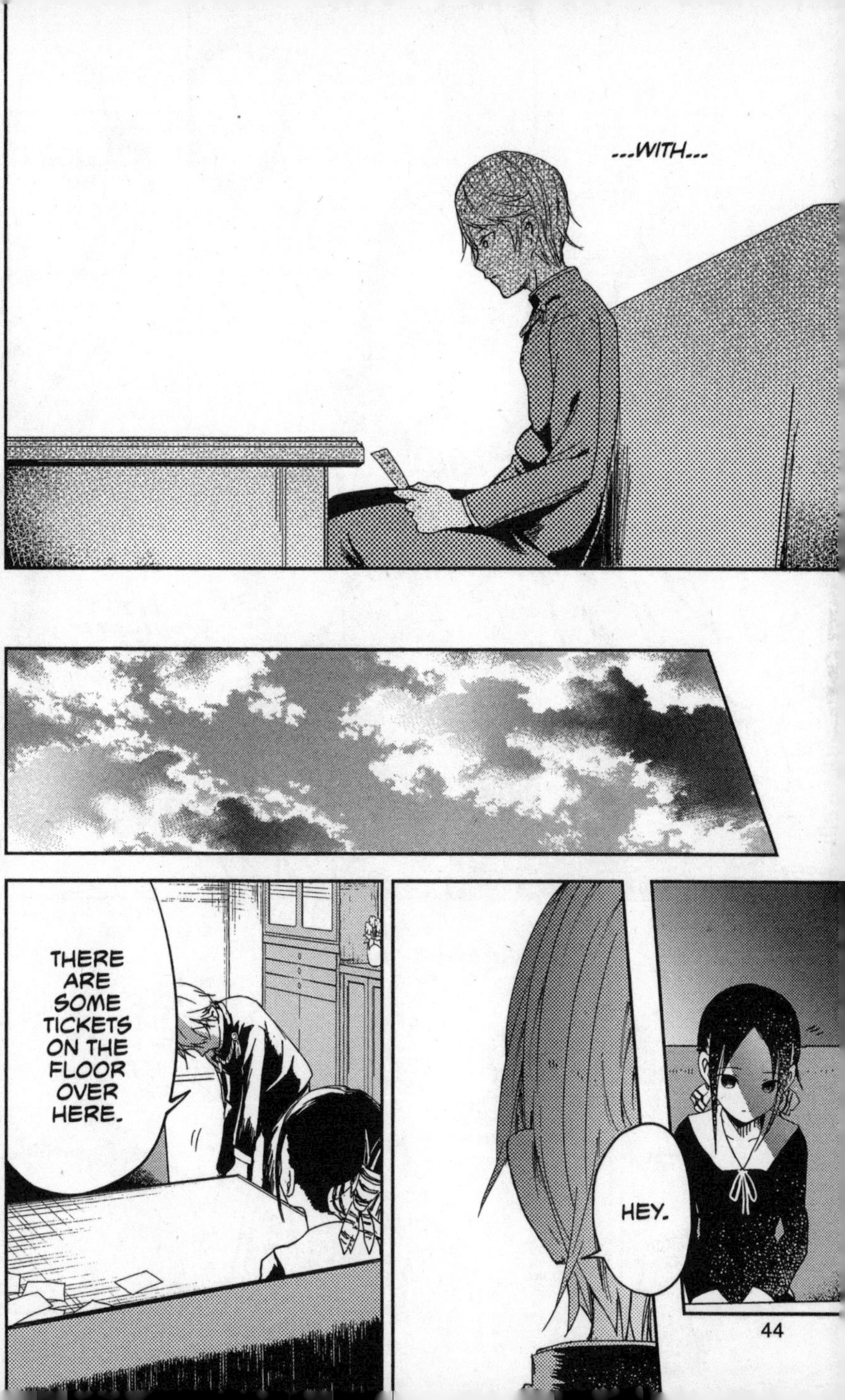
...WITH...
HEY.
THERE ARE SOME TICKETS ON THE FLOOR OVER HERE.

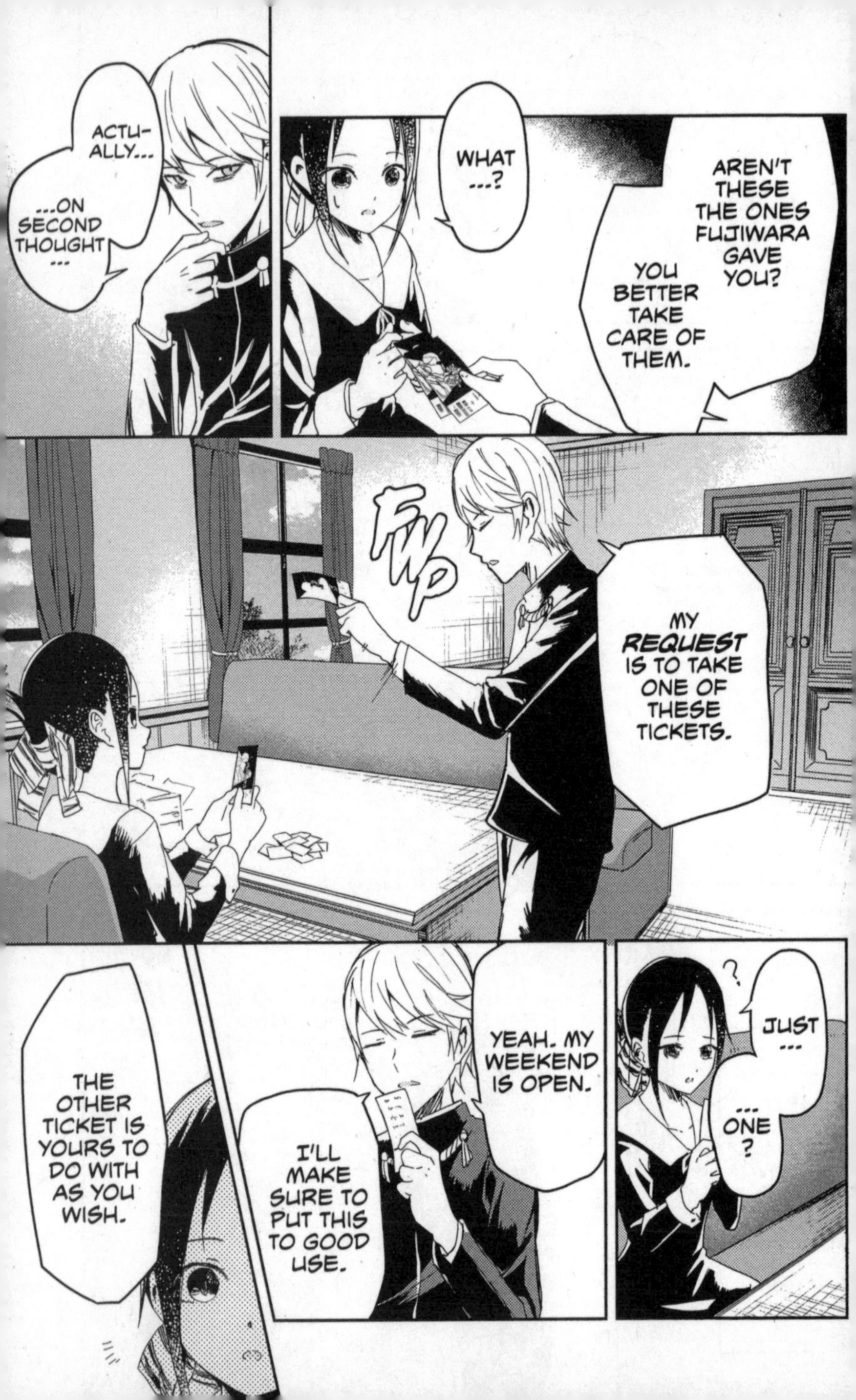
AREN'T THESE THE ONES FUJIWARA GAVE YOU?
YOU BETTER TAKE CARE OF THEM.
WHAT ...?
ACTU-ALLY...
...ON SECOND THOUGHT ...
FWP
MY **REQUEST** IS TO TAKE ONE OF THESE TICKETS.
JUST ...
... ONE ?
YEAH. MY WEEKEND IS OPEN.
I'LL MAKE SURE TO PUT THIS TO GOOD USE.
THE OTHER TICKET IS YOURS TO DO WITH AS YOU WISH.

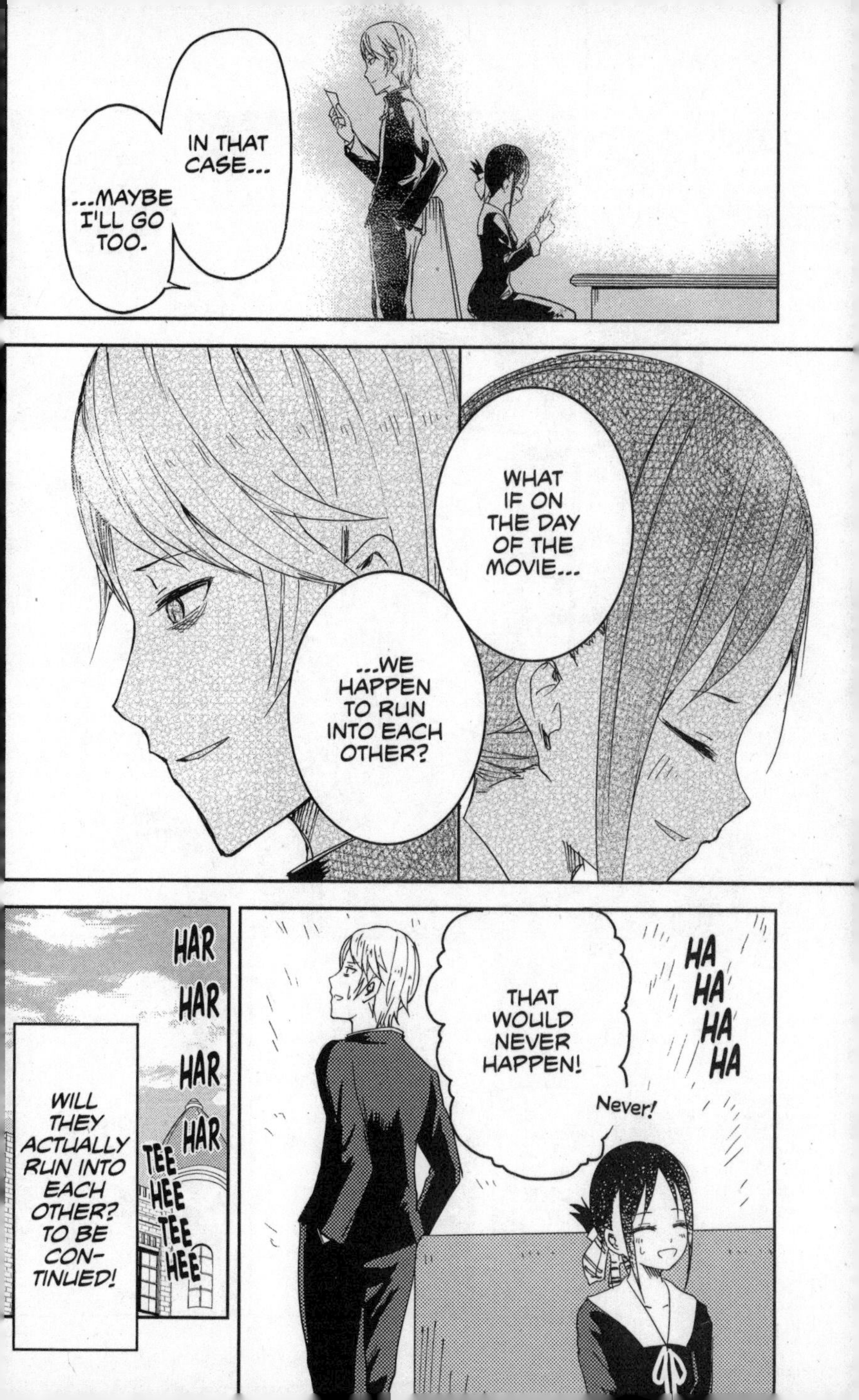
IN THAT CASE...
...MAYBE I'LL GO TOO.
WHAT IF ON THE DAY OF THE MOVIE...
...WE HAPPEN TO RUN INTO EACH OTHER?
HA HA HA HA
THAT WOULD NEVER HAPPEN!
Never!
HAR HAR HAR HAR
TEE HEE TEE HEE
WILL THEY ACTUALLY RUN INTO EACH OTHER? TO BE CON-TINUED!

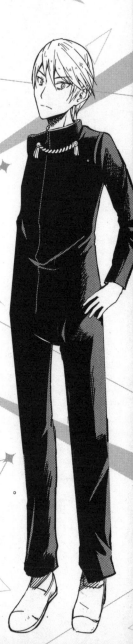

MIYUKI SHIROGANE

Miyuki Shirogane

◆ Shuchiin Academy
   High School Second-Year
◆ Student Council President
◆ Notable characteristics:
   penetrating eyes
◆ Main character in this story

A monster who ranks at the top of his class in national practice exams and is recognized as a genius for his exceptional schoolwork. He has strong administrative skills. However, it would be incorrect to classify these traits as innate. He is merely addicted to hard work.

It seems that his public image of accomplishments and brilliance is critical to his mental stability. His longing for approval is actually rather pathological. Consequently, it is taboo to utter the word "stupid" around him. At worst, unable to maintain his fragile ego, he might die an agonizing death.

Aside from his psychological issues, he is a good person.

He never turns down requests for a favor or advice, has the best of intentions, is unable to ignore those in need and naturally gravitates toward those in need of help. He spends ten hours a day studying and still manages to give his all to his part-time job. When he sleeps is unknown. His penetrating gaze might be a combination of lack of sleep and nearsightedness. He is also a serious caffeine addict and needs a dose every three hours or his battery goes dead and he abruptly falls asleep.

His hair color is just for manga illustrative purposes. He is 100 percent ethnically Japanese.

KAGUYA-SAMA
LOVE IS WAR

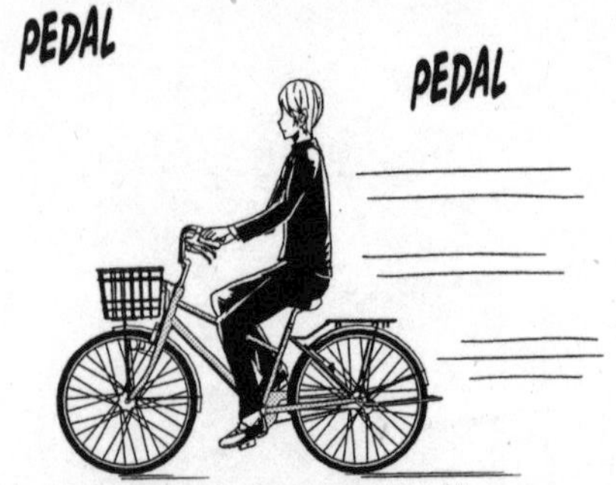
PEDAL
PEDAL

Battle 3 I Don't Know Kaguya All That Well

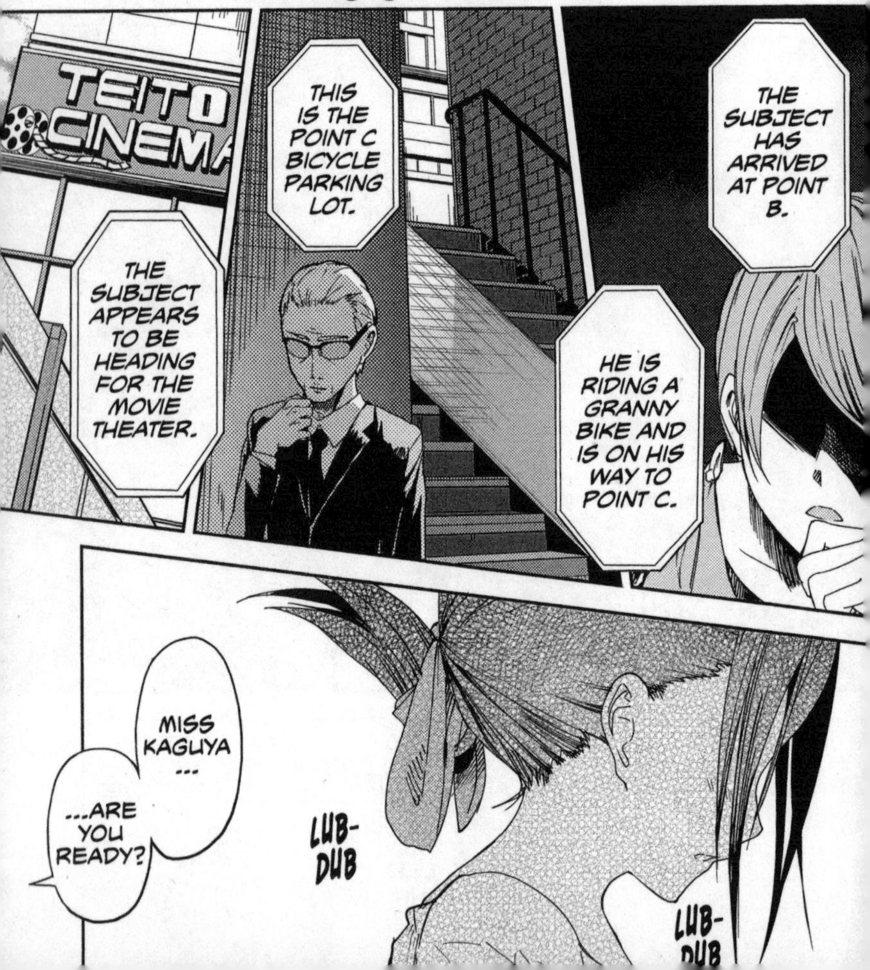
THE SUBJECT HAS ARRIVED AT POINT B.
HE IS RIDING A GRANNY BIKE AND IS ON HIS WAY TO POINT C.
THIS IS THE POINT C BICYCLE PARKING LOT.
THE SUBJECT APPEARS TO BE HEADING FOR THE MOVIE THEATER.
TEITO CINEMA
LUB-DUB
LUB-DUB
MISS KAGUYA...
...ARE YOU READY?

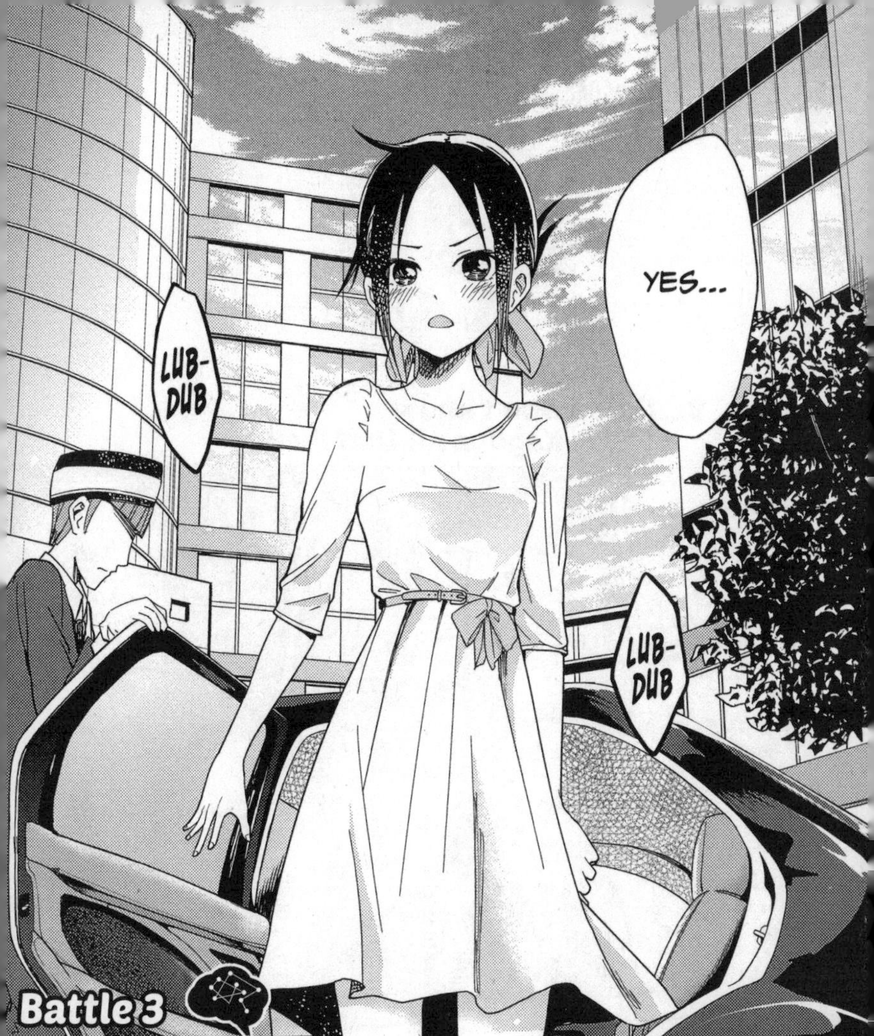
YES...
LUB-DUB
LUB-DUB
Battle 3
I Don't Know Kaguya All That Well

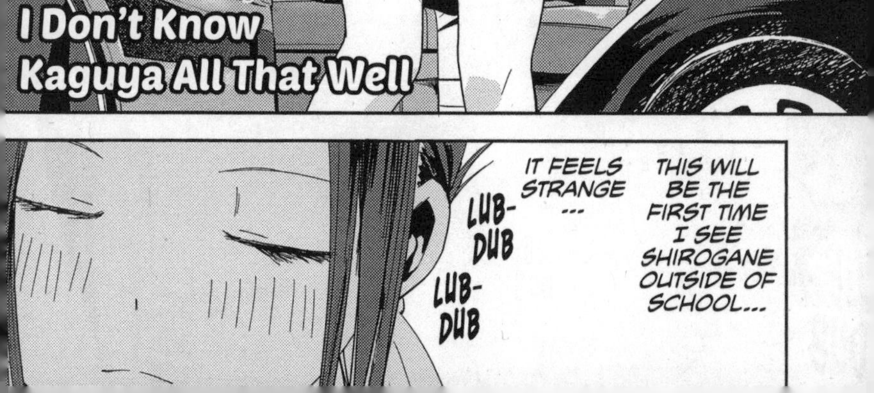
THIS WILL BE THE FIRST TIME I SEE SHIROGANE OUTSIDE OF SCHOOL...
IT FEELS STRANGE ...
LUB-DUB
LUB-DUB

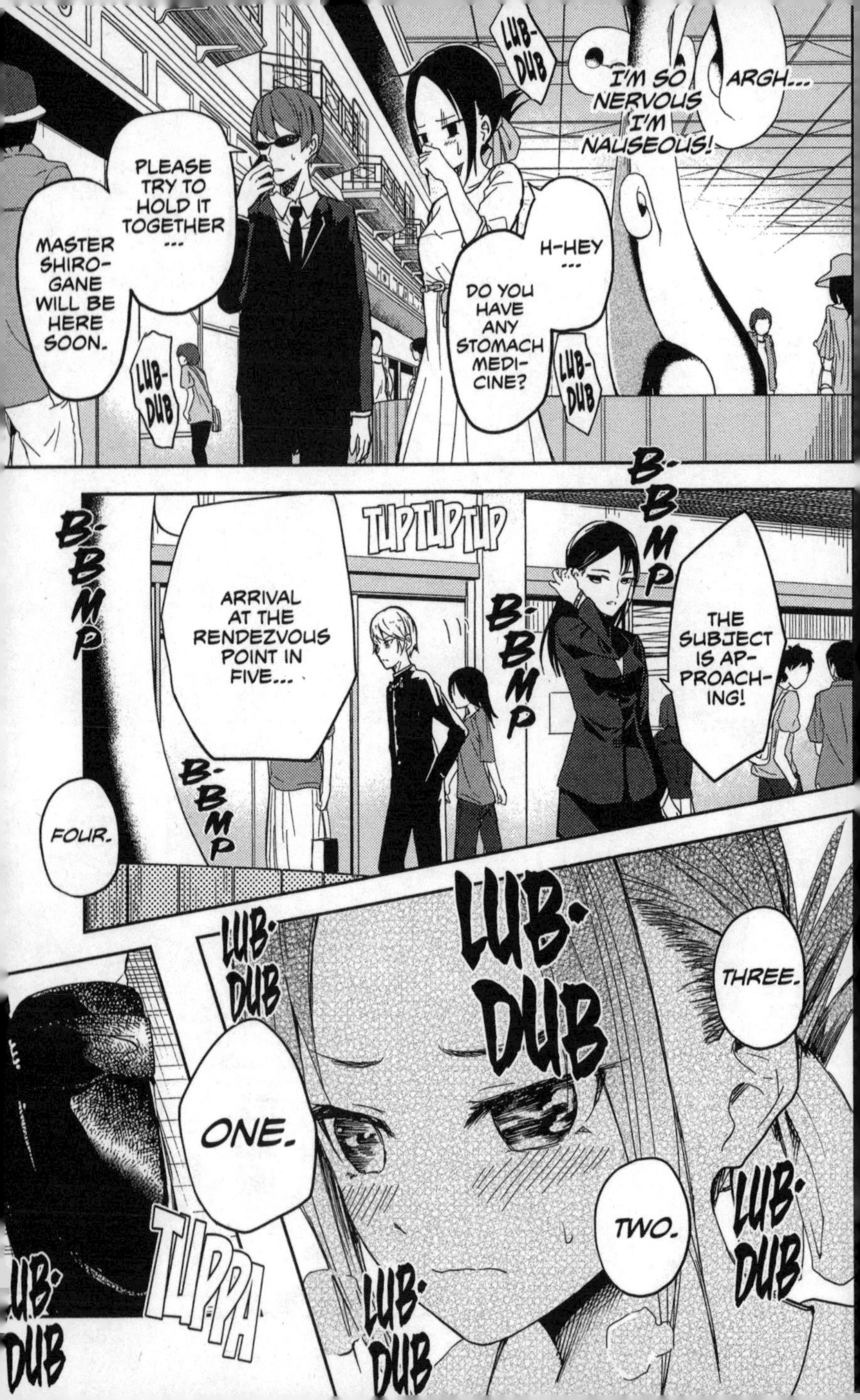
ARGH...
I'M SO NERVOUS I'M NAUSEOUS!
LUB-DUB
H-HEY... DO YOU HAVE ANY STOMACH MEDICINE?
LUB-DUB
PLEASE TRY TO HOLD IT TOGETHER...
MASTER SHIRO-GANE WILL BE HERE SOON.
LUB-DUB
B-B-MP
THE SUBJECT IS AP-PROACH-ING!
B-B-MP
TUP TUP TUP
ARRIVAL AT THE RENDEZVOUS POINT IN FIVE...
B-B-MP
B-B-MP
FOUR.
THREE.
LUB-DUB
LUB-DUB
TWO.
LUB-DUB
LUB-DUB
ONE.
LUB-DUB
TUPPA
LUB-DUB

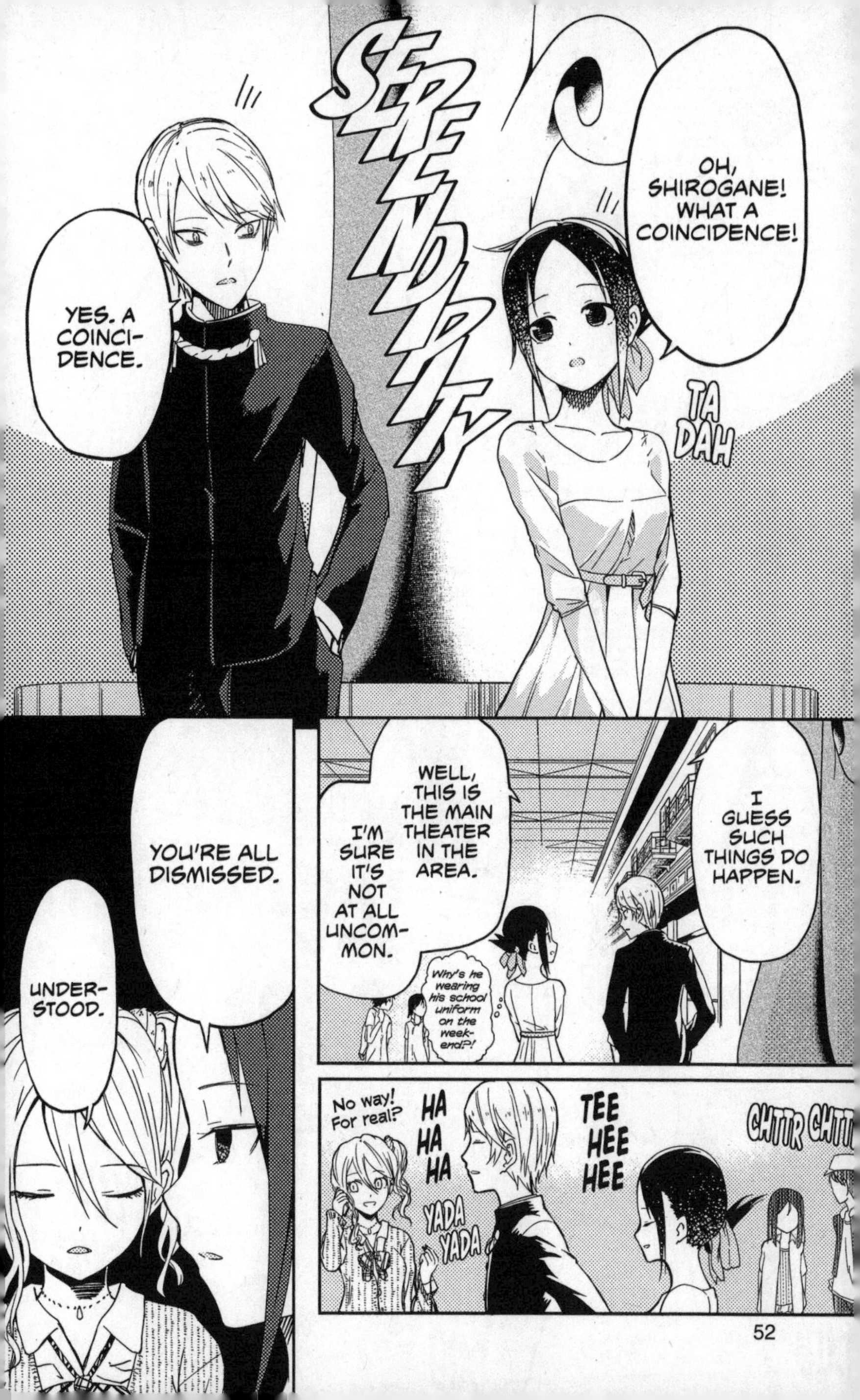
OH, SHIROGANE! WHAT A COINCIDENCE!
SERENDIPITY
TA DAH
YES. A COINCI-DENCE.
I GUESS SUCH THINGS DO HAPPEN.
WELL, THIS IS THE MAIN THEATER IN THE AREA.
I'M SURE IT'S NOT AT ALL UNCOM-MON.
Why's he wearing his school uniform on the week-end!?
CHTTR CHTT
TEE HEE HEE
HA HA HA
YADA YADA
No way! For real?
YOU'RE ALL DISMISSED.
UNDER-STOOD.

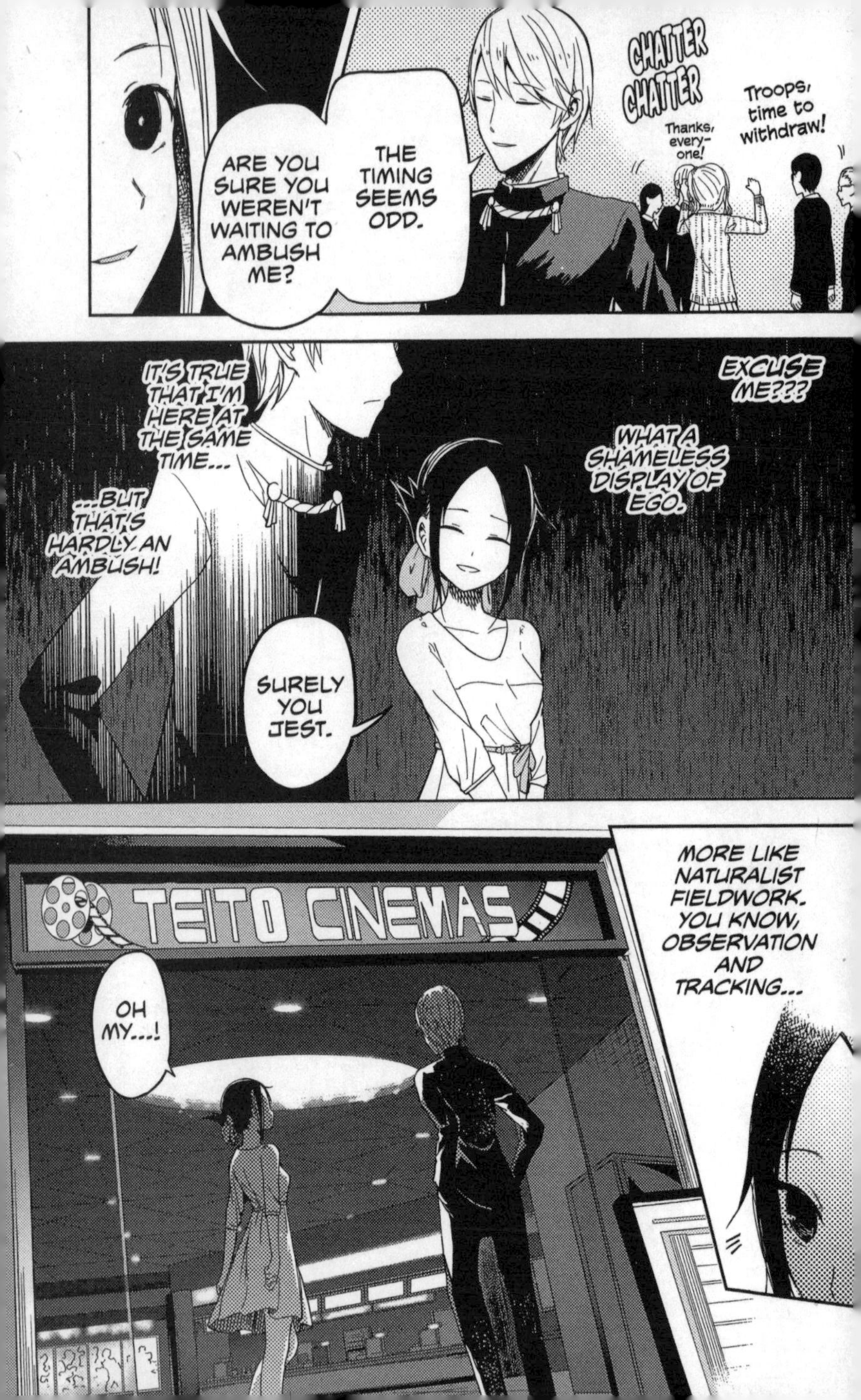
CHATTER CHATTER
Troops, time to withdraw!
Thanks, every-one!
THE TIMING SEEMS ODD.
ARE YOU SURE YOU WEREN'T WAITING TO AMBUSH ME?
EXCUSE ME???
WHAT A SHAMELESS DISPLAY OF EGO.
IT'S TRUE THAT I'M HERE AT THE SAME TIME...
...BUT THAT'S HARDLY AN AMBUSH!
SURELY YOU JEST.
MORE LIKE NATURALIST FIELDWORK. YOU KNOW, OBSERVATION AND TRACKING...
TEITO CINEMAS
OH MY...!

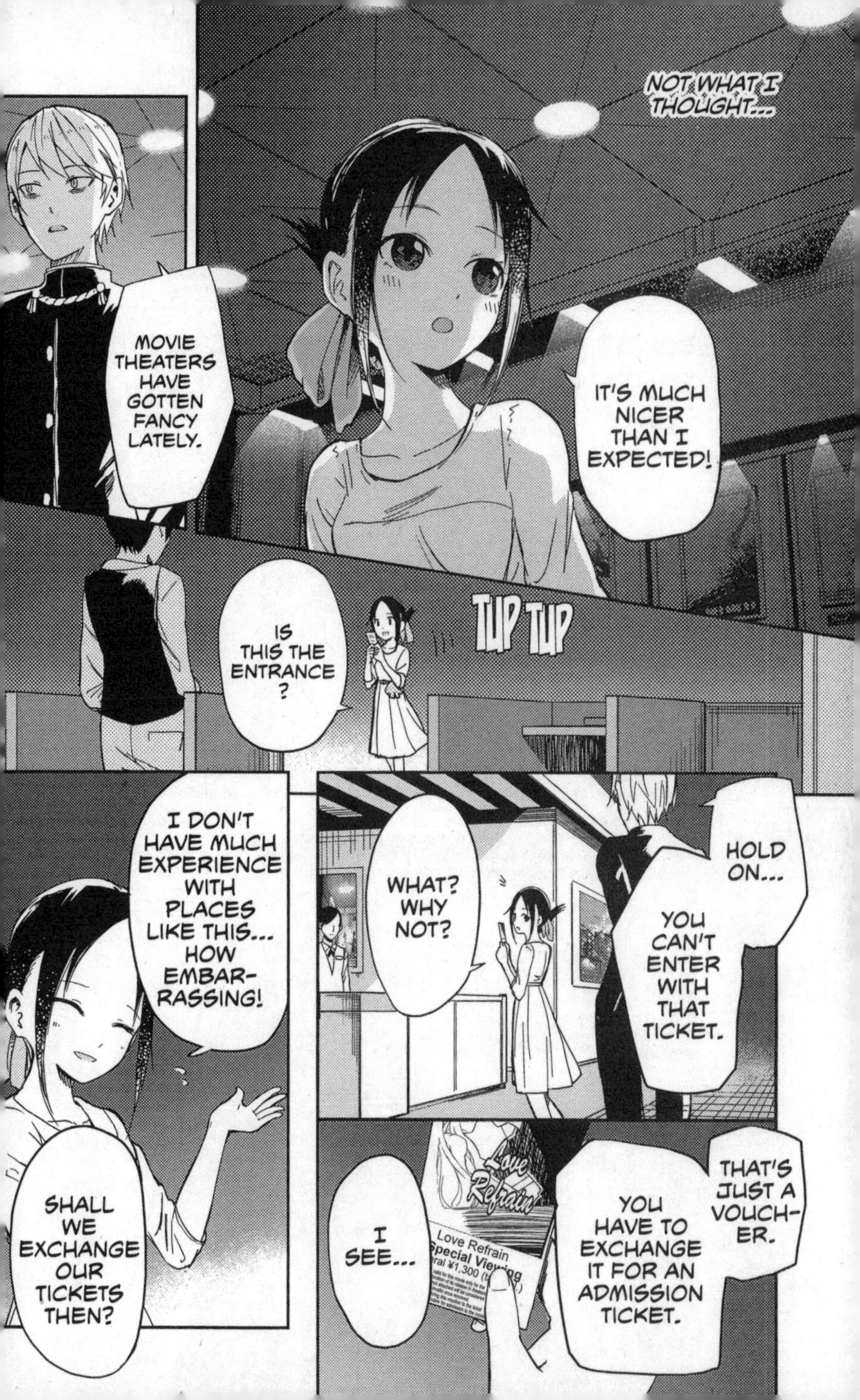
NOT WHAT I THOUGHT...
IT'S MUCH NICER THAN I EXPECTED!
MOVIE THEATERS HAVE GOTTEN FANCY LATELY.
TUP TUP
IS THIS THE ENTRANCE?
HOLD ON... YOU CAN'T ENTER WITH THAT TICKET.
WHAT? WHY NOT?
THAT'S JUST A VOUCHER.
YOU HAVE TO EXCHANGE IT FOR AN ADMISSION TICKET.
Love Refrain
Love Refrain Special Viewing
I SEE...
I DON'T HAVE MUCH EXPERIENCE WITH PLACES LIKE THIS... HOW EMBARRASSING!
SHALL WE EXCHANGE OUR TICKETS THEN?

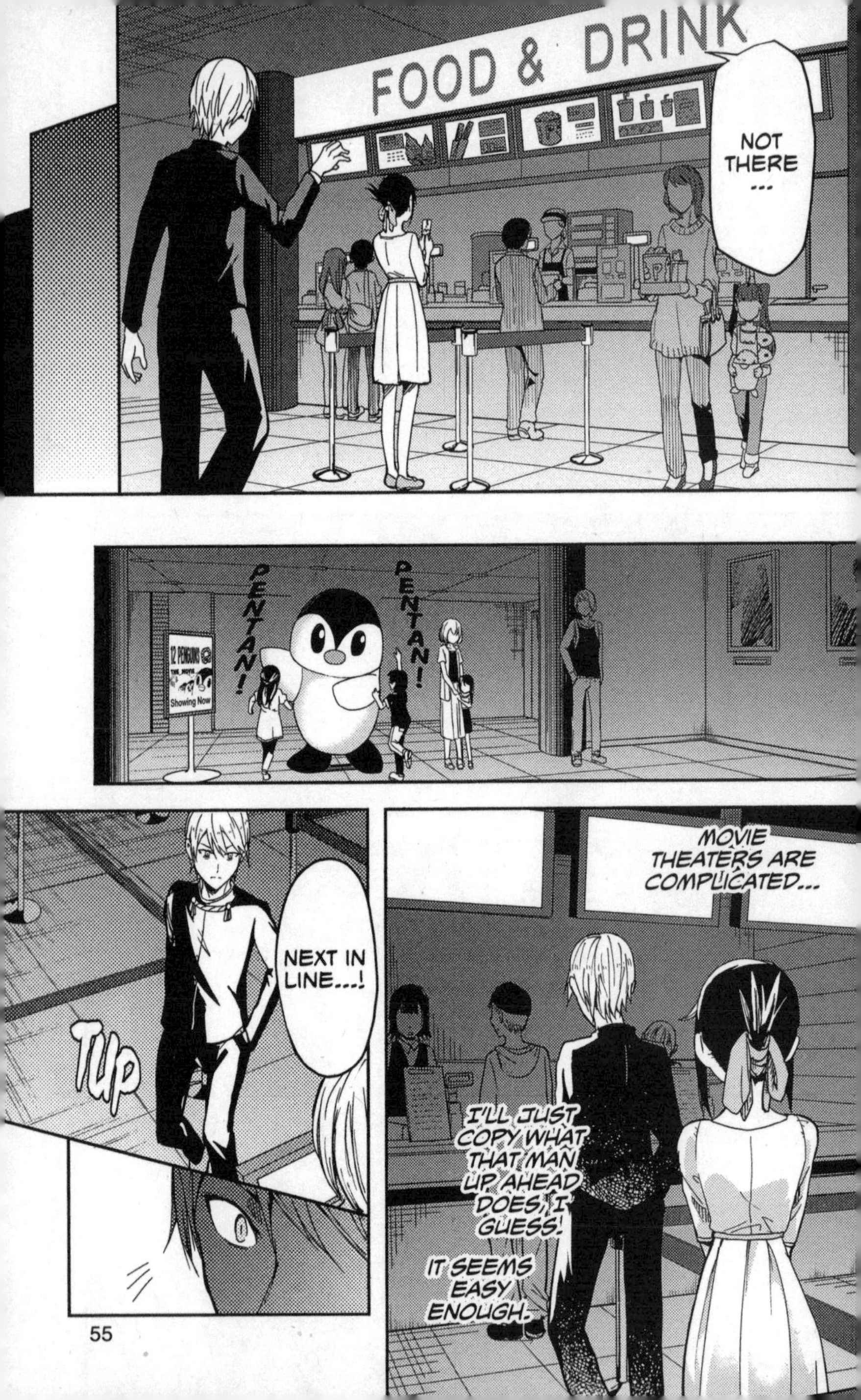
FOOD & DRINK
NOT THERE ...
PENTAN!
PENTAN!
12 PENGUINS THE MOVIE Showing Now
MOVIE THEATERS ARE COMPLICATED...
I'LL JUST COPY WHAT THAT MAN UP AHEAD DOES, I GUESS!
IT SEEMS EASY ENOUGH.
NEXT IN LINE...!
TUP

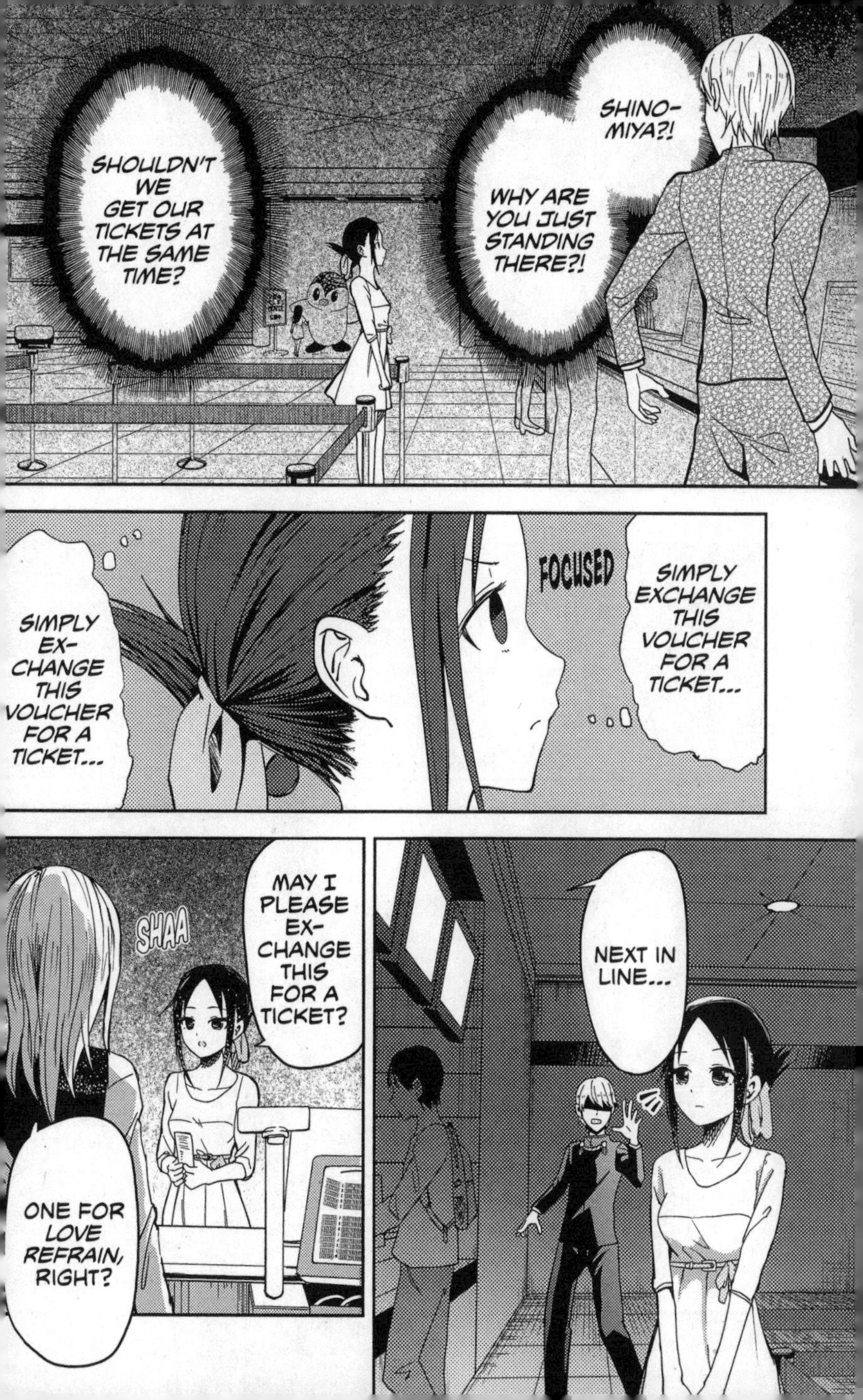
SHINO-MIYA?!
WHY ARE YOU JUST STANDING THERE?!
SHOULDN'T WE GET OUR TICKETS AT THE SAME TIME?
SIMPLY EXCHANGE THIS VOUCHER FOR A TICKET...
FOCUSED
SIMPLY EX-CHANGE THIS VOUCHER FOR A TICKET...
NEXT IN LINE...
MAY I PLEASE EX-CHANGE THIS FOR A TICKET?
SHAA
ONE FOR LOVE REFRAIN, RIGHT?

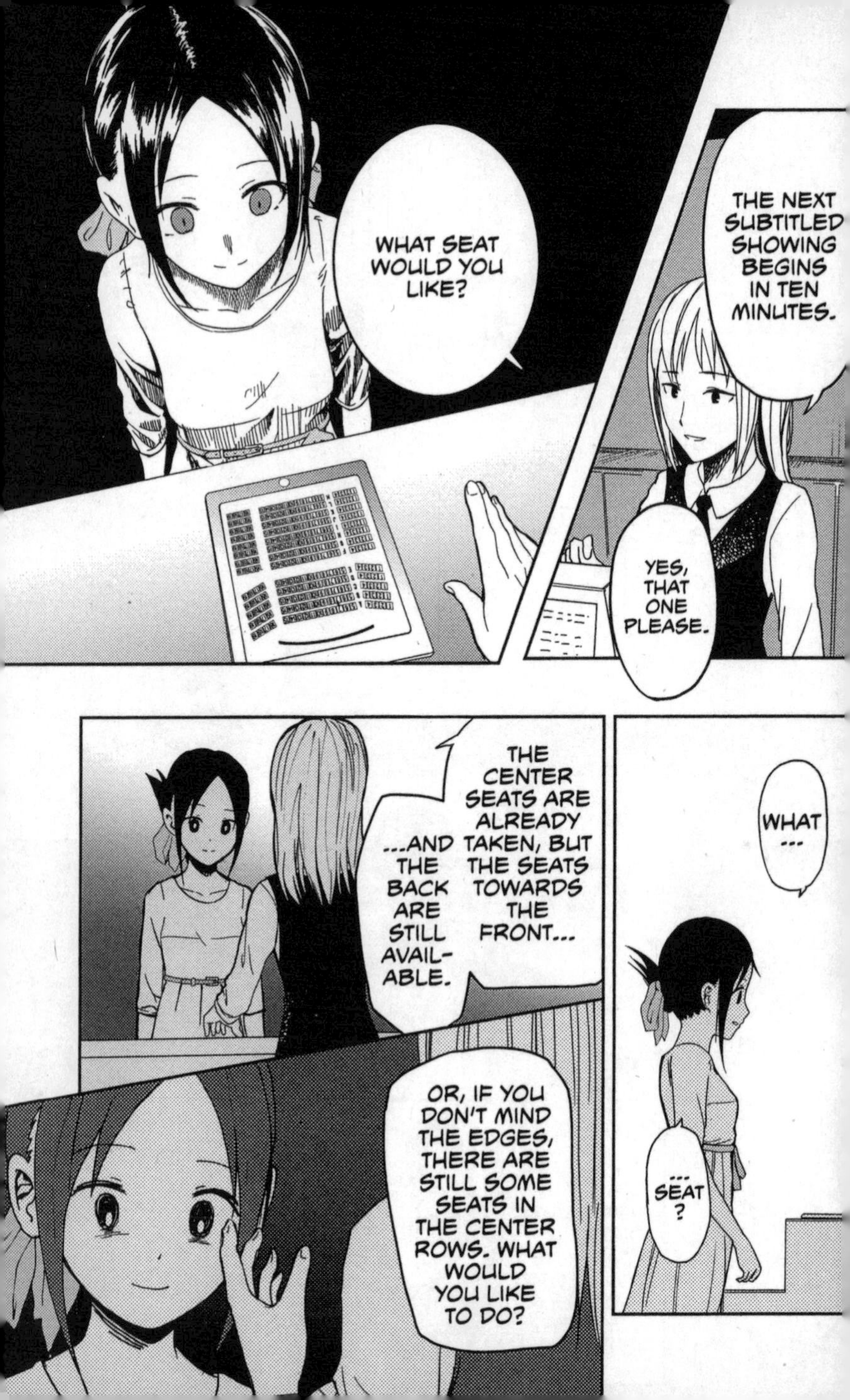
THE NEXT SUBTITLED SHOWING BEGINS IN TEN MINUTES.
WHAT SEAT WOULD YOU LIKE?
YES, THAT ONE PLEASE.
WHAT...
...SEAT?
THE CENTER SEATS ARE ALREADY TAKEN, BUT THE SEATS TOWARDS THE FRONT...
...AND THE BACK ARE STILL AVAIL-ABLE.
OR, IF YOU DON'T MIND THE EDGES, THERE ARE STILL SOME SEATS IN THE CENTER ROWS. WHAT WOULD YOU LIKE TO DO?

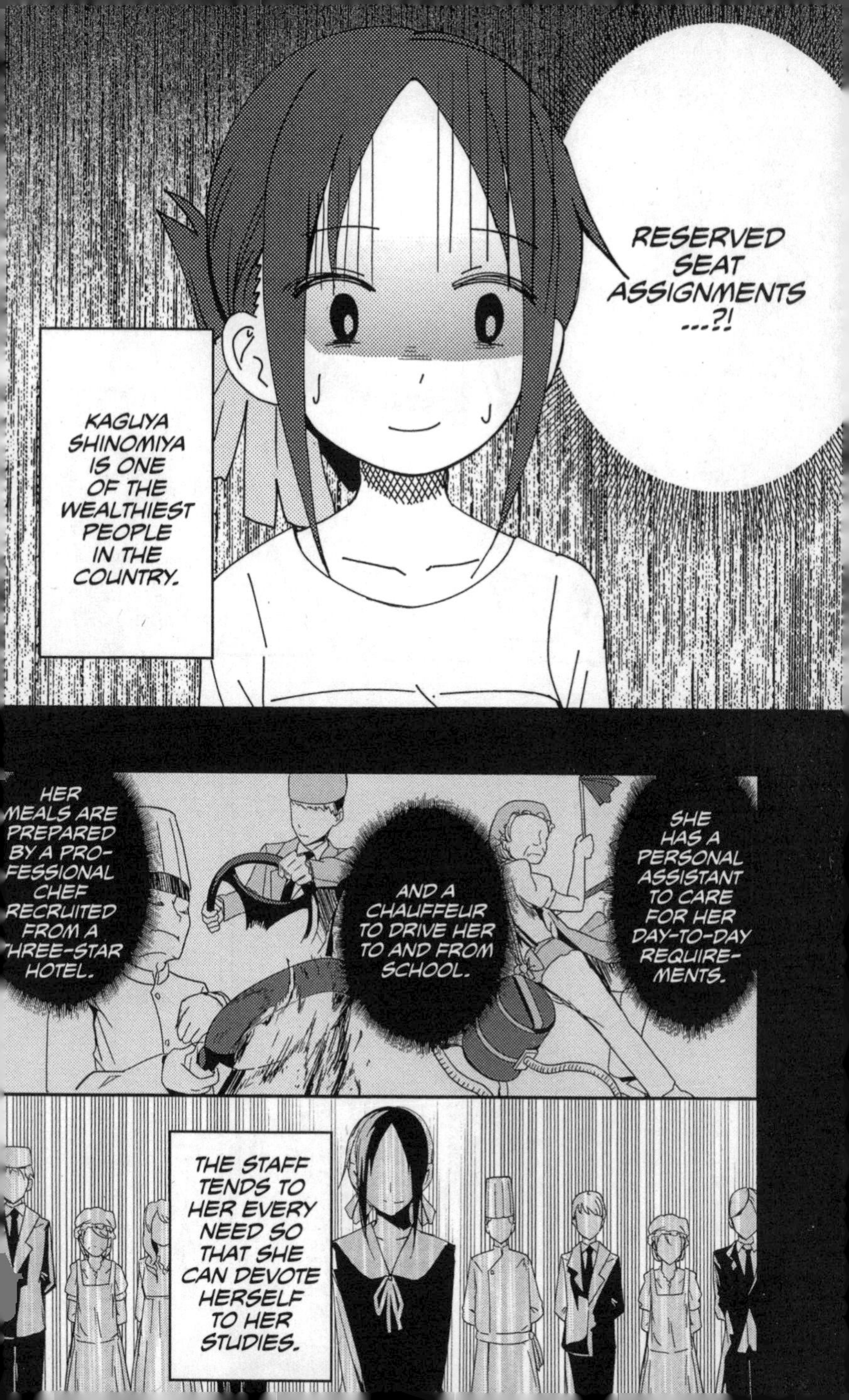
RESERVED SEAT ASSIGNMENTS ...?!
KAGUYA SHINOMIYA IS ONE OF THE WEALTHIEST PEOPLE IN THE COUNTRY.
SHE HAS A PERSONAL ASSISTANT TO CARE FOR HER DAY-TO-DAY REQUIRE-MENTS.
AND A CHAUFFEUR TO DRIVE HER TO AND FROM SCHOOL.
HER MEALS ARE PREPARED BY A PRO-FESSIONAL CHEF RECRUITED FROM A HREE-STAR HOTEL.
THE STAFF TENDS TO HER EVERY NEED SO THAT SHE CAN DEVOTE HERSELF TO HER STUDIES.

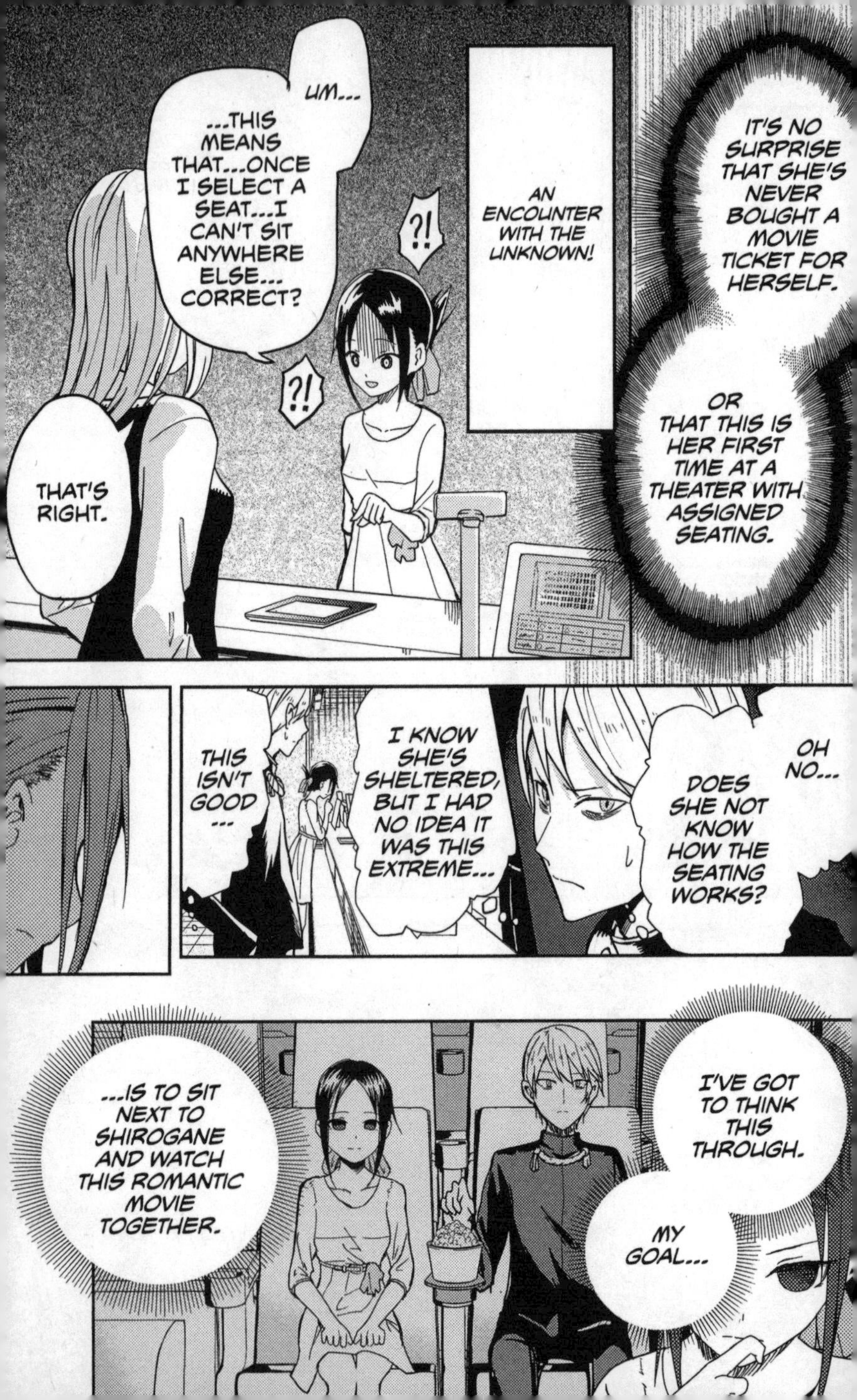
IT'S NO SURPRISE THAT SHE'S NEVER BOUGHT A MOVIE TICKET FOR HERSELF.
OR THAT THIS IS HER FIRST TIME AT A THEATER WITH ASSIGNED SEATING.
AN ENCOUNTER WITH THE UNKNOWN!
UM...
...THIS MEANS THAT...ONCE I SELECT A SEAT...I CAN'T SIT ANYWHERE ELSE... CORRECT?
?!
?!
THAT'S RIGHT.
OH NO...
DOES SHE NOT KNOW HOW THE SEATING WORKS?
I KNOW SHE'S SHELTERED, BUT I HAD NO IDEA IT WAS THIS EXTREME...
THIS ISN'T GOOD...
I'VE GOT TO THINK THIS THROUGH.
MY GOAL...
...IS TO SIT NEXT TO SHIROGANE AND WATCH THIS ROMANTIC MOVIE TOGETHER.

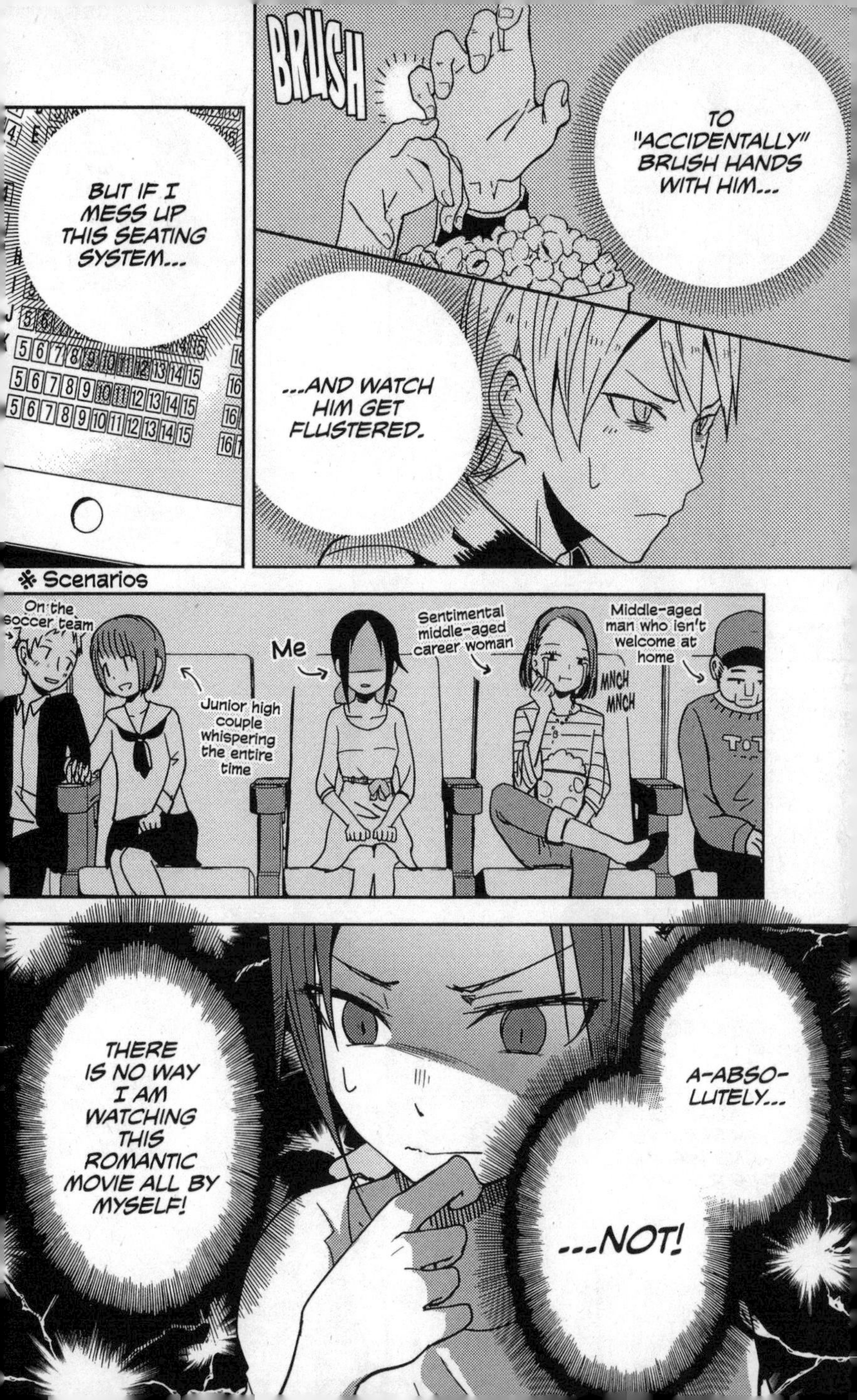
BRUSH
TO "ACCIDENTALLY" BRUSH HANDS WITH HIM...
...AND WATCH HIM GET FLUSTERED.
BUT IF I MESS UP THIS SEATING SYSTEM...
※ Scenarios
Middle-aged man who isn't welcome at home
MNCH MNCH
Sentimental middle-aged career woman
Me
Junior high couple whispering the entire time
On the soccer team
A-ABSO-LUTELY...
...NOT!
THERE IS NO WAY I AM WATCHING THIS ROMANTIC MOVIE ALL BY MYSELF!

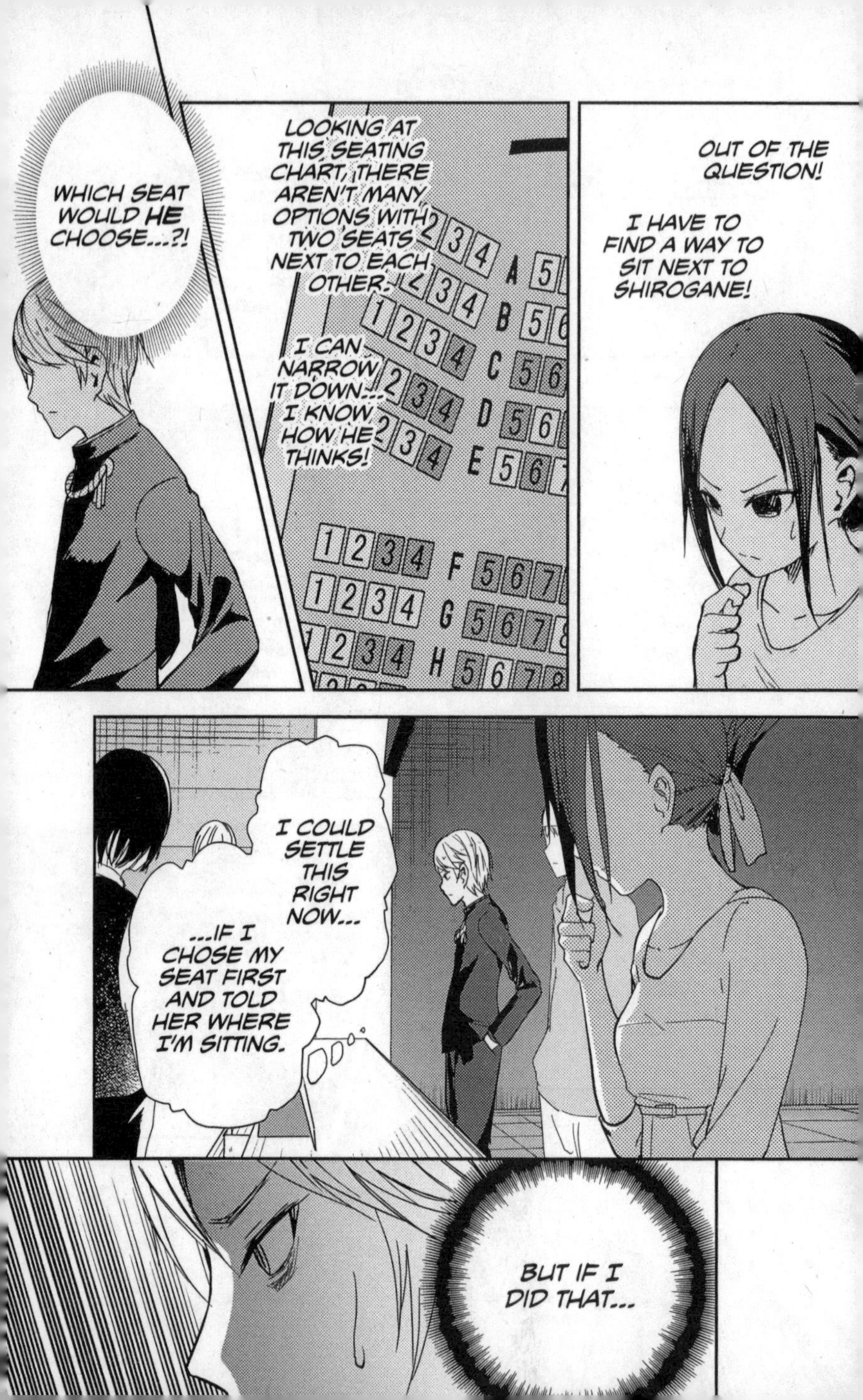
OUT OF THE QUESTION!
I HAVE TO FIND A WAY TO SIT NEXT TO SHIROGANE!
LOOKING AT THIS SEATING CHART, THERE AREN'T MANY OPTIONS WITH TWO SEATS NEXT TO EACH OTHER.
I CAN NARROW IT DOWN... I KNOW HOW HE THINKS!
WHICH SEAT WOULD HE CHOOSE...?!
I COULD SETTLE THIS RIGHT NOW...
...IF I CHOSE MY SEAT FIRST AND TOLD HER WHERE I'M SITTING.
BUT IF I DID THAT...

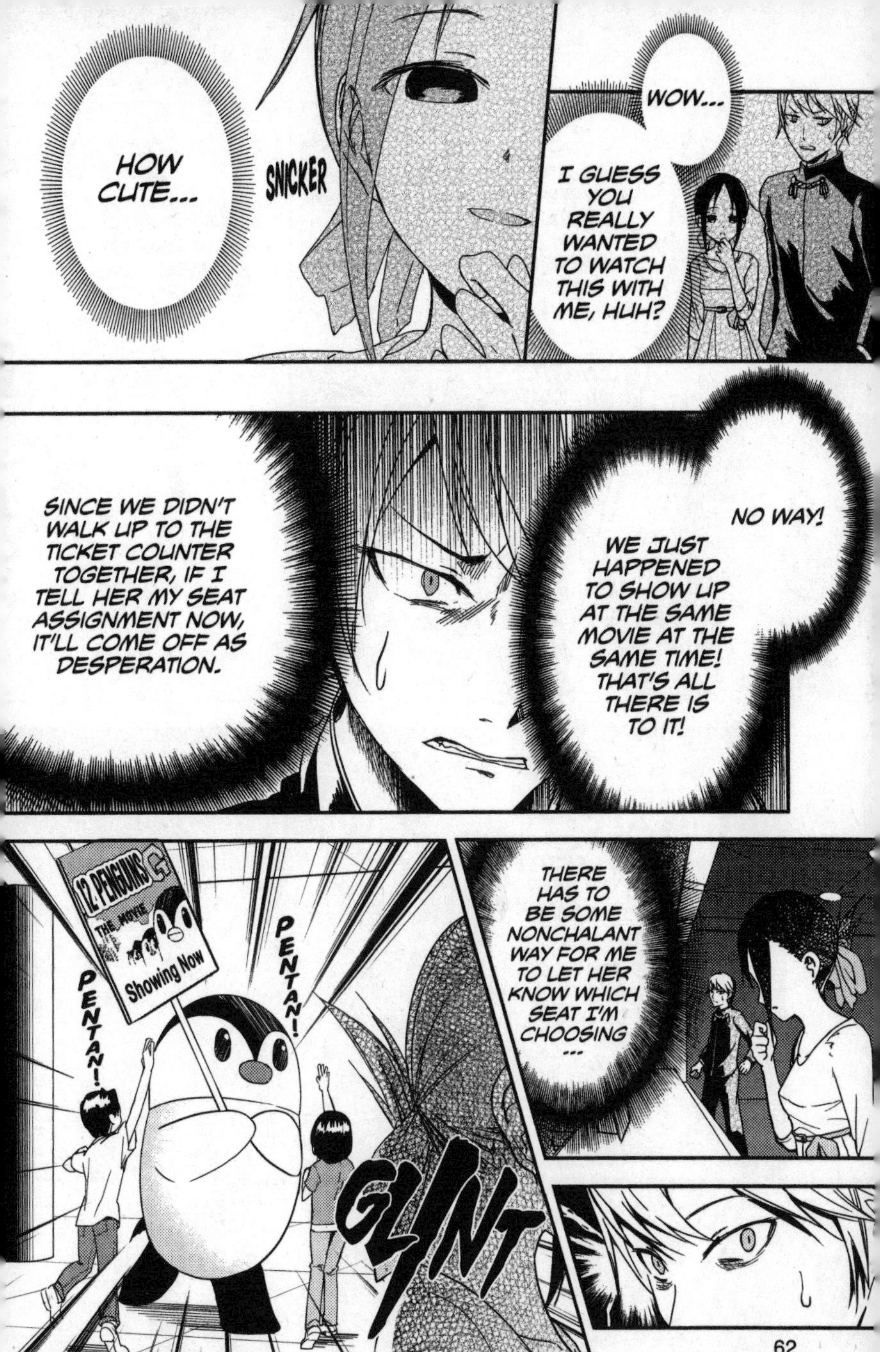
WOW...
I GUESS YOU REALLY WANTED TO WATCH THIS WITH ME, HUH?
HOW CUTE...
SNICKER
NO WAY!
WE JUST HAPPENED TO SHOW UP AT THE SAME MOVIE AT THE SAME TIME! THAT'S ALL THERE IS TO IT!
SINCE WE DIDN'T WALK UP TO THE TICKET COUNTER TOGETHER, IF I TELL HER MY SEAT ASSIGNMENT NOW, IT'LL COME OFF AS DESPERATION.
THERE HAS TO BE SOME NONCHALANT WAY FOR ME TO LET HER KNOW WHICH SEAT I'M CHOOSING...
GLINT
12 PENGUINS G
THE MOVIE
Showing Now
PENTAN!
PENTAN!

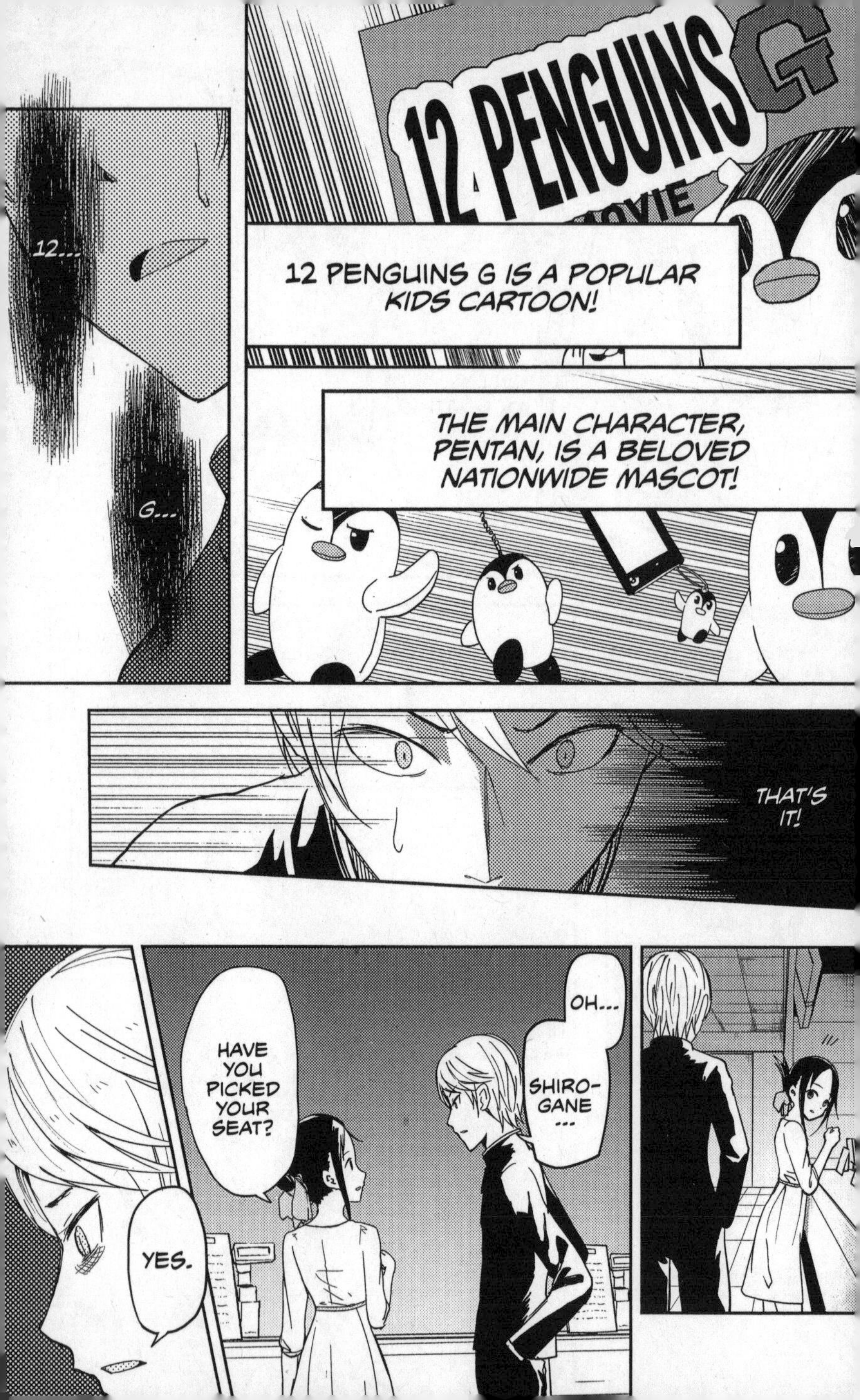
12 PENGUINS G
12 PENGUINS G IS A POPULAR KIDS CARTOON!
THE MAIN CHARACTER, PENTAN, IS A BELOVED NATIONWIDE MASCOT!
12...
G...
THAT'S IT!
OH...
SHIRO-GANE...
HAVE YOU PICKED YOUR SEAT?
YES.

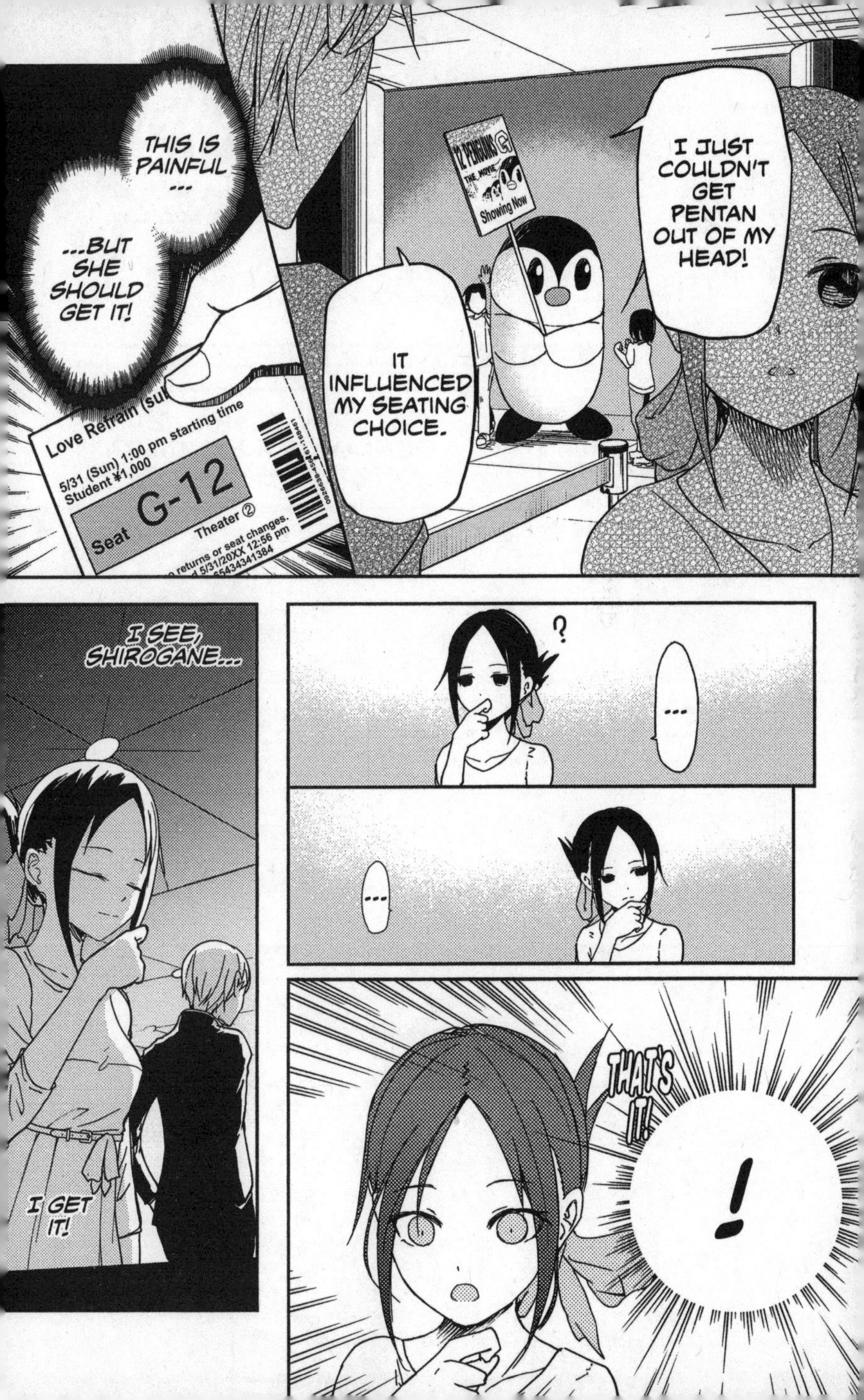

I JUST COULDN'T GET PENTAN OUT OF MY HEAD!
12 PENGUINS THE MOVIE Showing Now
IT INFLUENCED MY SEATING CHOICE.
THIS IS PAINFUL...
...BUT SHE SHOULD GET IT!
Love Refrain
5/31 (Sun) 1:00 pm starting time
Student ¥1,000
Seat G-12
Theater ②
?
...
...
THAT'S IT!
!
I SEE, SHIROGANE...
I GET IT!

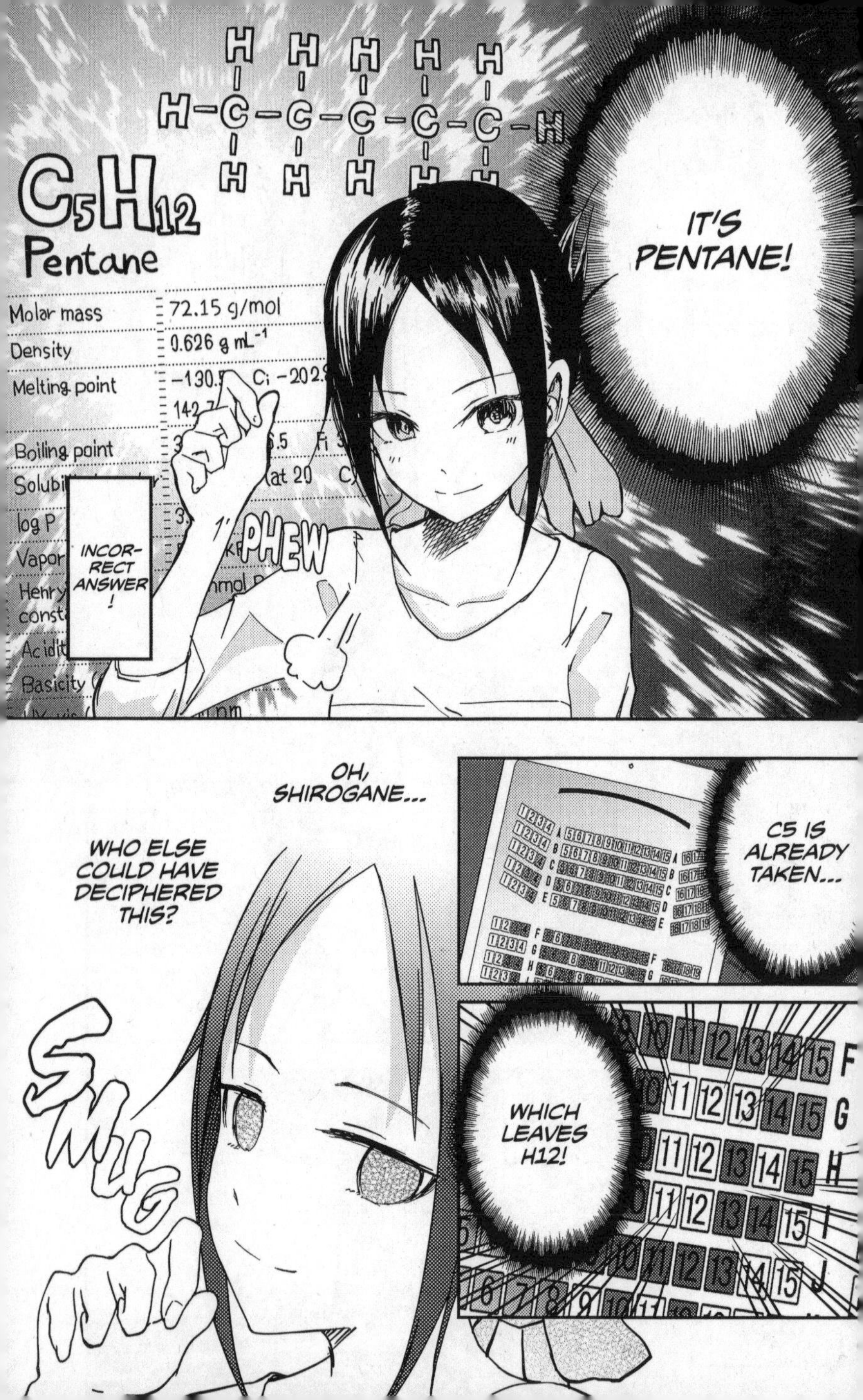
IT'S PENTANE!
C5H12
Pentane
Molar mass 72.15 g/mol
Density 0.626 g mL-1
Melting point
Boiling point
INCORRECT ANSWER!
PHEW
C5 IS ALREADY TAKEN...
WHICH LEAVES H12!
OH, SHIROGANE...
WHO ELSE COULD HAVE DECIPHERED THIS?
SMUG

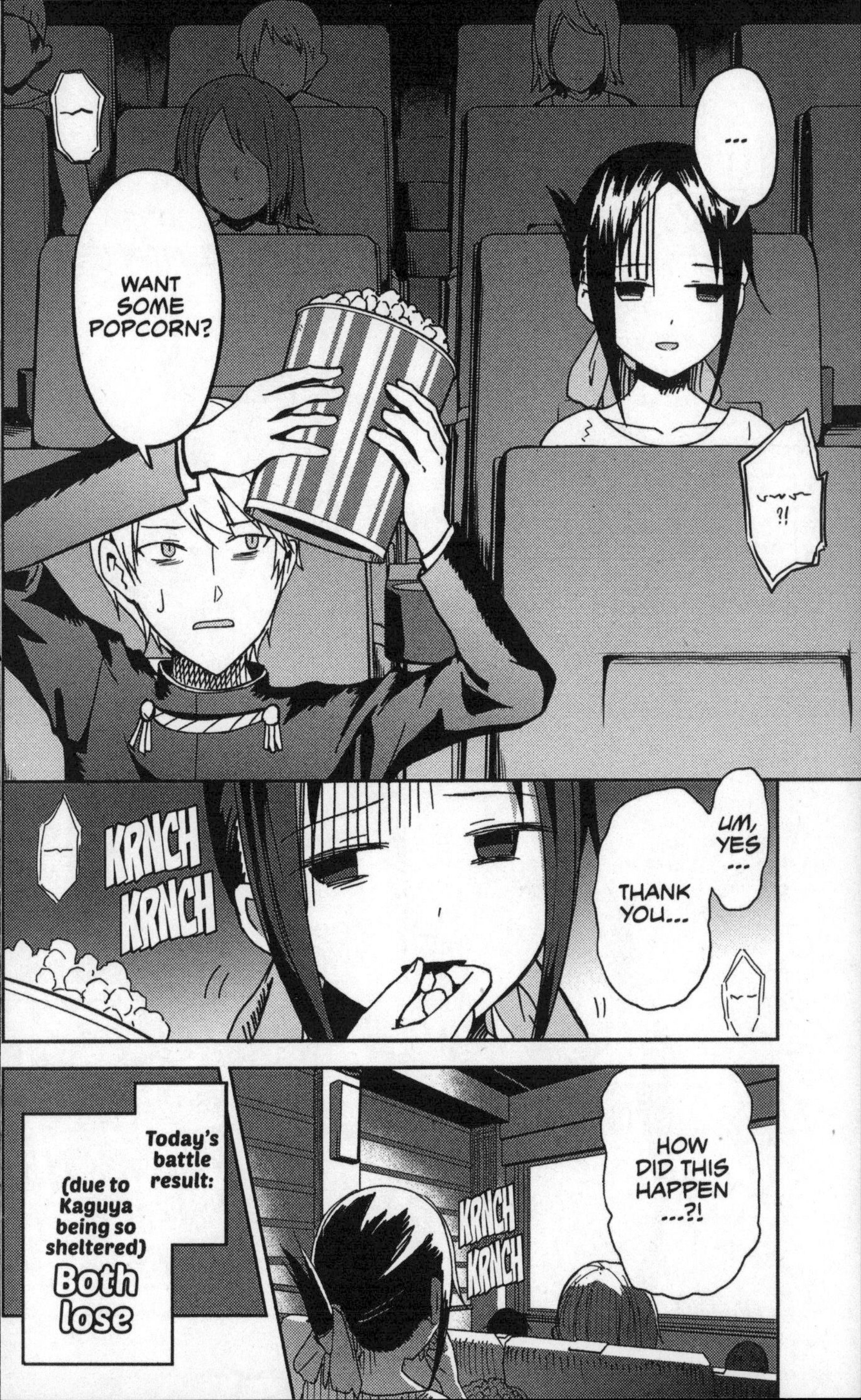
...
WANT SOME POPCORN?
?!
UM, YES ... THANK YOU...
KRNCH KRNCH
HOW DID THIS HAPPEN ...?!
KRNCH KRNCH
Today's battle result:
(due to Kaguya being so sheltered)
Both lose

KAGUYA SHINOMIYA

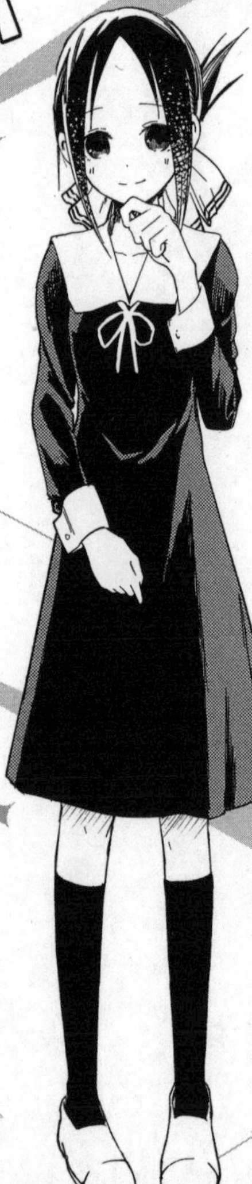

Kaguya Shinomiya

- Shuchiin Academy High School Second-Year
- Student Council Vice President
- Notable characteristics: stunning beauty
- Main character in this story

The daughter of the Shinomiya Group, one of the top four business conglomerates in the country. A universal genius, skilled at just about everything.

She naturally looks down upon others, and her first thought is how to use other people for her benefit. It is unclear whether she was born this way or if it is the result of the Shinomiya family's sense of entitlement being ingrained in her.

Kaguya had little interaction with others before joining the student council, but her social ties appear to be expanding.

She is a 100 percent pure, innocent and sheltered girl. Her naïveté is revealed when we least expect it.

She doesn't understand love. It's going to take a while.

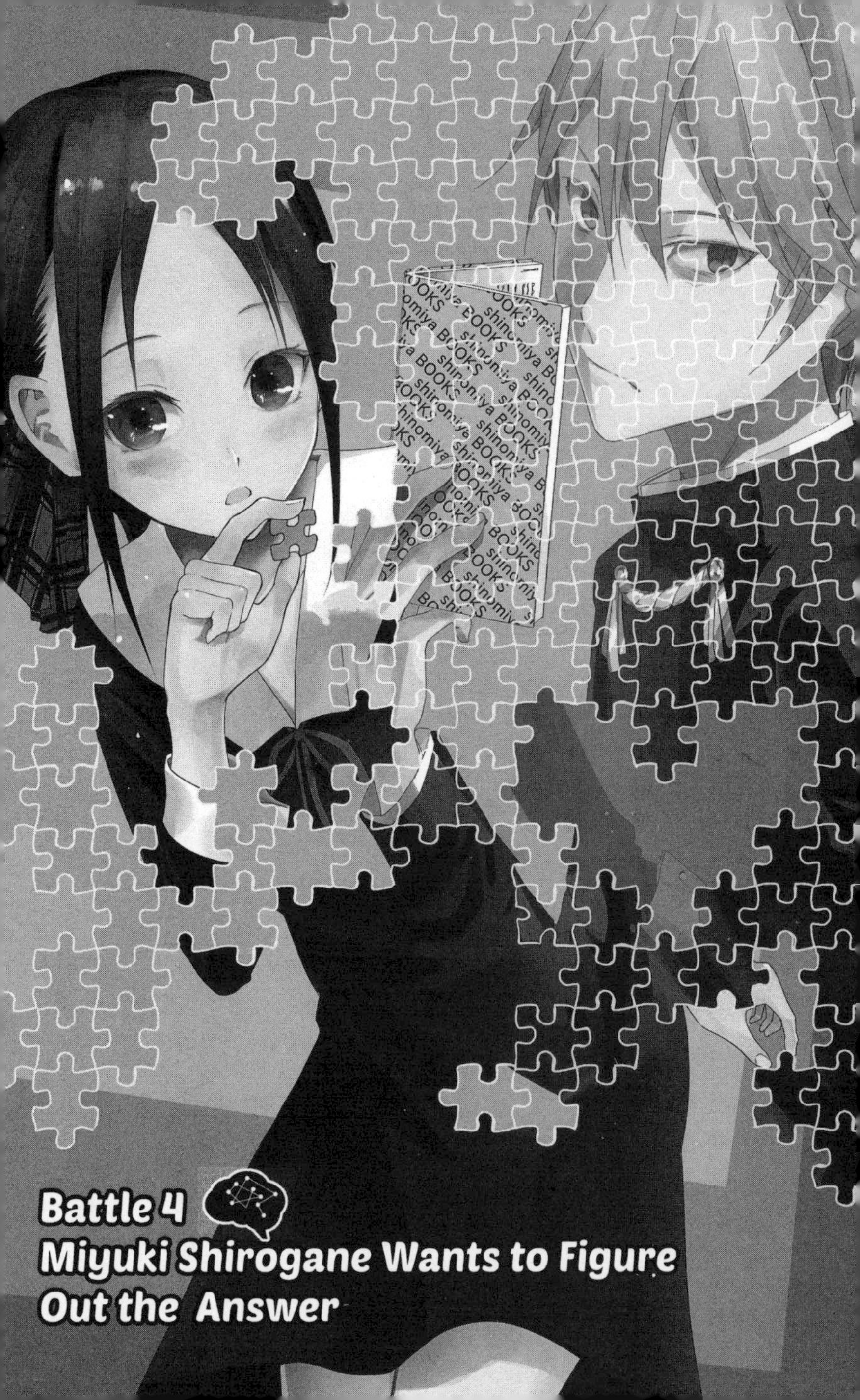
shinomiya BOOKS

Battle 4
Miyuki Shirogane Wants to Figure Out the Answer

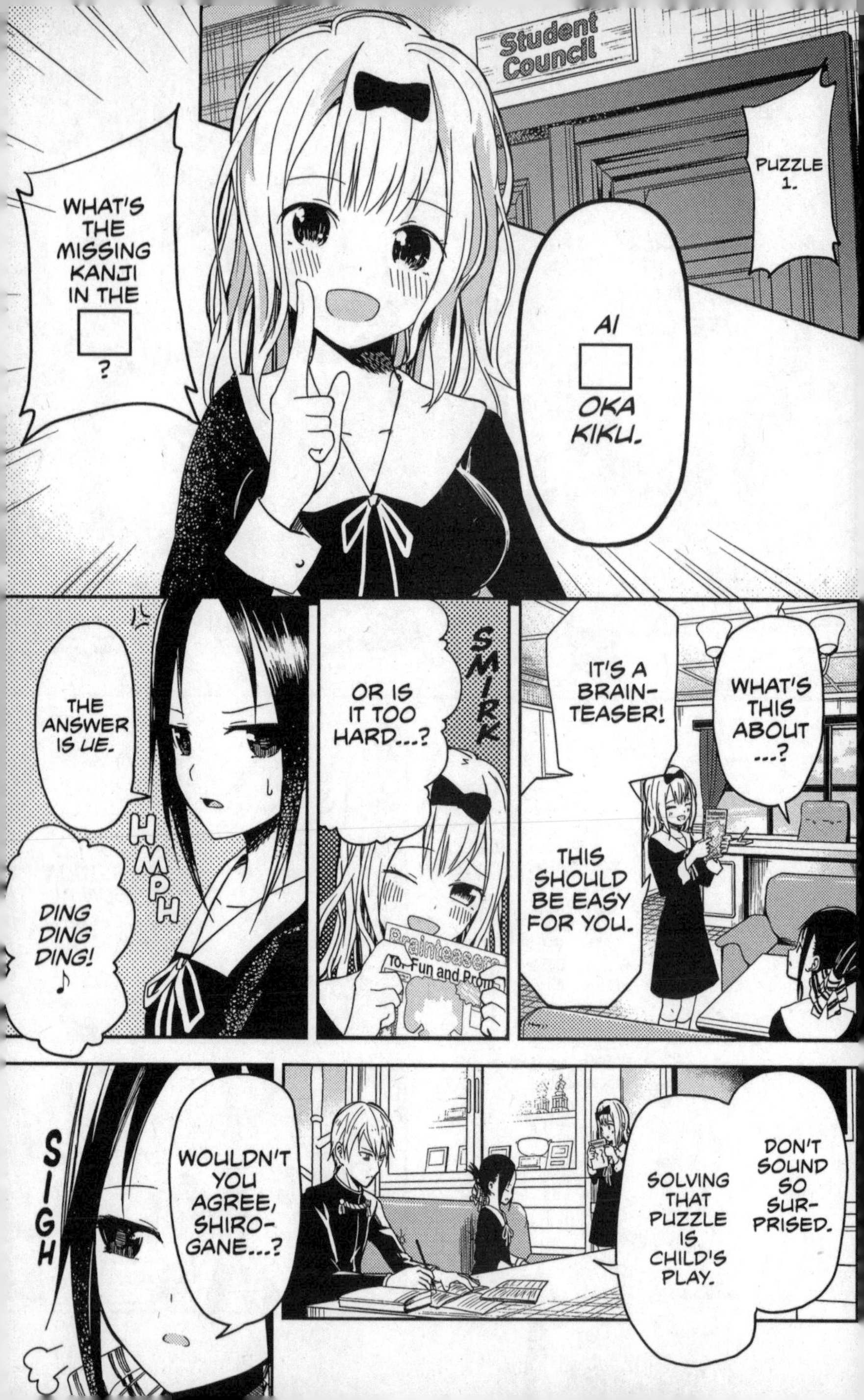
Student Council
PUZZLE 1.
AI □ OKA KIKU.
WHAT'S THE MISSING KANJI IN THE □ ?
WHAT'S THIS ABOUT ...?
IT'S A BRAIN-TEASER!
THIS SHOULD BE EASY FOR YOU.
SMIRK
OR IS IT TOO HARD...?
Brainteasers
THE ANSWER IS UE.
HMPH
DING DING DING! ♪
DON'T SOUND SO SUR-PRISED.
SOLVING THAT PUZZLE IS CHILD'S PLAY.
WOULDN'T YOU AGREE, SHIRO-GANE...?
SIGH

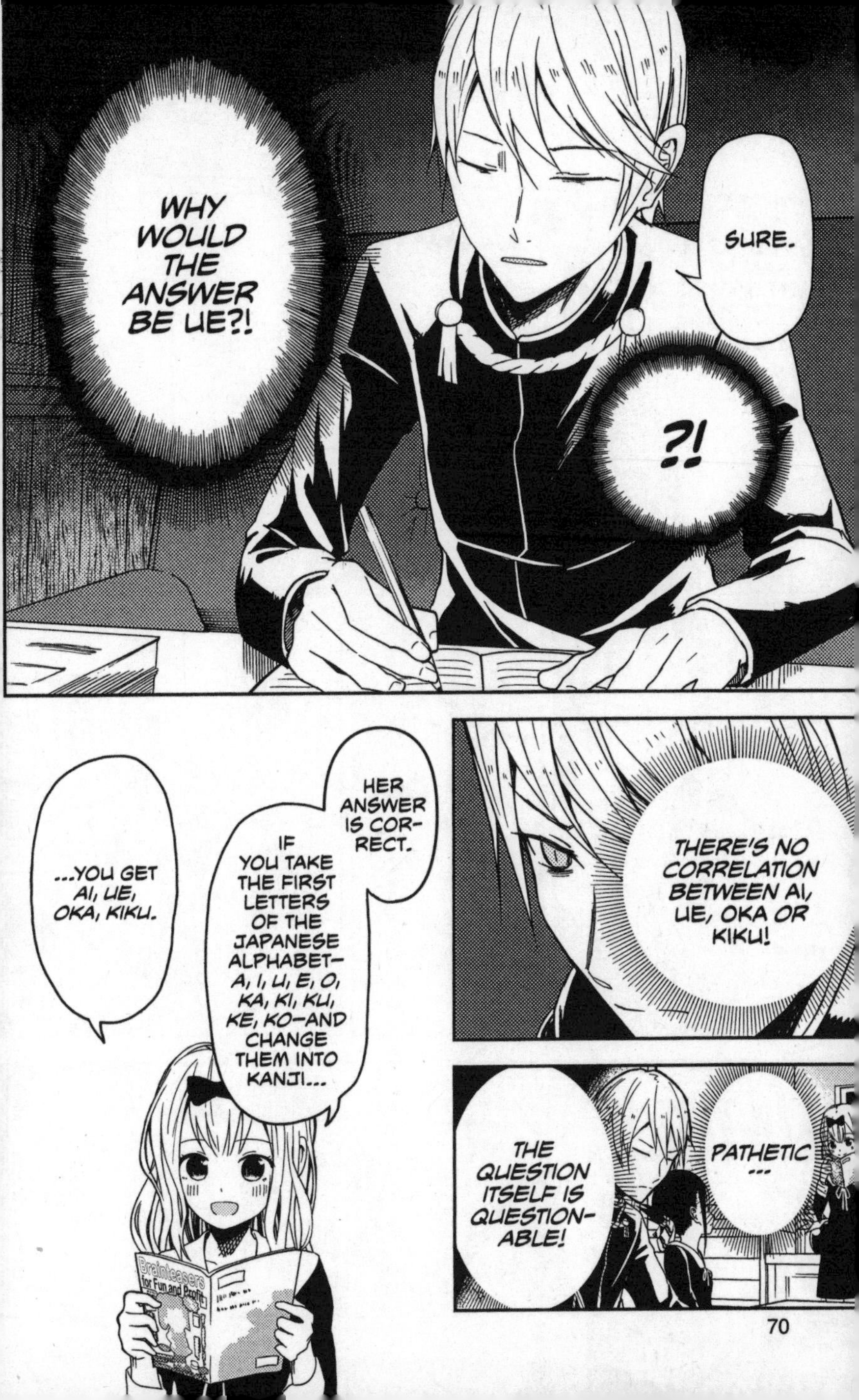
SURE.
?!
WHY WOULD THE ANSWER BE UE?!
THERE'S NO CORRELATION BETWEEN AI, UE, OKA OR KIKU!
PATHETIC...
THE QUESTION ITSELF IS QUESTION-ABLE!
HER ANSWER IS COR-RECT.
IF YOU TAKE THE FIRST LETTERS OF THE JAPANESE ALPHABET—A, I, U, E, O, KA, KI, KU, KE, KO—AND CHANGE THEM INTO KANJI...
...YOU GET AI, UE, OKA, KIKU.
Brainteasers for Fun and Profit

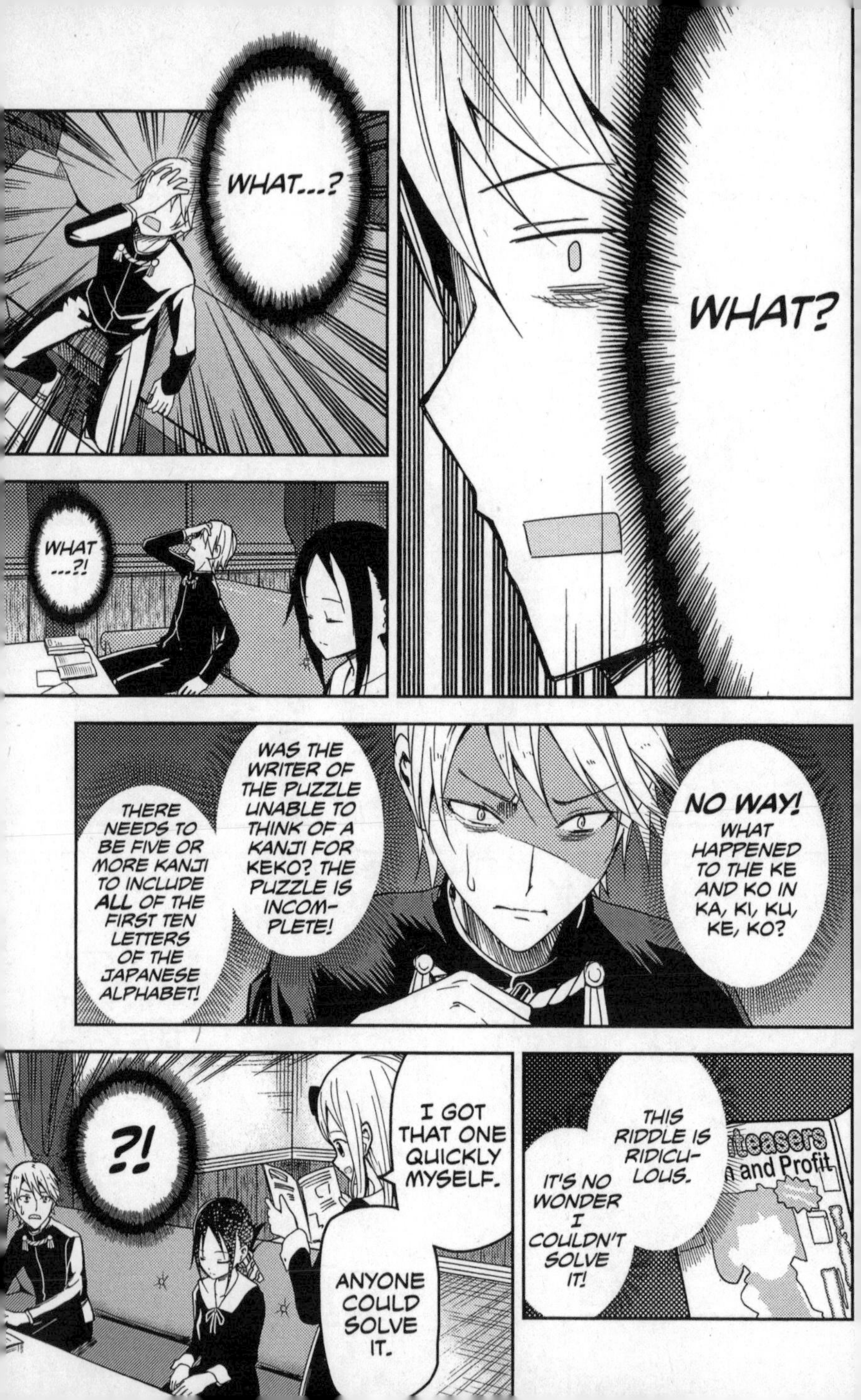
WHAT?
WHAT...?
WHAT ...?!
NO WAY! WHAT HAPPENED TO THE KE AND KO IN KA, KI, KU, KE, KO?
WAS THE WRITER OF THE PUZZLE UNABLE TO THINK OF A KANJI FOR KEKO? THE PUZZLE IS INCOMPLETE!
THERE NEEDS TO BE FIVE OR MORE KANJI TO INCLUDE ALL OF THE FIRST TEN LETTERS OF THE JAPANESE ALPHABET!
THIS RIDDLE IS RIDICULOUS.
IT'S NO WONDER I COULDN'T SOLVE IT!
I GOT THAT ONE QUICKLY MYSELF.
?!
ANYONE COULD SOLVE IT.

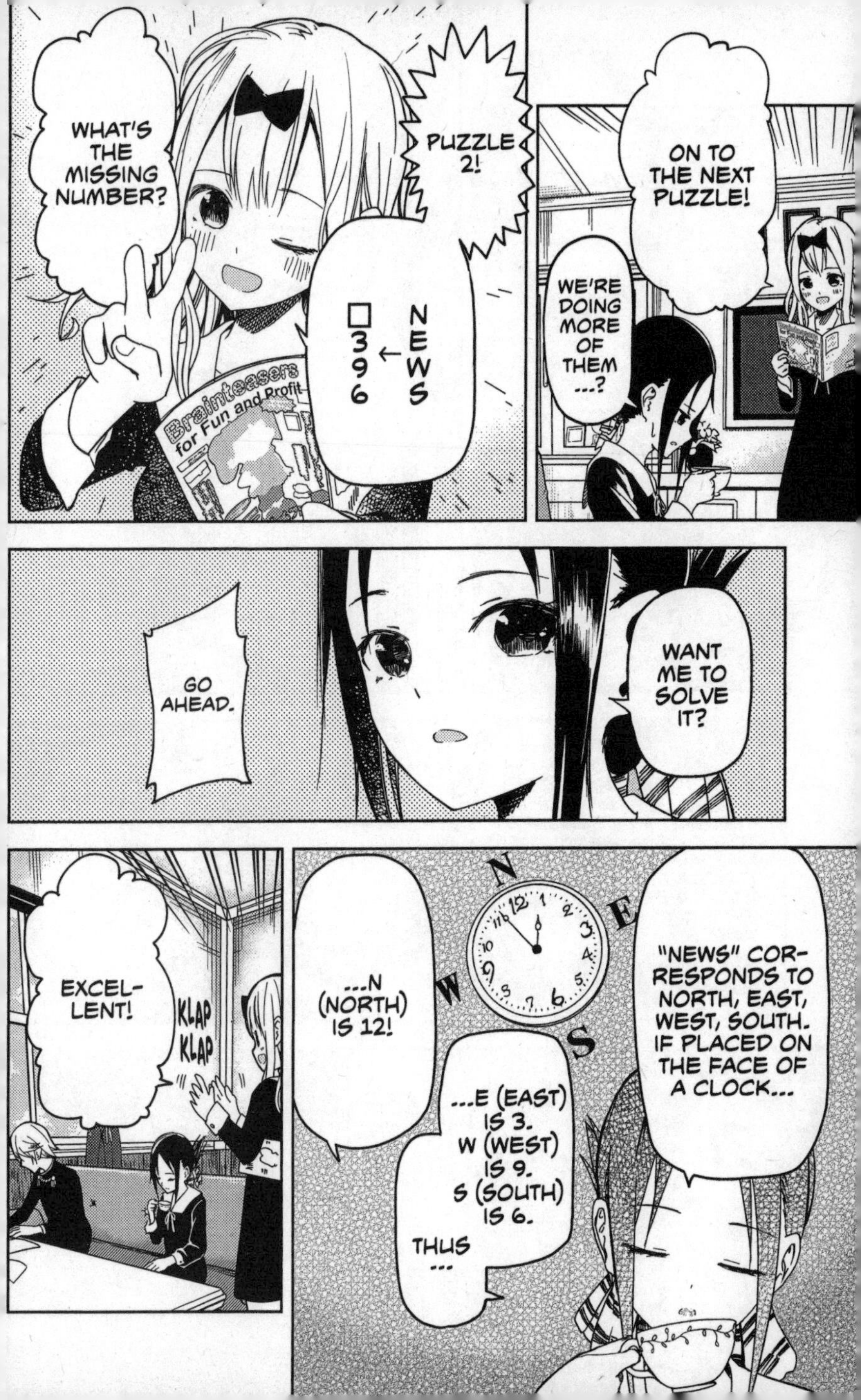
ON TO THE NEXT PUZZLE!
WE'RE DOING MORE OF THEM ...?
PUZZLE 2!
NEWS ← □396
Brainteasers for Fun and Profit
WHAT'S THE MISSING NUMBER?
WANT ME TO SOLVE IT?
GO AHEAD.
"NEWS" COR-RESPONDS TO NORTH, EAST, WEST, SOUTH. IF PLACED ON THE FACE OF A CLOCK...
N E W S
...N (NORTH) IS 12!
...E (EAST) IS 3. W (WEST) IS 9. S (SOUTH) IS 6.
THUS ...
EXCEL-LENT!
KLAP KLAP

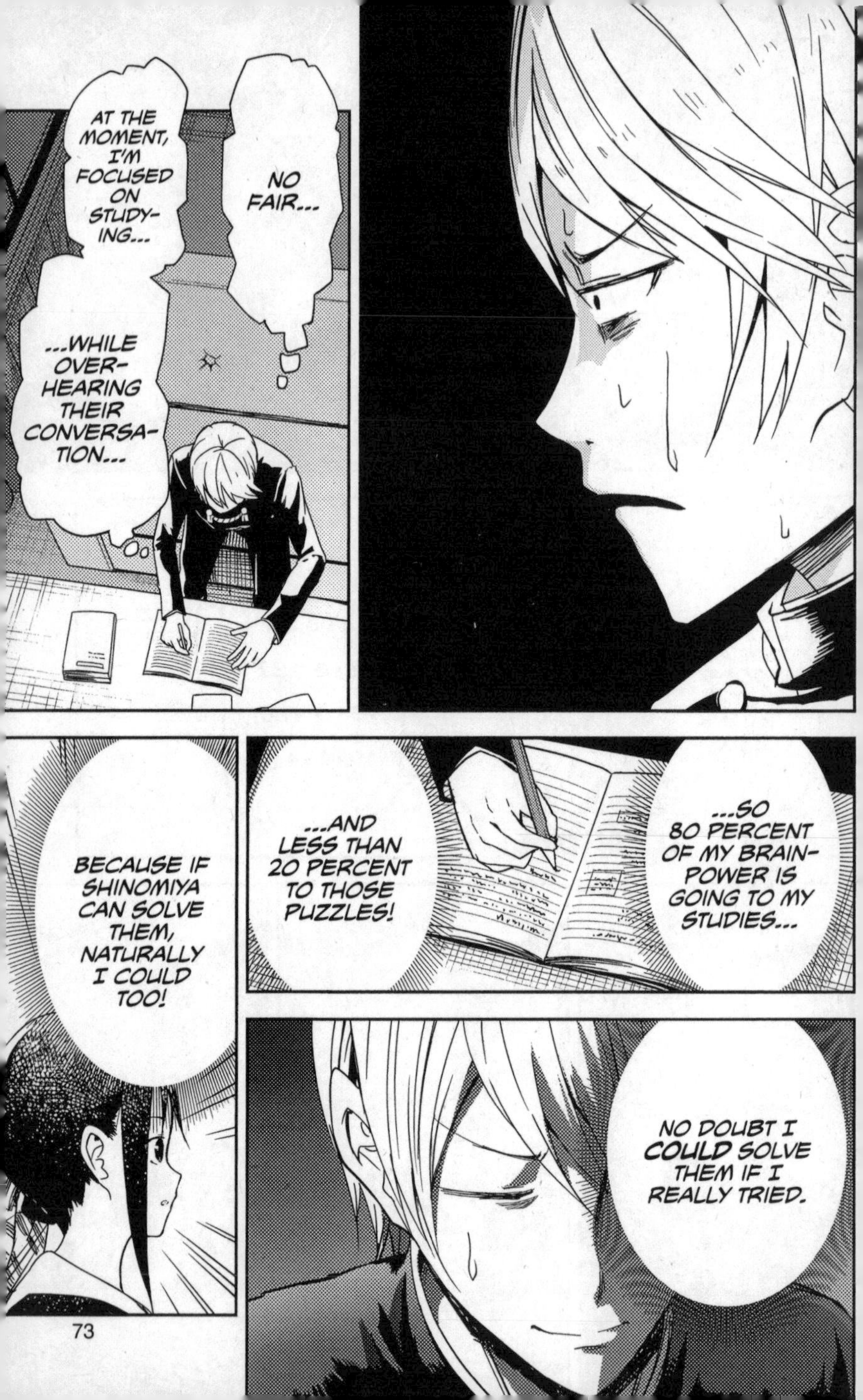
NO FAIR...
AT THE MOMENT, I'M FOCUSED ON STUDYING...
...WHILE OVERHEARING THEIR CONVERSATION...
...SO 80 PERCENT OF MY BRAINPOWER IS GOING TO MY STUDIES...
...AND LESS THAN 20 PERCENT TO THOSE PUZZLES!
NO DOUBT I COULD SOLVE THEM IF I REALLY TRIED.
BECAUSE IF SHINOMIYA CAN SOLVE THEM, NATURALLY I COULD TOO!

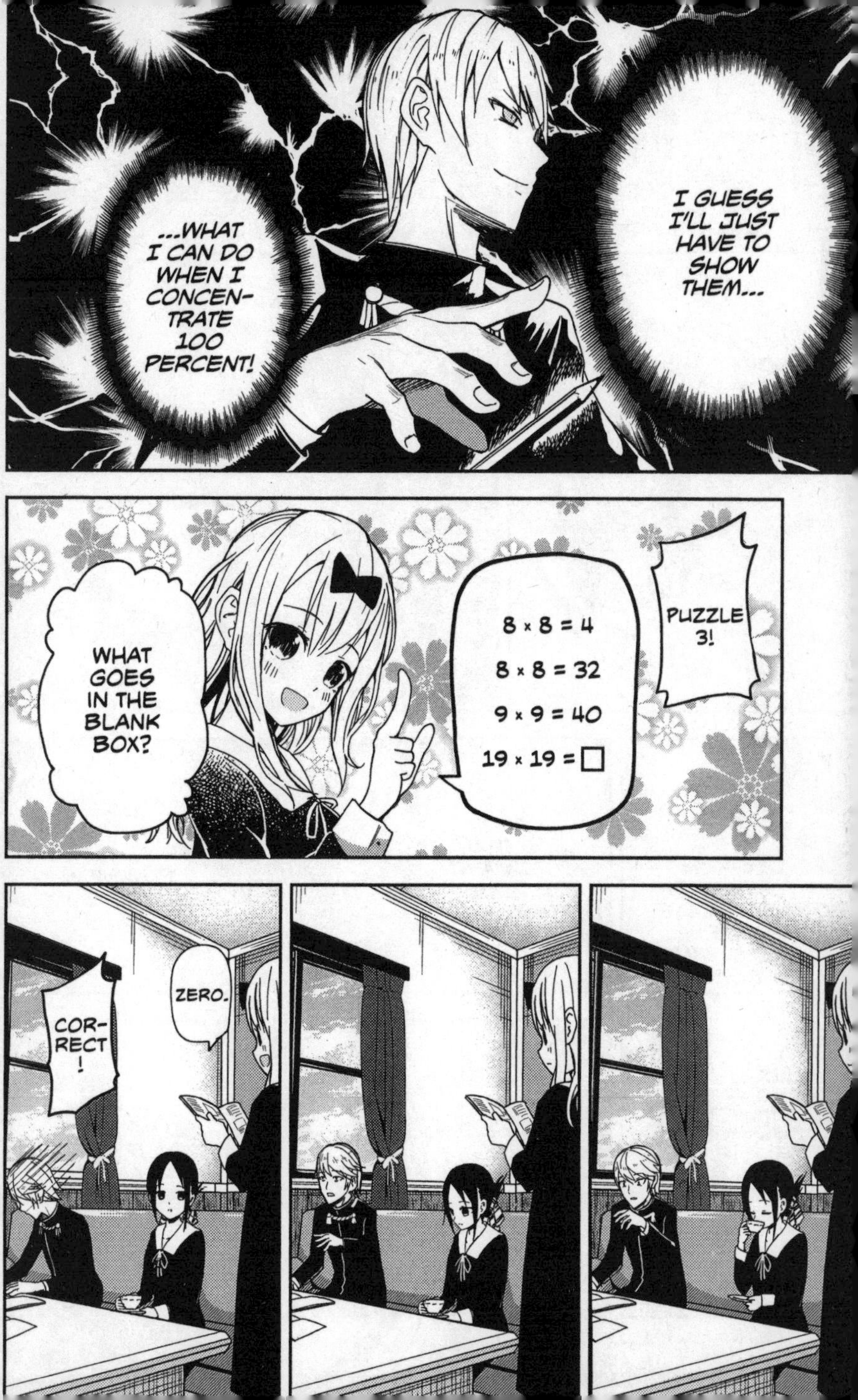
I GUESS I'LL JUST HAVE TO SHOW THEM...
...WHAT I CAN DO WHEN I CONCENTRATE 100 PERCENT!
PUZZLE 3!
8 × 8 = 4
8 × 8 = 32
9 × 9 = 40
19 × 19 = □
WHAT GOES IN THE BLANK BOX?
ZERO.
CORRECT!

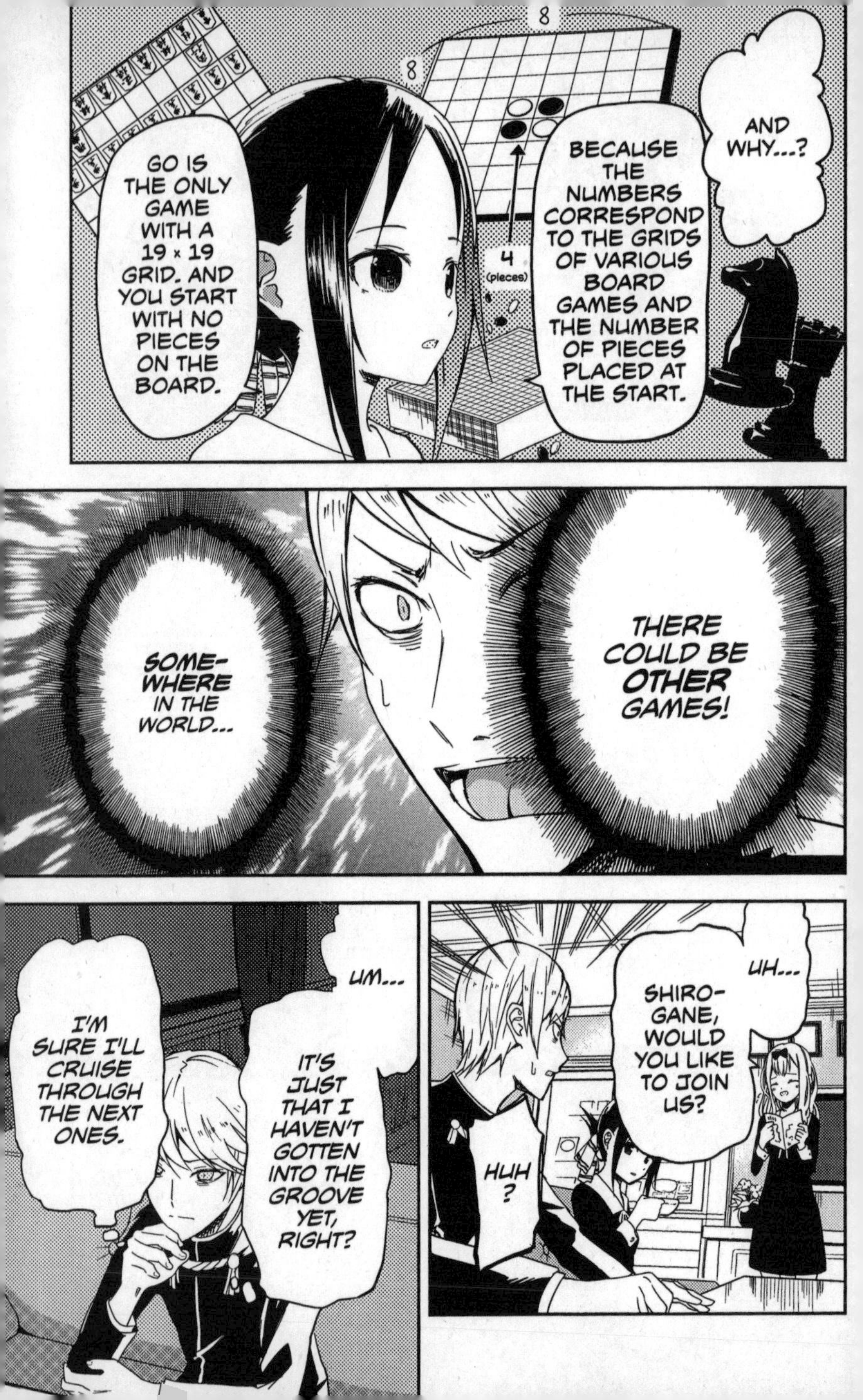
AND WHY...?
8
8
4 (pieces)
BECAUSE THE NUMBERS CORRESPOND TO THE GRIDS OF VARIOUS BOARD GAMES AND THE NUMBER OF PIECES PLACED AT THE START.
GO IS THE ONLY GAME WITH A 19 × 19 GRID. AND YOU START WITH NO PIECES ON THE BOARD.
THERE COULD BE OTHER GAMES!
SOME-WHERE IN THE WORLD...
UH...
SHIRO-GANE, WOULD YOU LIKE TO JOIN US?
HUH?
UM...
IT'S JUST THAT I HAVEN'T GOTTEN INTO THE GROOVE YET, RIGHT?
I'M SURE I'LL CRUISE THROUGH THE NEXT ONES.

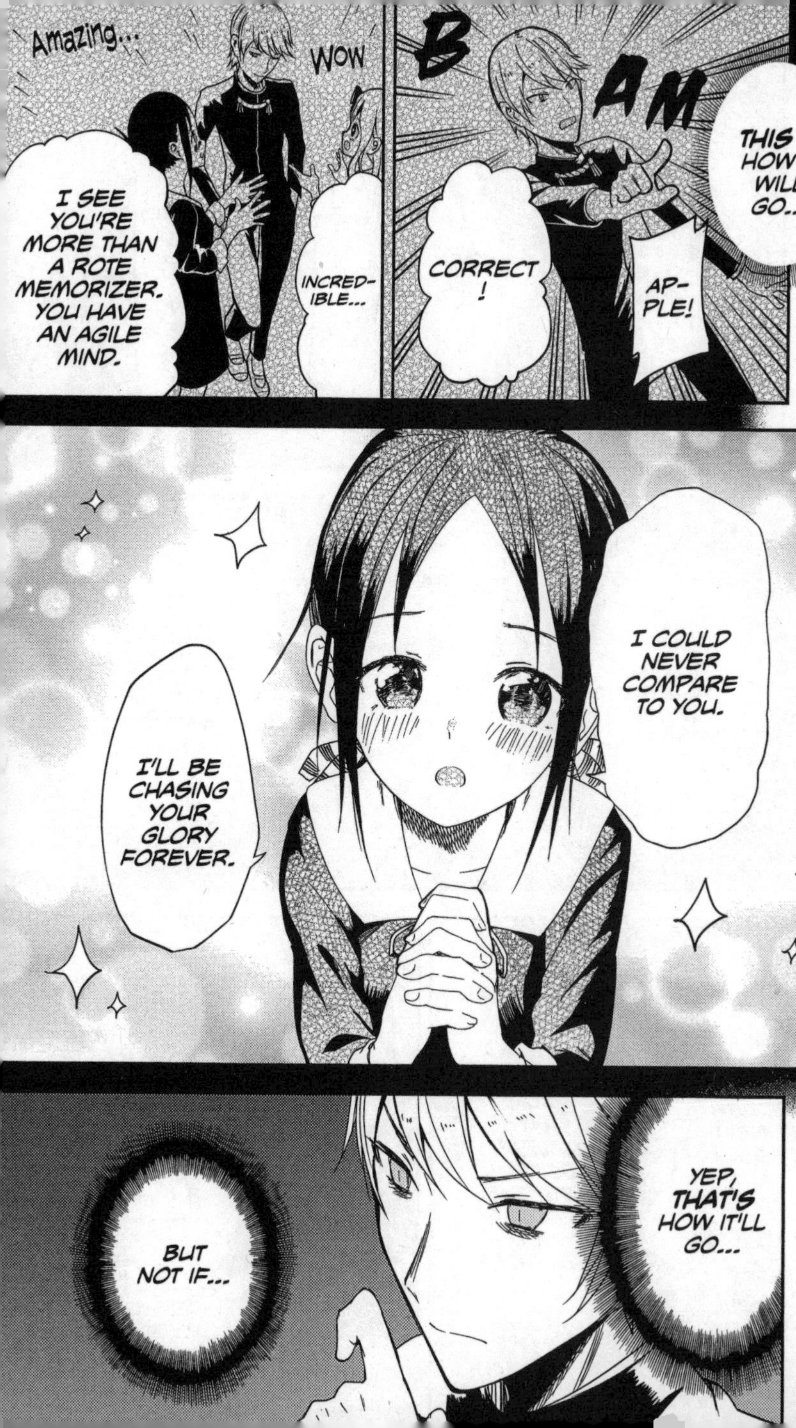

THIS IS HOW IT WILL GO...
BAM
AP-PLE!
CORRECT!
WOW
Amazing...
INCREDIBLE...
I SEE YOU'RE MORE THAN A ROTE MEMORIZER. YOU HAVE AN AGILE MIND.
I COULD NEVER COMPARE TO YOU.
I'LL BE CHASING YOUR GLORY FOREVER.
YEP, THAT'S HOW IT'LL GO...
BUT NOT IF...

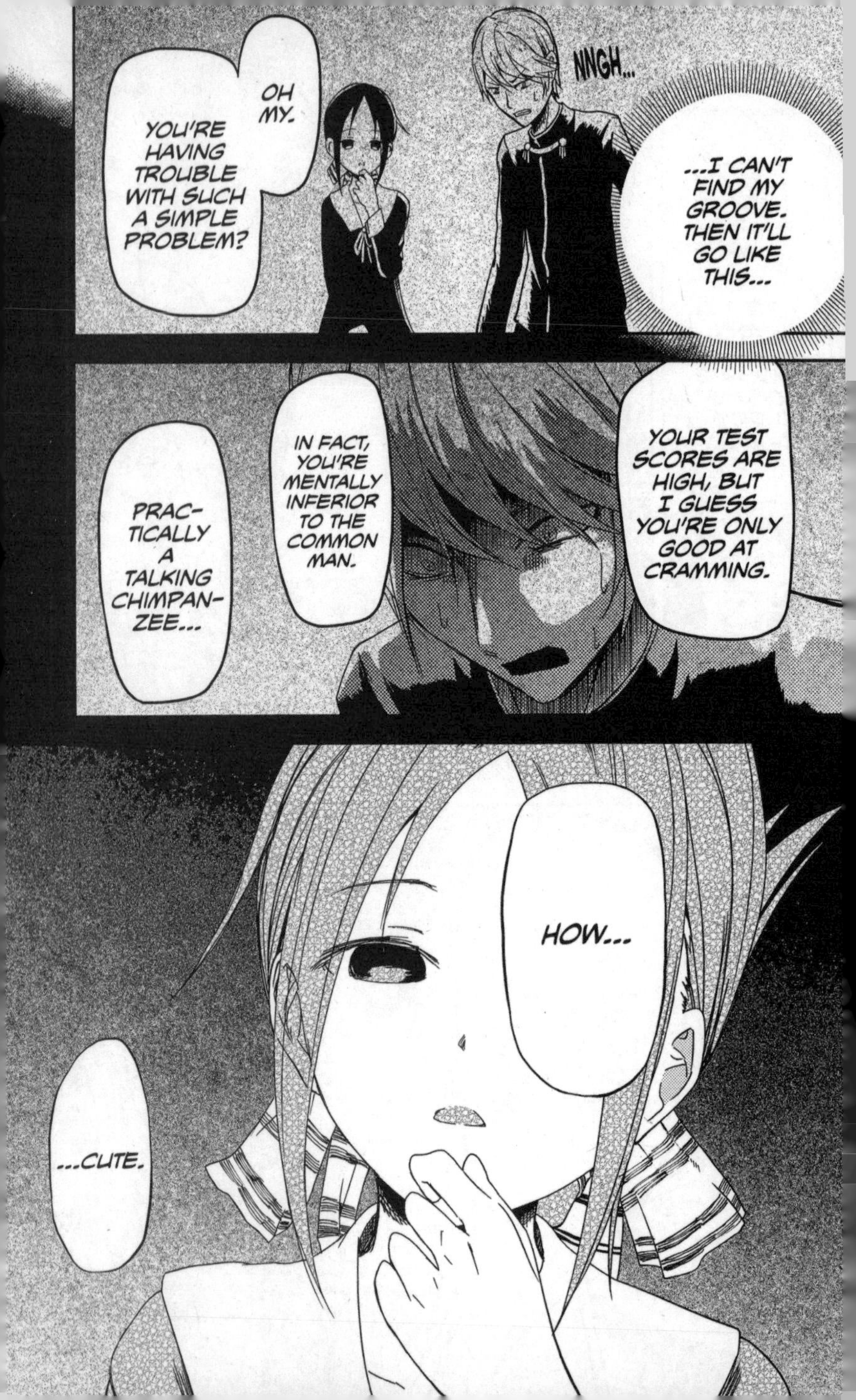
NNGH...
...I CAN'T FIND MY GROOVE. THEN IT'LL GO LIKE THIS...
OH MY.
YOU'RE HAVING TROUBLE WITH SUCH A SIMPLE PROBLEM?
YOUR TEST SCORES ARE HIGH, BUT I GUESS YOU'RE ONLY GOOD AT CRAMMING.
IN FACT, YOU'RE MENTALLY INFERIOR TO THE COMMON MAN.
PRAC-TICALLY A TALKING CHIMPAN-ZEE...
HOW...
...CUTE.

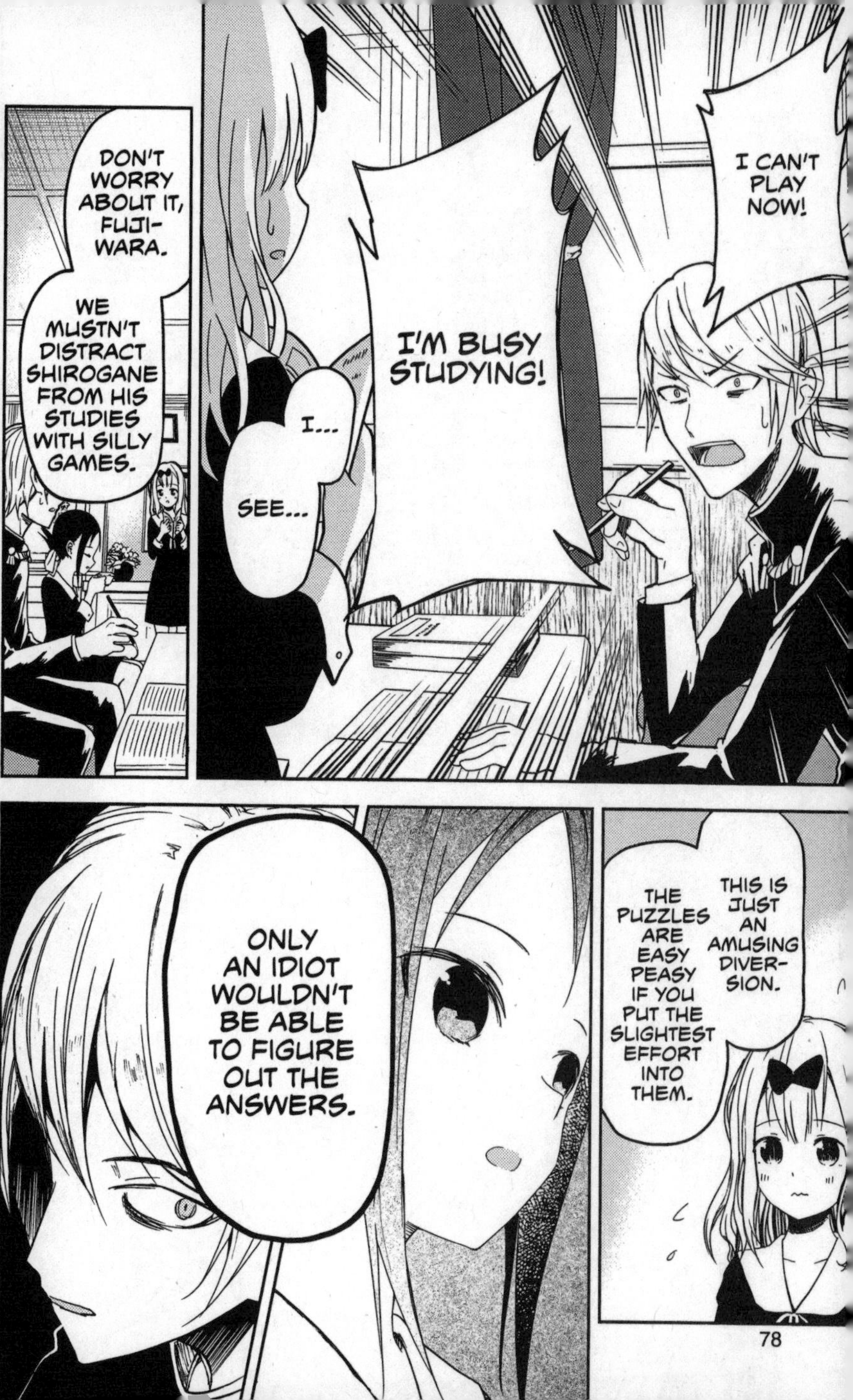
I CAN'T PLAY NOW!
I'M BUSY STUDYING!
I...
SEE...
DON'T WORRY ABOUT IT, FUJIWARA.
WE MUSTN'T DISTRACT SHIROGANE FROM HIS STUDIES WITH SILLY GAMES.
THIS IS JUST AN AMUSING DIVERSION.
THE PUZZLES ARE EASY PEASY IF YOU PUT THE SLIGHTEST EFFORT INTO THEM.
ONLY AN IDIOT WOULDN'T BE ABLE TO FIGURE OUT THE ANSWERS.

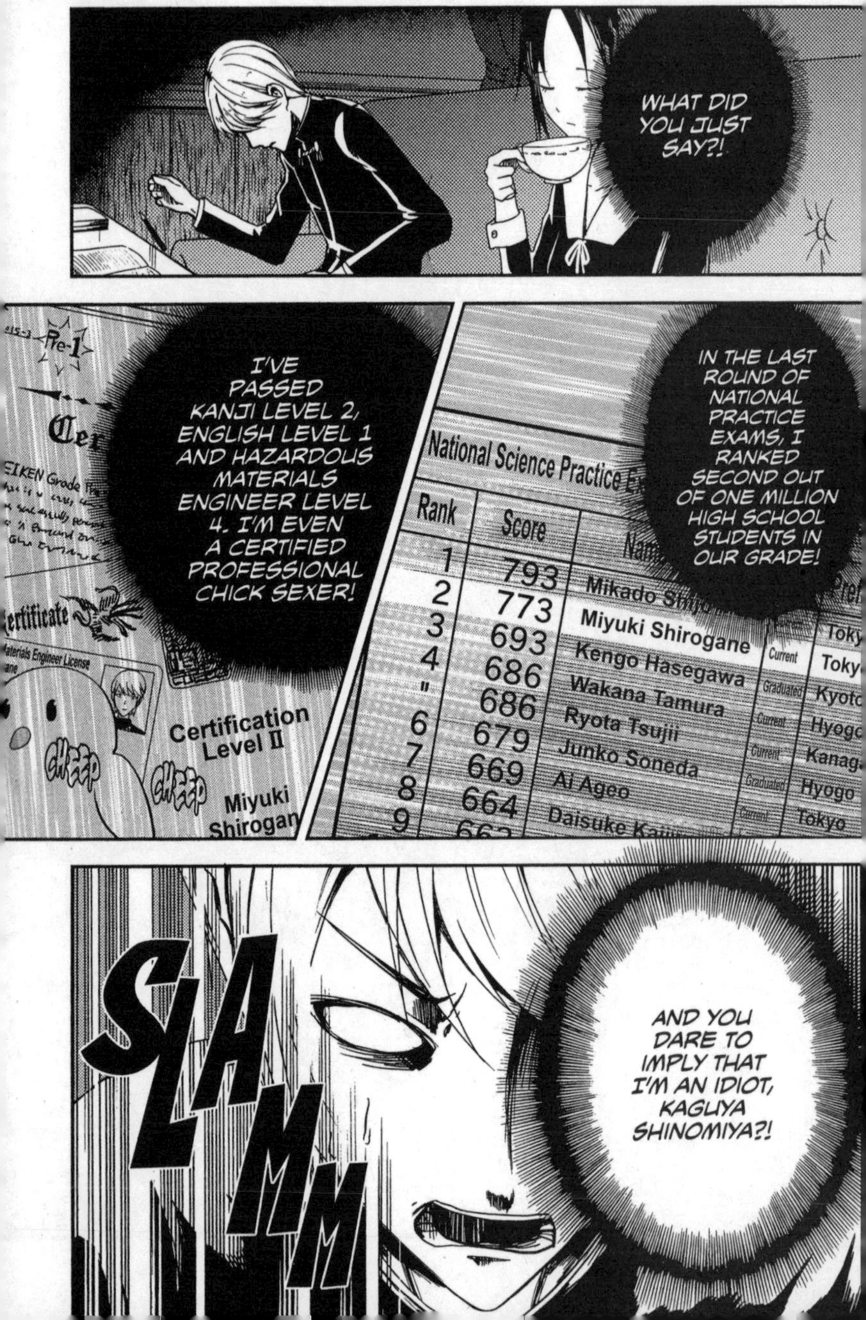
WHAT DID YOU JUST SAY?!
IN THE LAST ROUND OF NATIONAL PRACTICE EXAMS, I RANKED SECOND OUT OF ONE MILLION HIGH SCHOOL STUDENTS IN OUR GRADE!
National Science Practice Ex
Rank
Score
1 793 Mikado Shijo
2 773 Miyuki Shirogane Tokyo
3 693 Kengo Hasegawa Current Tokyo
4 686 Wakana Tamura Graduated Kyoto
" 686 Ryota Tsujii Current Hyogo
6 679 Junko Soneda Current Kanaga
7 669 Ai Ageo Graduated Hyogo
8 664 Daisuke Kaiji Current Tokyo
9
I'VE PASSED KANJI LEVEL 2, ENGLISH LEVEL 1 AND HAZARDOUS MATERIALS ENGINEER LEVEL 4. I'M EVEN A CERTIFIED PROFESSIONAL CHICK SEXER!
Pre-1
Cer
EIKEN Grade Pre
ertificate
Materials Engineer License
Certification Level II
Miyuki Shirogan
CHEEP
CHEEP
AND YOU DARE TO IMPLY THAT I'M AN IDIOT, KAGUYA SHINOMIYA?!
SLAMM

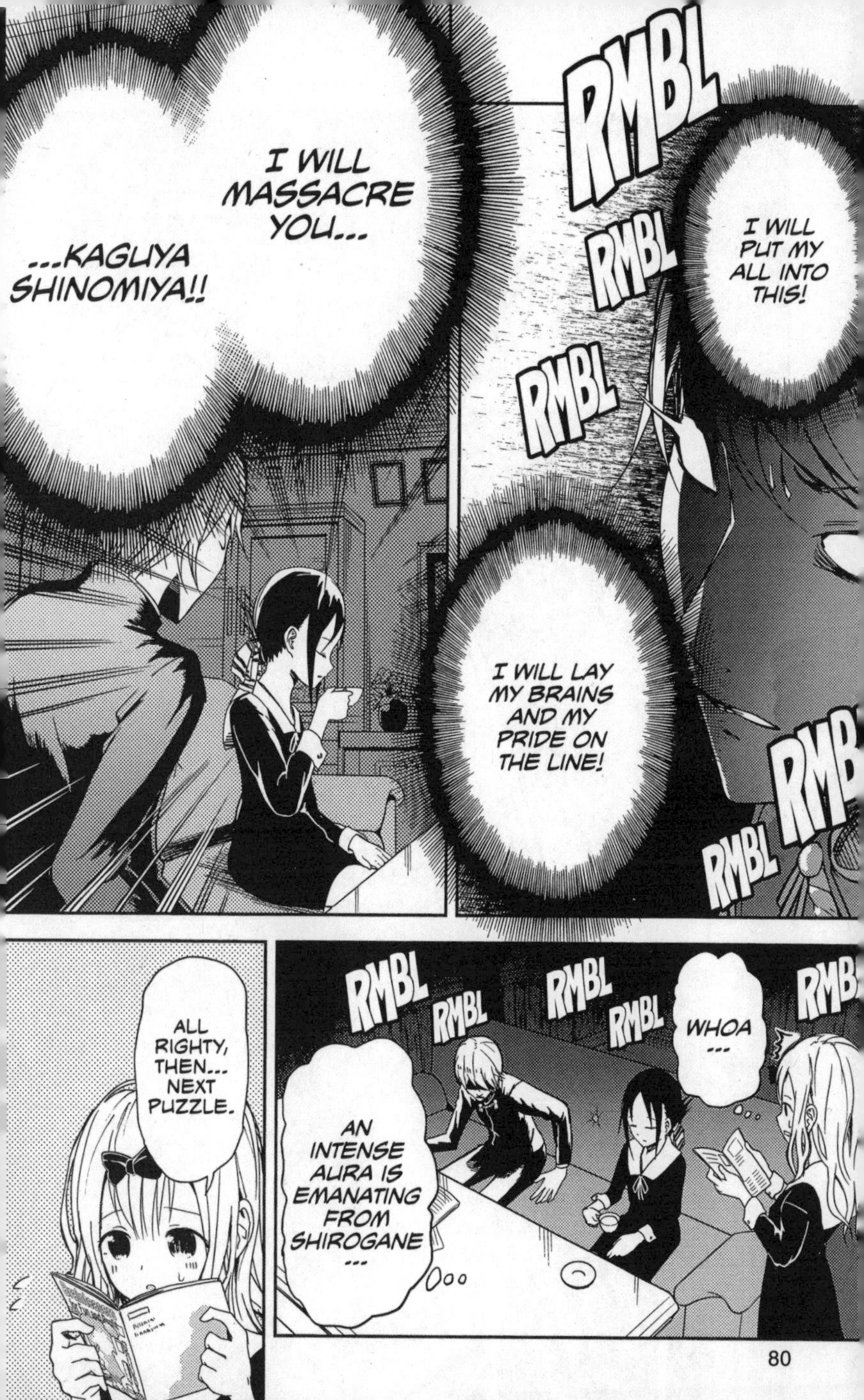

RMBL
RMBL
I WILL PUT MY ALL INTO THIS!
RMBL
I WILL LAY MY BRAINS AND MY PRIDE ON THE LINE!
RMB
RMBL
I WILL MASSACRE YOU...
...KAGUYA SHINOMIYA!!
RMB
WHOA ...
RMBL
RMBL
RMBL
RMBL
AN INTENSE AURA IS EMANATING FROM SHIROGANE ...
ALL RIGHTY, THEN... NEXT PUZZLE.

※ HIDE THE LEFT SIDE OF THIS PAGE TO PARTICIPATE IN THE BRAINTEASER. PROCEED WITH CAUTION, AS THE QUALITY OF THESE PUZZLES IS NOT VERY HIGH.

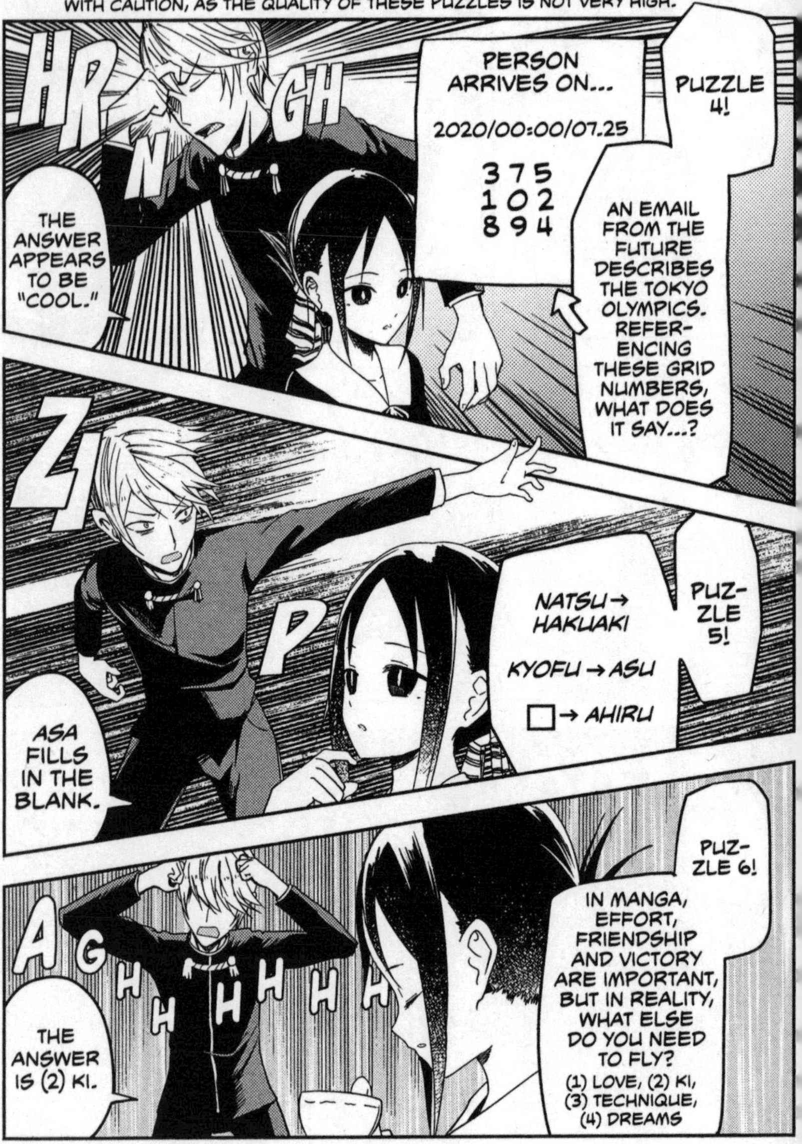
PUZZLE 4!
PERSON ARRIVES ON...
2020/00:00/07.25
375
102
894
AN EMAIL FROM THE FUTURE DESCRIBES THE TOKYO OLYMPICS. REFERENCING THESE GRID NUMBERS, WHAT DOES IT SAY...?
HRNGH
THE ANSWER APPEARS TO BE "COOL."
PUZZLE 5!
NATSU → HAKUAKI
KYOFU → ASU
□ → AHIRU
ZIP
ASA FILLS IN THE BLANK.
PUZZLE 6!
IN MANGA, EFFORT, FRIENDSHIP AND VICTORY ARE IMPORTANT, BUT IN REALITY, WHAT ELSE DO YOU NEED TO FLY?
(1) LOVE, (2) KI, (3) TECHNIQUE, (4) DREAMS
AGHHHHHH
THE ANSWER IS (2) KI.

← Explanations on page 87

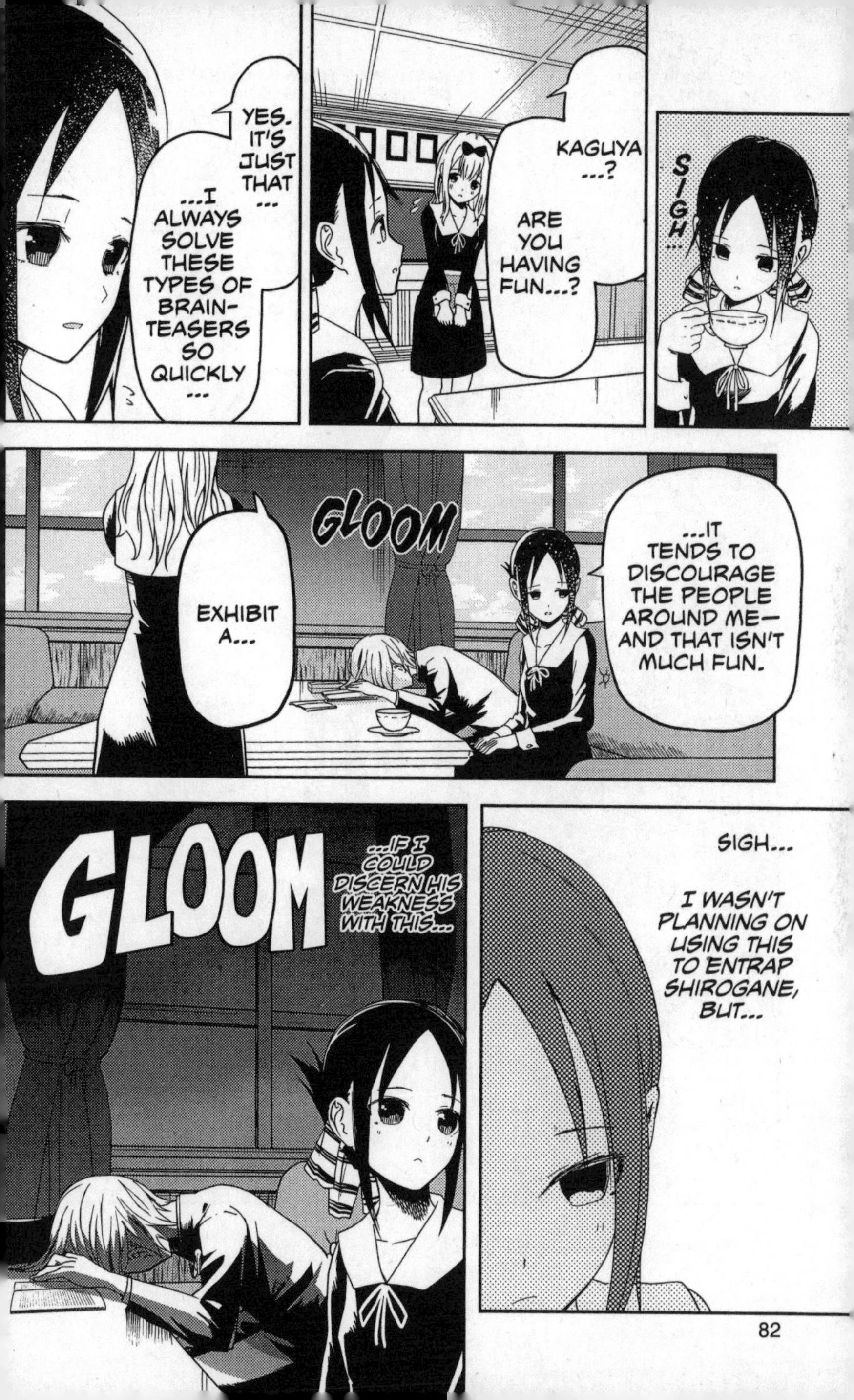
SIGH...
KAGUYA...?
ARE YOU HAVING FUN...?
YES. IT'S JUST THAT...
...I ALWAYS SOLVE THESE TYPES OF BRAIN-TEASERS SO QUICKLY...
...IT TENDS TO DISCOURAGE THE PEOPLE AROUND ME—AND THAT ISN'T MUCH FUN.
GLOOM
EXHIBIT A...
SIGH...
I WASN'T PLANNING ON USING THIS TO ENTRAP SHIROGANE, BUT...
...IF I COULD DISCERN HIS WEAKNESS WITH THIS...
GLOOM

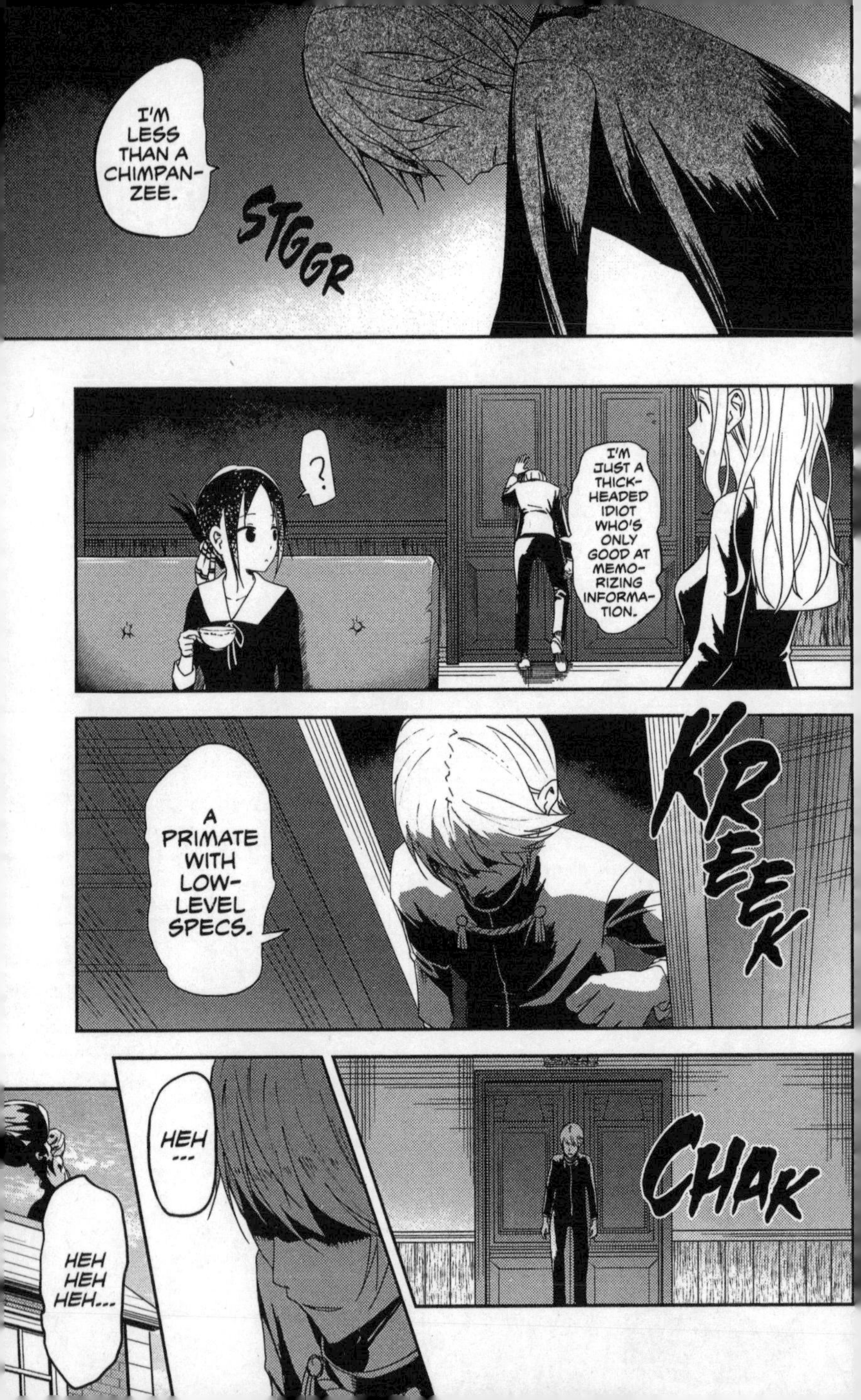
I'M LESS THAN A CHIMPAN-ZEE.
STGGR
I'M JUST A THICK-HEADED IDIOT WHO'S ONLY GOOD AT MEMO-RIZING INFORMA-TION.
?
KREEEK
A PRIMATE WITH LOW-LEVEL SPECS.
CHAK
HEH ...
HEH HEH HEH...

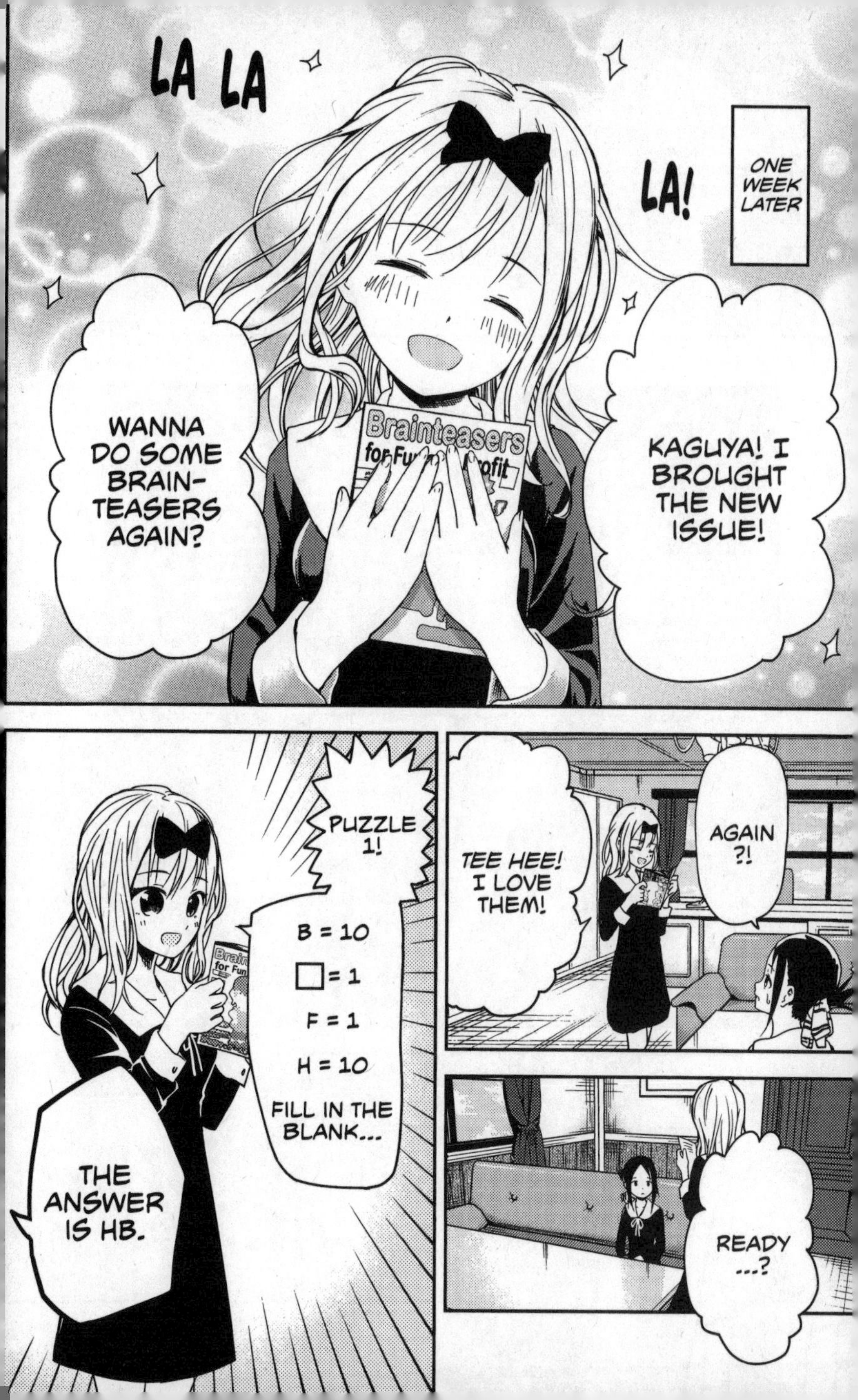
ONE WEEK LATER
LA LA LA!
Brainteasers
KAGUYA! I BROUGHT THE NEW ISSUE!
WANNA DO SOME BRAIN-TEASERS AGAIN?
AGAIN ?!
TEE HEE! I LOVE THEM!
READY ...?
PUZZLE 1!
B = 10
□ = 1
F = 1
H = 10
FILL IN THE BLANK...
THE ANSWER IS HB.

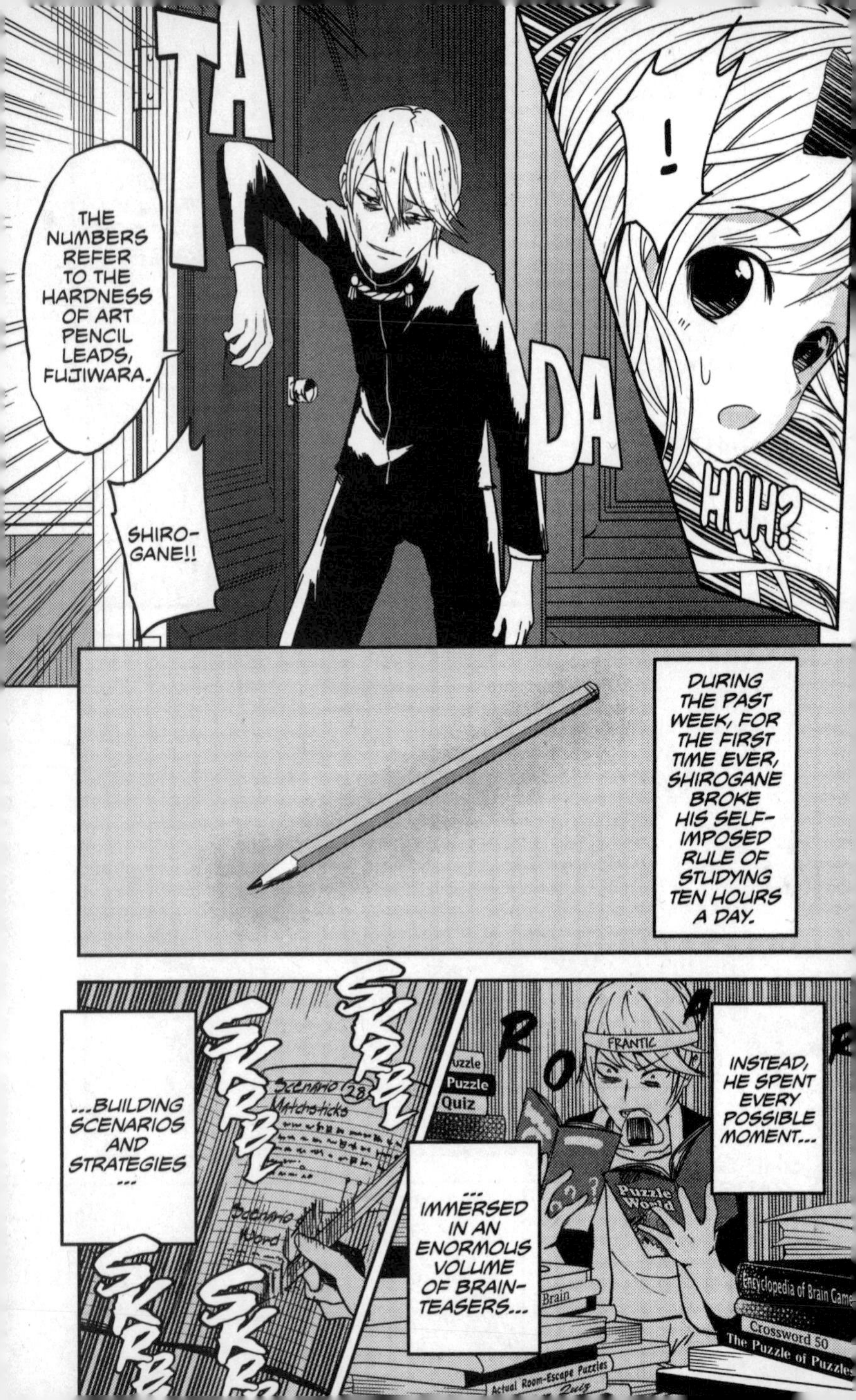
!
HUH?
TA
DA
THE NUMBERS REFER TO THE HARDNESS OF ART PENCIL LEADS, FUJIWARA.
SHIRO-GANE!!
DURING THE PAST WEEK, FOR THE FIRST TIME EVER, SHIROGANE BROKE HIS SELF-IMPOSED RULE OF STUDYING TEN HOURS A DAY.
ROAR
INSTEAD, HE SPENT EVERY POSSIBLE MOMENT...
FRANTIC
Puzzle
Quiz
Puzzle World
Crossword 50
The Puzzle of Puzzles
Actual Room-Escape Puzzles
...IMMERSED IN AN ENORMOUS VOLUME OF BRAIN-TEASERS...
SKRBL SKRBL
Scenario 28 Matchsticks
...BUILDING SCENARIOS AND STRATEGIES...
SKRBL SKRBL

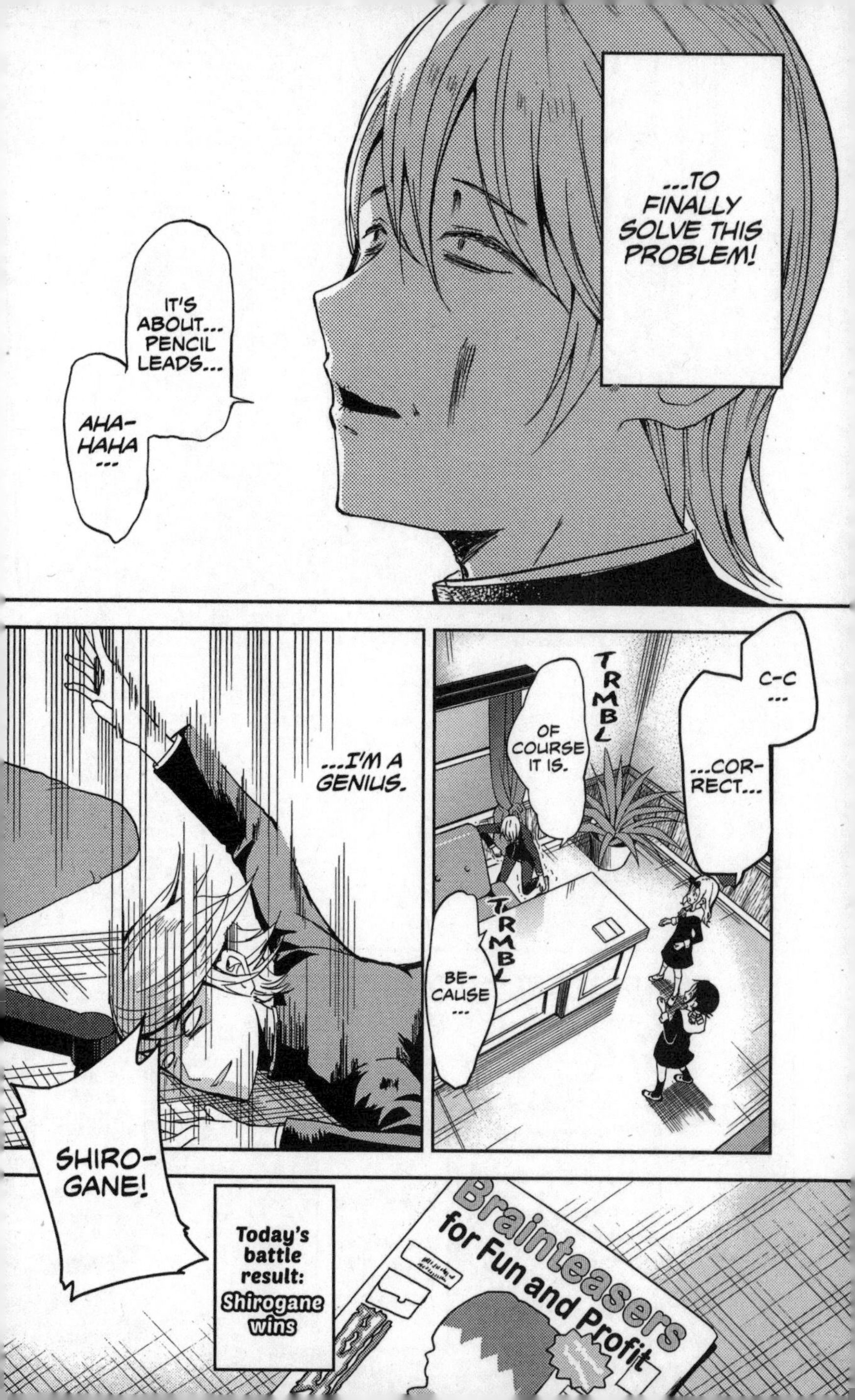
...TO FINALLY SOLVE THIS PROBLEM!
IT'S ABOUT... PENCIL LEADS...
AHA-HAHA...
C-C...
...COR-RECT...
TRMBL
OF COURSE IT IS.
TRMBL
BE-CAUSE...
...I'M A GENIUS.
Brainteasers for Fun and Profit
Today's battle result: Shirogane wins
SHIRO-GANE!

3 7 5
1 0 2
8 9 4
A COOL

Puzzle 4
The numbers at the top represent the time stamp for the email from the future. This time stamp is split up into four sections: the year, the hour, the minutes and the date, respectively. If you create four copies of the grid (one for each section of the time stamp) and black out all of the numbers that *don't* appear in each given section, the shapes of the remaining boxes spell out an English word.

2020 makes "C," 00 makes "O," 00 makes "O," and, finally, 0725 makes "L." Put them together and they spell out the word "COOL."

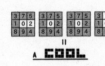

Passage of time
Summer → Fall
Today → Tomorrow
Morning → Afternoon

***Natsu* (means "summer") →**
***Hakuaki* (means "Cretaceous Period";**
***Aki* means "fall")**

***Kyofu* (means "fear";**
***Kyo* means "today") →**
***Asu* (means "tomorrow")**

[blank box: (answer is "morning")] →
***Ahiru* (means "duck";**
***Hiru* means "afternoon")**

Puzzle 5
Understanding and solving this puzzle requires a knowledge of the phonetic reading of kanji. The phonetic reading of the Japanese word on one side of the arrow (on the right, left and then the right again) includes a word that when paired with the word on the other side reflects the passage of time. For example, the word "Fall" on the right is part of the full Japanese word on that line. Fall matches with "Summer" on the left, because fall comes after summer. Following this pattern, Kaguya deduces that since the word "Afternoon" is embedded in the word on the right in the last line, the word on the left should be the word "Morning."

***Do ry o ku* (means "effort")**
***Yu u j o u* (means "friendship")**
***Sh o u ri* (means "victory")**
Answer: (2) *ki*

Puzzle 6:
In this puzzle, if you take the last hiragana letter of each of the words mentioned (*doryoku*, *yuujou* and *shouri*), you get *kuuri*. Adding *ki* to this makes *kuuriki*, which means "aerodynamics"—which is related to "flying."

KAGUYA-SAMA
LOVE IS WAR

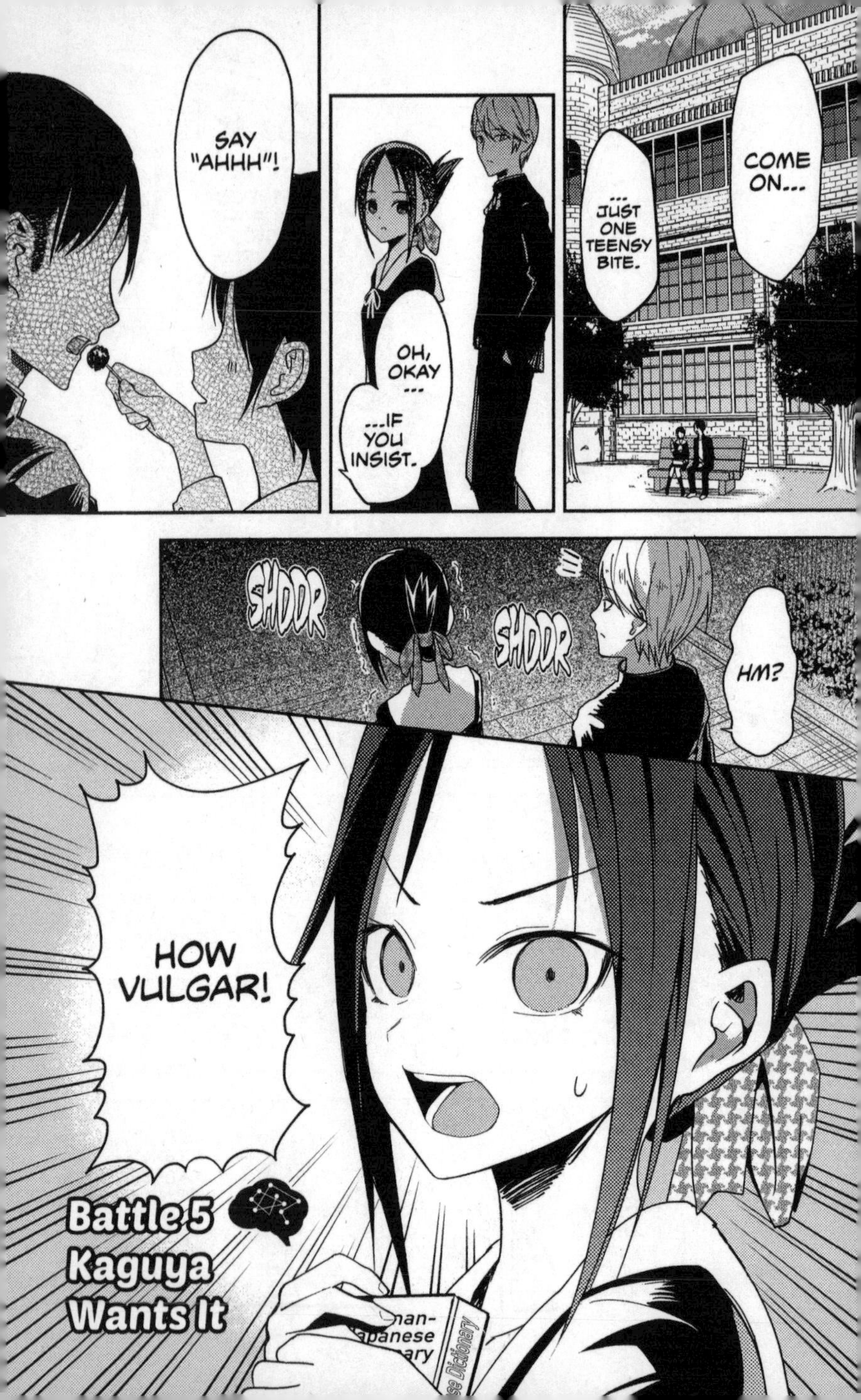
COME ON...
...JUST ONE TEENSY BITE.
OH, OKAY...
...IF YOU INSIST.
SAY "AHHH"!
HM?
SHDDR
SHDDR
HOW VULGAR!
Battle 5 Kaguya Wants It

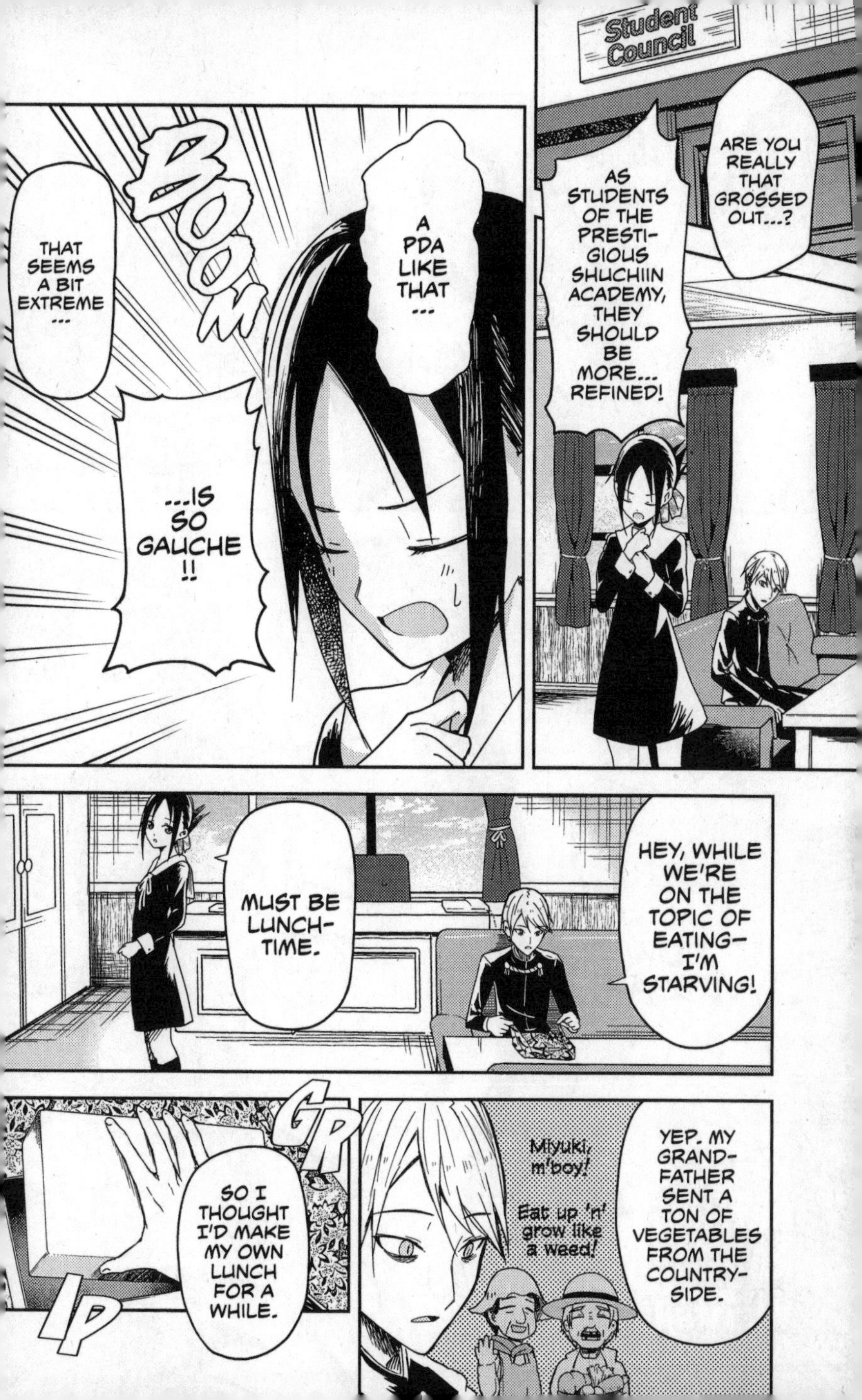
Student Council
ARE YOU REALLY THAT GROSSED OUT...?
AS STUDENTS OF THE PRESTI-GIOUS SHUCHIIN ACADEMY, THEY SHOULD BE MORE... REFINED!
A PDA LIKE THAT...
BOOM
...IS SO GAUCHE!!
THAT SEEMS A BIT EXTREME...
HEY, WHILE WE'RE ON THE TOPIC OF EATING— I'M STARVING!
MUST BE LUNCH-TIME.
YEP. MY GRAND-FATHER SENT A TON OF VEGETABLES FROM THE COUNTRY-SIDE.
Miyuki, m'boy!
Eat up 'n' grow like a weed!
GRIP
SO I THOUGHT I'D MAKE MY OWN LUNCH FOR A WHILE.

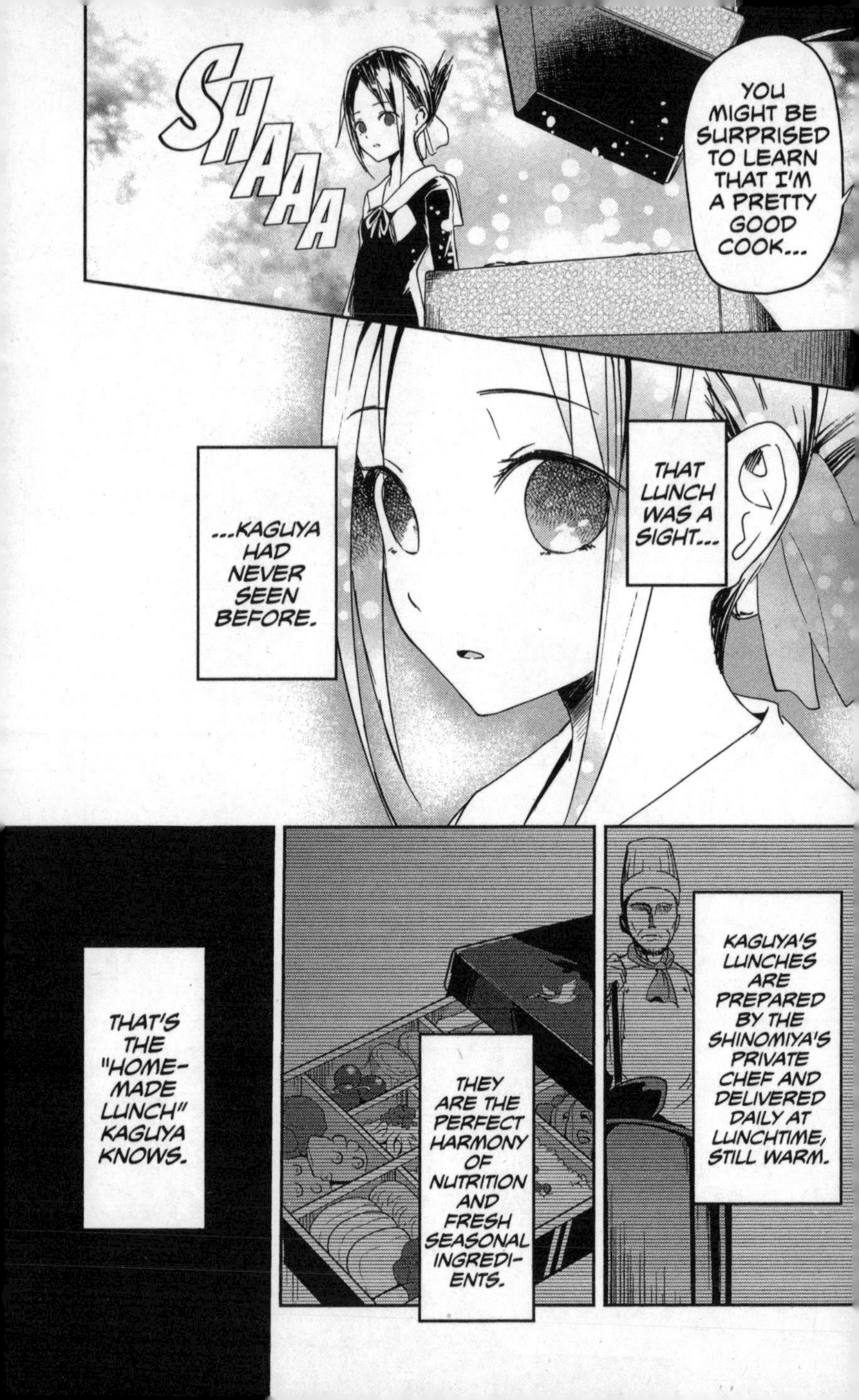
YOU MIGHT BE SURPRISED TO LEARN THAT I'M A PRETTY GOOD COOK...
SHAAAA
THAT LUNCH WAS A SIGHT...
...KAGUYA HAD NEVER SEEN BEFORE.
KAGUYA'S LUNCHES ARE PREPARED BY THE SHINOMIYA'S PRIVATE CHEF AND DELIVERED DAILY AT LUNCHTIME, STILL WARM.
THEY ARE THE PERFECT HARMONY OF NUTRITION AND FRESH SEASONAL INGREDI-ENTS.
THAT'S THE "HOME-MADE LUNCH" KAGUYA KNOWS.

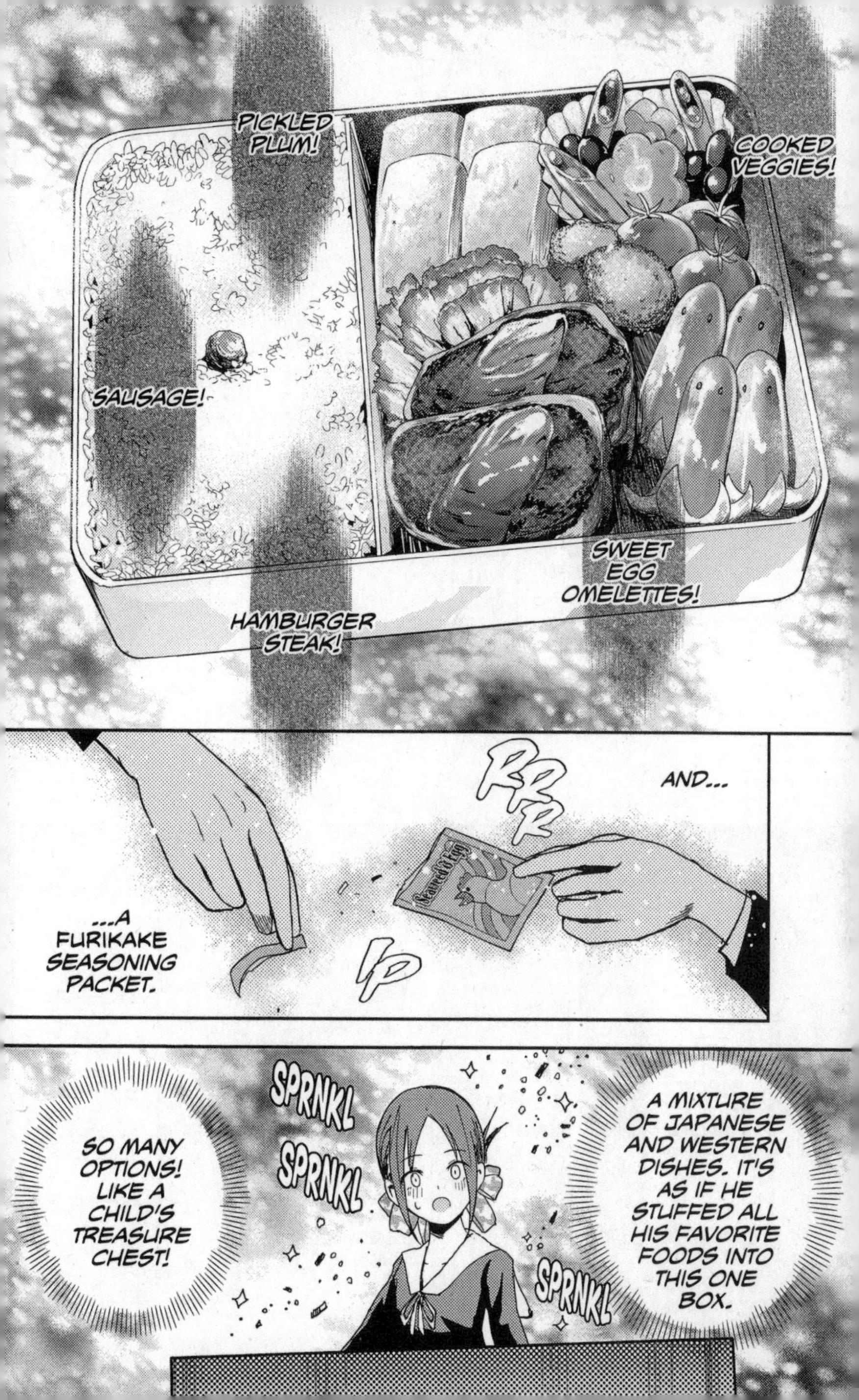

COOKED VEGGIES!
PICKLED PLUM!
SAUSAGE!
SWEET EGG OMELETTES!
HAMBURGER STEAK!
AND...
RRR
...A FURIKAKE SEASONING PACKET.
IP
A MIXTURE OF JAPANESE AND WESTERN DISHES. IT'S AS IF HE STUFFED ALL HIS FAVORITE FOODS INTO THIS ONE BOX.
SPRNKL
SPRNKL
SPRNKL
SO MANY OPTIONS! LIKE A CHILD'S TREASURE CHEST!

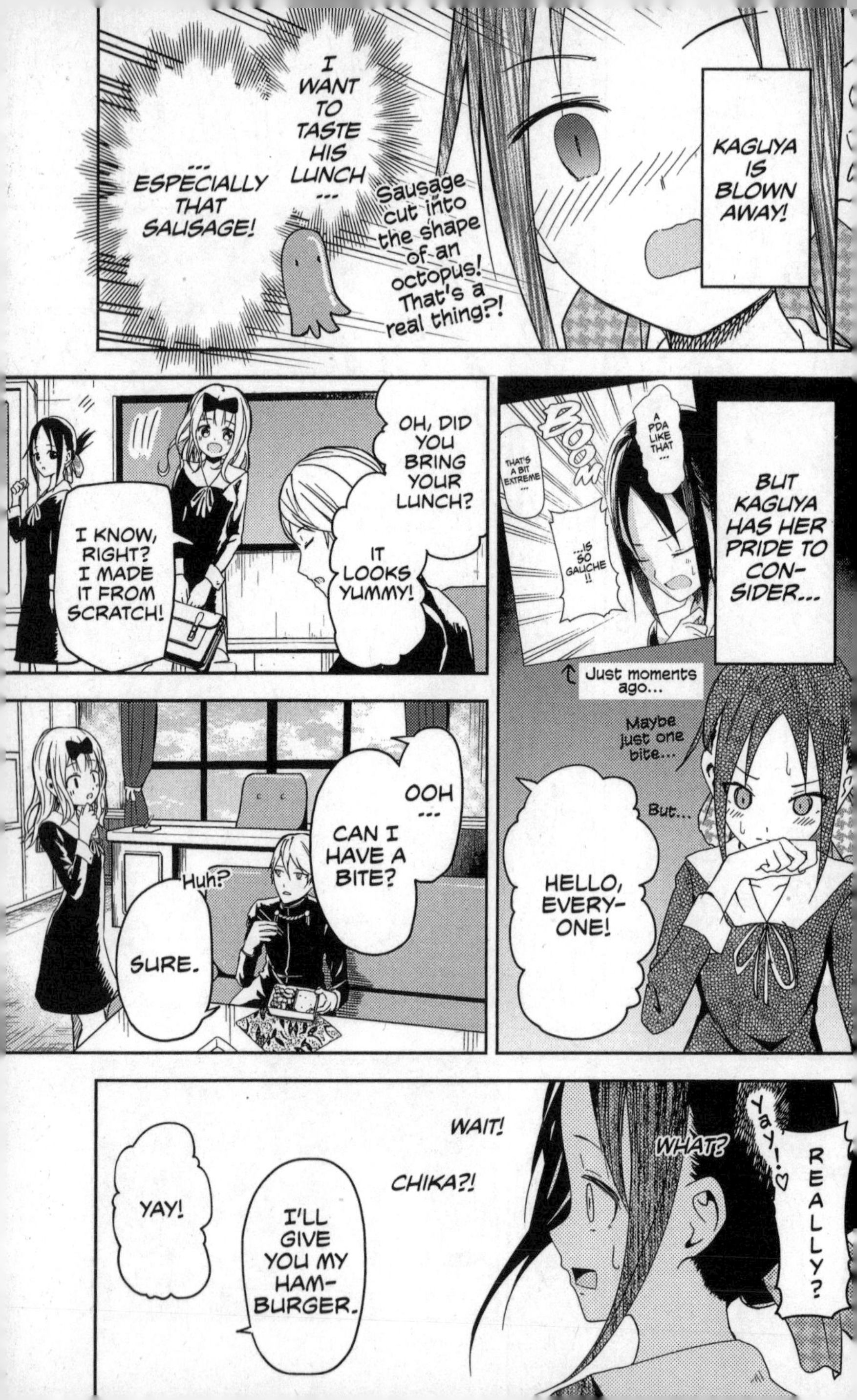
KAGUYA IS BLOWN AWAY!
Sausage cut into the shape of an octopus! That's a real thing?!
I WANT TO TASTE HIS LUNCH...
...ESPECIALLY THAT SAUSAGE!
BUT KAGUYA HAS HER PRIDE TO CON-SIDER...
A PDA LIKE THAT...
...IS SO GAUCHE!!
THAT'S A BIT EXTREME...
BOOM
Just moments ago...
Maybe just one bite...
But...
HELLO, EVERY-ONE!
OH, DID YOU BRING YOUR LUNCH?
IT LOOKS YUMMY!
I KNOW, RIGHT? I MADE IT FROM SCRATCH!
OOH... CAN I HAVE A BITE?
Huh?
SURE.
REALLY?
Yay!♡
WHAT?
WAIT!
CHIKA?!
I'LL GIVE YOU MY HAM-BURGER.
YAY!

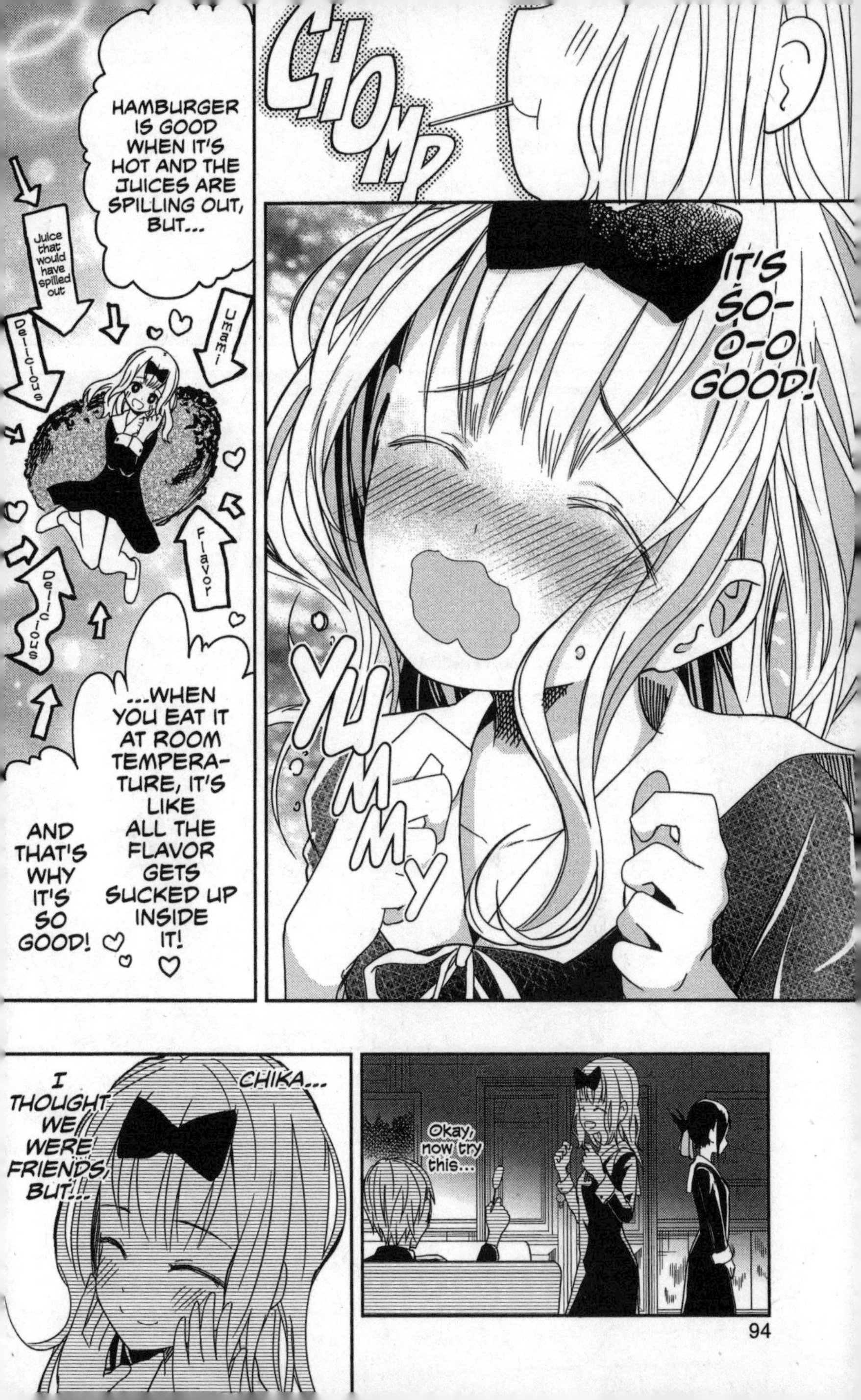
CHOMP
IT'S SO-O-O GOOD!
YUMMY
HAMBURGER IS GOOD WHEN IT'S HOT AND THE JUICES ARE SPILLING OUT, BUT...
Juice that would have spilled out
Umami
Delicious
Flavor
Delicious
...WHEN YOU EAT IT AT ROOM TEMPERA-TURE, IT'S LIKE ALL THE FLAVOR GETS SUCKED UP INSIDE IT!
AND THAT'S WHY IT'S SO GOOD!
Okay, now try this...
CHIKA...
I THOUGHT WE WERE FRIENDS, BUT...

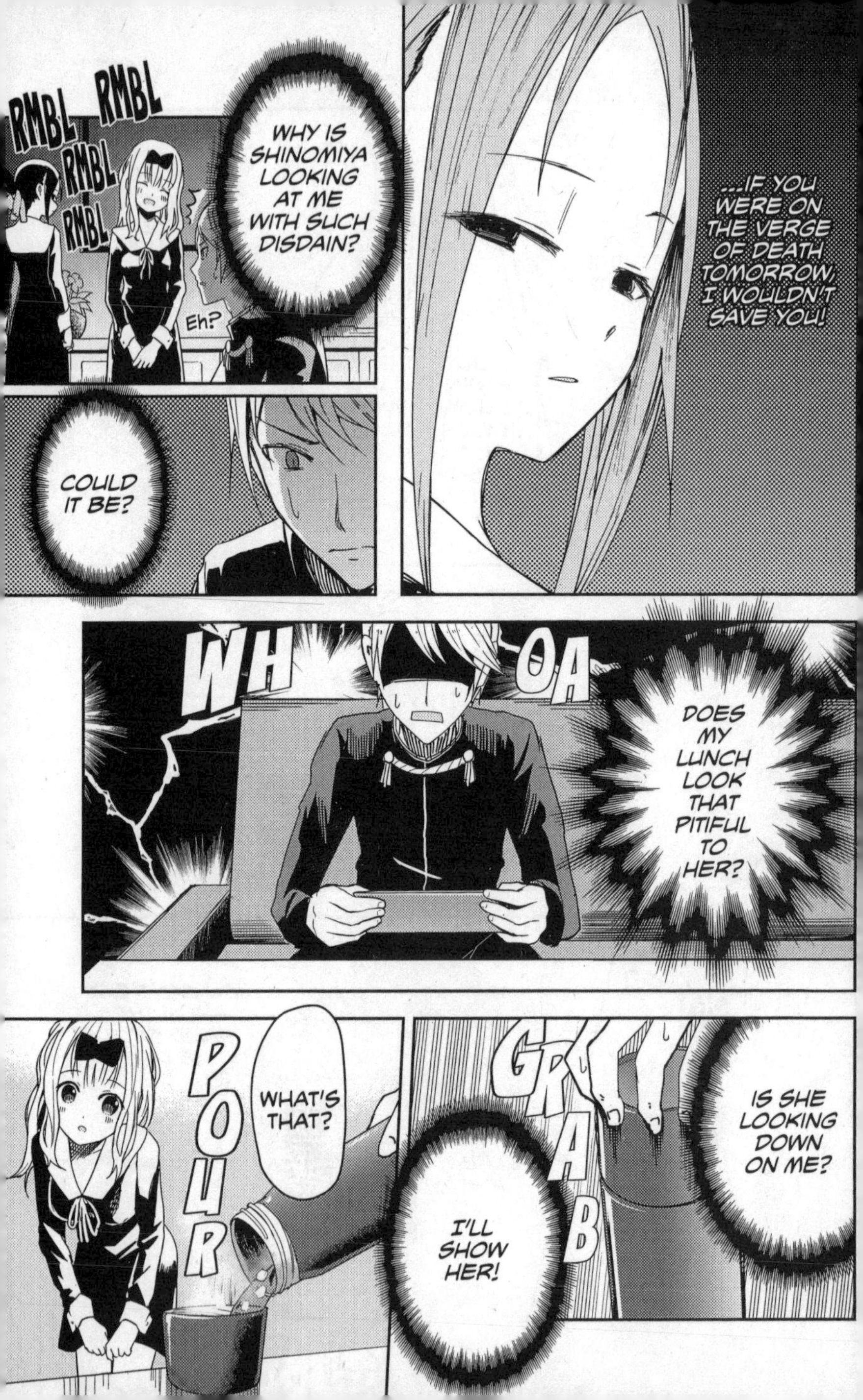
...IF YOU WERE ON THE VERGE OF DEATH TOMORROW, I WOULDN'T SAVE YOU!
RMBL RMBL RMBL RMBL
WHY IS SHINOMIYA LOOKING AT ME WITH SUCH DISDAIN?
Eh?
COULD IT BE?
WHOA
DOES MY LUNCH LOOK THAT PITIFUL TO HER?
GRAB
IS SHE LOOKING DOWN ON ME?
I'LL SHOW HER!
WHAT'S THAT?
POUR

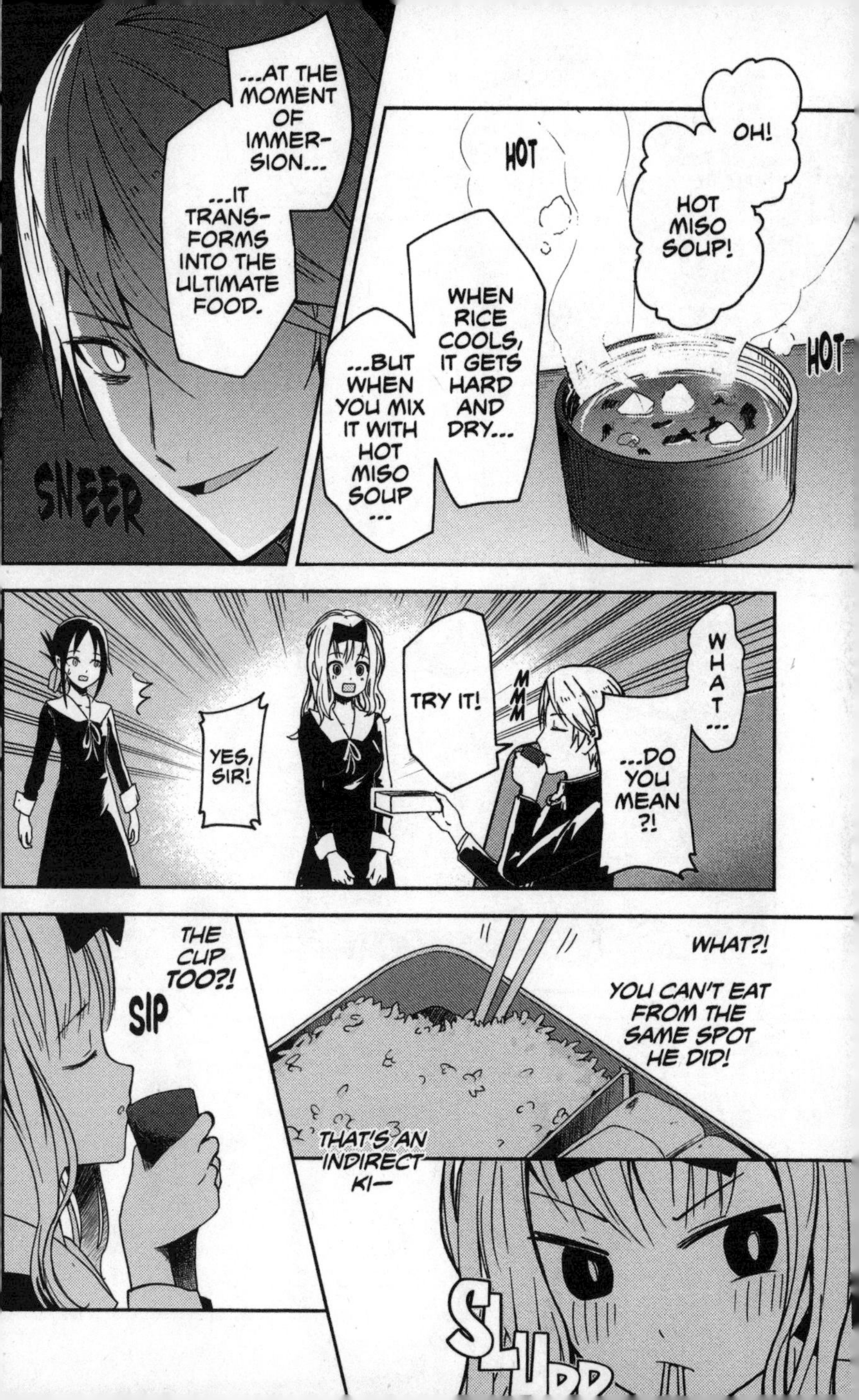
OH!
HOT MISO SOUP!
HOT
HOT
WHEN RICE COOLS, IT GETS HARD AND DRY...
...BUT WHEN YOU MIX IT WITH HOT MISO SOUP...
...AT THE MOMENT OF IMMERSION...
...IT TRANSFORMS INTO THE ULTIMATE FOOD.
SNEER
WHAT...
...DO YOU MEAN?!
MMM
TRY IT!
YES, SIR!
WHAT?!
YOU CAN'T EAT FROM THE SAME SPOT HE DID!
THAT'S AN INDIRECT KI—
THE CUP TOO?!
SIP

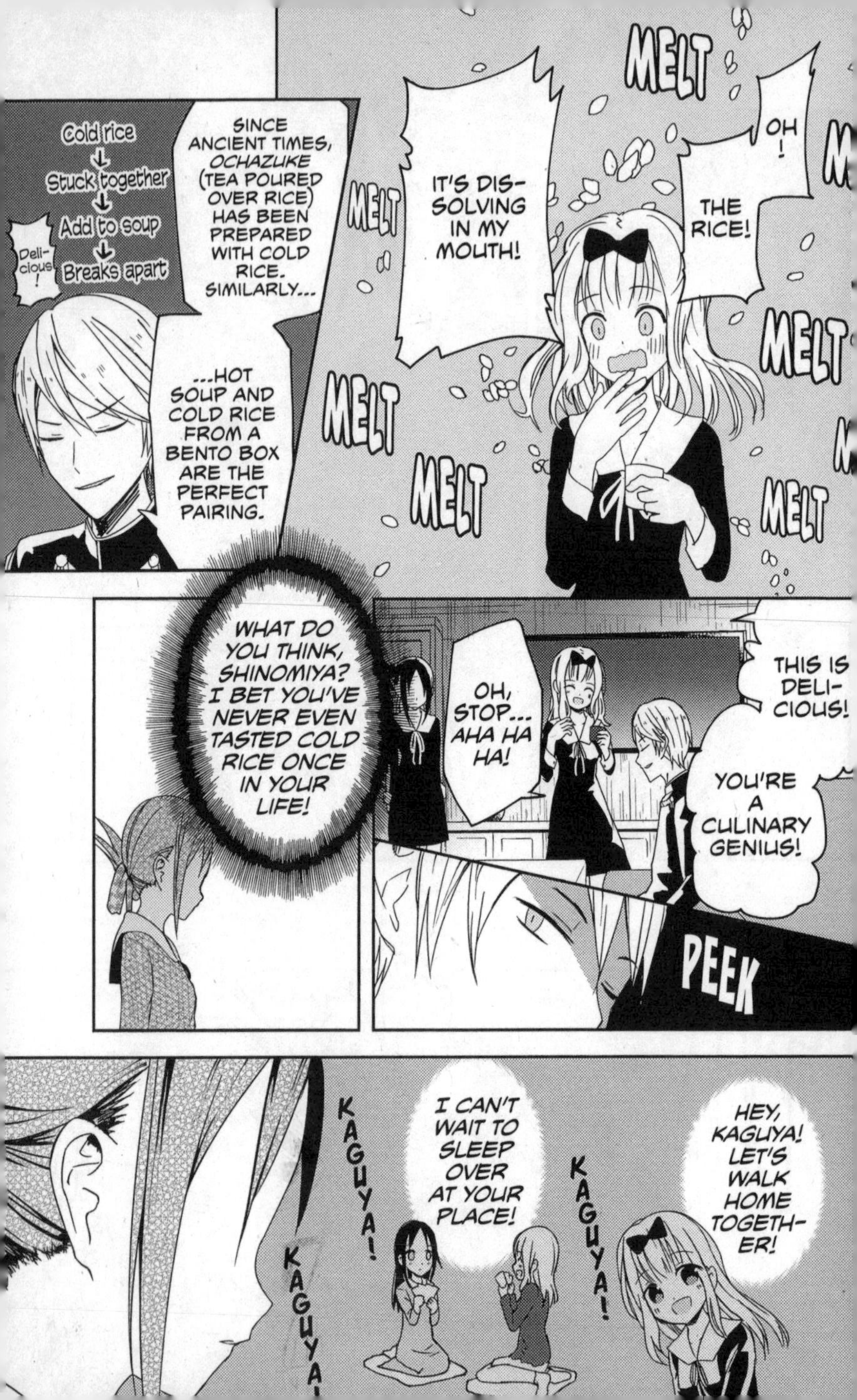
MELT
OH! THE RICE!
IT'S DIS-SOLVING IN MY MOUTH!
MELT
MELT
MELT
MELT
MELT
SINCE ANCIENT TIMES, OCHAZUKE (TEA POURED OVER RICE) HAS BEEN PREPARED WITH COLD RICE. SIMILARLY...
Cold rice ↓ Stuck together ↓ Add to soup ↓ Breaks apart
Deli-cious!
...HOT SOUP AND COLD RICE FROM A BENTO BOX ARE THE PERFECT PAIRING.
THIS IS DELI-CIOUS!
YOU'RE A CULINARY GENIUS!
OH, STOP... AHA HA HA!
PEEK
WHAT DO YOU THINK, SHINOMIYA? I BET YOU'VE NEVER EVEN TASTED COLD RICE ONCE IN YOUR LIFE!
HEY, KAGUYA! LET'S WALK HOME TOGETH-ER!
KAGUYA!
I CAN'T WAIT TO SLEEP OVER AT YOUR PLACE!
KAGUYA!
KAGUYA!
KAGUYA!

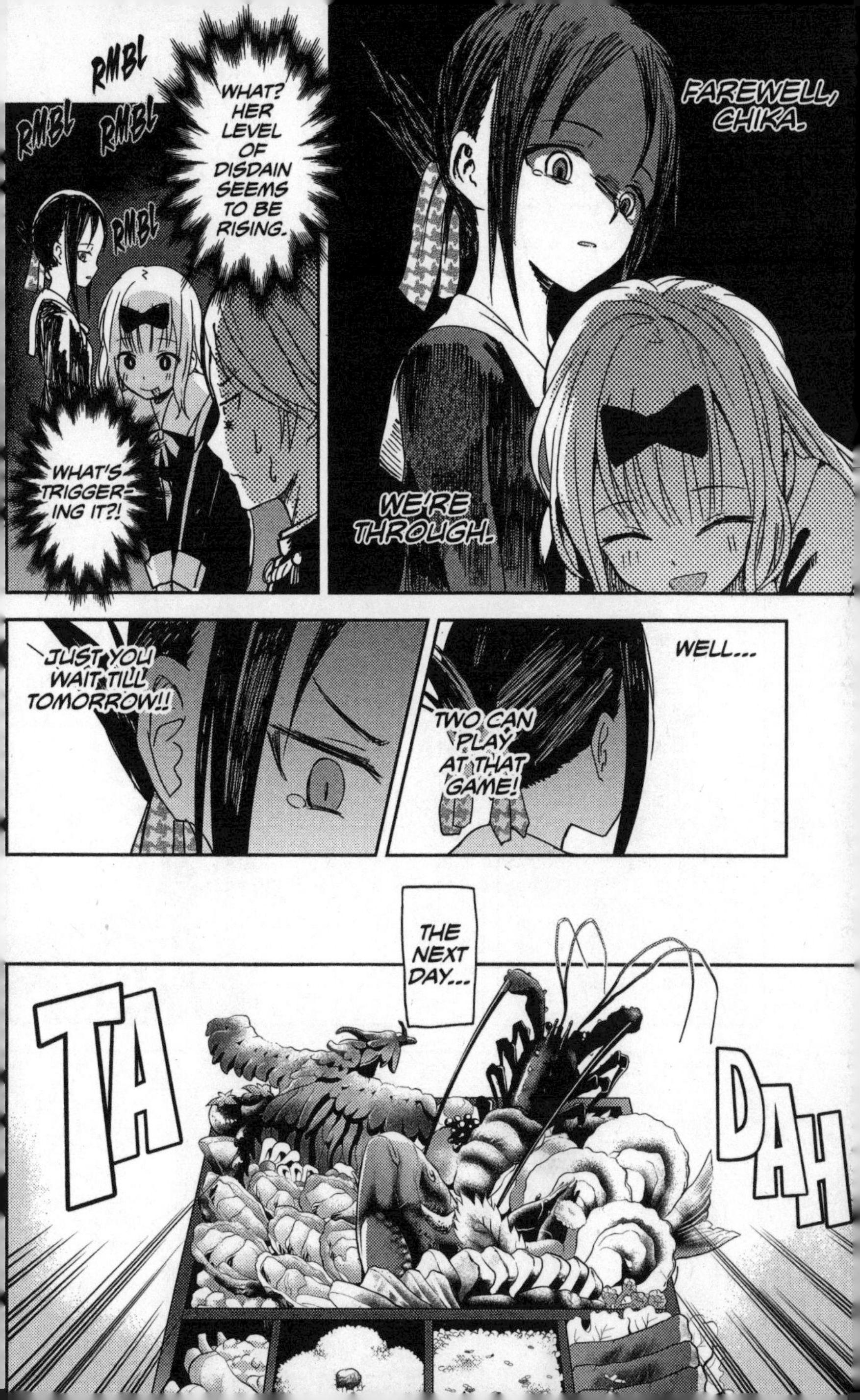
FAREWELL, CHIKA.
WE'RE THROUGH.
RMBL
RMBL
RMBL
RMBL
WHAT? HER LEVEL OF DISDAIN SEEMS TO BE RISING.
WHAT'S TRIGGERING IT?!
WELL...
TWO CAN PLAY AT THAT GAME!
JUST YOU WAIT TILL TOMORROW!!
THE NEXT DAY...
TA
DAH

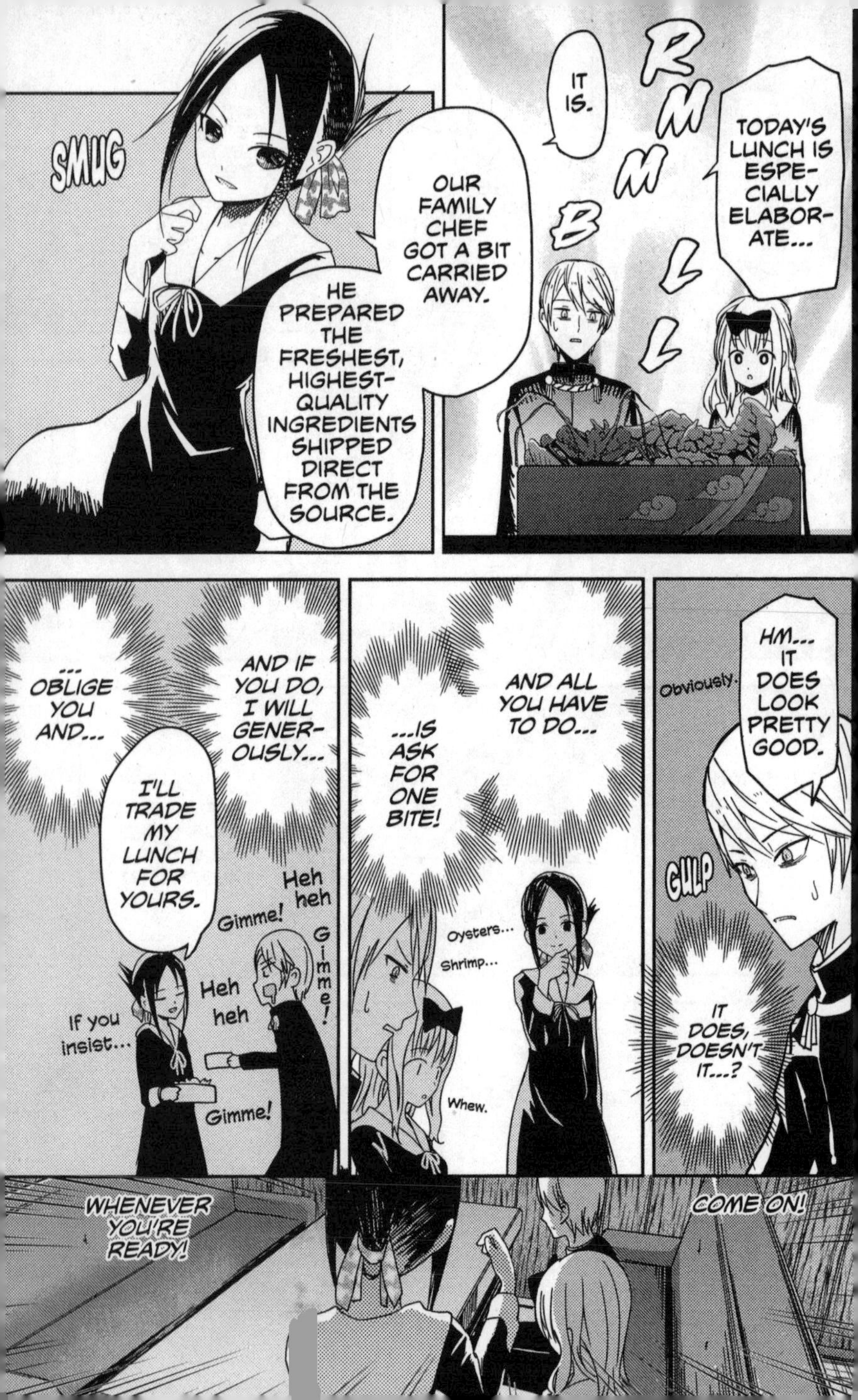
RMMBLL
TODAY'S LUNCH IS ESPECIALLY ELABORATE...
IT IS.
SMUG
OUR FAMILY CHEF GOT A BIT CARRIED AWAY.
HE PREPARED THE FRESHEST, HIGHEST-QUALITY INGREDIENTS SHIPPED DIRECT FROM THE SOURCE.
HM... IT DOES LOOK PRETTY GOOD.
Obviously.
GULP
IT DOES, DOESN'T IT...?
AND ALL YOU HAVE TO DO...
...IS ASK FOR ONE BITE!
Oysters...
Shrimp...
Whew.
AND IF YOU DO, I WILL GENEROUSLY...
...OBLIGE YOU AND...
I'LL TRADE MY LUNCH FOR YOURS.
Heh heh
Gimme!
Gimme!
Heh heh
If you insist...
Gimme!
COME ON!
WHENEVER YOU'RE READY!

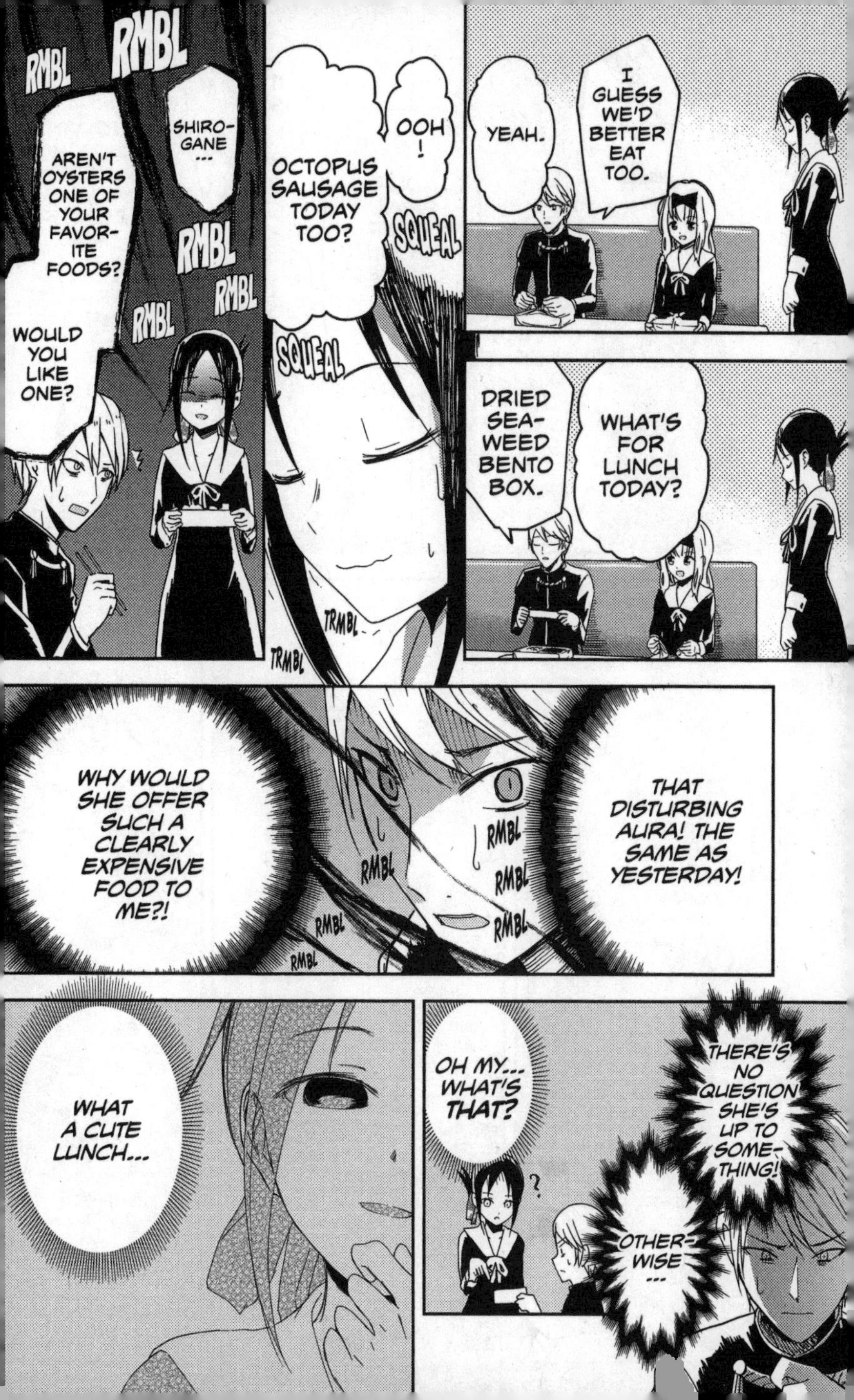
I GUESS WE'D BETTER EAT TOO.
YEAH.
WHAT'S FOR LUNCH TODAY?
DRIED SEA-WEED BENTO BOX.
OOH!
OCTOPUS SAUSAGE TODAY TOO?
SQUEAL
SQUEAL
TRMBL
TRMBL
RMBL
RMBL
SHIRO-GANE...
AREN'T OYSTERS ONE OF YOUR FAVOR-ITE FOODS?
RMBL
RMBL
RMBL
WOULD YOU LIKE ONE?
THAT DISTURBING AURA! THE SAME AS YESTERDAY!
RMBL
RMBL
RMBL
RMBL
RMBL
RMBL
WHY WOULD SHE OFFER SUCH A CLEARLY EXPENSIVE FOOD TO ME?!
THERE'S NO QUESTION SHE'S UP TO SOME-THING!
OTHER-WISE...
OH MY... WHAT'S THAT?
?
WHAT A CUTE LUNCH...

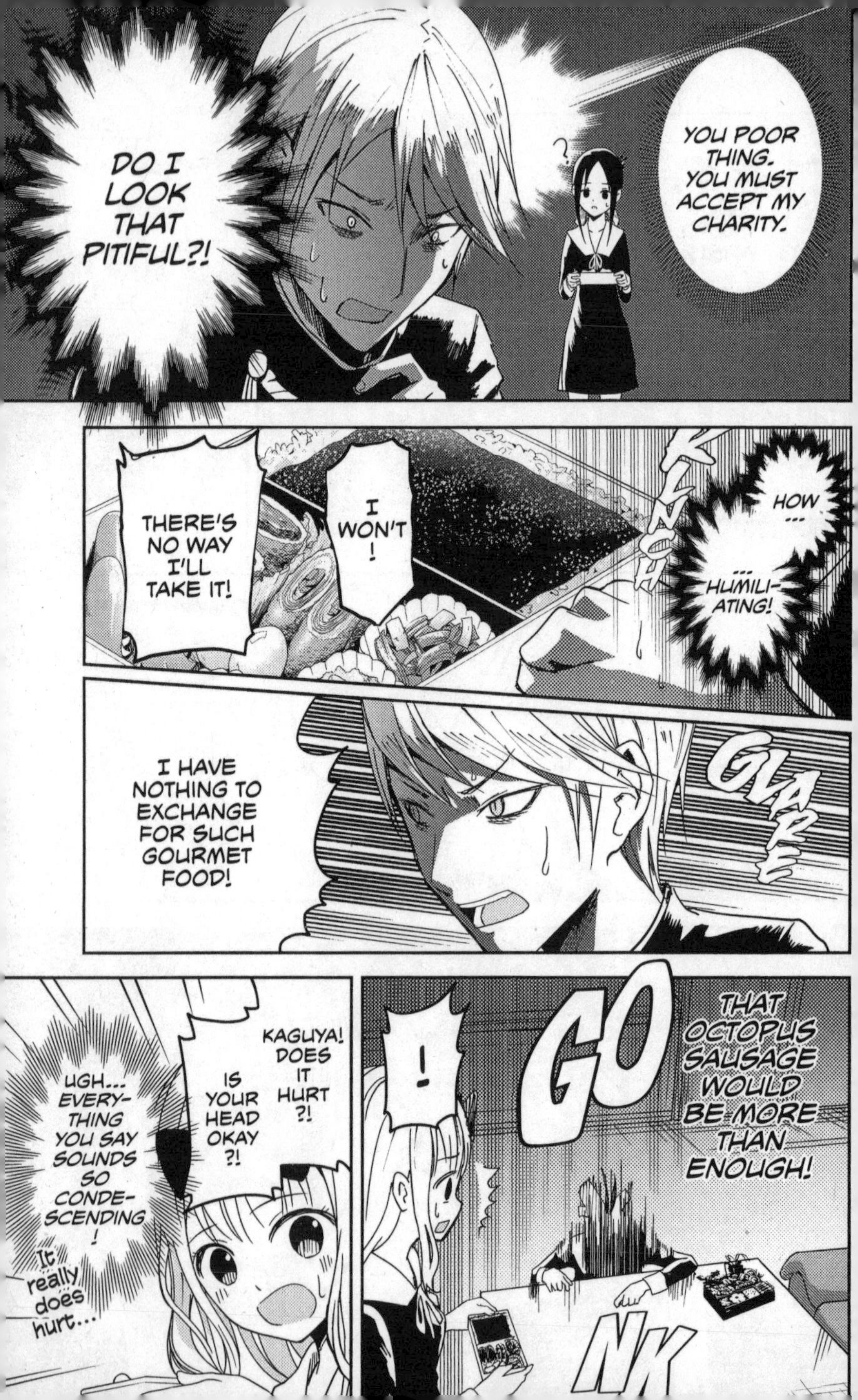

YOU POOR THING. YOU MUST ACCEPT MY CHARITY.
?
DO I LOOK THAT PITIFUL?!
HOW... ...HUMILIATING!
I WON'T!
THERE'S NO WAY I'LL TAKE IT!
GLARE
I HAVE NOTHING TO EXCHANGE FOR SUCH GOURMET FOOD!
THAT OCTOPUS SAUSAGE WOULD BE MORE THAN ENOUGH!
GO
NK
!
KAGUYA! DOES IT HURT?!
IS YOUR HEAD OKAY?!
UGH... EVERYTHING YOU SAY SOUNDS SO CONDESCENDING!
It really... does hurt...

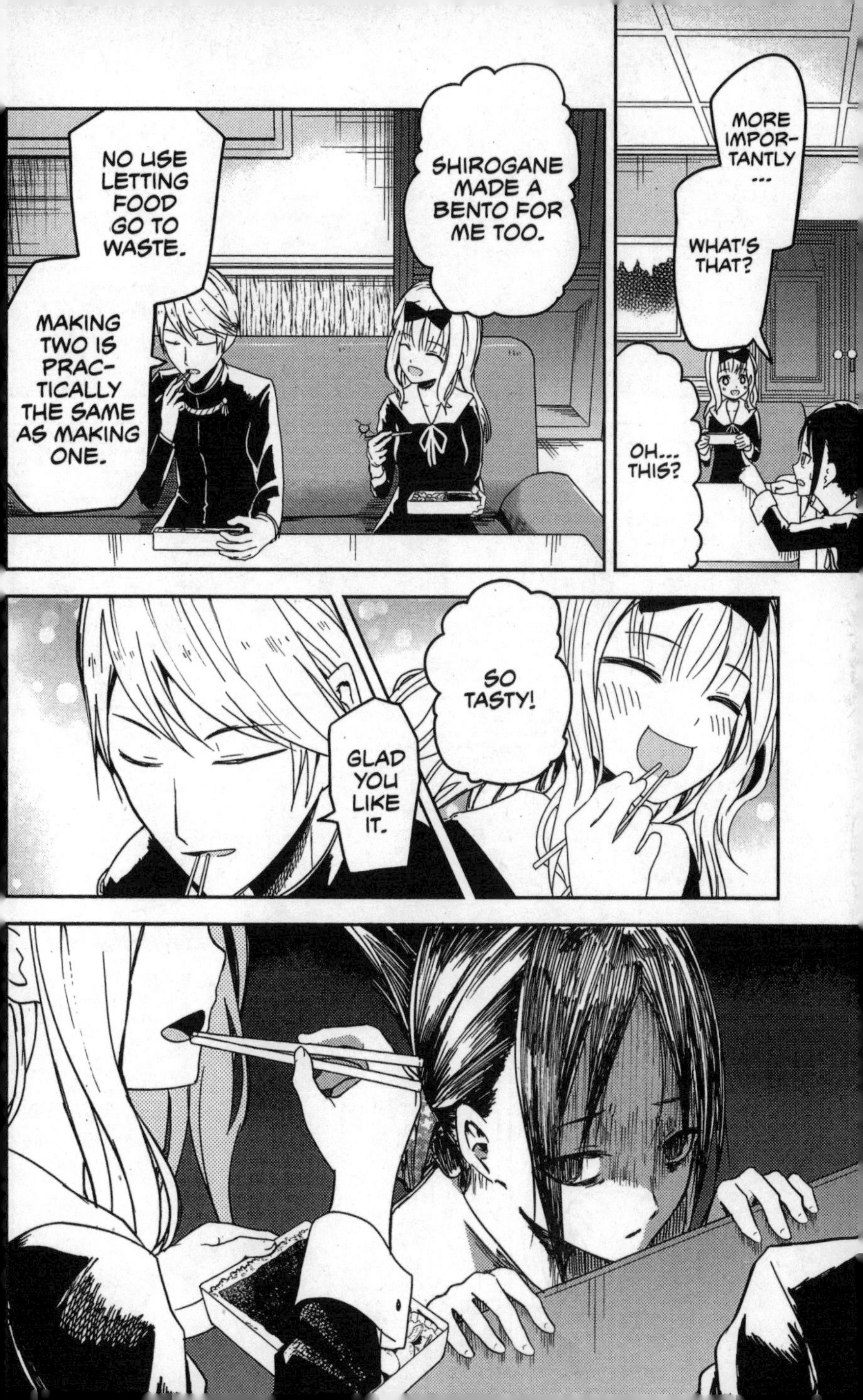
MORE IMPORTANTLY...
WHAT'S THAT?
OH... THIS?
SHIROGANE MADE A BENTO FOR ME TOO.
NO USE LETTING FOOD GO TO WASTE.
MAKING TWO IS PRACTICALLY THE SAME AS MAKING ONE.
SO TASTY!
GLAD YOU LIKE IT.

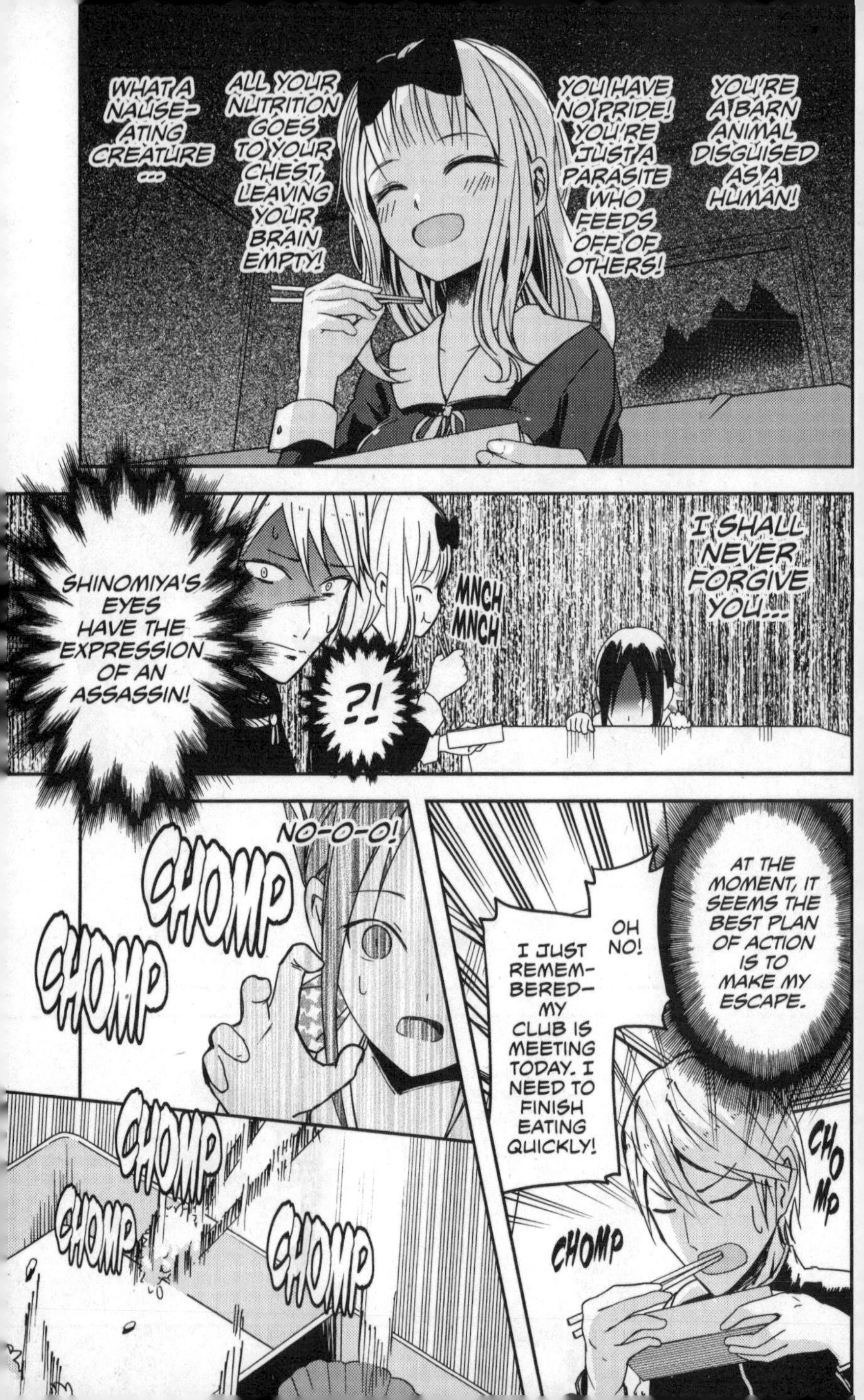
YOU'RE A BARN ANIMAL DISGUISED AS A HUMAN!
YOU HAVE NO PRIDE! YOU'RE JUST A PARASITE WHO FEEDS OFF OF OTHERS!
ALL YOUR NUTRITION GOES TO YOUR CHEST, LEAVING YOUR BRAIN EMPTY!
WHAT A NAUSEATING CREATURE...
I SHALL NEVER FORGIVE YOU...
MNCH MNCH
?!
SHINOMIYA'S EYES HAVE THE EXPRESSION OF AN ASSASSIN!
AT THE MOMENT, IT SEEMS THE BEST PLAN OF ACTION IS TO MAKE MY ESCAPE.
CHOMP
CHOMP
OH NO!
I JUST REMEMBERED—MY CLUB IS MEETING TODAY. I NEED TO FINISH EATING QUICKLY!
NO-O-O!
CHOMP
CHOMP
CHOMP
CHOMP
CHOMP

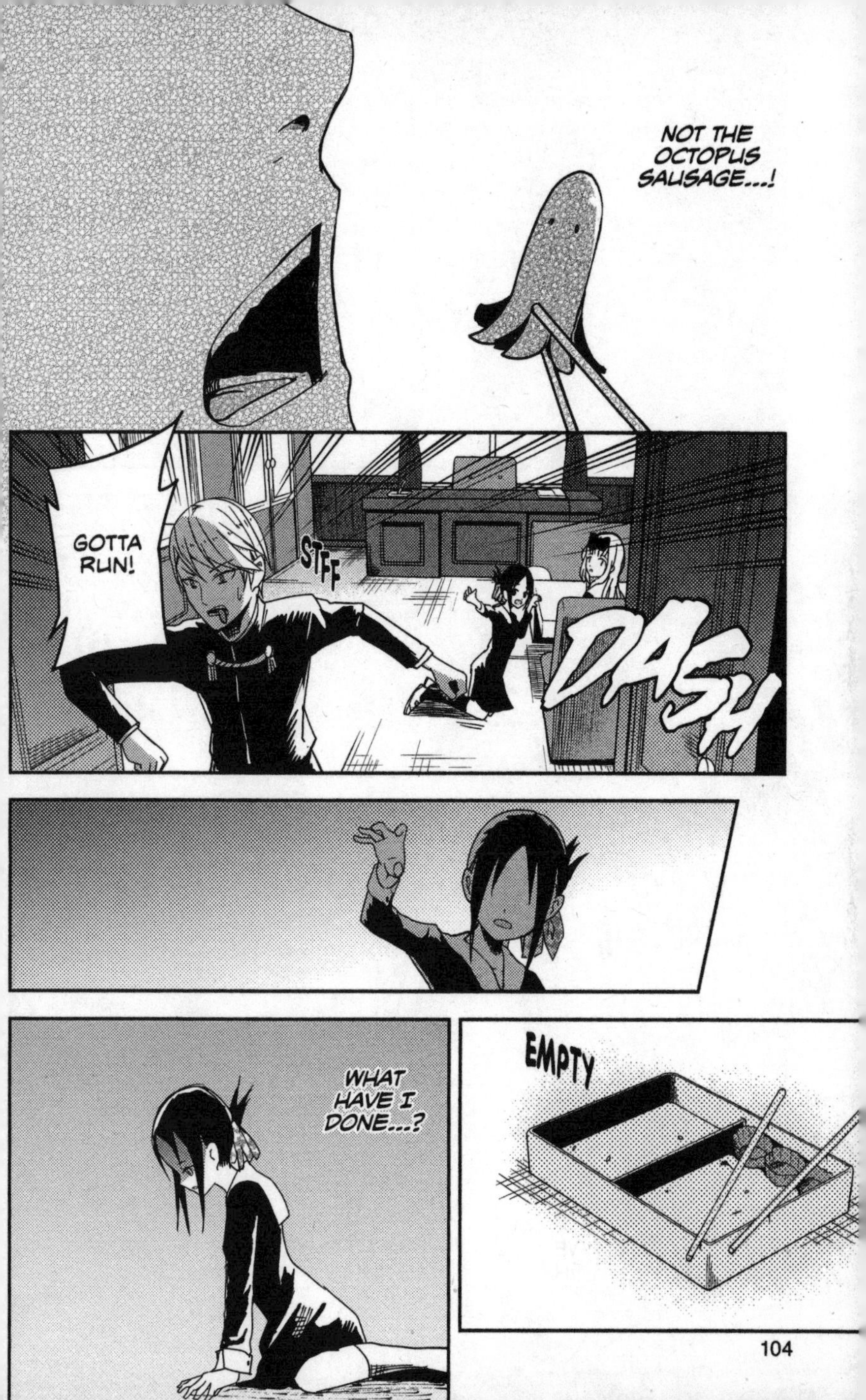
NOT THE OCTOPUS SAUSAGE...!
DASH
STIFF
GOTTA RUN!
EMPTY
WHAT HAVE I DONE...?

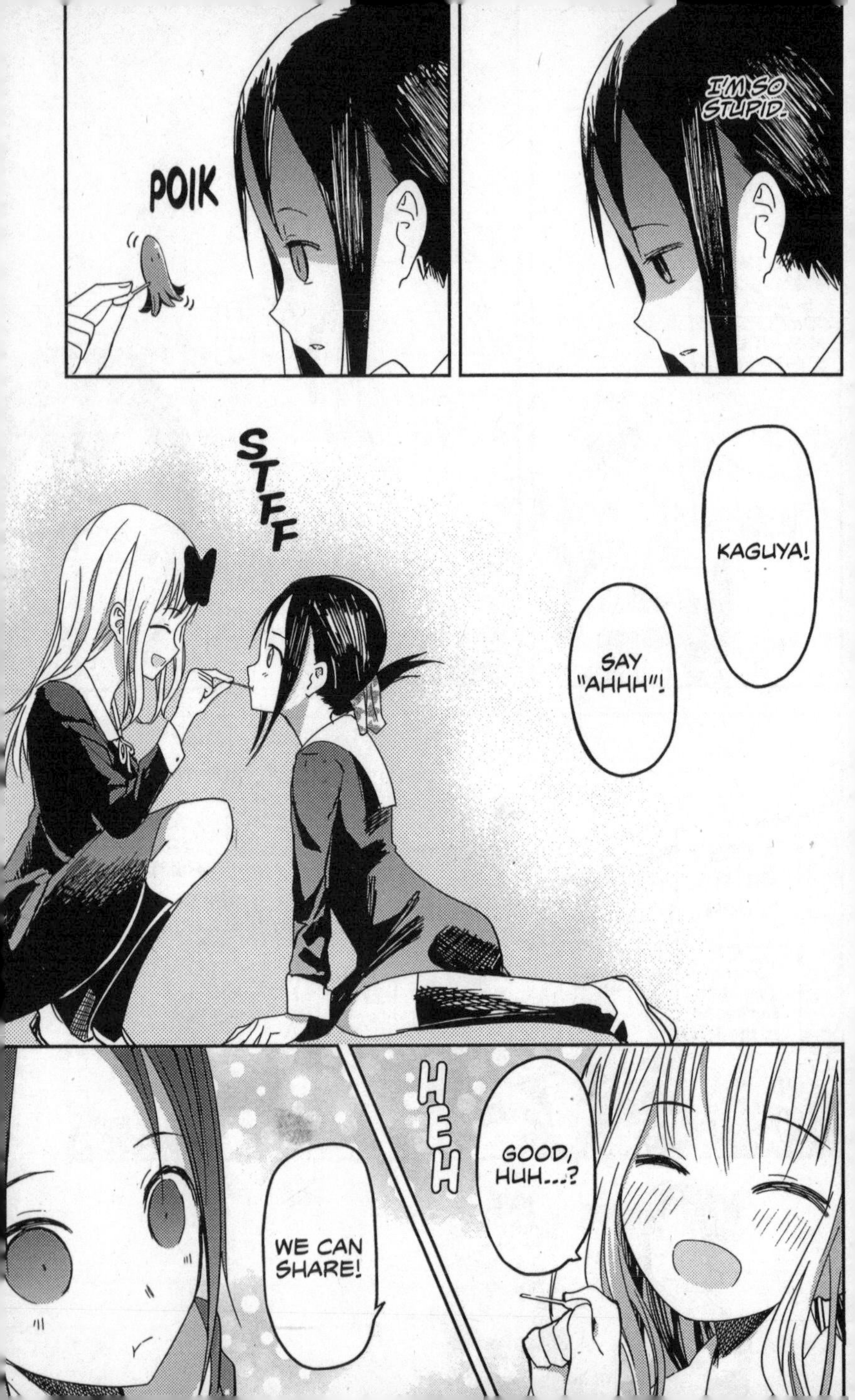
I'M SO STUPID.
POIK
KAGUYA!
SAY "AHHH"!
STFF
HEH
GOOD, HUH...?
WE CAN SHARE!

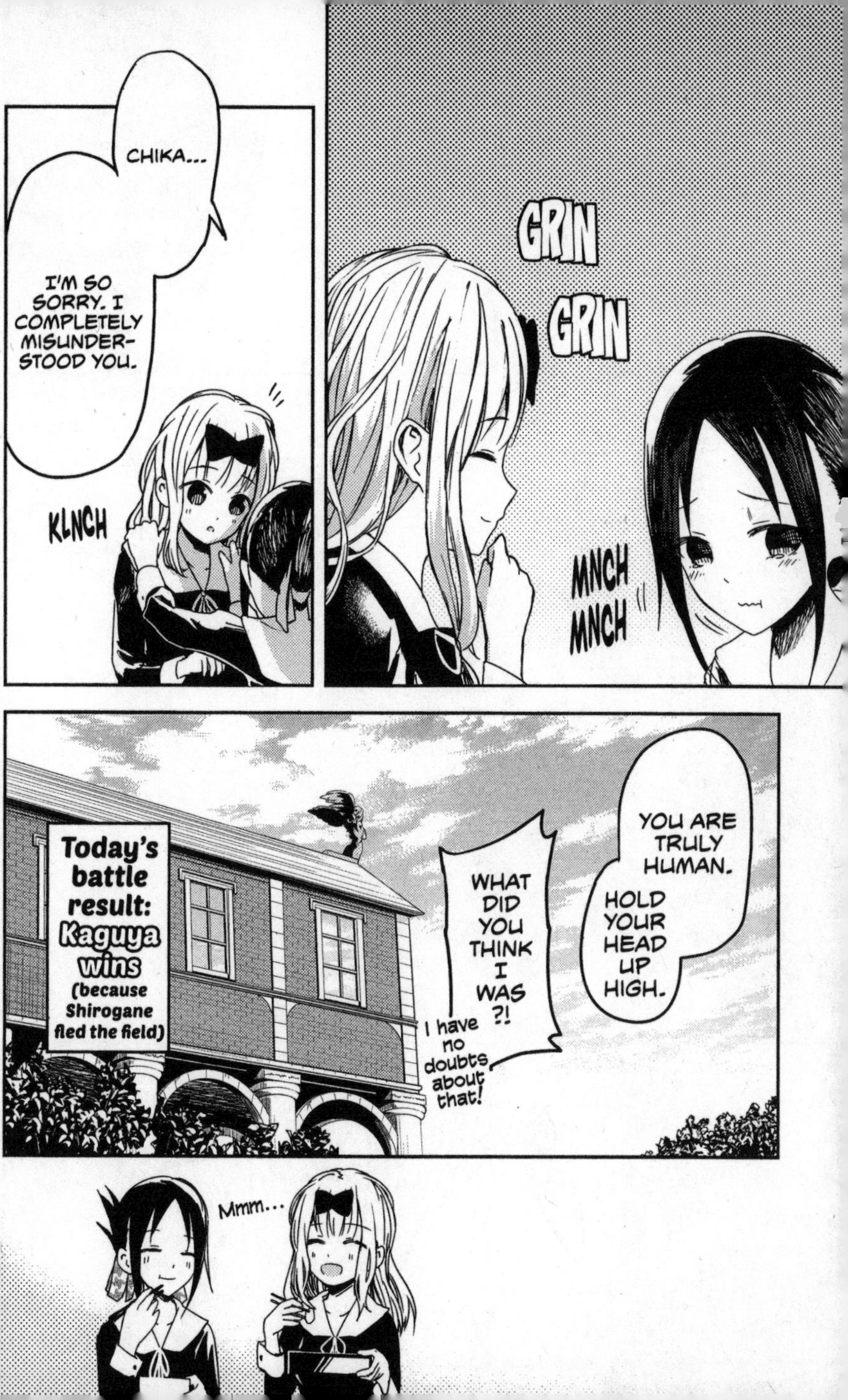
GRIN
GRIN
MNCH
MNCH
CHIKA...
I'M SO SORRY. I COMPLETELY MISUNDER-STOOD YOU.
KLNCH
YOU ARE TRULY HUMAN.
HOLD YOUR HEAD UP HIGH.
WHAT DID YOU THINK I WAS?!
I have no doubts about that!
Today's battle result: Kaguya wins (because Shirogane fled the field)
Mmm...

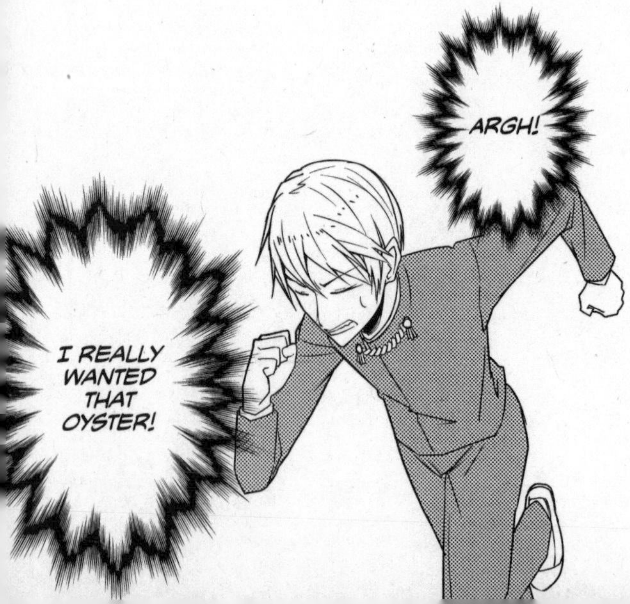
ARGH!
I REALLY WANTED THAT OYSTER!

KAGUYA-SAMA
LOVE IS WAR

Battle 6
Miyuki Shirogane Wants to Hide His Ignorance

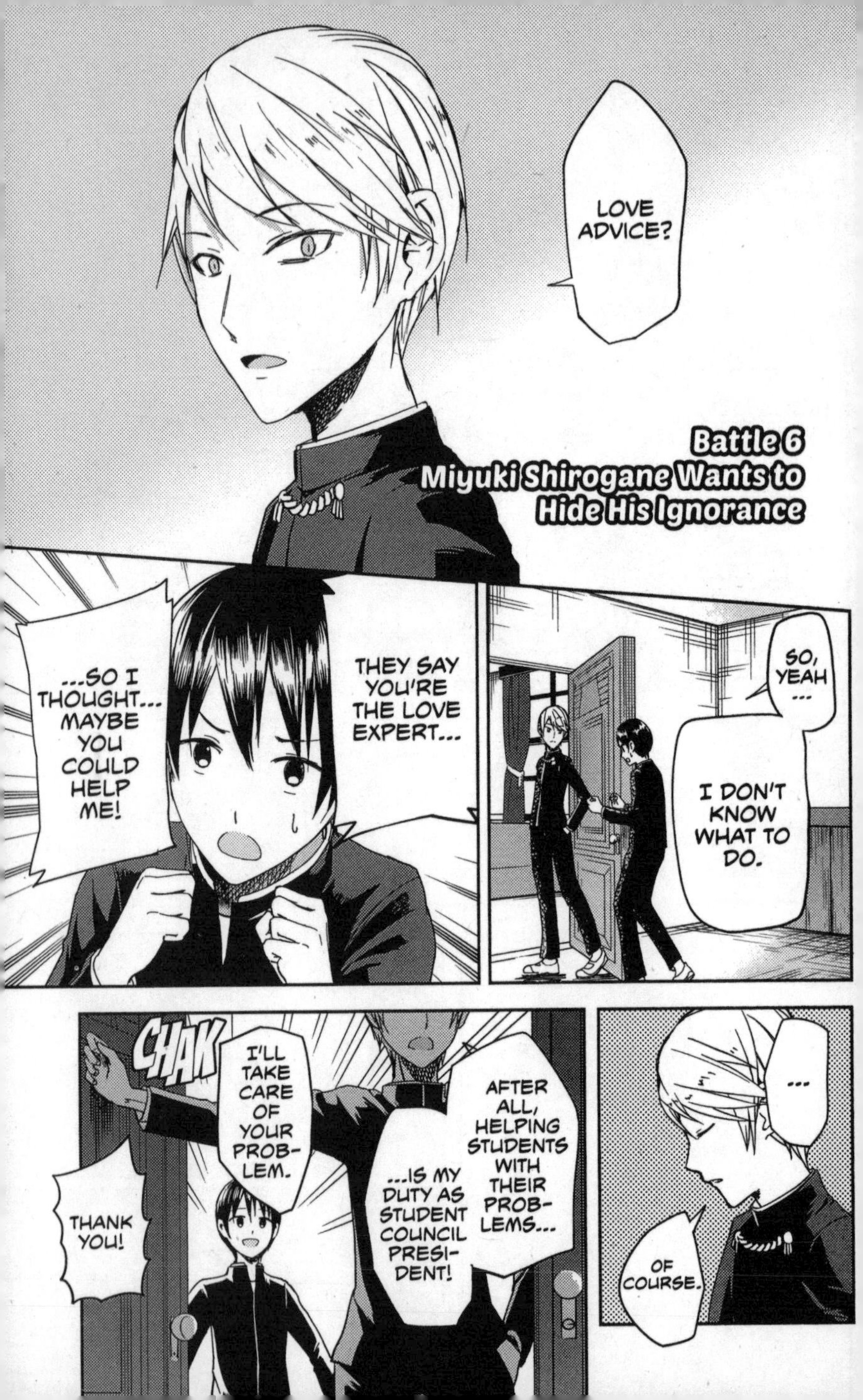
LOVE ADVICE?
SO, YEAH ...
I DON'T KNOW WHAT TO DO.
THEY SAY YOU'RE THE LOVE EXPERT...
...SO I THOUGHT... MAYBE YOU COULD HELP ME!
...
OF COURSE.
AFTER ALL, HELPING STUDENTS WITH THEIR PROB-LEMS...
...IS MY DUTY AS STUDENT COUNCIL PRESI-DENT!
I'LL TAKE CARE OF YOUR PROB-LEM.
CHAK
THANK YOU!

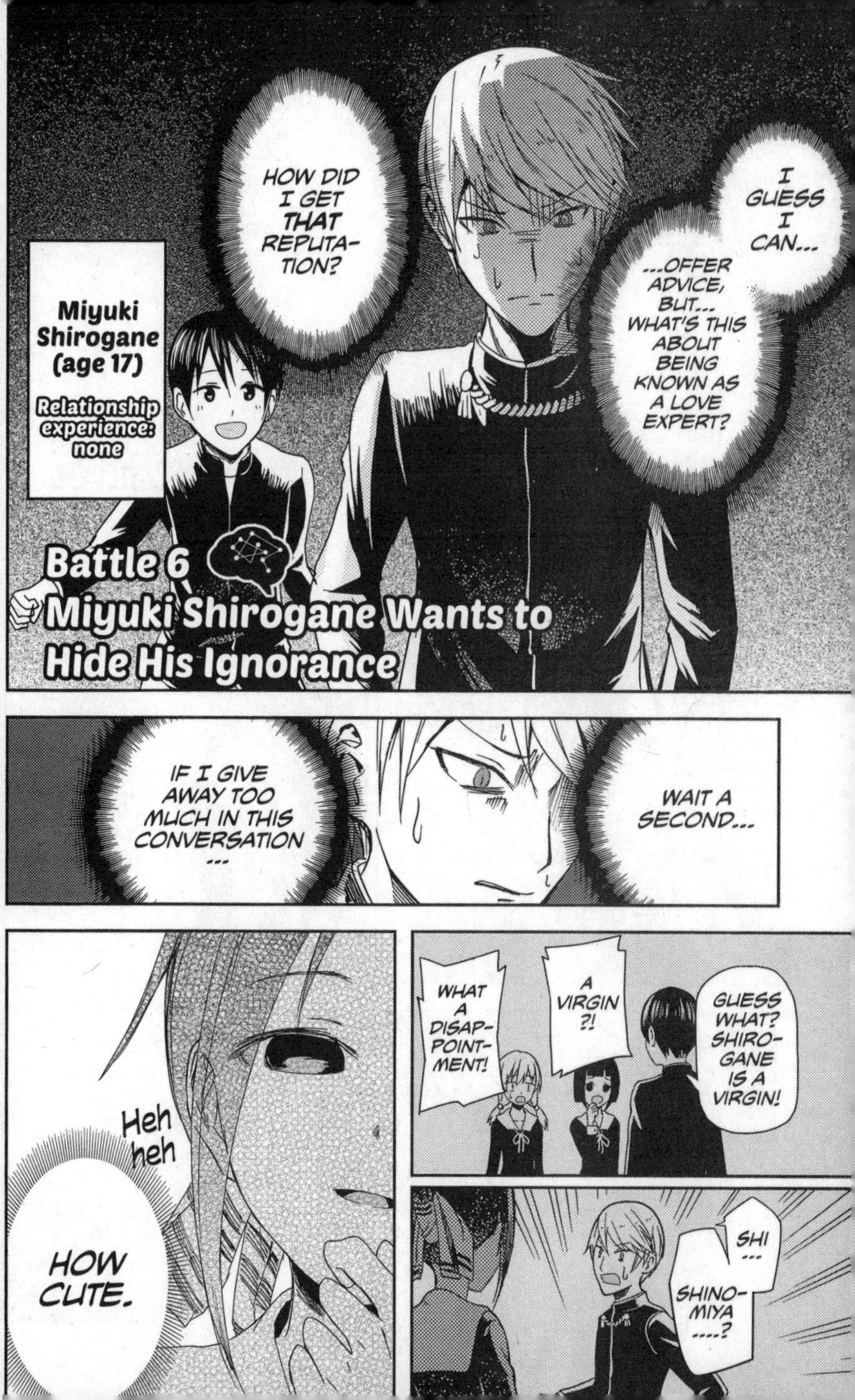
I GUESS I CAN...
...OFFER ADVICE, BUT... WHAT'S THIS ABOUT BEING KNOWN AS A LOVE EXPERT?
HOW DID I GET THAT REPUTATION?
Miyuki Shirogane (age 17)
Relationship experience: none
Battle 6
Miyuki Shirogane Wants to Hide His Ignorance
WAIT A SECOND...
IF I GIVE AWAY TOO MUCH IN THIS CONVERSATION...
GUESS WHAT? SHIROGANE IS A VIRGIN!
A VIRGIN?!
WHAT A DISAPPOINTMENT!
SHI... SHINOMIYA...?
Heh heh
HOW CUTE.

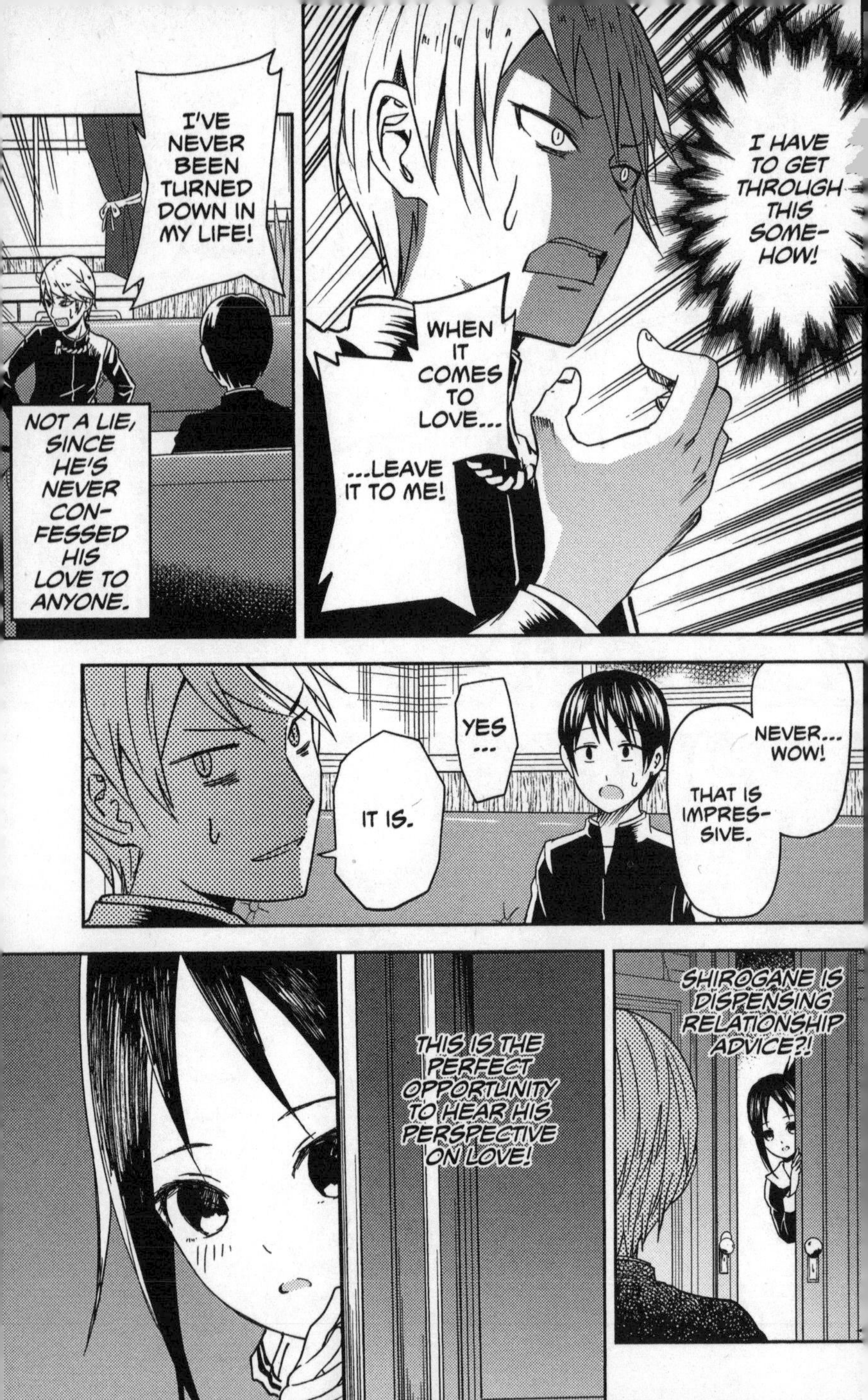
I HAVE TO GET THROUGH THIS SOME-HOW!
WHEN IT COMES TO LOVE...
...LEAVE IT TO ME!
I'VE NEVER BEEN TURNED DOWN IN MY LIFE!
NOT A LIE, SINCE HE'S NEVER CON-FESSED HIS LOVE TO ANYONE.
NEVER... WOW!
THAT IS IMPRES-SIVE.
YES...
IT IS.
SHIROGANE IS DISPENSING RELATIONSHIP ADVICE?!
THIS IS THE PERFECT OPPORTUNITY TO HEAR HIS PERSPECTIVE ON LOVE!

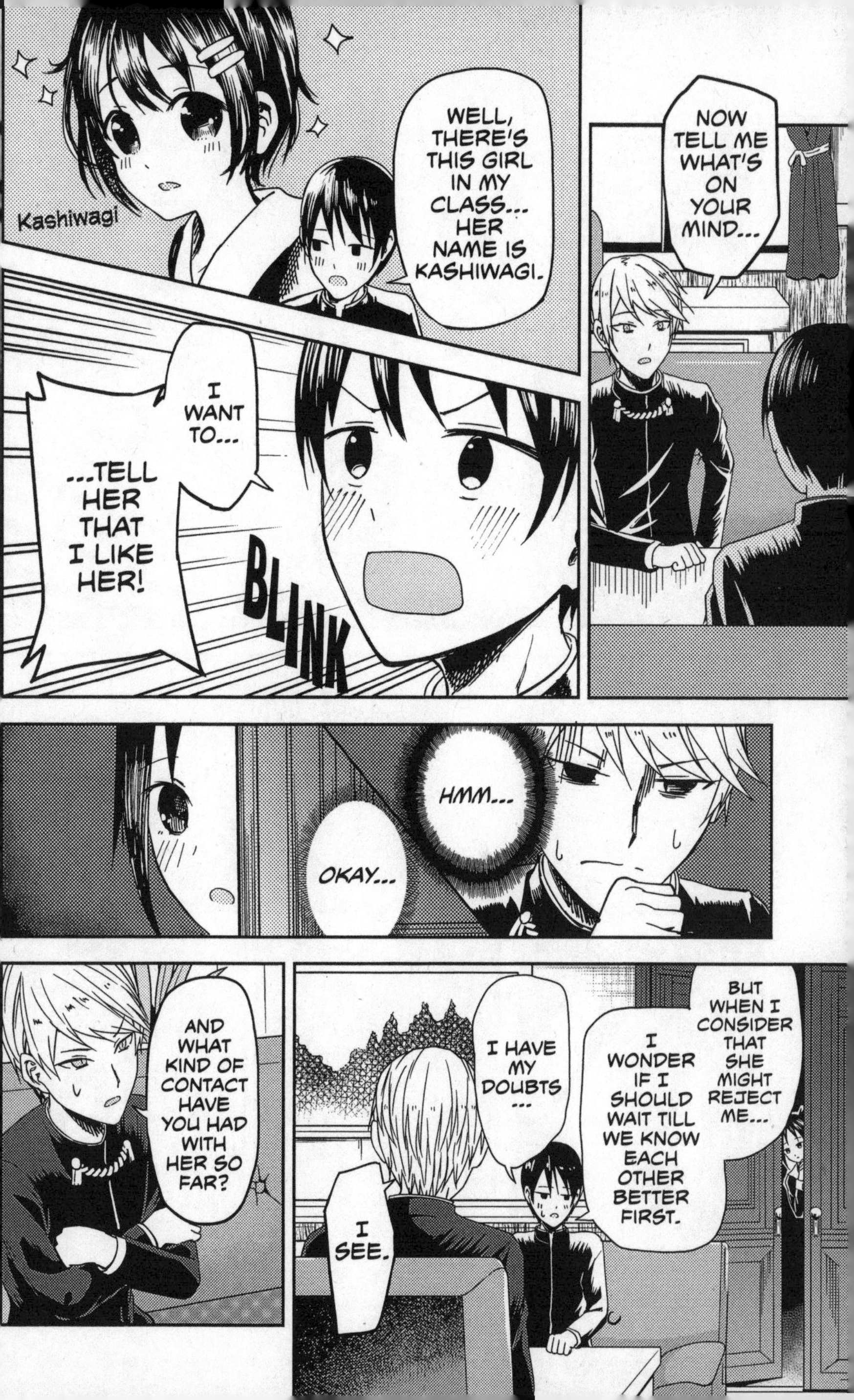
NOW TELL ME WHAT'S ON YOUR MIND...
WELL, THERE'S THIS GIRL IN MY CLASS... HER NAME IS KASHIWAGI.
Kashiwagi
I WANT TO...
...TELL HER THAT I LIKE HER!
BLINK
HMM...
OKAY...
BUT WHEN I CONSIDER THAT SHE MIGHT REJECT ME...
I WONDER IF I SHOULD WAIT TILL WE KNOW EACH OTHER BETTER FIRST.
I HAVE MY DOUBTS...
I SEE.
AND WHAT KIND OF CONTACT HAVE YOU HAD WITH HER SO FAR?

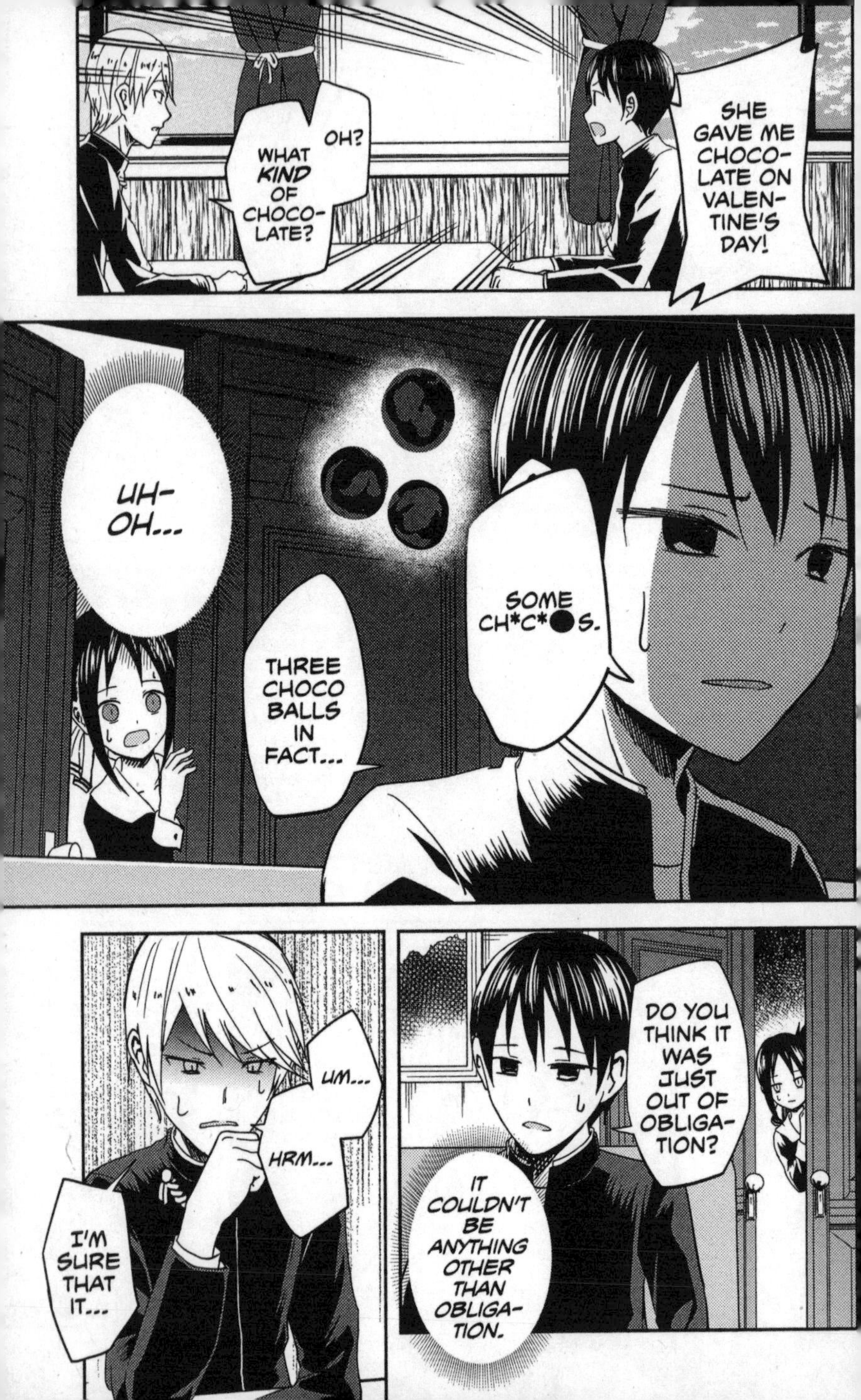
SHE GAVE ME CHOCOLATE ON VALENTINE'S DAY!
OH? WHAT *KIND* OF CHOCOLATE?
SOME CH*C*●S.
THREE CHOCO BALLS IN FACT...
UH-OH...
DO YOU THINK IT WAS JUST OUT OF OBLIGATION?
IT COULDN'T BE ANYTHING OTHER THAN OBLIGATION.
UM...
HRM...
I'M SURE THAT IT...

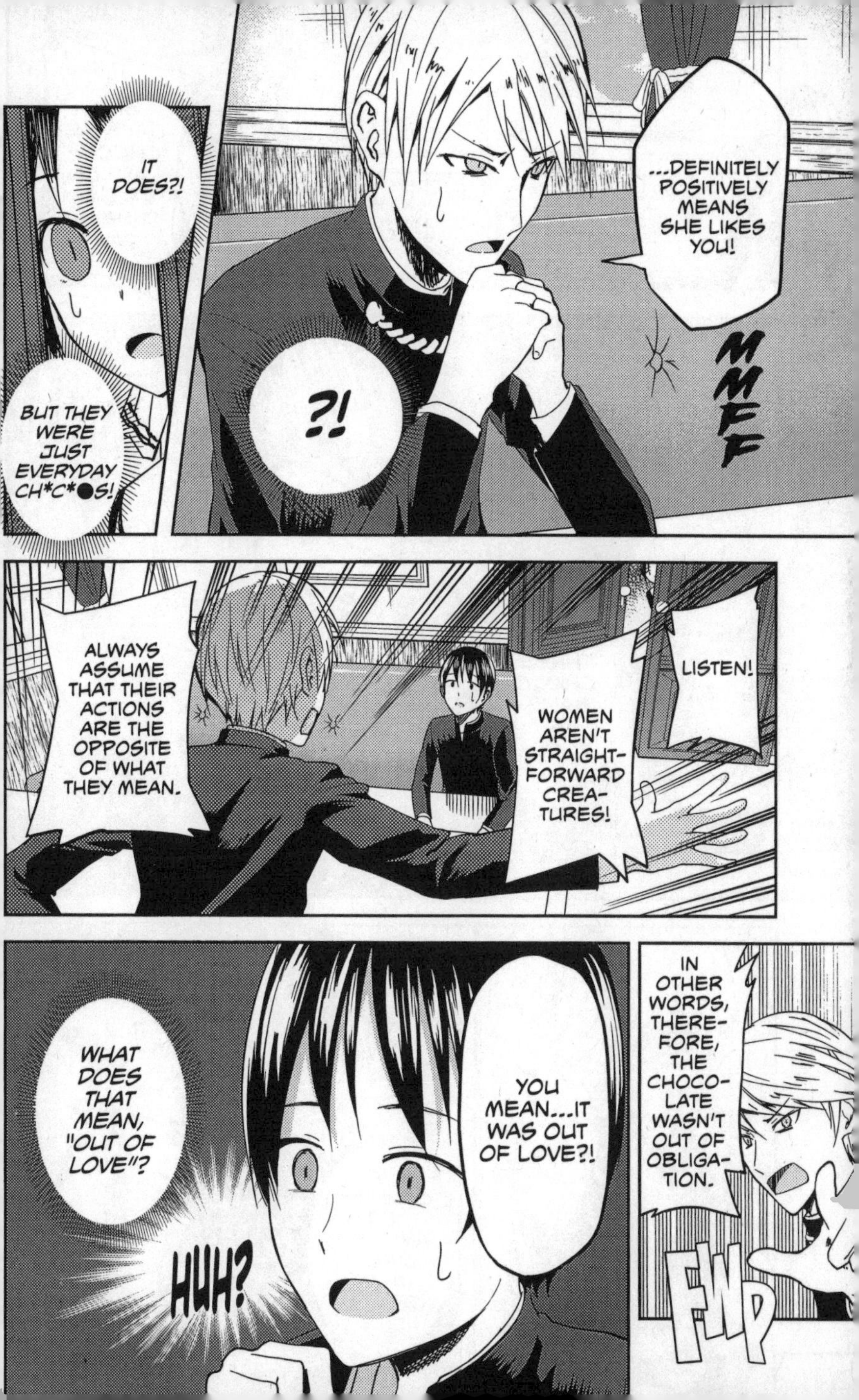
...DEFINITELY POSITIVELY MEANS SHE LIKES YOU!
MMFF
?!
IT DOES?!
BUT THEY WERE JUST EVERYDAY CH*C*●S!
LISTEN!
WOMEN AREN'T STRAIGHT-FORWARD CREA-TURES!
ALWAYS ASSUME THAT THEIR ACTIONS ARE THE OPPOSITE OF WHAT THEY MEAN.
IN OTHER WORDS, THERE-FORE, THE CHOCO-LATE WASN'T OUT OF OBLIGA-TION.
FWP
YOU MEAN...IT WAS OUT OF LOVE?!
WHAT DOES THAT MEAN, "OUT OF LOVE"?
HUH?

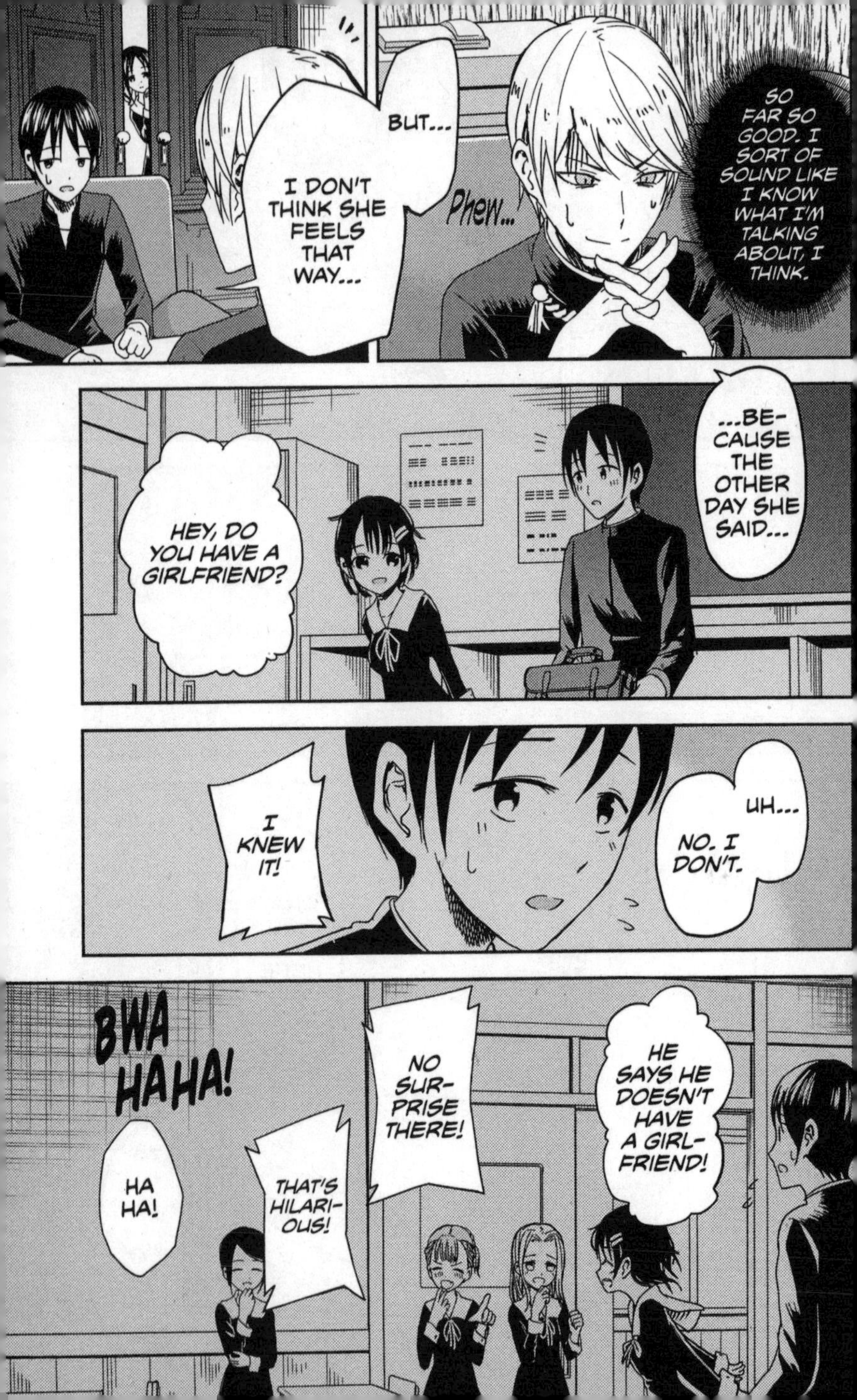

SO FAR SO GOOD. I SORT OF SOUND LIKE I KNOW WHAT I'M TALKING ABOUT, I THINK.
Phew...
BUT...
I DON'T THINK SHE FEELS THAT WAY...
...BE-CAUSE THE OTHER DAY SHE SAID...
HEY, DO YOU HAVE A GIRLFRIEND?
UH...
NO. I DON'T.
I KNEW IT!
HE SAYS HE DOESN'T HAVE A GIRL-FRIEND!
NO SUR-PRISE THERE!
BWA HAHA!
THAT'S HILARI-OUS!
HA HA!

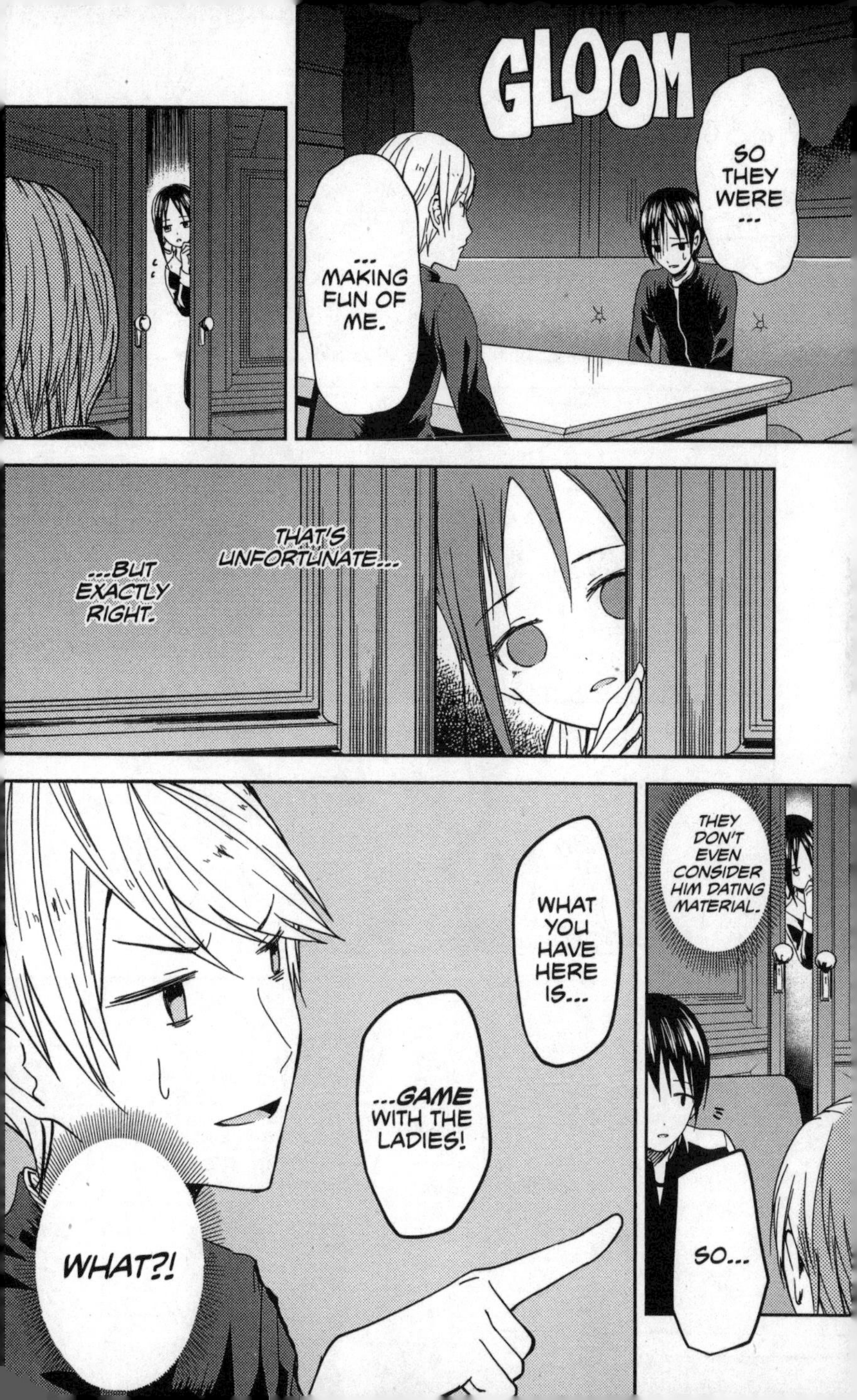
GLOOM
SO THEY WERE...
...MAKING FUN OF ME.
THAT'S UNFORTUNATE...
...BUT EXACTLY RIGHT.
THEY DON'T EVEN CONSIDER HIM DATING MATERIAL.
SO...
WHAT YOU HAVE HERE IS...
...GAME WITH THE LADIES!
WHAT?!

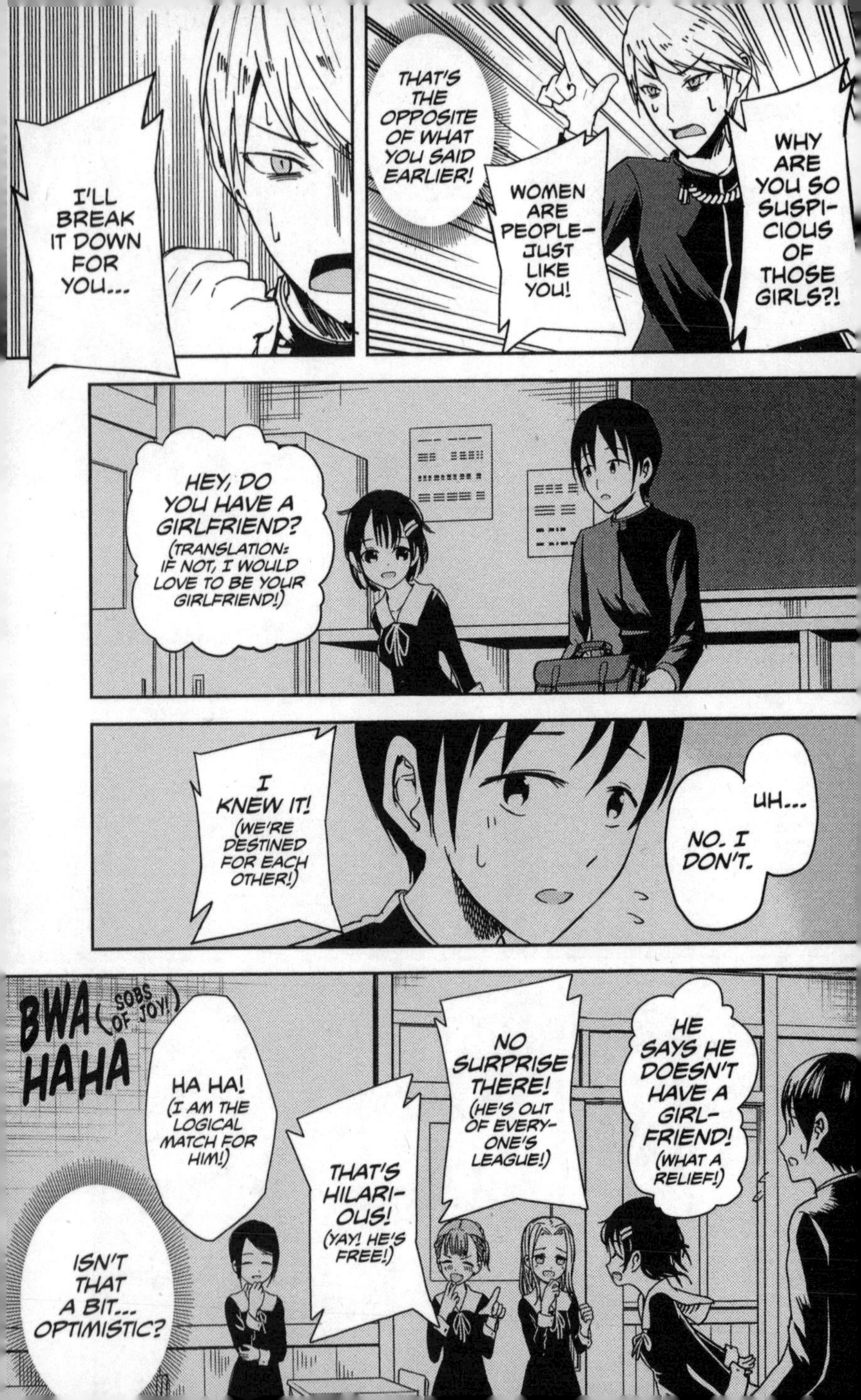
WHY ARE YOU SO SUSPICIOUS OF THOSE GIRLS?!
WOMEN ARE PEOPLE— JUST LIKE YOU!
THAT'S THE OPPOSITE OF WHAT YOU SAID EARLIER!
I'LL BREAK IT DOWN FOR YOU...
HEY, DO YOU HAVE A GIRLFRIEND? (TRANSLATION: IF NOT, I WOULD LOVE TO BE YOUR GIRLFRIEND!)
UH...
NO. I DON'T.
I KNEW IT! (WE'RE DESTINED FOR EACH OTHER!)
HE SAYS HE DOESN'T HAVE A GIRLFRIEND! (WHAT A RELIEF!)
NO SURPRISE THERE! (HE'S OUT OF EVERYONE'S LEAGUE!)
THAT'S HILARIOUS! (YAY! HE'S FREE!)
HA HA! (I AM THE LOGICAL MATCH FOR HIM!)
BWA HAHA
(SOBS OF JOY!)
ISN'T THAT A BIT... OPTIMISTIC?

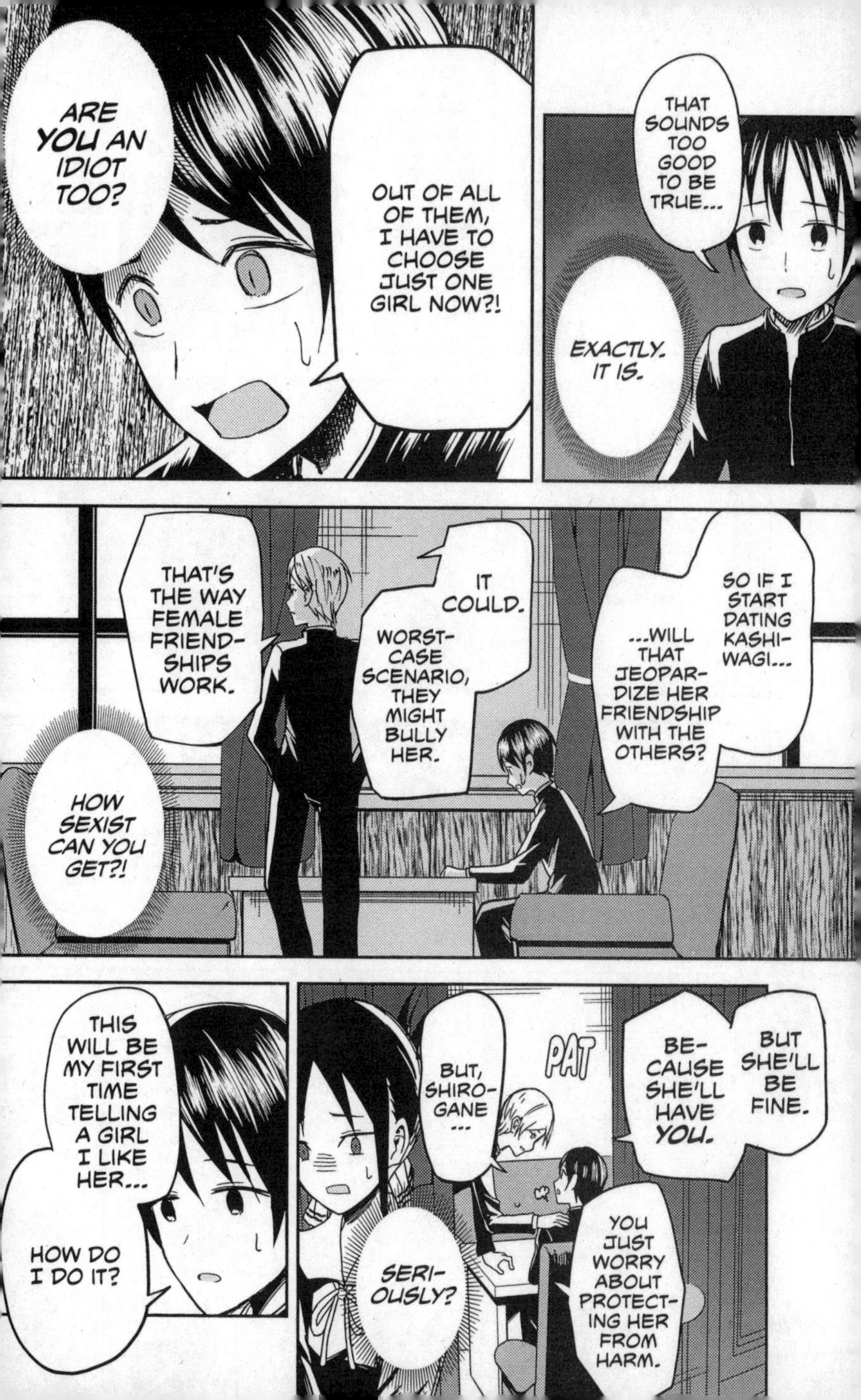
THAT SOUNDS TOO GOOD TO BE TRUE...
EXACTLY. IT IS.
OUT OF ALL OF THEM, I HAVE TO CHOOSE JUST ONE GIRL NOW?!
ARE YOU AN IDIOT TOO?
SO IF I START DATING KASHIWAGI...
...WILL THAT JEOPARDIZE HER FRIENDSHIP WITH THE OTHERS?
IT COULD.
WORST-CASE SCENARIO, THEY MIGHT BULLY HER.
THAT'S THE WAY FEMALE FRIENDSHIPS WORK.
HOW SEXIST CAN YOU GET?!
BUT SHE'LL BE FINE.
BECAUSE SHE'LL HAVE YOU.
PAT
BUT, SHIROGANE...
YOU JUST WORRY ABOUT PROTECTING HER FROM HARM.
SERIOUSLY?
THIS WILL BE MY FIRST TIME TELLING A GIRL I LIKE HER...
HOW DO I DO IT?

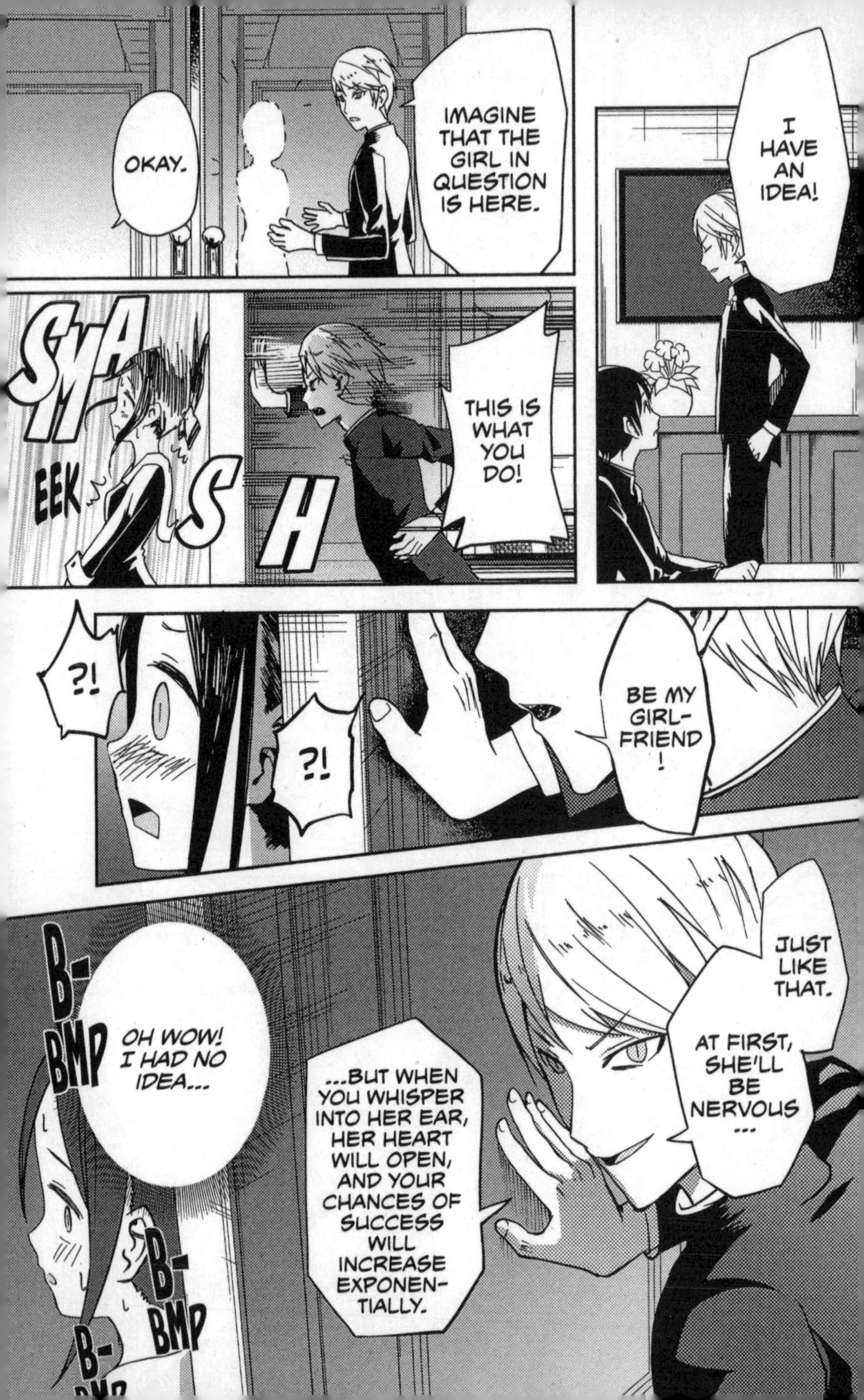
I HAVE AN IDEA!
IMAGINE THAT THE GIRL IN QUESTION IS HERE.
OKAY.
THIS IS WHAT YOU DO!
SHASH
EEK
BE MY GIRLFRIEND!
?!
?!
JUST LIKE THAT.
AT FIRST, SHE'LL BE NERVOUS...
...BUT WHEN YOU WHISPER INTO HER EAR, HER HEART WILL OPEN, AND YOUR CHANCES OF SUCCESS WILL INCREASE EXPONENTIALLY.
OH WOW! I HAD NO IDEA...
B-BMP
B-BMP
B-

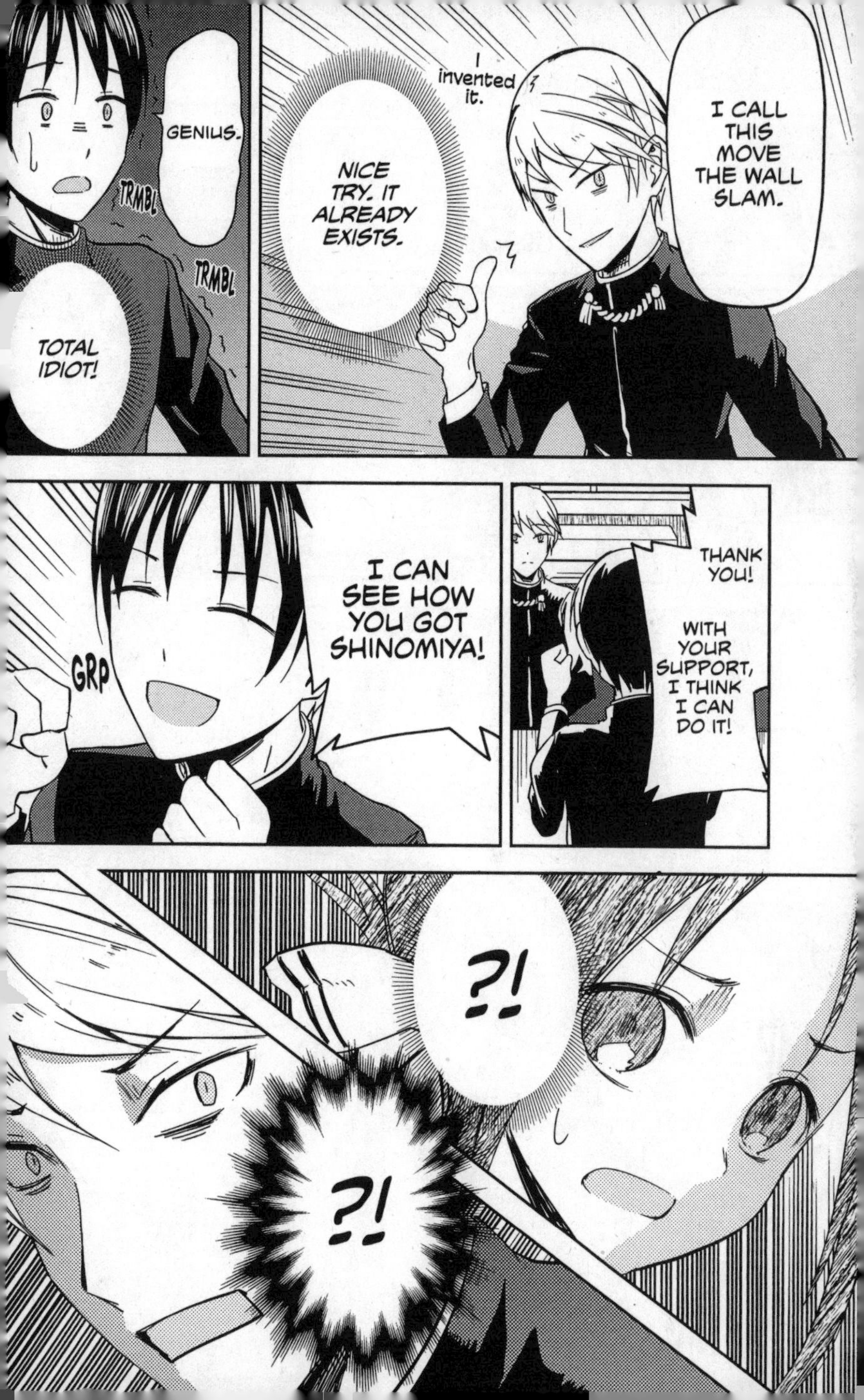
I CALL THIS MOVE THE WALL SLAM.
I invented it.
NICE TRY. IT ALREADY EXISTS.
GENIUS.
TRMBL
TRMBL
TOTAL IDIOT!
THANK YOU!
WITH YOUR SUPPORT, I THINK I CAN DO IT!
I CAN SEE HOW YOU GOT SHINOMIYA!
GRP
?!
?!

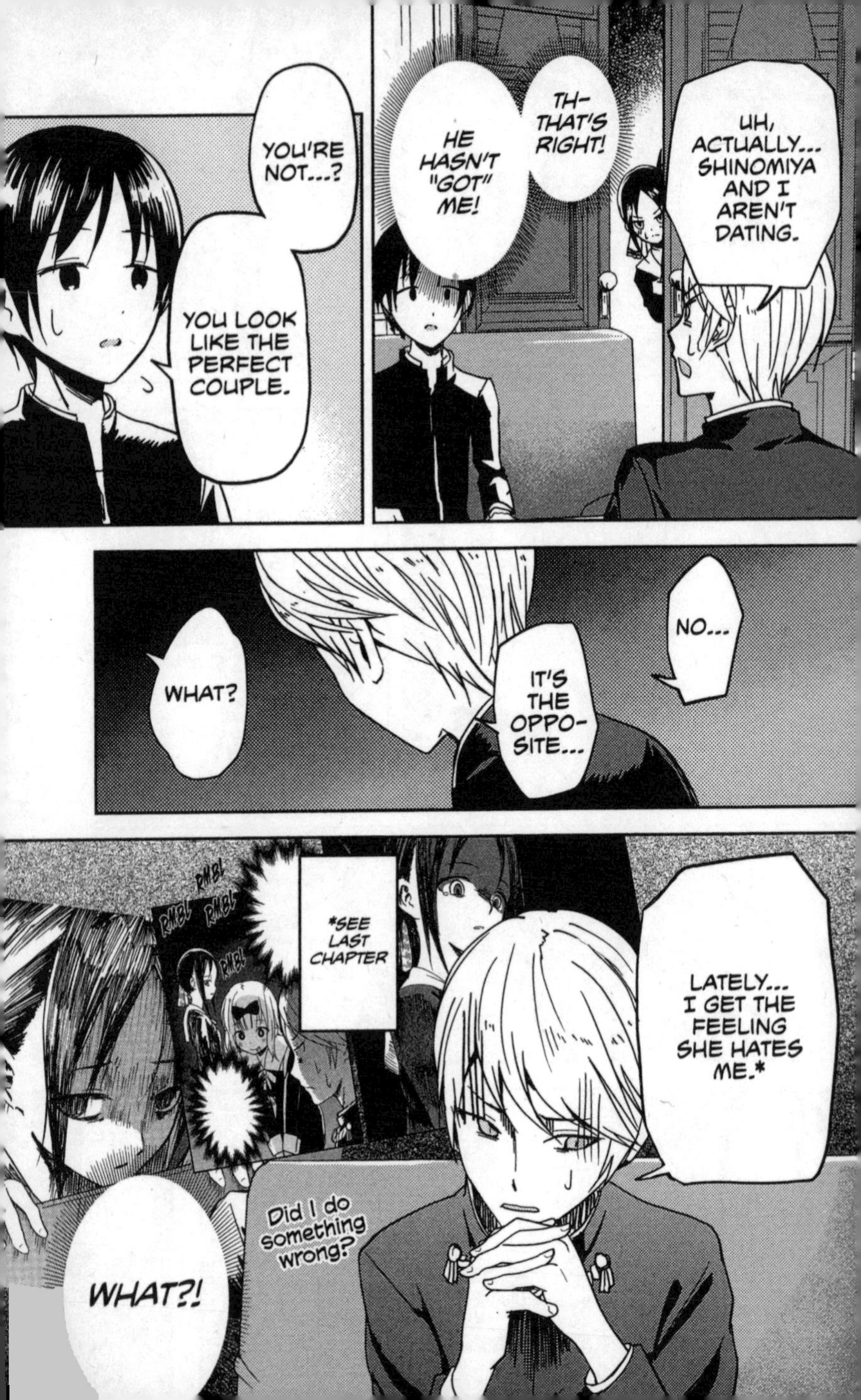

UH, ACTUALLY... SHINOMIYA AND I AREN'T DATING.
TH-THAT'S RIGHT!
HE HASN'T "GOT" ME!
YOU'RE NOT...?
YOU LOOK LIKE THE PERFECT COUPLE.
NO...
IT'S THE OPPO-SITE...
WHAT?
LATELY... I GET THE FEELING SHE HATES ME.*
*SEE LAST CHAPTER
Did I do something wrong?
RMBL RMBL RMBL RMBL
WHAT?!

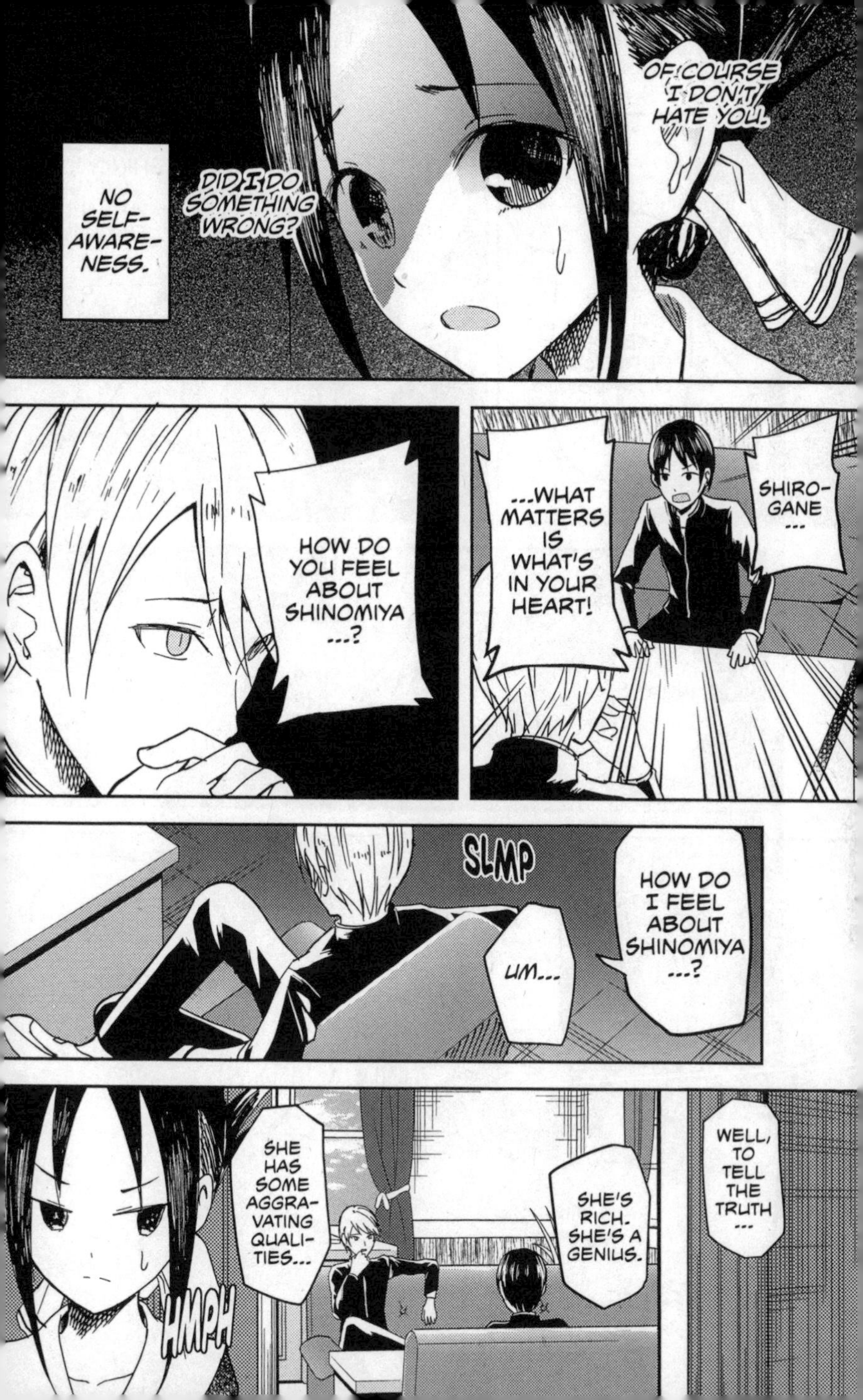
OF COURSE I DON'T HATE YOU.
DID I DO SOMETHING WRONG?
NO SELF-AWARENESS.
SHIRO-GANE ...
...WHAT MATTERS IS WHAT'S IN YOUR HEART!
HOW DO YOU FEEL ABOUT SHINOMIYA ...?
HOW DO I FEEL ABOUT SHINOMIYA ...?
SLMP
UM...
WELL, TO TELL THE TRUTH ...
SHE'S RICH. SHE'S A GENIUS.
SHE HAS SOME AGGRAVATING QUALITIES...
HMPH

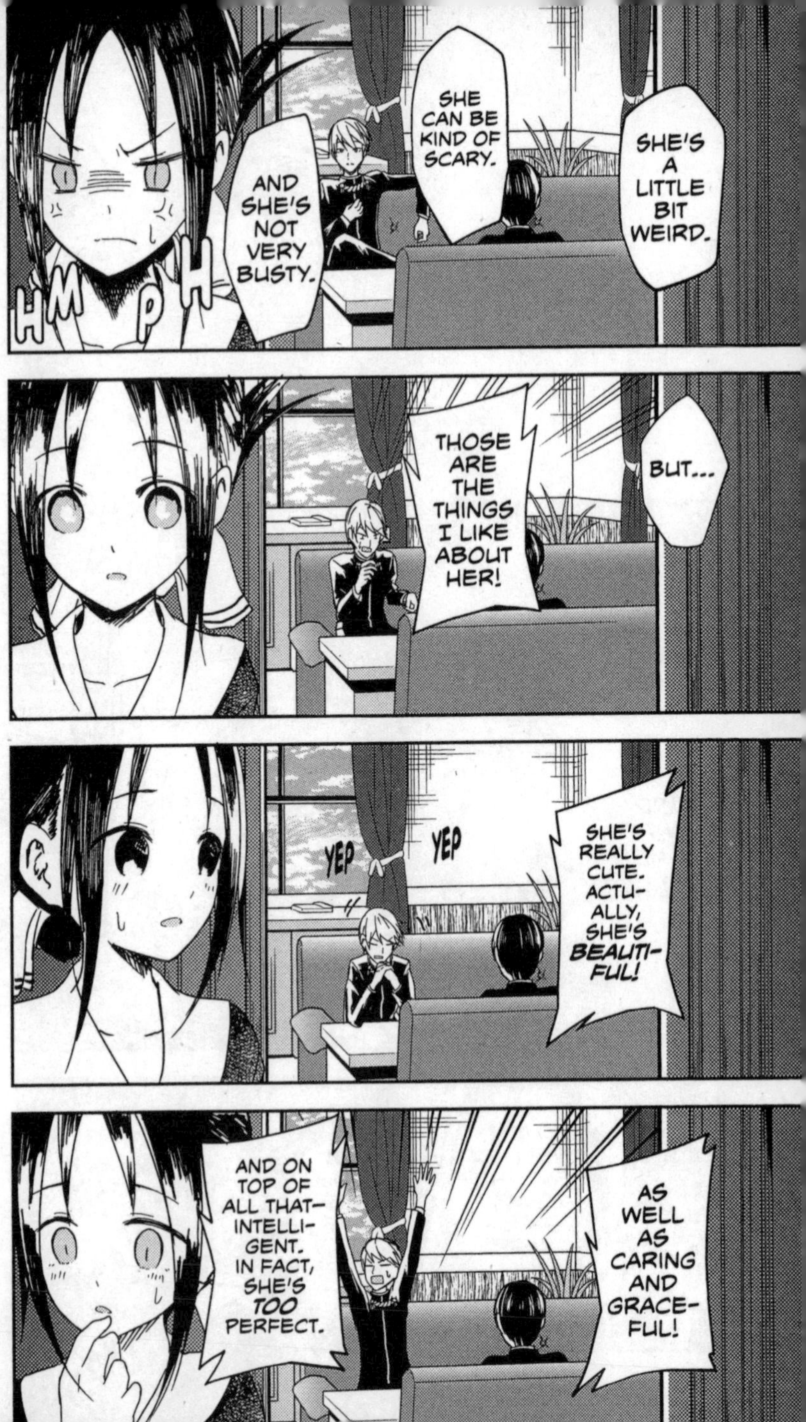
SHE'S A LITTLE BIT WEIRD.
SHE CAN BE KIND OF SCARY.
AND SHE'S NOT VERY BUSTY.
HMPH
BUT...
THOSE ARE THE THINGS I LIKE ABOUT HER!
SHE'S REALLY CUTE. ACTUALLY, SHE'S *BEAUTIFUL!*
YEP
YEP
AS WELL AS CARING AND GRACEFUL!
AND ON TOP OF ALL THAT—INTELLIGENT. IN FACT, SHE'S *TOO* PERFECT.

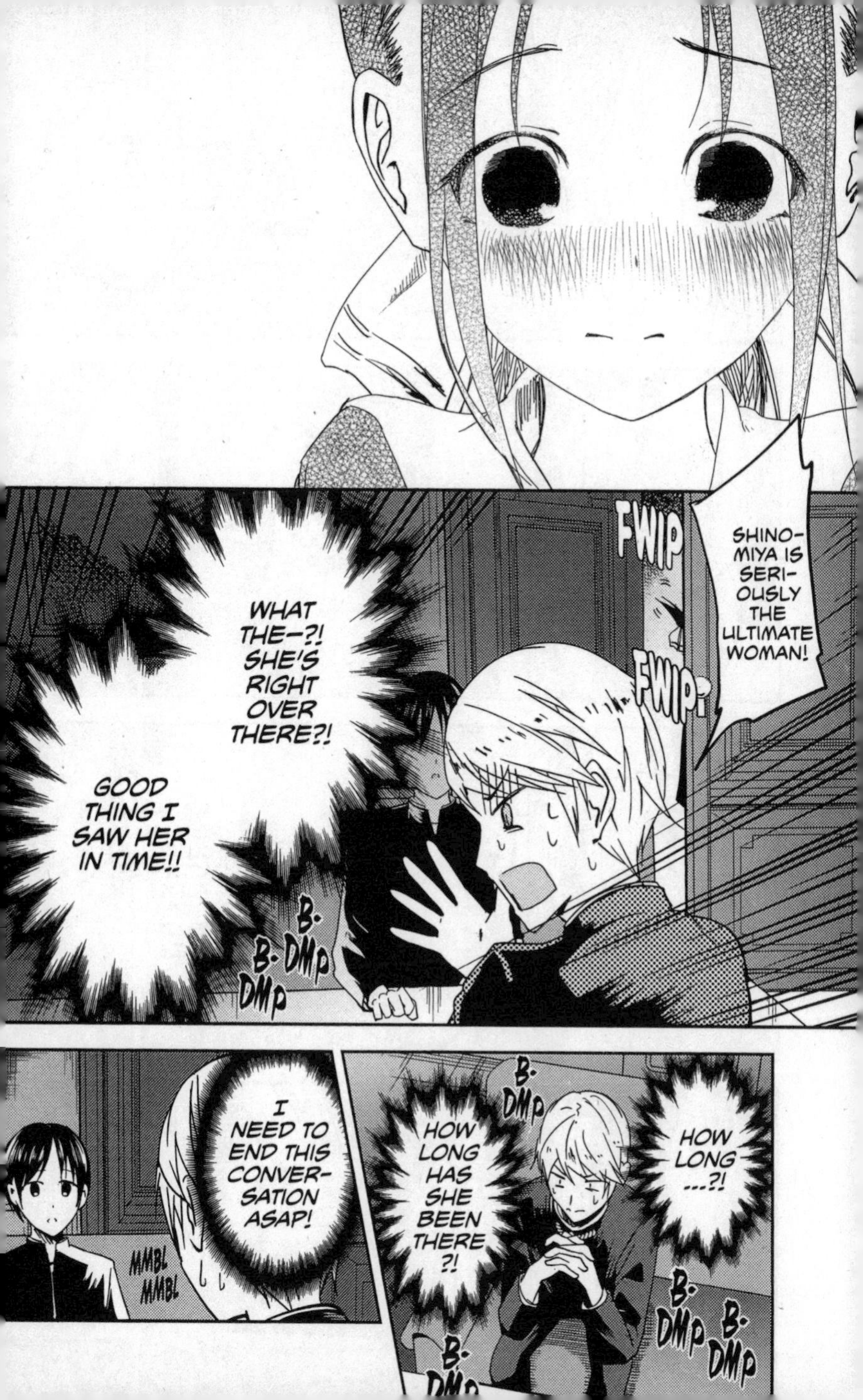
SHINOMIYA IS SERIOUSLY THE ULTIMATE WOMAN!
FWIP
FWIP
WHAT THE—?! SHE'S RIGHT OVER THERE?!
GOOD THING I SAW HER IN TIME!!
B-DMP
B-DMP
HOW LONG...?!
B-DMP
HOW LONG HAS SHE BEEN THERE?!
B-DMP
B-DMP
B-DMP
I NEED TO END THIS CONVERSATION ASAP!
MMBL MMBL

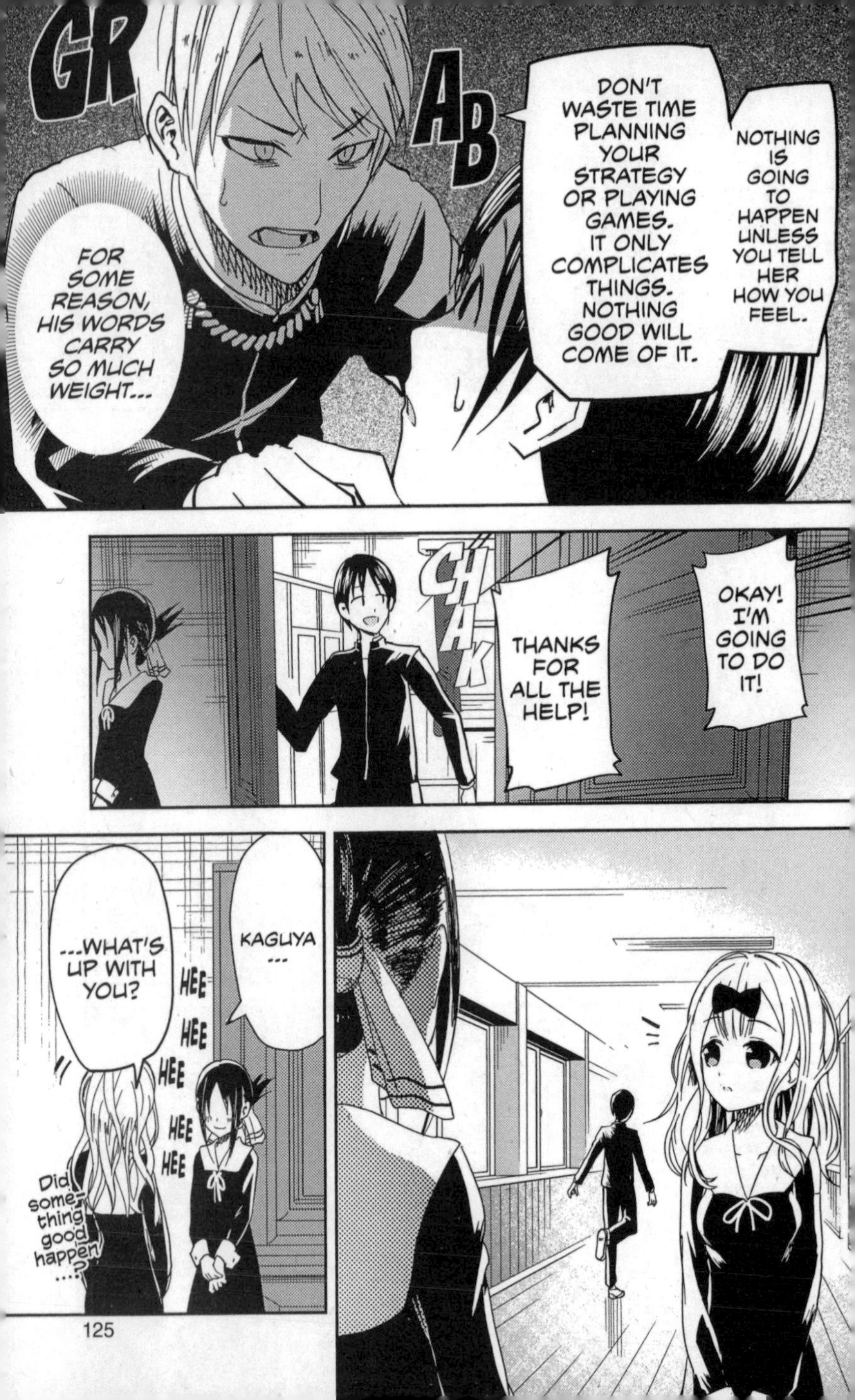
GRAB
NOTHING IS GOING TO HAPPEN UNLESS YOU TELL HER HOW YOU FEEL.
DON'T WASTE TIME PLANNING YOUR STRATEGY OR PLAYING GAMES. IT ONLY COMPLICATES THINGS. NOTHING GOOD WILL COME OF IT.
FOR SOME REASON, HIS WORDS CARRY SO MUCH WEIGHT...
OKAY! I'M GOING TO DO IT!
THANKS FOR ALL THE HELP!
CHAK
KAGUYA...
...WHAT'S UP WITH YOU?
HEE HEE HEE HEE HEE
Did something good happen...?

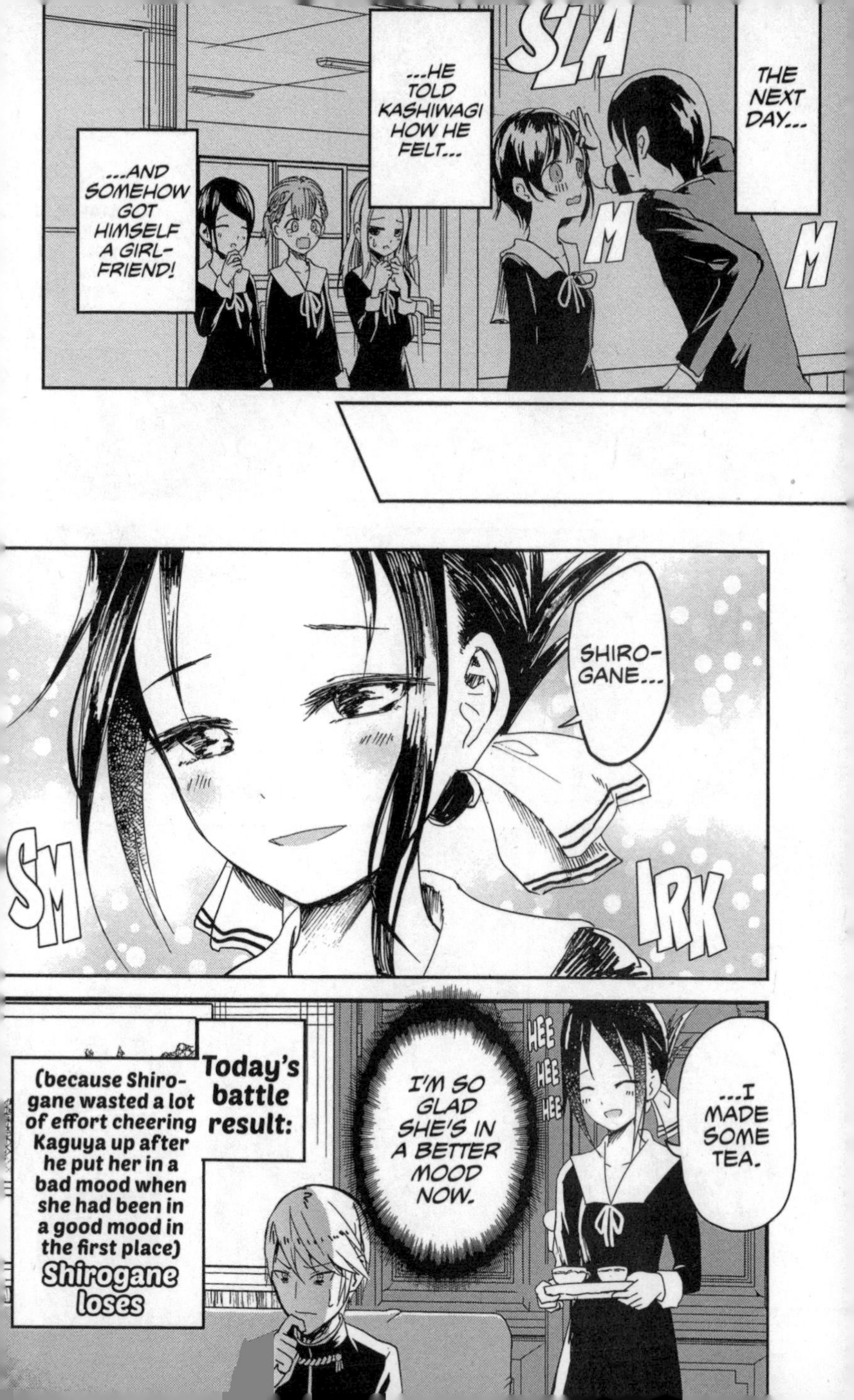
THE NEXT DAY...
SLAMM
...HE TOLD KASHIWAGI HOW HE FELT...
...AND SOMEHOW GOT HIMSELF A GIRLFRIEND!
SHIRO-GANE...
SMIRK
...I MADE SOME TEA.
HEE HEE HEE
I'M SO GLAD SHE'S IN A BETTER MOOD NOW.
Today's battle result:
(because Shirogane wasted a lot of effort cheering Kaguya up after he put her in a bad mood when she had been in a good mood in the first place)
Shirogane loses

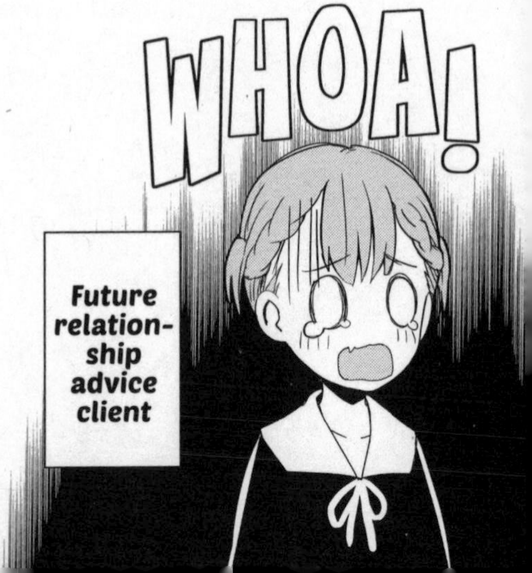
WHOA!
Future relationship-ship advice client

KAGUYA-SAMA
LOVE IS WAR

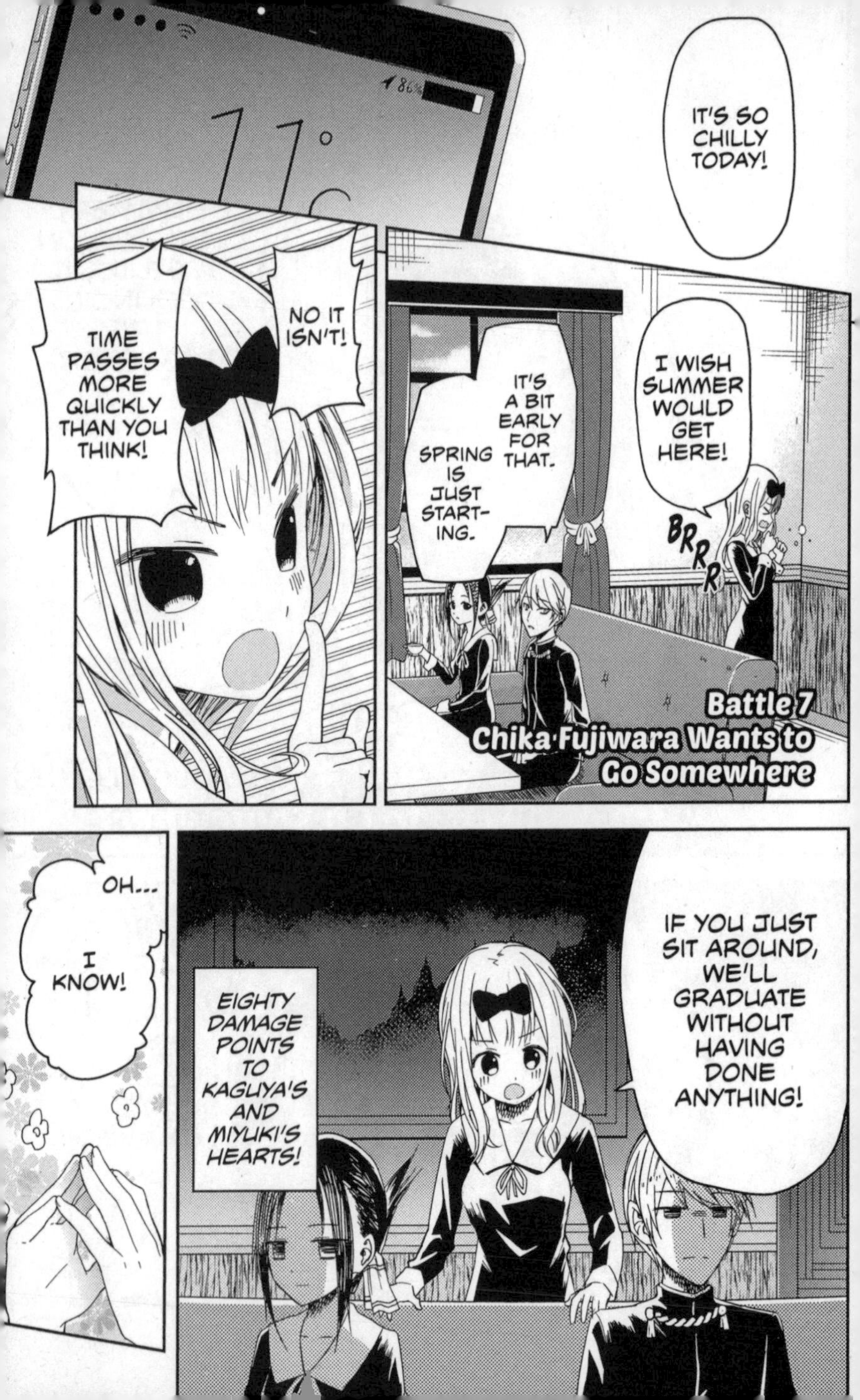
IT'S SO CHILLY TODAY!
I WISH SUMMER WOULD GET HERE!
BRRR
IT'S A BIT EARLY FOR THAT.
SPRING IS JUST START-ING.
Battle 7
Chika Fujiwara Wants to Go Somewhere
NO IT ISN'T!
TIME PASSES MORE QUICKLY THAN YOU THINK!
IF YOU JUST SIT AROUND, WE'LL GRADUATE WITHOUT HAVING DONE ANYTHING!
EIGHTY DAMAGE POINTS TO KAGUYA'S AND MIYUKI'S HEARTS!
OH...
I KNOW!

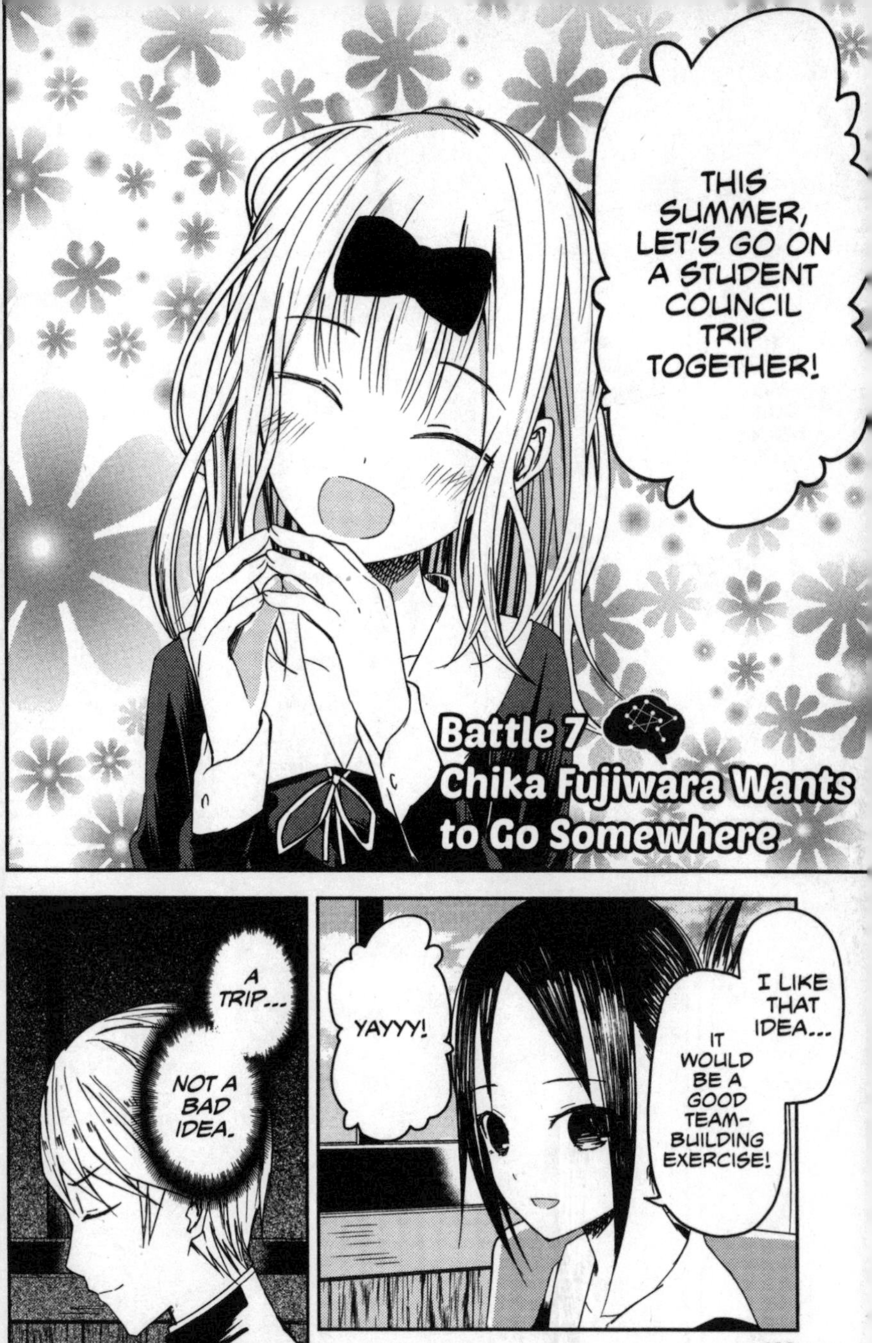
THIS SUMMER, LET'S GO ON A STUDENT COUNCIL TRIP TOGETHER!
Battle 7 Chika Fujiwara Wants to Go Somewhere
I LIKE THAT IDEA...
IT WOULD BE A GOOD TEAM-BUILDING EXERCISE!
YAYYY!
A TRIP...
NOT A BAD IDEA.

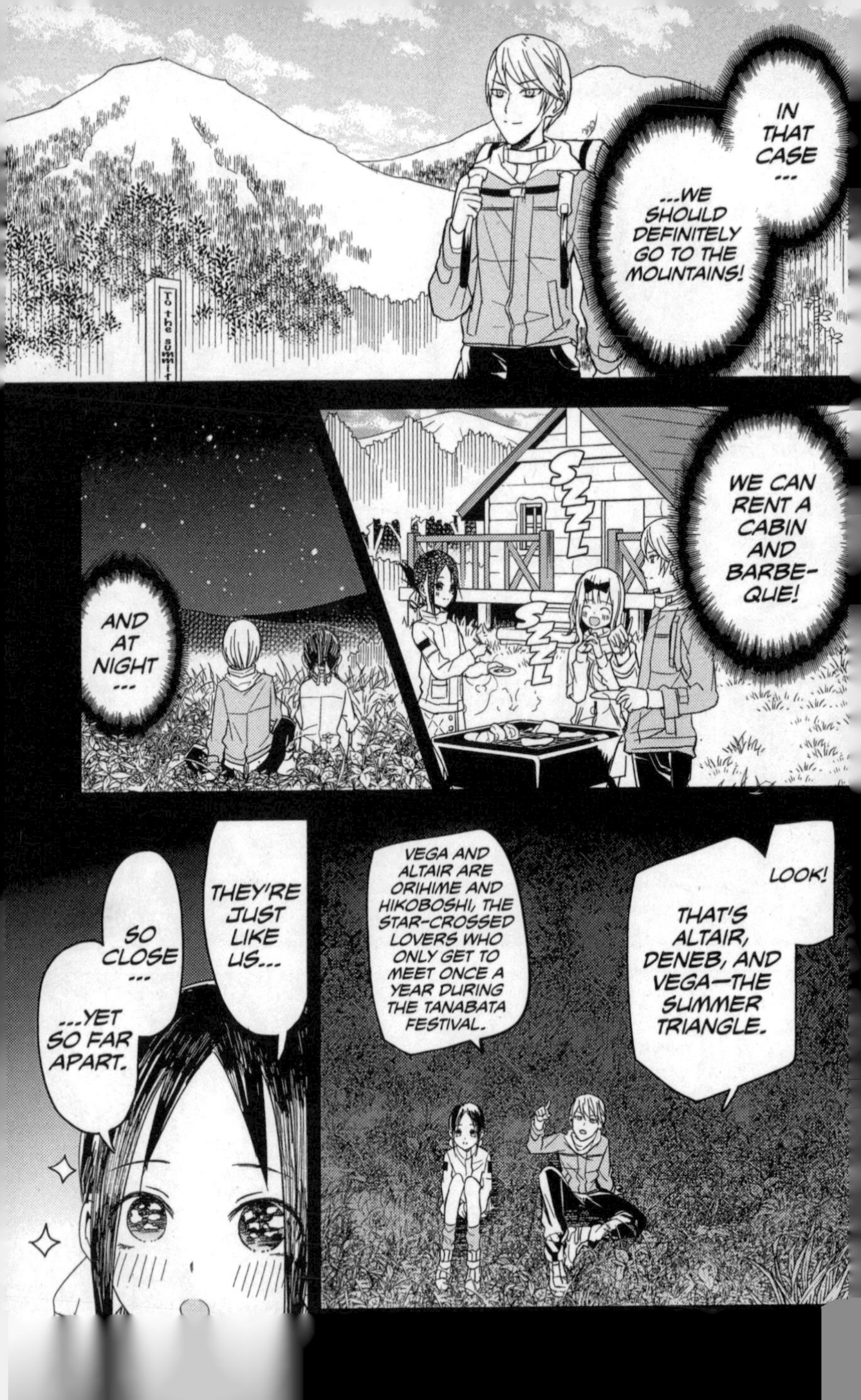
IN THAT CASE...
...WE SHOULD DEFINITELY GO TO THE MOUNTAINS!
To the summit
WE CAN RENT A CABIN AND BARBE-QUE!
SZZZL
SZZZL
AND AT NIGHT...
LOOK!
THAT'S ALTAIR, DENEB, AND VEGA—THE SUMMER TRIANGLE.
VEGA AND ALTAIR ARE ORIHIME AND HIKOBOSHI, THE STAR-CROSSED LOVERS WHO ONLY GET TO MEET ONCE A YEAR DURING THE TANABATA FESTIVAL.
THEY'RE JUST LIKE US...
SO CLOSE...
...YET SO FAR APART.

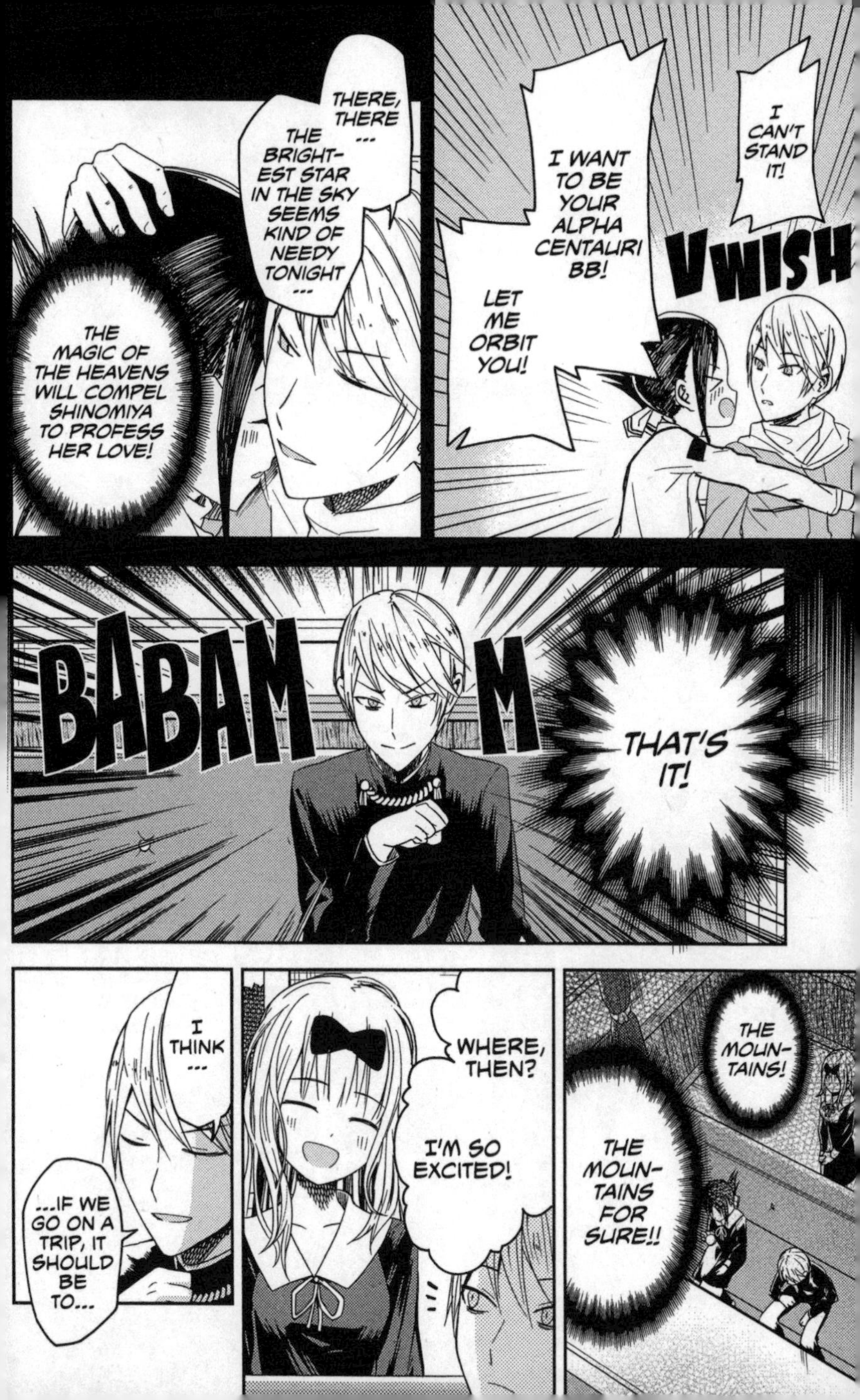
I CAN'T STAND IT!
I WANT TO BE YOUR ALPHA CENTAURI BB!
LET ME ORBIT YOU!
VWISH
THERE, THERE ...
THE BRIGHTEST STAR IN THE SKY SEEMS KIND OF NEEDY TONIGHT ...
THE MAGIC OF THE HEAVENS WILL COMPEL SHINOMIYA TO PROFESS HER LOVE!
THAT'S IT!
BABAM M
THE MOUNTAINS!
THE MOUNTAINS FOR SURE!!
WHERE, THEN?
I'M SO EXCITED!
I THINK ...
...IF WE GO ON A TRIP, IT SHOULD BE TO...

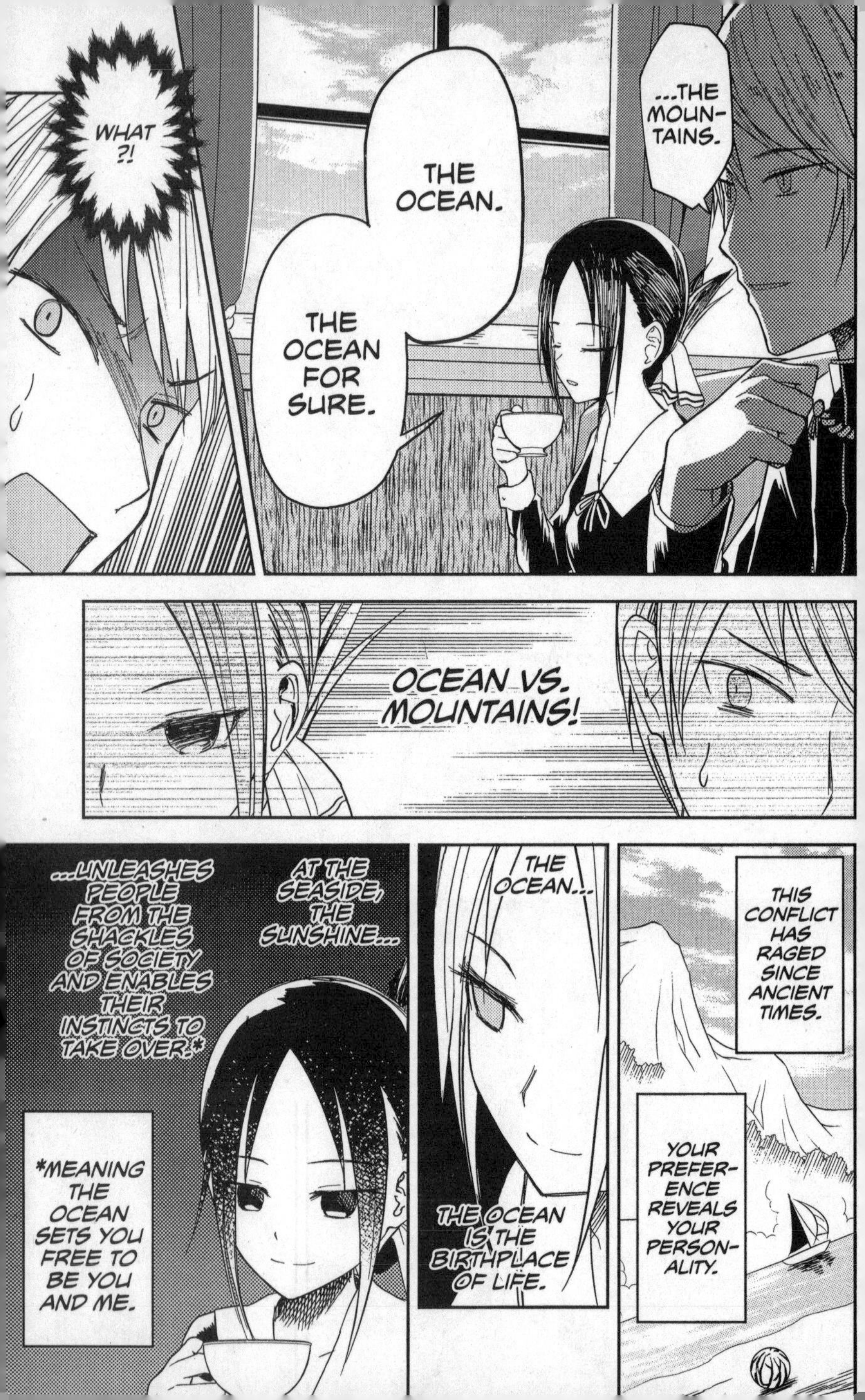

...THE MOUNTAINS.
THE OCEAN.
THE OCEAN FOR SURE.
WHAT ?!
OCEAN VS. MOUNTAINS!
THIS CONFLICT HAS RAGED SINCE ANCIENT TIMES.
YOUR PREFERENCE REVEALS YOUR PERSONALITY.
THE OCEAN...
THE OCEAN IS THE BIRTHPLACE OF LIFE.
AT THE SEASIDE, THE SUNSHINE...
...UNLEASHES PEOPLE FROM THE SHACKLES OF SOCIETY AND ENABLES THEIR INSTINCTS TO TAKE OVER.*
*MEANING THE OCEAN SETS YOU FREE TO BE YOU AND ME.

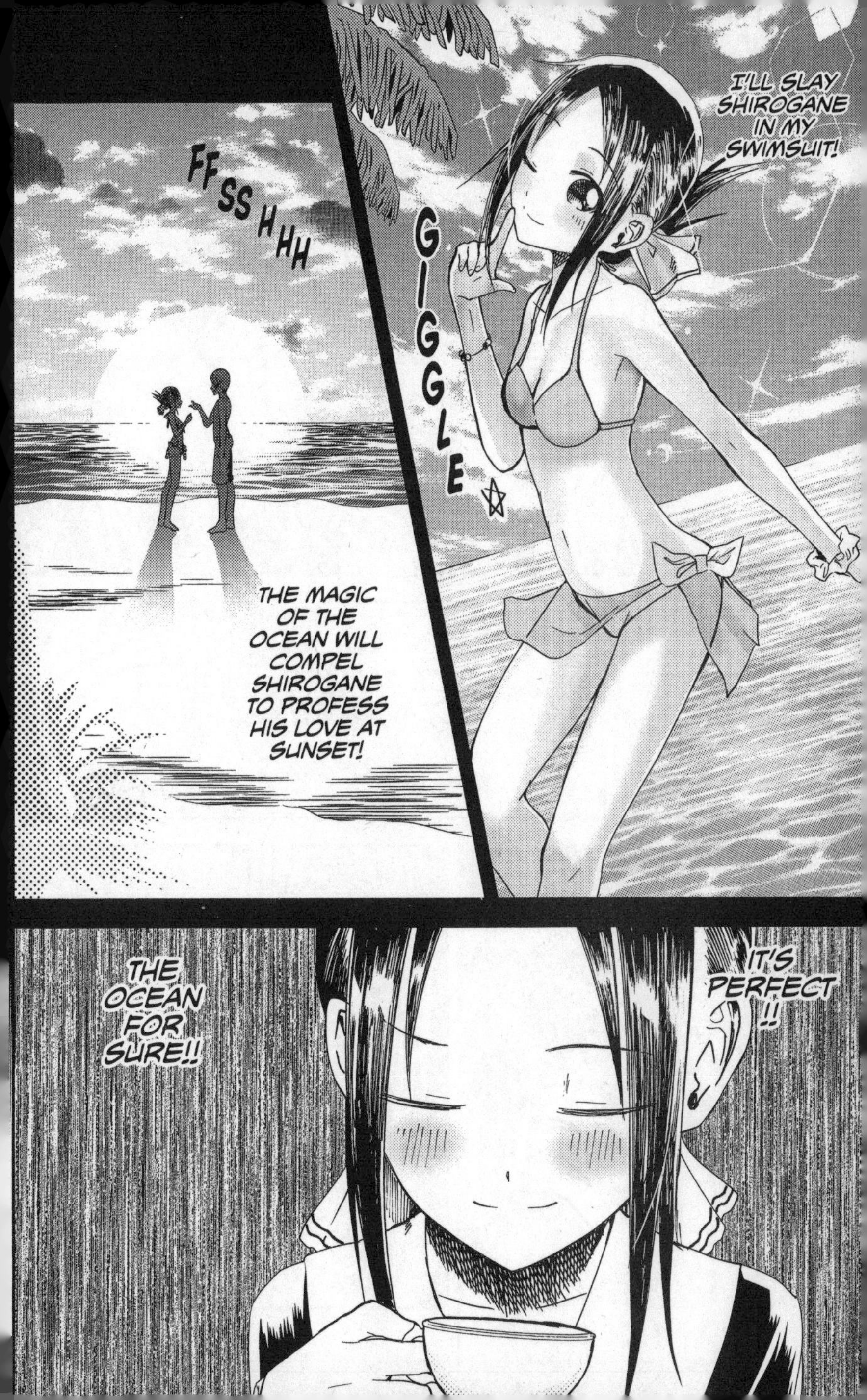
I'LL SLAY SHIROGANE IN MY SWIMSUIT!
GIGGLE
FFSSHHH
THE MAGIC OF THE OCEAN WILL COMPEL SHIROGANE TO PROFESS HIS LOVE AT SUNSET!
IT'S PERFECT!!
THE OCEAN FOR SURE!!

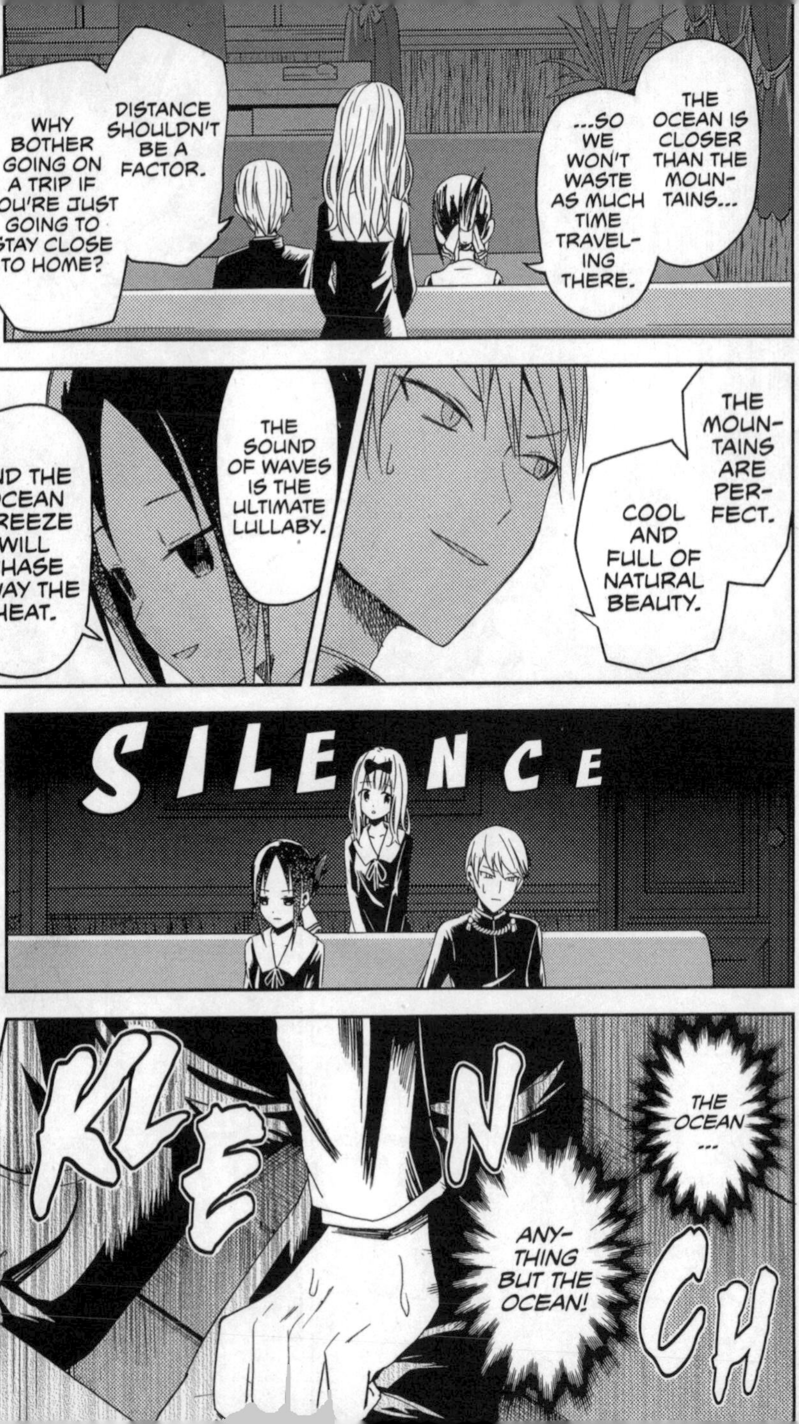
THE OCEAN IS CLOSER THAN THE MOUNTAINS...
...SO WE WON'T WASTE AS MUCH TIME TRAVELING THERE.
DISTANCE SHOULDN'T BE A FACTOR.
WHY BOTHER GOING ON A TRIP IF YOU'RE JUST GOING TO STAY CLOSE TO HOME?
THE MOUNTAINS ARE PERFECT.
COOL AND FULL OF NATURAL BEAUTY.
THE SOUND OF WAVES IS THE ULTIMATE LULLABY.
AND THE OCEAN BREEZE WILL CHASE AWAY THE HEAT.
SILENCE
THE OCEAN...
ANYTHING BUT THE OCEAN!
KLENCH

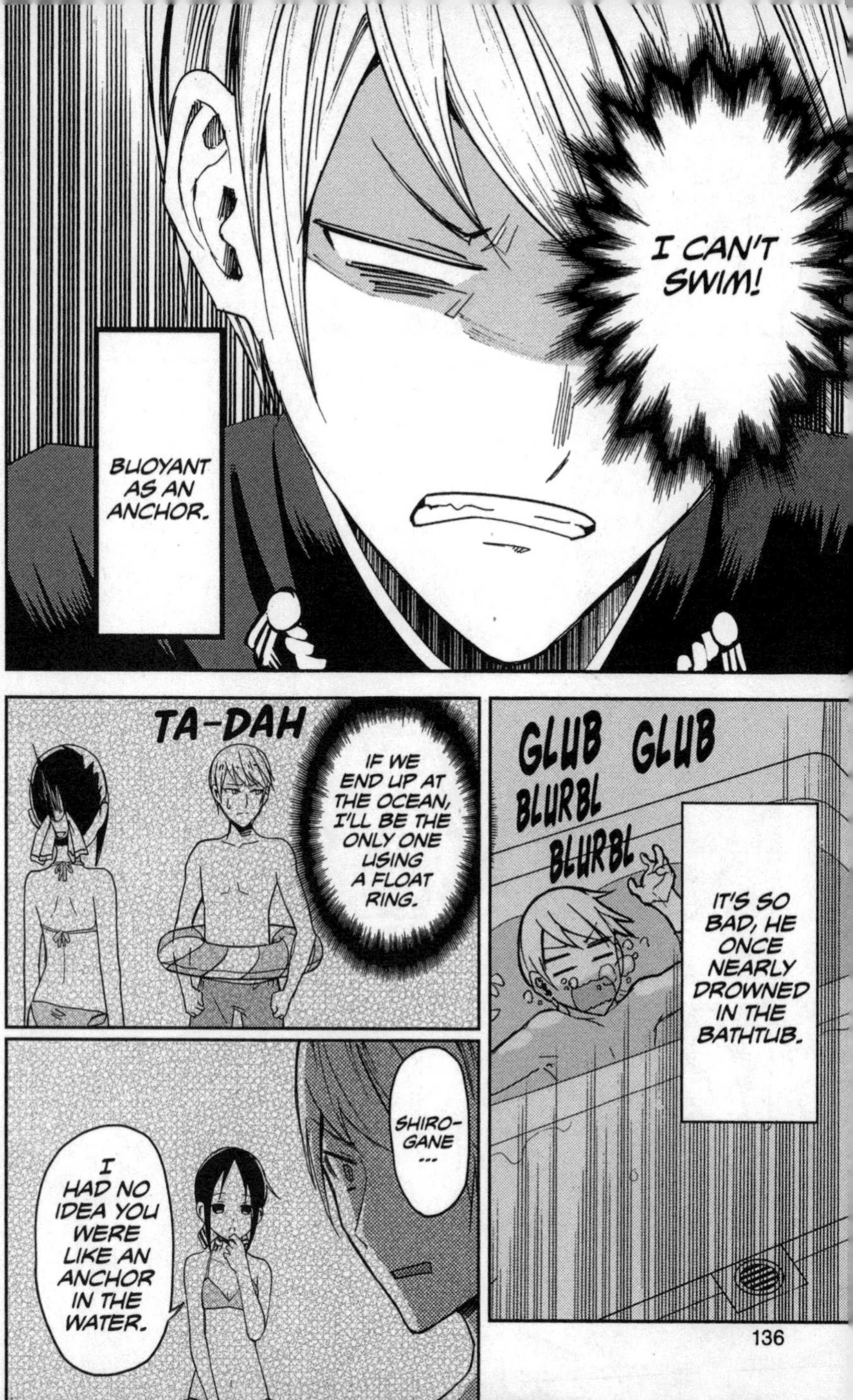
I CAN'T SWIM!
BUOYANT AS AN ANCHOR.
GLUB GLUB
BLURBL
BLURBL
IT'S SO BAD, HE ONCE NEARLY DROWNED IN THE BATHTUB.
TA-DAH
IF WE END UP AT THE OCEAN, I'LL BE THE ONLY ONE USING A FLOAT RING.
SHIROGANE...
I HAD NO IDEA YOU WERE LIKE AN ANCHOR IN THE WATER.

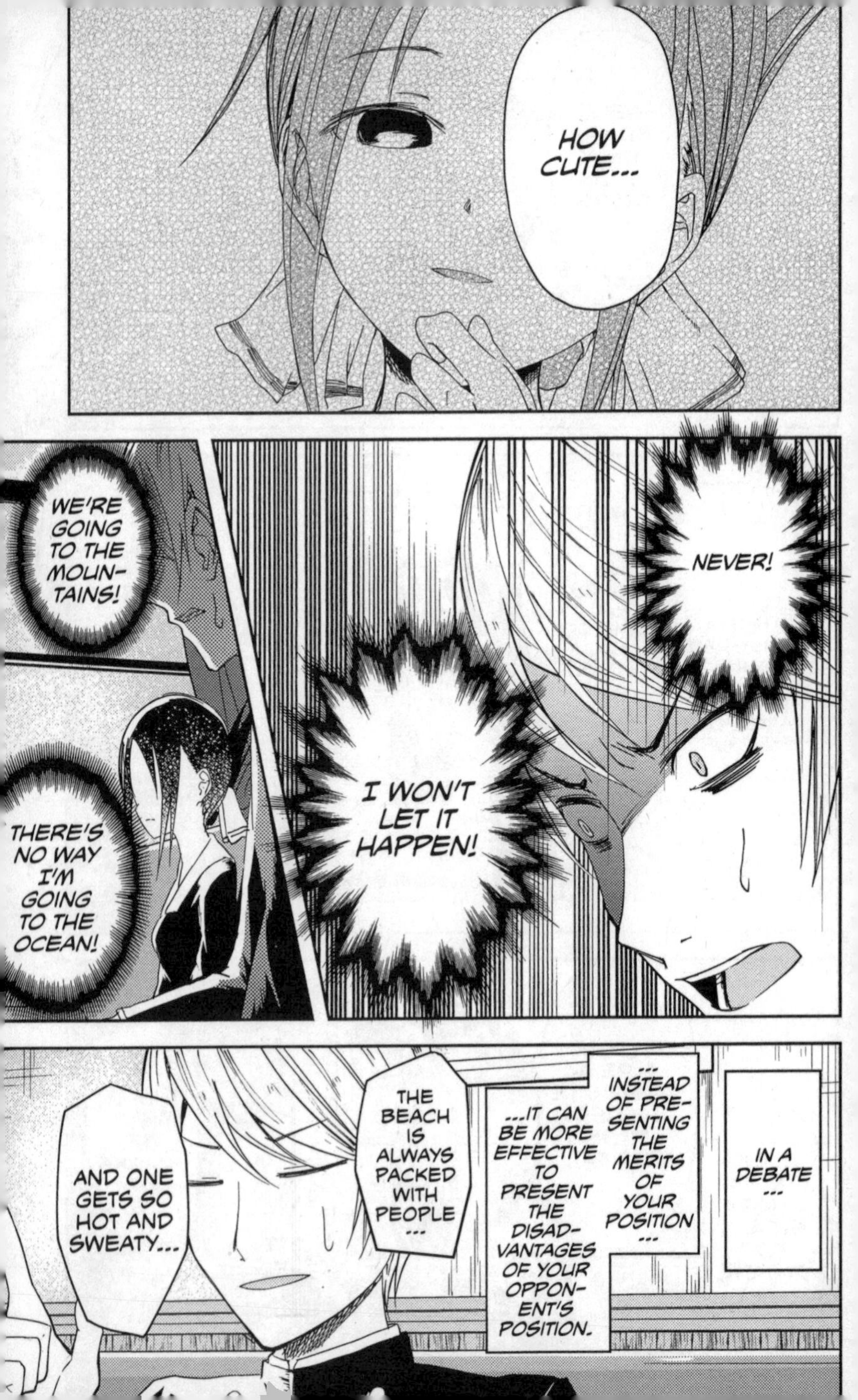
HOW CUTE...
NEVER!
I WON'T LET IT HAPPEN!
WE'RE GOING TO THE MOUNTAINS!
THERE'S NO WAY I'M GOING TO THE OCEAN!
IN A DEBATE...
...INSTEAD OF PRESENTING THE MERITS OF YOUR POSITION...
...IT CAN BE MORE EFFECTIVE TO PRESENT THE DISADVANTAGES OF YOUR OPPONENT'S POSITION.
THE BEACH IS ALWAYS PACKED WITH PEOPLE...
AND ONE GETS SO HOT AND SWEATY...

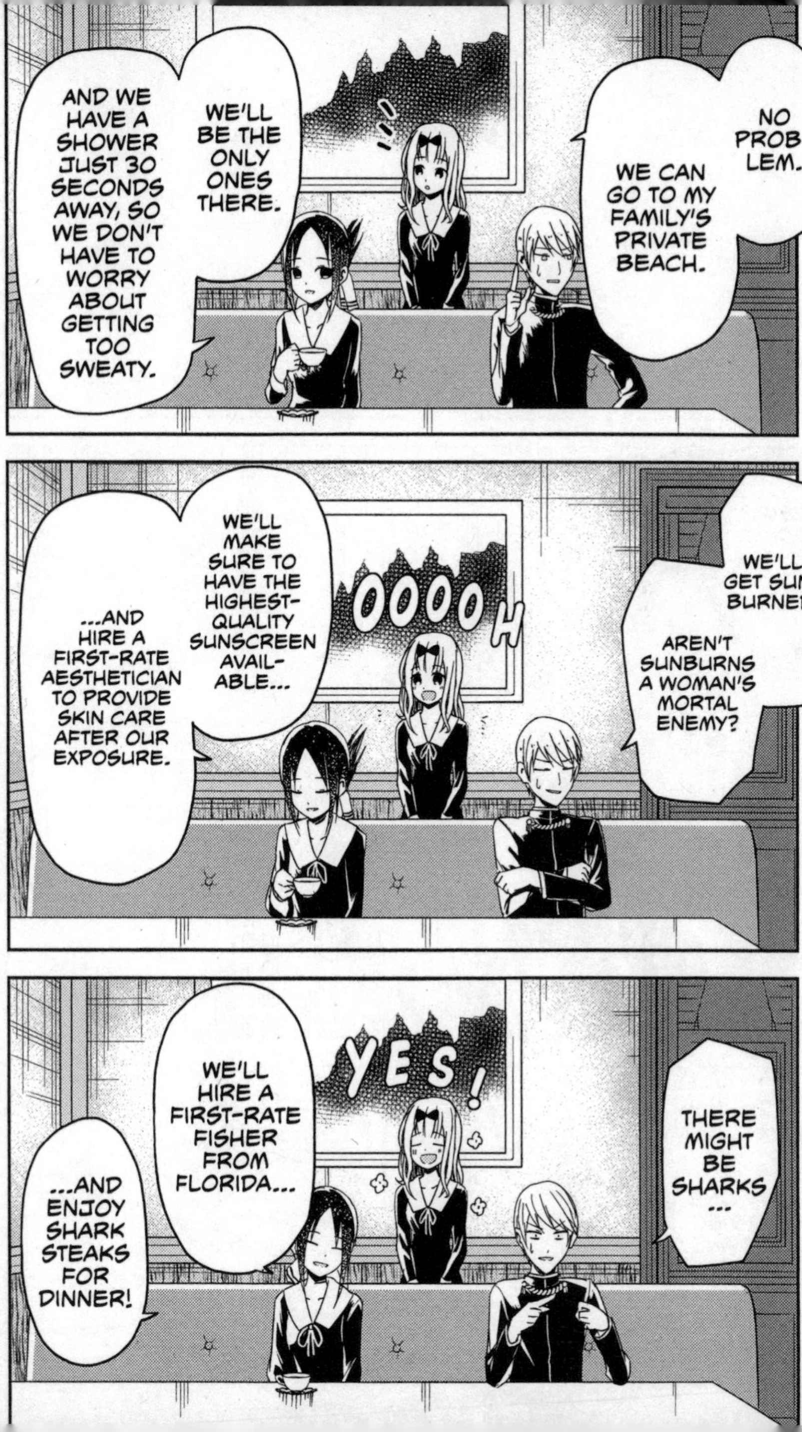
NO PROBLEM.
WE CAN GO TO MY FAMILY'S PRIVATE BEACH.
WE'LL BE THE ONLY ONES THERE.
AND WE HAVE A SHOWER JUST 30 SECONDS AWAY, SO WE DON'T HAVE TO WORRY ABOUT GETTING TOO SWEATY.
WE'LL GET SUNBURNED.
AREN'T SUNBURNS A WOMAN'S MORTAL ENEMY?
OOOOH
WE'LL MAKE SURE TO HAVE THE HIGHEST-QUALITY SUNSCREEN AVAILABLE...
...AND HIRE A FIRST-RATE AESTHETICIAN TO PROVIDE SKIN CARE AFTER OUR EXPOSURE.
THERE MIGHT BE SHARKS...
YES!
WE'LL HIRE A FIRST-RATE FISHER FROM FLORIDA...
...AND ENJOY SHARK STEAKS FOR DINNER!

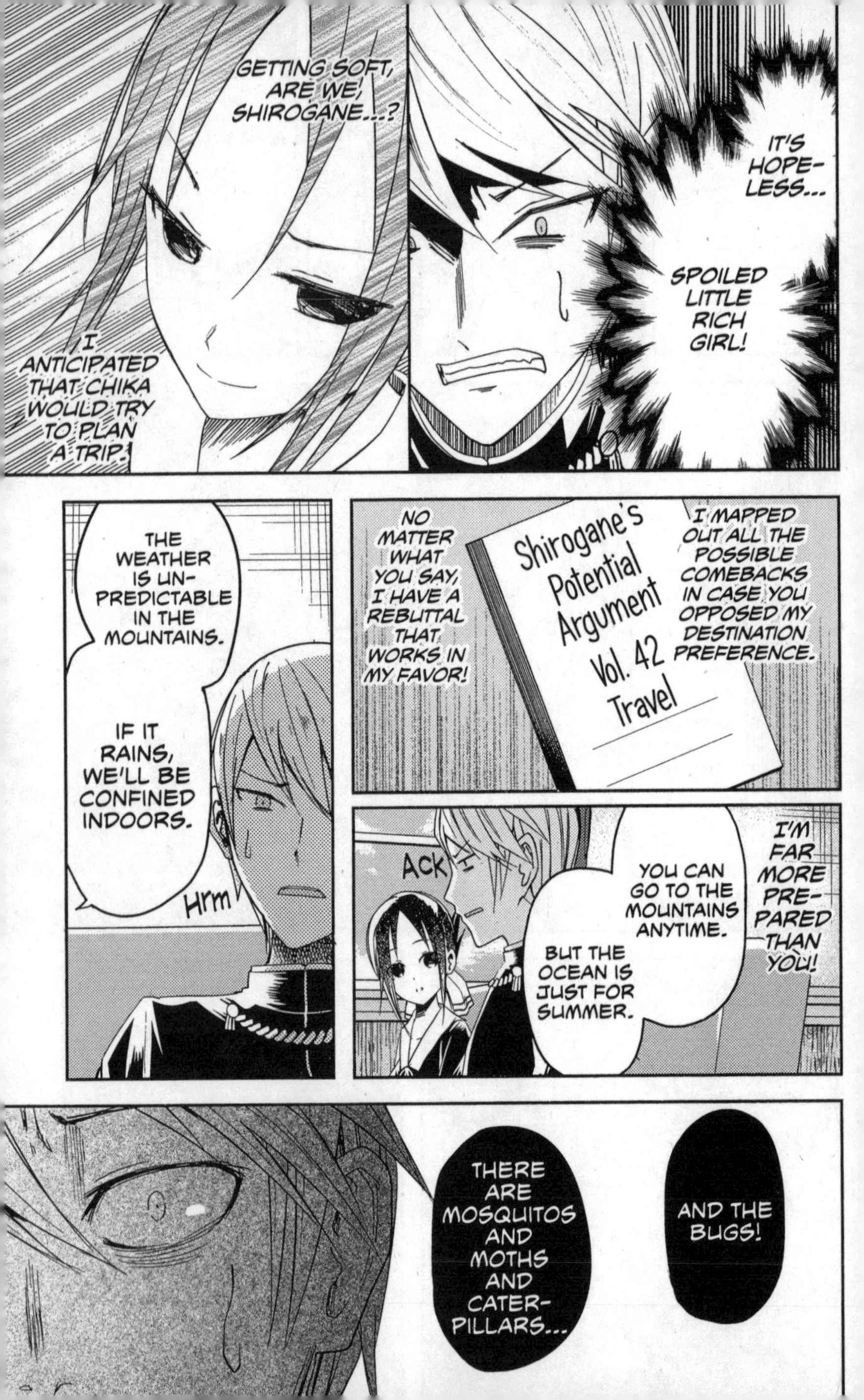
IT'S HOPELESS...
SPOILED LITTLE RICH GIRL!
GETTING SOFT, ARE WE, SHIROGANE...?
I ANTICIPATED THAT CHIKA WOULD TRY TO PLAN A TRIP!
I MAPPED OUT ALL THE POSSIBLE COMEBACKS IN CASE YOU OPPOSED MY DESTINATION PREFERENCE.
Shirogane's Potential Argument Vol. 42 Travel
NO MATTER WHAT YOU SAY, I HAVE A REBUTTAL THAT WORKS IN MY FAVOR!
I'M FAR MORE PREPARED THAN YOU!
YOU CAN GO TO THE MOUNTAINS ANYTIME.
BUT THE OCEAN IS JUST FOR SUMMER.
ACK
THE WEATHER IS UNPREDICTABLE IN THE MOUNTAINS.
IF IT RAINS, WE'LL BE CONFINED INDOORS.
Hrm
AND THE BUGS!
THERE ARE MOSQUITOS AND MOTHS AND CATERPILLARS...

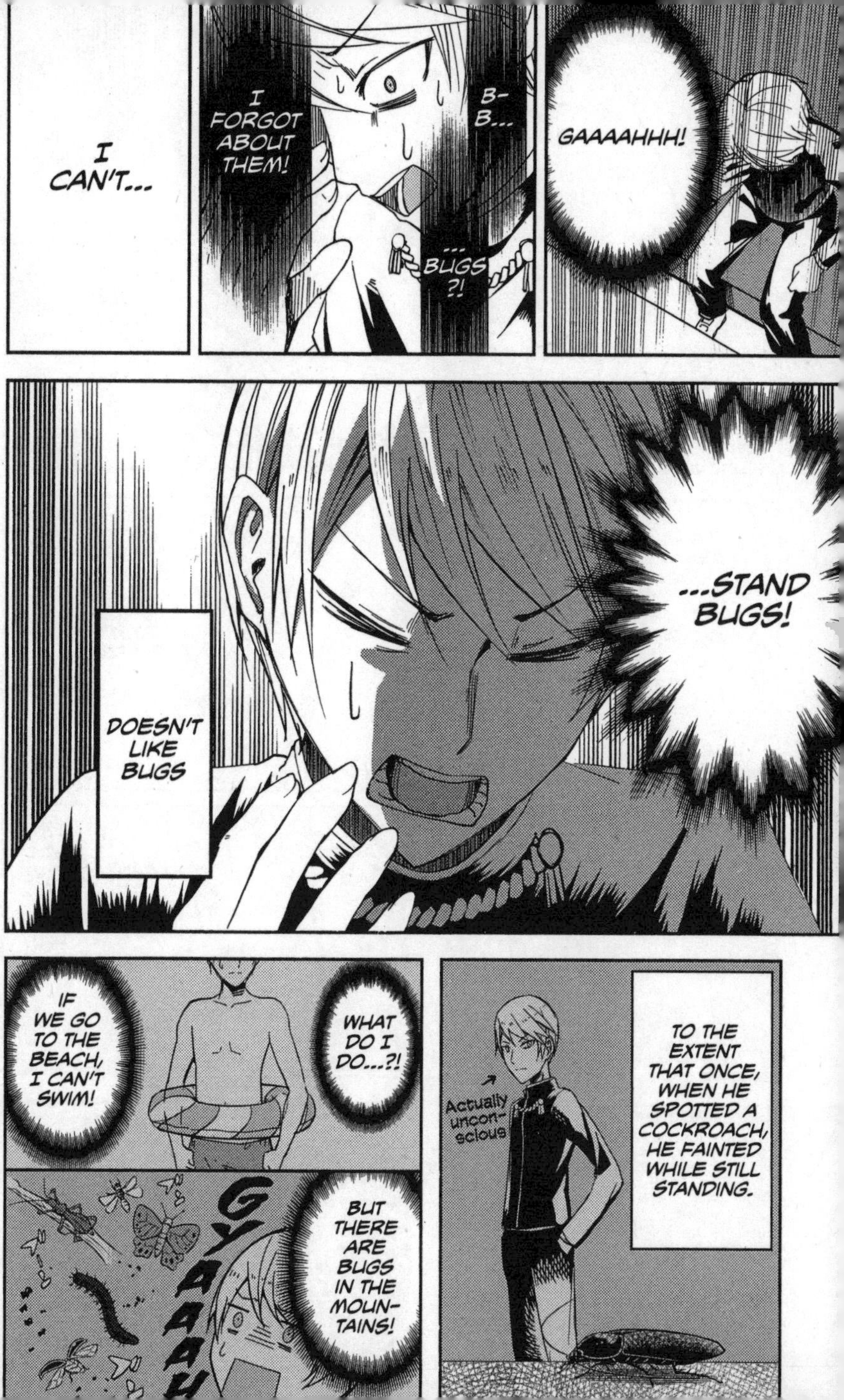
GAAAAHHH!
B-B...
I FORGOT ABOUT THEM!
...BUGS?!
I CAN'T...
...STAND BUGS!
DOESN'T LIKE BUGS
TO THE EXTENT THAT ONCE, WHEN HE SPOTTED A COCKROACH, HE FAINTED WHILE STILL STANDING.
Actually unconscious
WHAT DO I DO...?!
IF WE GO TO THE BEACH, I CAN'T SWIM!
BUT THERE ARE BUGS IN THE MOUNTAINS!
GYAAAAU

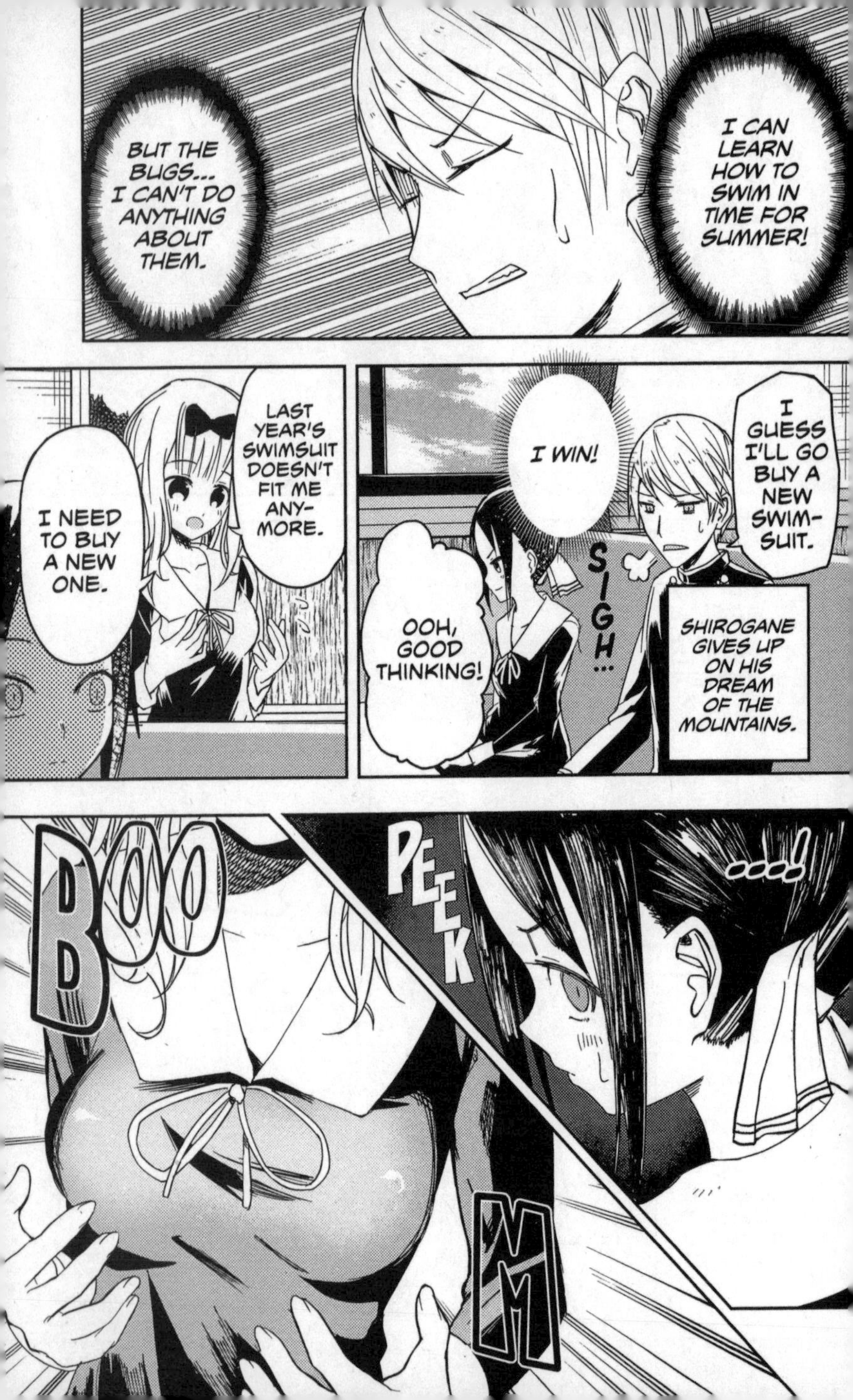

I CAN LEARN HOW TO SWIM IN TIME FOR SUMMER!
BUT THE BUGS... I CAN'T DO ANYTHING ABOUT THEM.
I GUESS I'LL GO BUY A NEW SWIMSUIT.
SHIROGANE GIVES UP ON HIS DREAM OF THE MOUNTAINS.
SIGH...
I WIN!
OOH, GOOD THINKING!
LAST YEAR'S SWIMSUIT DOESN'T FIT ME ANYMORE.
I NEED TO BUY A NEW ONE.
...!
PEEK
BOO
MM

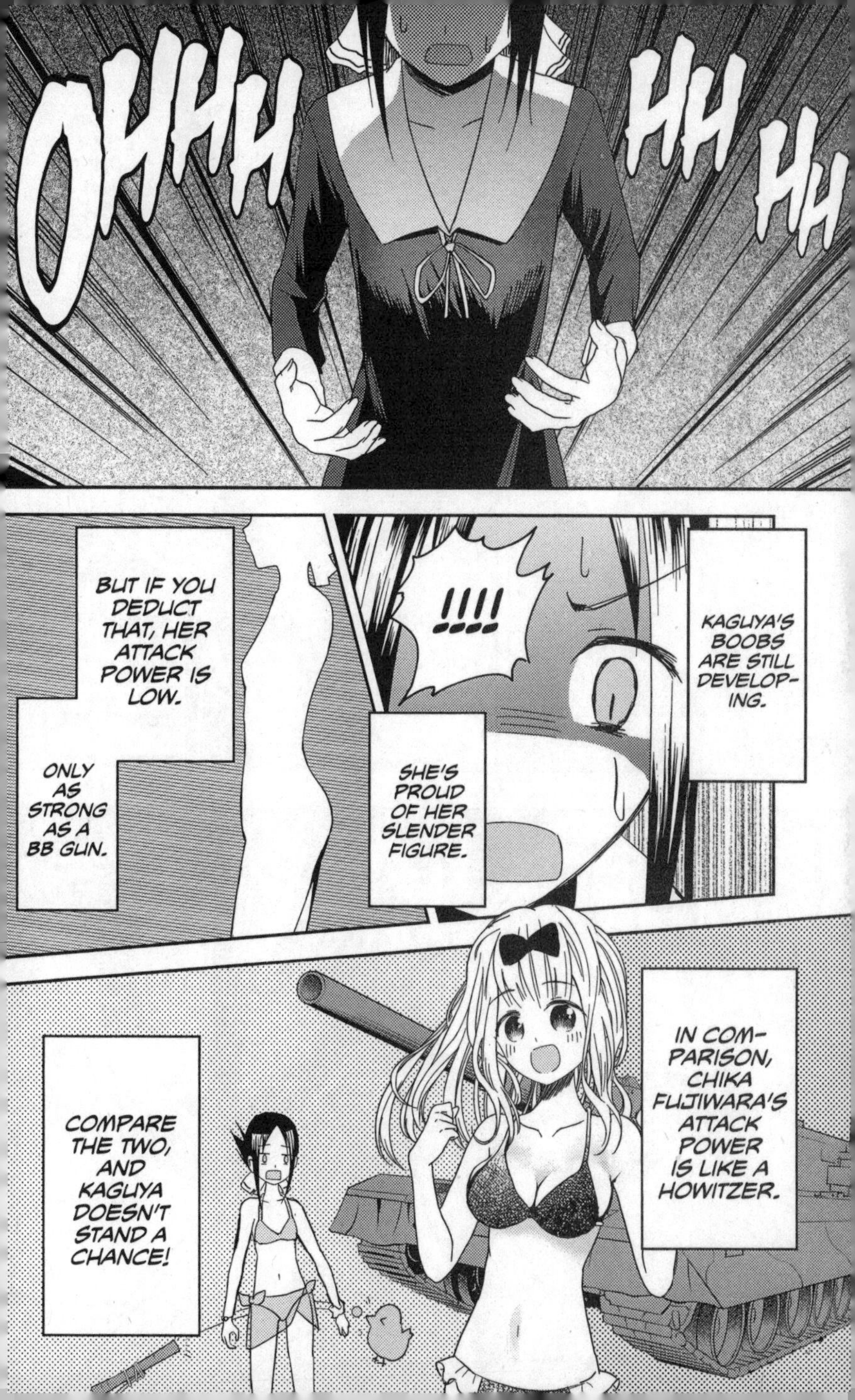
OHHH HH HH
KAGUYA'S BOOBS ARE STILL DEVELOP-ING.
!!!!
SHE'S PROUD OF HER SLENDER FIGURE.
BUT IF YOU DEDUCT THAT, HER ATTACK POWER IS LOW.
ONLY AS STRONG AS A BB GUN.
IN COM-PARISON, CHIKA FUJIWARA'S ATTACK POWER IS LIKE A HOWITZER.
COMPARE THE TWO, AND KAGUYA DOESN'T STAND A CHANCE!

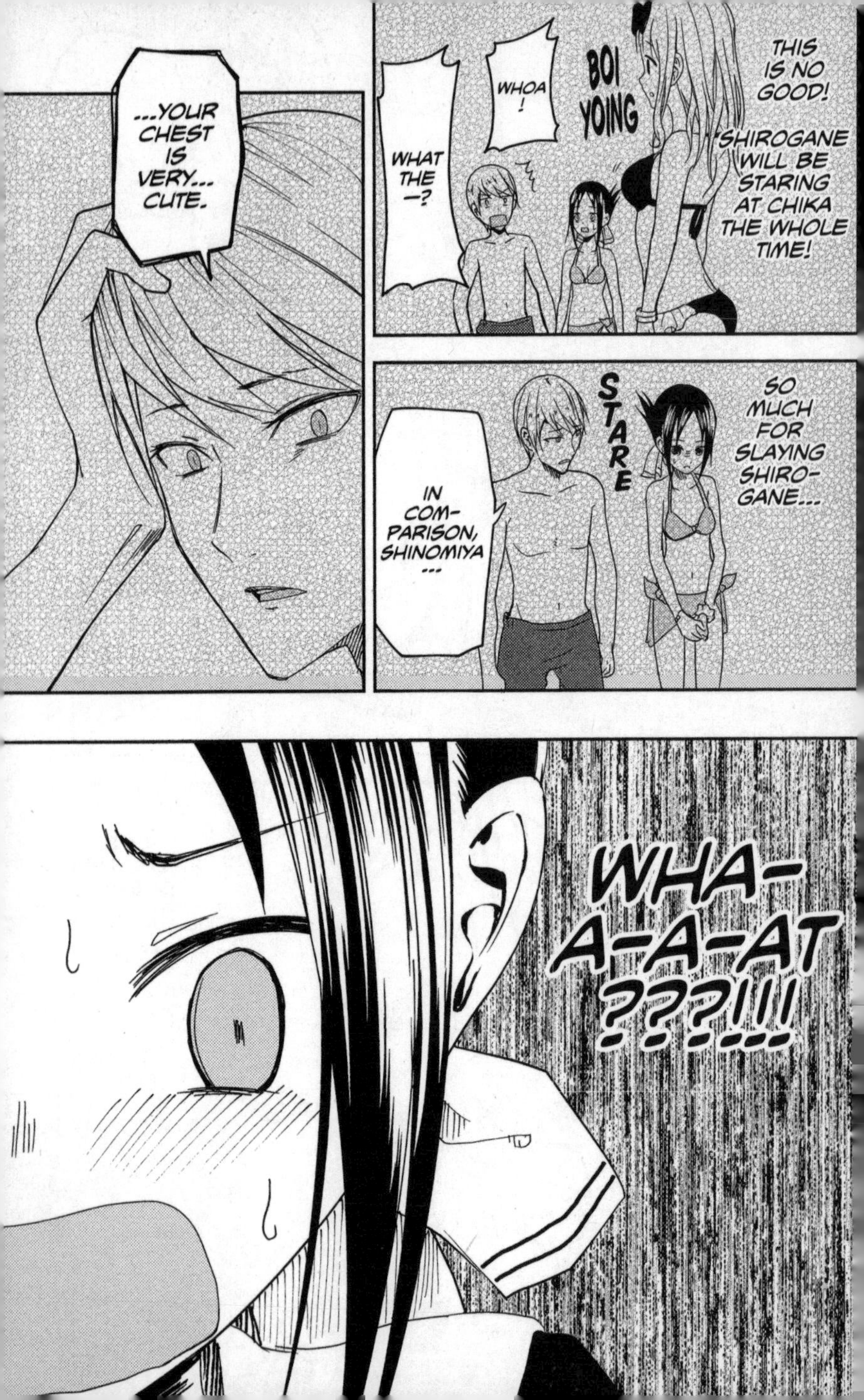
THIS IS NO GOOD!
SHIROGANE WILL BE STARING AT CHIKA THE WHOLE TIME!
BOI YOING
WHOA!
WHAT THE—?
SO MUCH FOR SLAYING SHIRO-GANE...
STARE
IN COM-PARISON, SHINOMIYA...
...YOUR CHEST IS VERY... CUTE.
WHA-A-A-AT???!!!

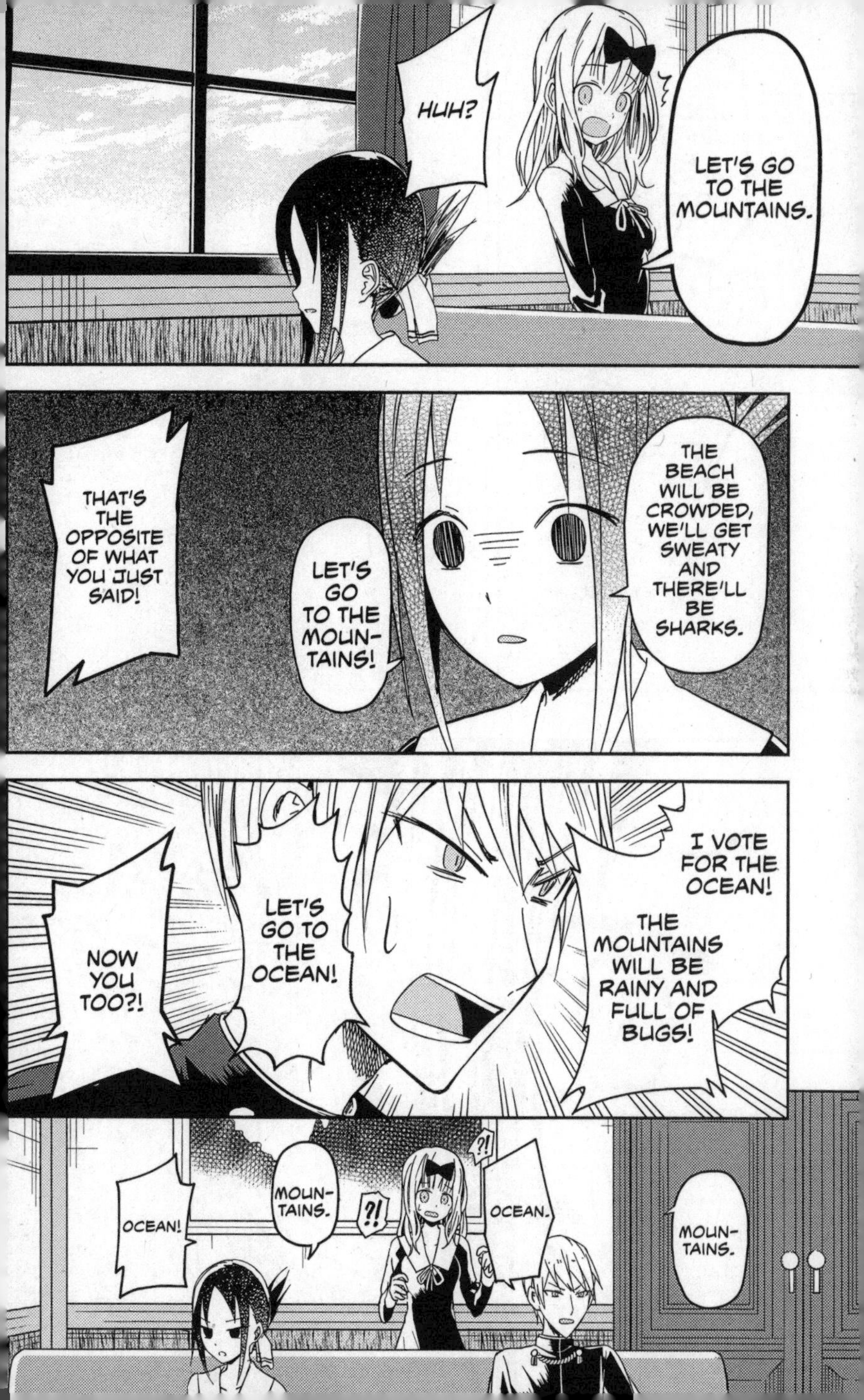
LET'S GO TO THE MOUNTAINS.
HUH?
THE BEACH WILL BE CROWDED, WE'LL GET SWEATY AND THERE'LL BE SHARKS.
LET'S GO TO THE MOUN-TAINS!
THAT'S THE OPPOSITE OF WHAT YOU JUST SAID!
I VOTE FOR THE OCEAN!
THE MOUNTAINS WILL BE RAINY AND FULL OF BUGS!
LET'S GO TO THE OCEAN!
NOW YOU TOO?!
MOUN-TAINS.
?!
OCEAN.
?!
MOUN-TAINS.
OCEAN!

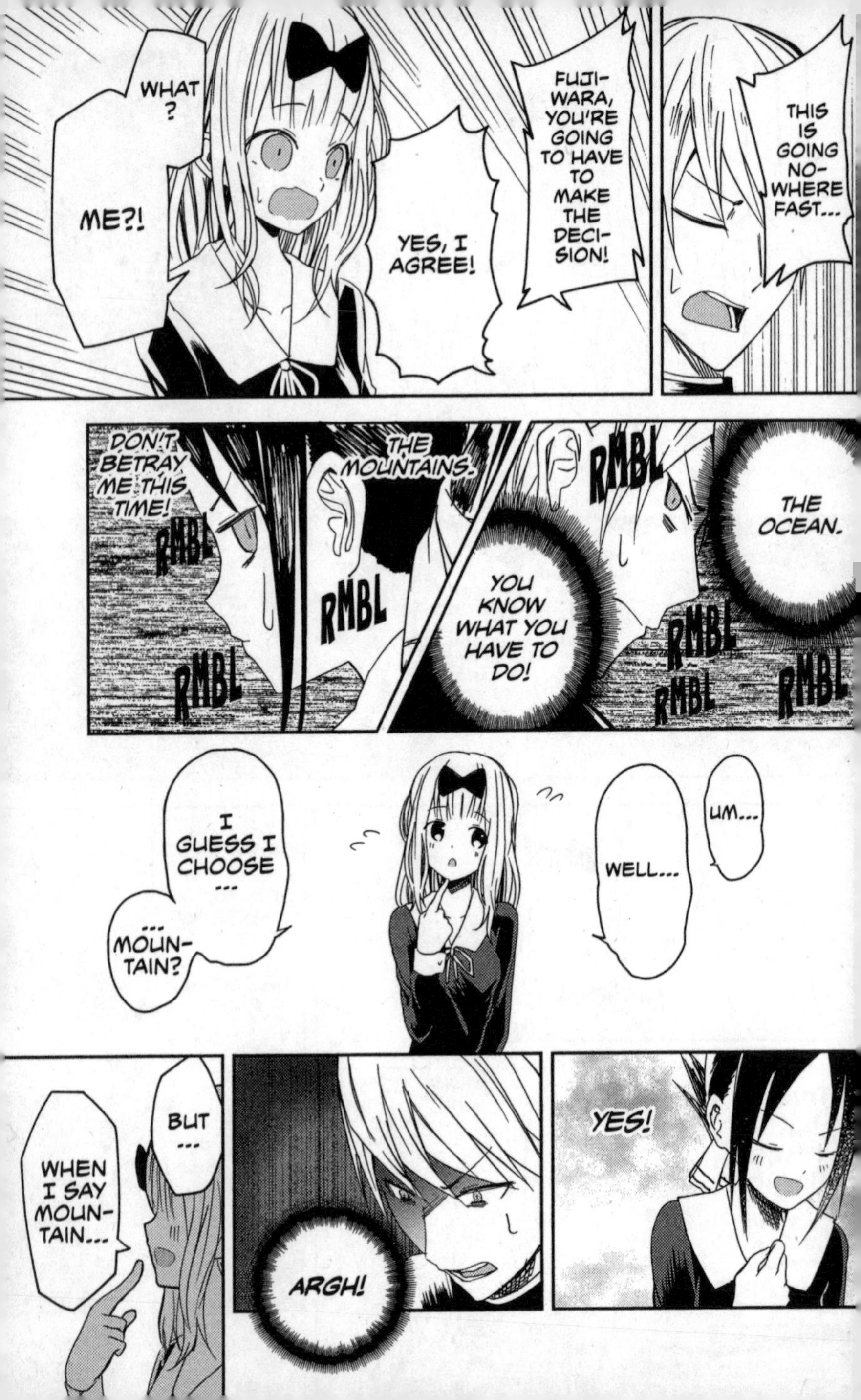
THIS IS GOING NOWHERE FAST...
FUJIWARA, YOU'RE GOING TO HAVE TO MAKE THE DECISION!
YES, I AGREE!
WHAT?
ME?!
THE OCEAN.
RMBL
YOU KNOW WHAT YOU HAVE TO DO!
RMBL RMBL RMBL
THE MOUNTAINS.
DON'T BETRAY ME THIS TIME!
RMBL RMBL RMBL
UM...
WELL...
I GUESS I CHOOSE...
...MOUNTAIN?
YES!
ARGH!
BUT...
WHEN I SAY MOUNTAIN...

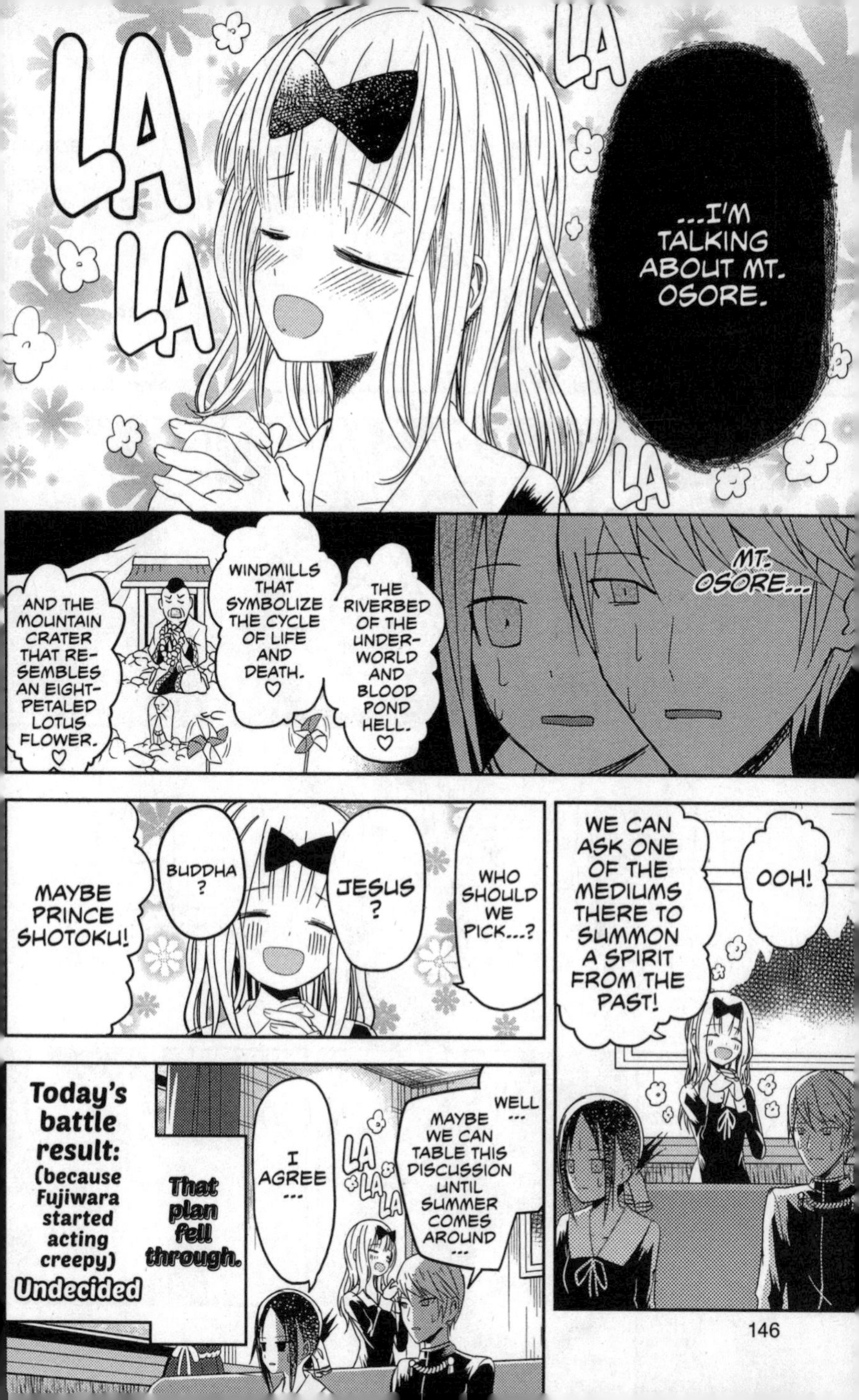
LA
...I'M TALKING ABOUT MT. OSORE.
LA
LA LA
MT. OSORE...
THE RIVERBED OF THE UNDER-WORLD AND BLOOD POND HELL. ♡
WINDMILLS THAT SYMBOLIZE THE CYCLE OF LIFE AND DEATH. ♡
AND THE MOUNTAIN CRATER THAT RE-SEMBLES AN EIGHT-PETALED LOTUS FLOWER. ♡
OOH!
WE CAN ASK ONE OF THE MEDIUMS THERE TO SUMMON A SPIRIT FROM THE PAST!
WHO SHOULD WE PICK...?
JESUS?
BUDDHA?
MAYBE PRINCE SHOTOKU!
WELL...
MAYBE WE CAN TABLE THIS DISCUSSION UNTIL SUMMER COMES AROUND...
LA LA LA
I AGREE...
Today's battle result:
(because Fujiwara started acting creepy)
That plan fell through.
Undecided

CHIKA FUJIWARA

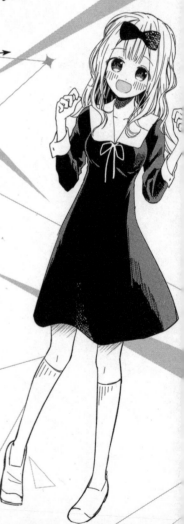

Chika Fujiwara

- Shuchiin Academy High School Second-Year
- Student Council Secretary
- Notable characteristics: soft, poofy, large boobs
- A main character in this story

From a prominent political family. Her great-grandfather was a prime minister, and her uncle is currently a minister in the government.

Although she is rather overprotected, she grew up in a loving home and has a kind heart.

Since video games and other forms of popular entertainment are forbidden in her household, she escapes reality by seriously devoting herself to her hobbies.

She enjoys German strategy board games, puzzles and various subcultures—essentially, anything that isn't mainstream.

She's not a liar, but when it comes to games like Werewolf or poker, she can hold her bluff and is a worthy opponent.

Kaguya has been her close friend since junior high school, and they often have sleepovers—although they don't appear to be that friendly due to Kaguya's demeanor.

The direction of this story has yet to be determined. There is no guarantee that Miyuki and Kaguya will get together and live happily ever after. The outcome will be up to the characters.

KAGUYA-SAMA

LOVE IS WAR

Battle 8
Kaguya Wants to Be Figured Out

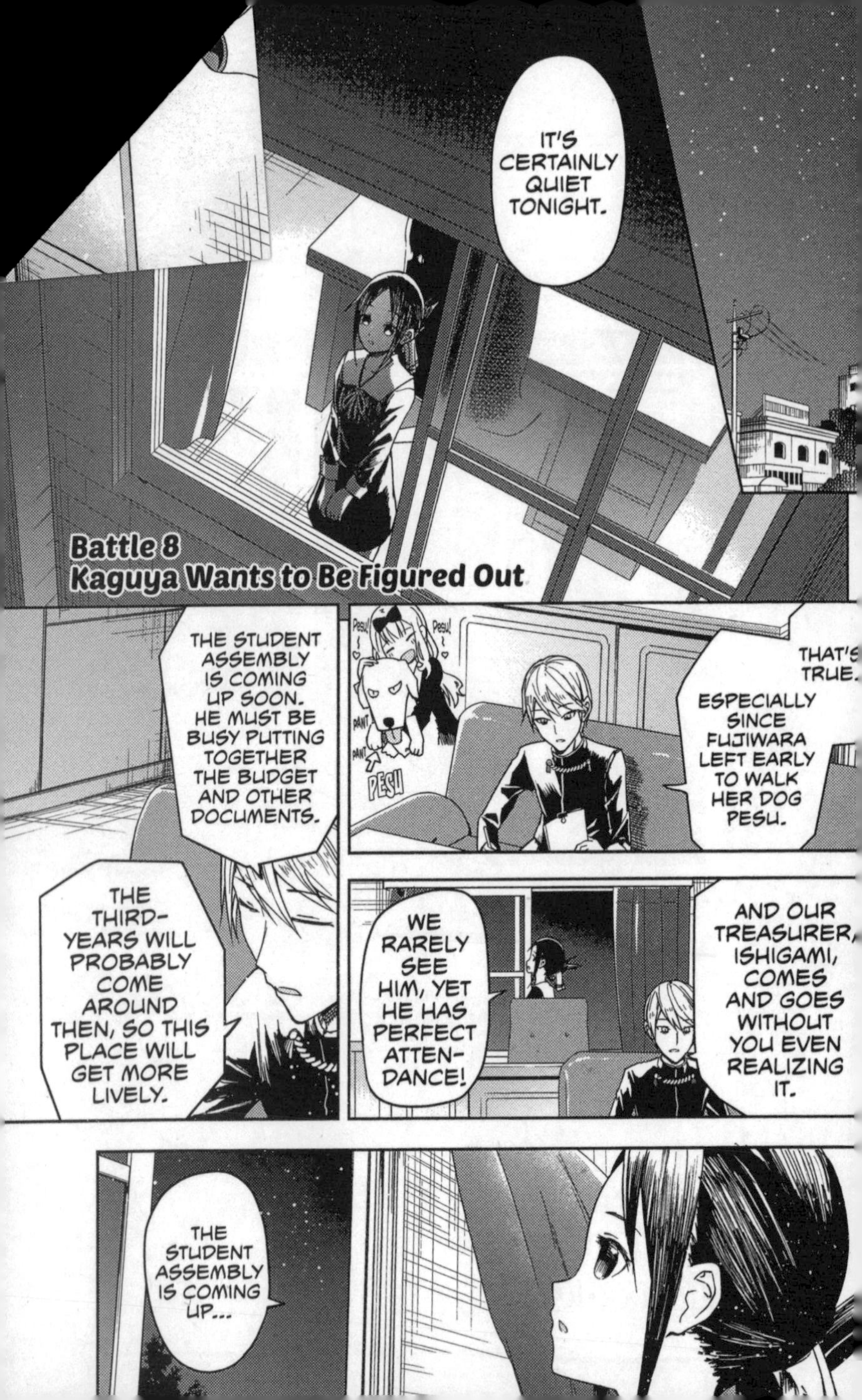
IT'S CERTAINLY QUIET TONIGHT.
THAT'S TRUE.
ESPECIALLY SINCE FUJIWARA LEFT EARLY TO WALK HER DOG PESU.
Pesu!
Pesu!
PANT
PANT
PESU
THE STUDENT ASSEMBLY IS COMING UP SOON. HE MUST BE BUSY PUTTING TOGETHER THE BUDGET AND OTHER DOCUMENTS.
AND OUR TREASURER, ISHIGAMI, COMES AND GOES WITHOUT YOU EVEN REALIZING IT.
WE RARELY SEE HIM, YET HE HAS PERFECT ATTEN-DANCE!
THE THIRD-YEARS WILL PROBABLY COME AROUND THEN, SO THIS PLACE WILL GET MORE LIVELY.
THE STUDENT ASSEMBLY IS COMING UP...

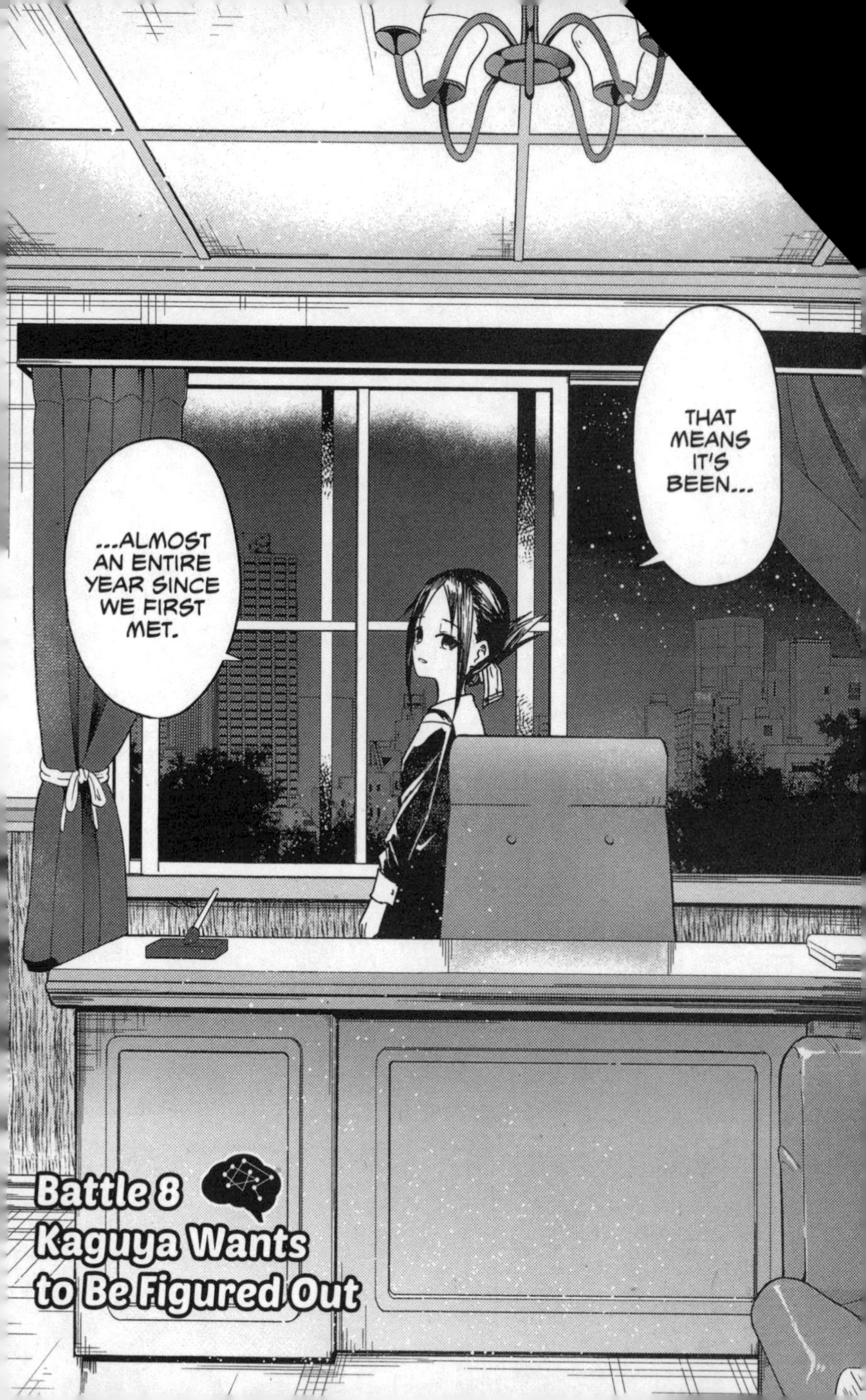
THAT MEANS IT'S BEEN...
...ALMOST AN ENTIRE YEAR SINCE WE FIRST MET.
Battle 8 Kaguya Wants to Be Figured Out

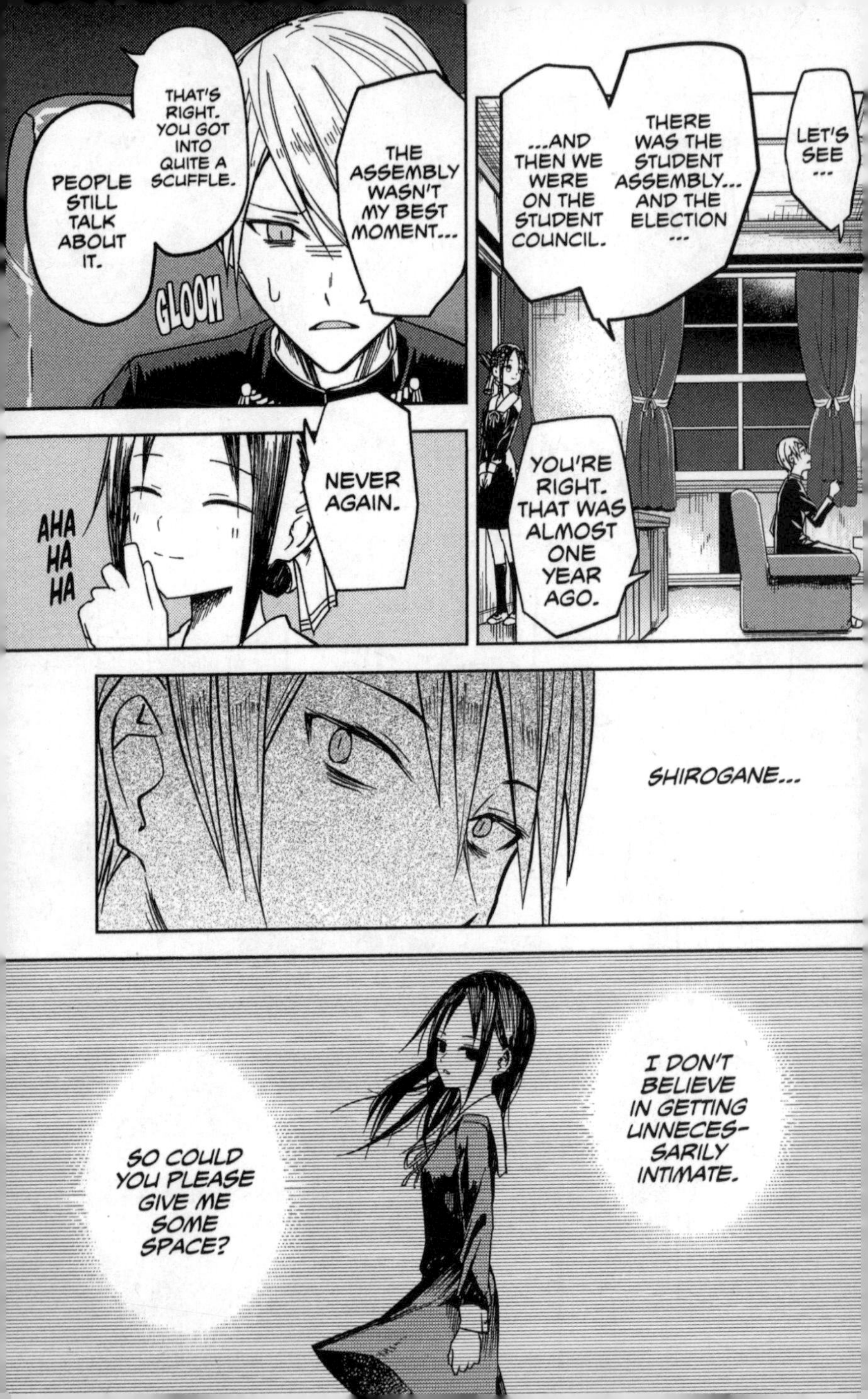
LET'S SEE ...
THERE WAS THE STUDENT ASSEMBLY... AND THE ELECTION ...
...AND THEN WE WERE ON THE STUDENT COUNCIL.
YOU'RE RIGHT. THAT WAS ALMOST ONE YEAR AGO.
THE ASSEMBLY WASN'T MY BEST MOMENT...
THAT'S RIGHT. YOU GOT INTO QUITE A SCUFFLE.
PEOPLE STILL TALK ABOUT IT.
GLOOM
NEVER AGAIN.
AHA HA HA
SHIROGANE...
I DON'T BELIEVE IN GETTING UNNECES-SARILY INTIMATE.
SO COULD YOU PLEASE GIVE ME SOME SPACE?

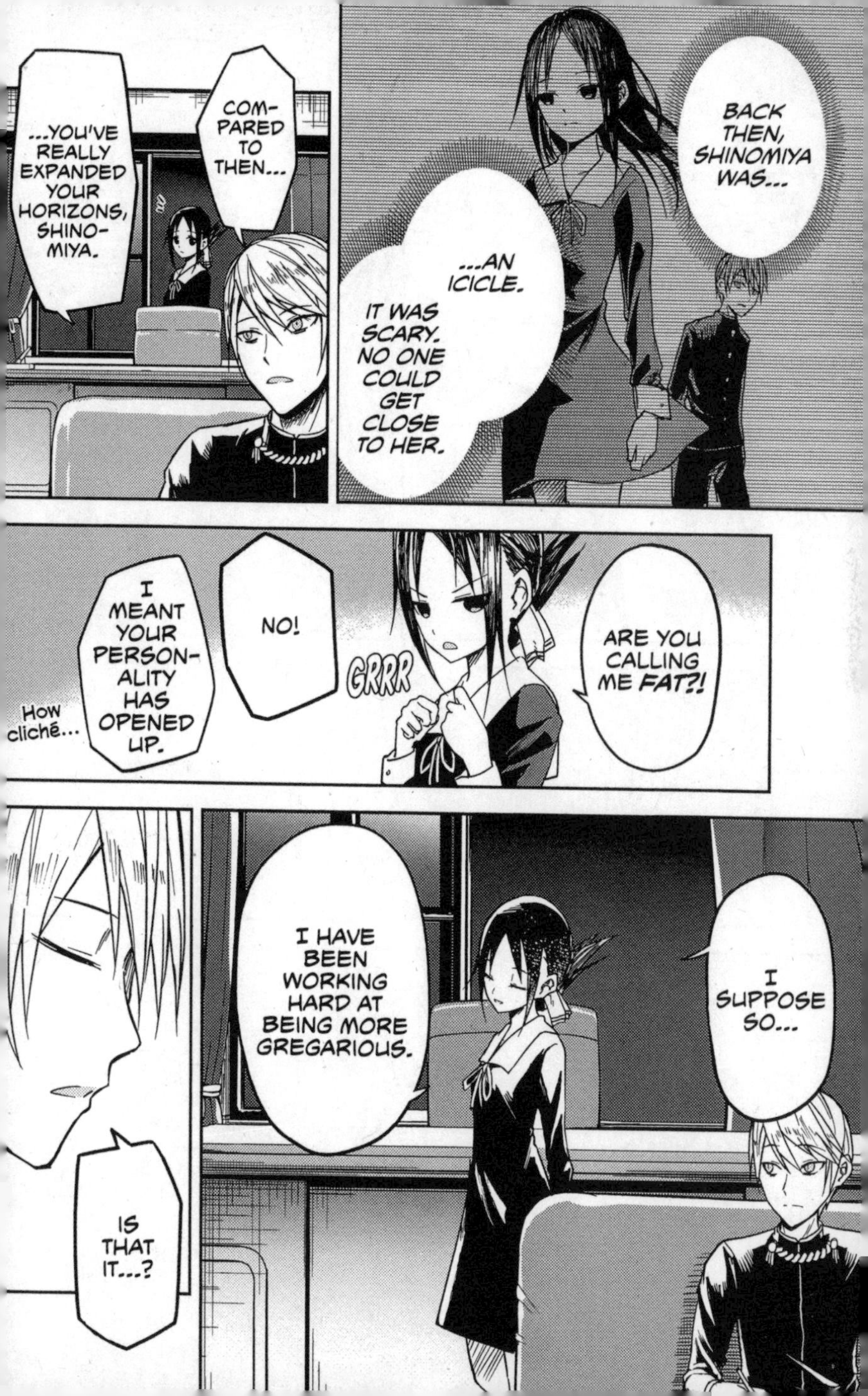
BACK THEN, SHINOMIYA WAS...
...AN ICICLE.
IT WAS SCARY. NO ONE COULD GET CLOSE TO HER.
COMPARED TO THEN...
...YOU'VE REALLY EXPANDED YOUR HORIZONS, SHINOMIYA.
ARE YOU CALLING ME FAT?!
GRRR
NO!
I MEANT YOUR PERSONALITY HAS OPENED UP.
How cliché...
I SUPPOSE SO...
I HAVE BEEN WORKING HARD AT BEING MORE GREGARIOUS.
IS THAT IT...?

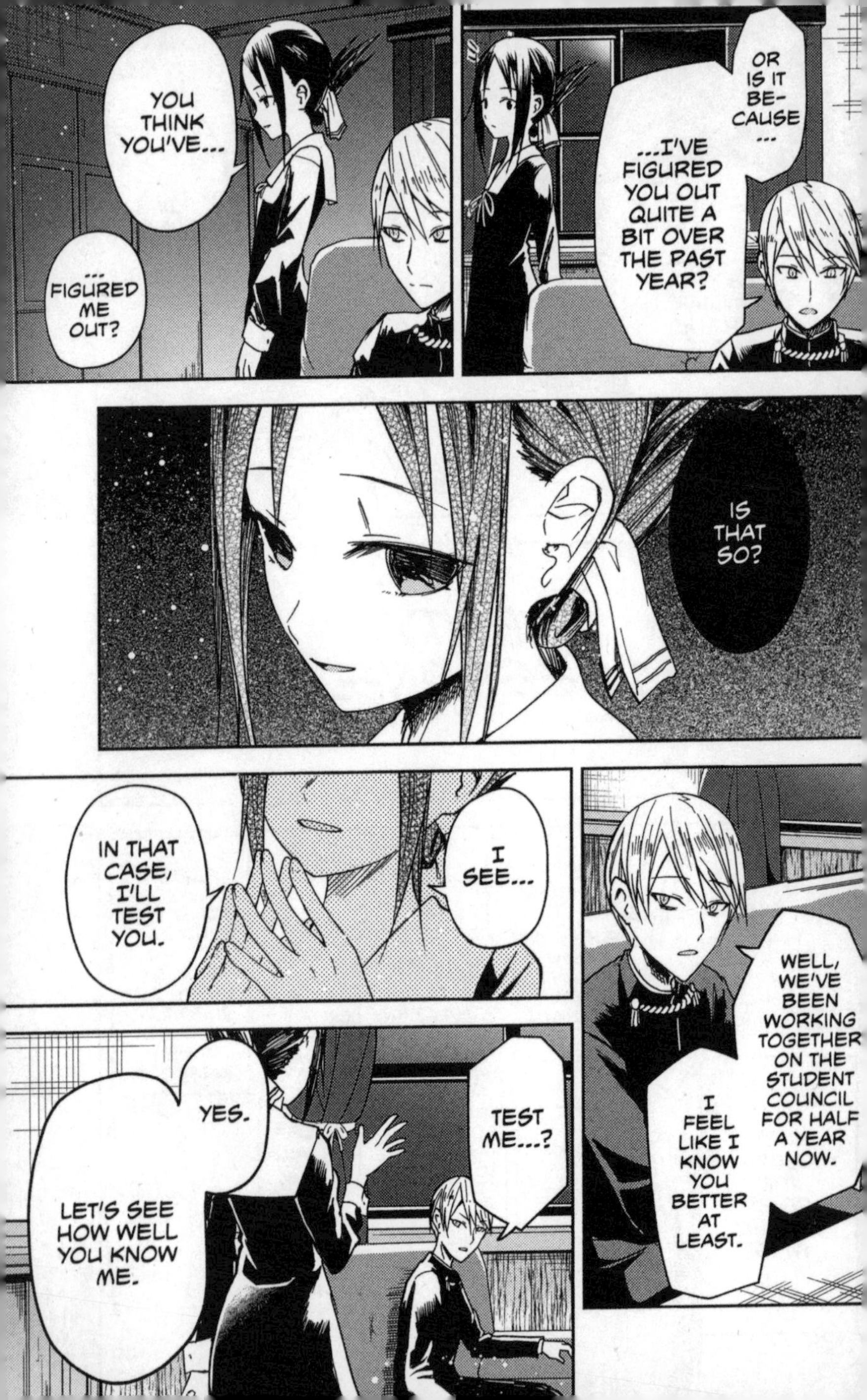
OR IS IT BE-CAUSE...
...I'VE FIGURED YOU OUT QUITE A BIT OVER THE PAST YEAR?
YOU THINK YOU'VE...
...FIGURED ME OUT?
IS THAT SO?
WELL, WE'VE BEEN WORKING TOGETHER ON THE STUDENT COUNCIL FOR HALF A YEAR NOW.
I FEEL LIKE I KNOW YOU BETTER AT LEAST.
I SEE...
IN THAT CASE, I'LL TEST YOU.
TEST ME...?
YES.
LET'S SEE HOW WELL YOU KNOW ME.

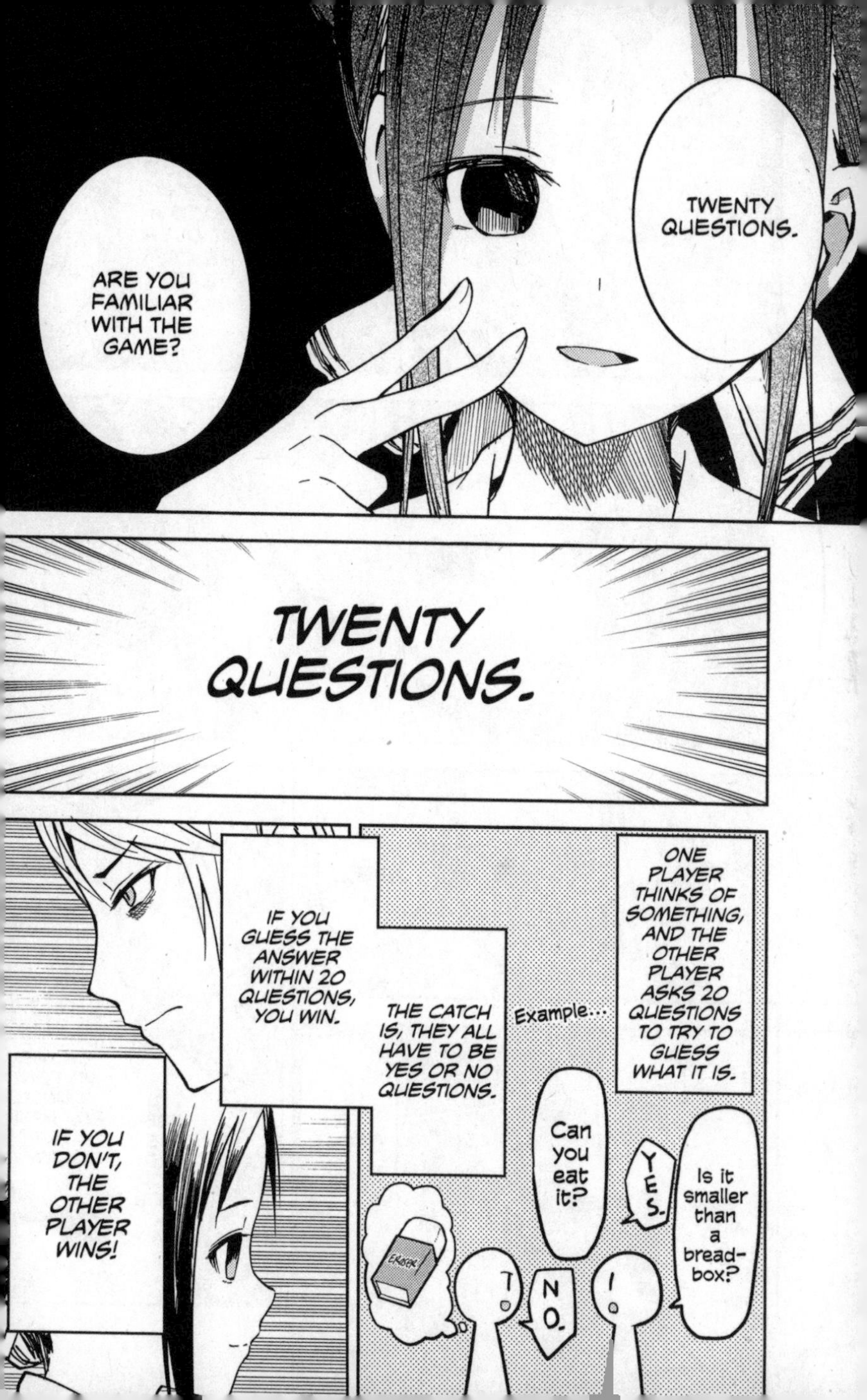
TWENTY QUESTIONS.
ARE YOU FAMILIAR WITH THE GAME?
TWENTY QUESTIONS.
ONE PLAYER THINKS OF SOMETHING, AND THE OTHER PLAYER ASKS 20 QUESTIONS TO TRY TO GUESS WHAT IT IS.
Example...
Is it smaller than a bread-box?
YES.
Can you eat it?
NO.
IF YOU GUESS THE ANSWER WITHIN 20 QUESTIONS, YOU WIN.
THE CATCH IS, THEY ALL HAVE TO BE YES OR NO QUESTIONS.
IF YOU DON'T, THE OTHER PLAYER WINS!

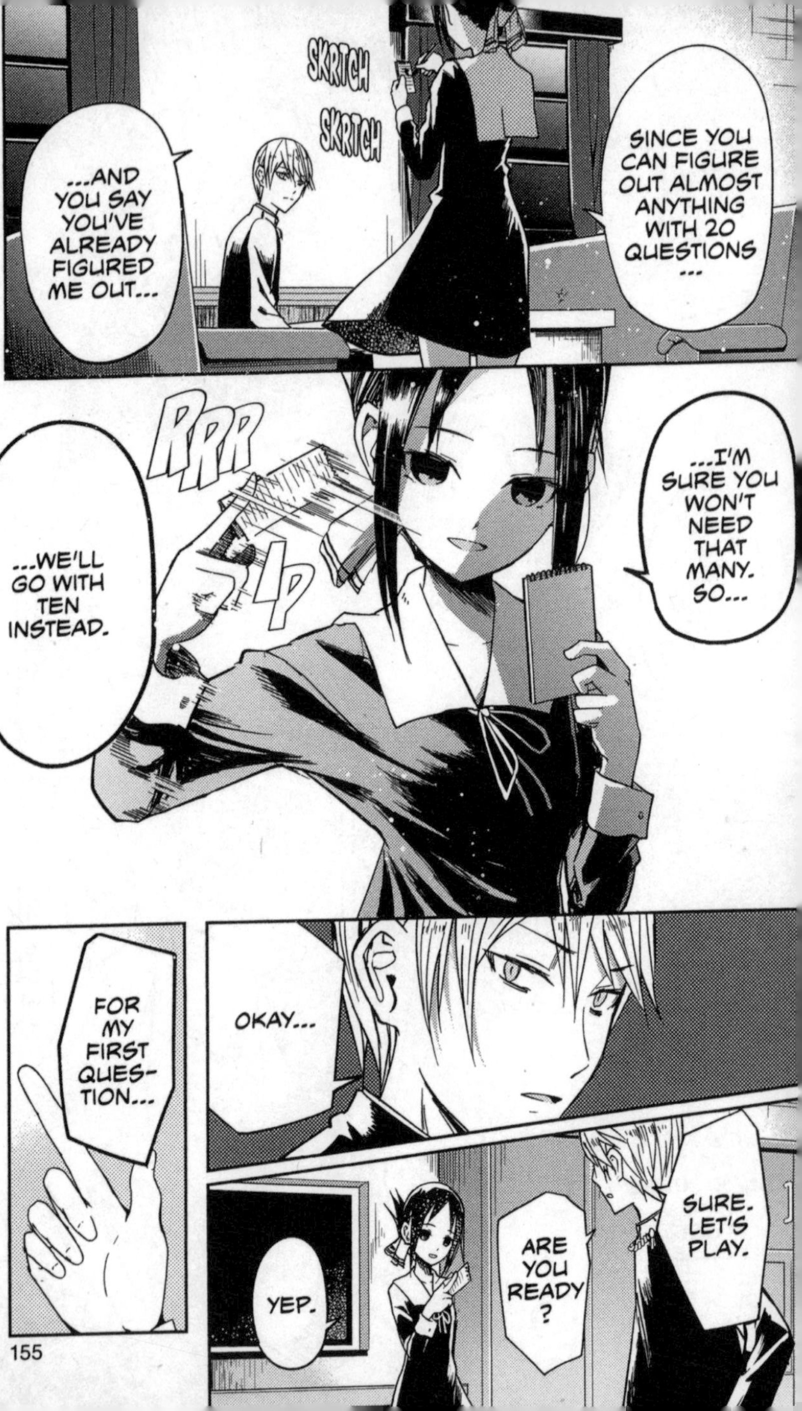
SINCE YOU CAN FIGURE OUT ALMOST ANYTHING WITH 20 QUESTIONS ...
SKRTCH
SKRTCH
...AND YOU SAY YOU'VE ALREADY FIGURED ME OUT...
...I'M SURE YOU WON'T NEED THAT MANY. SO...
RRR
RIP
...WE'LL GO WITH TEN INSTEAD.
OKAY...
SURE. LET'S PLAY.
ARE YOU READY?
YEP.
FOR MY FIRST QUES-TION...

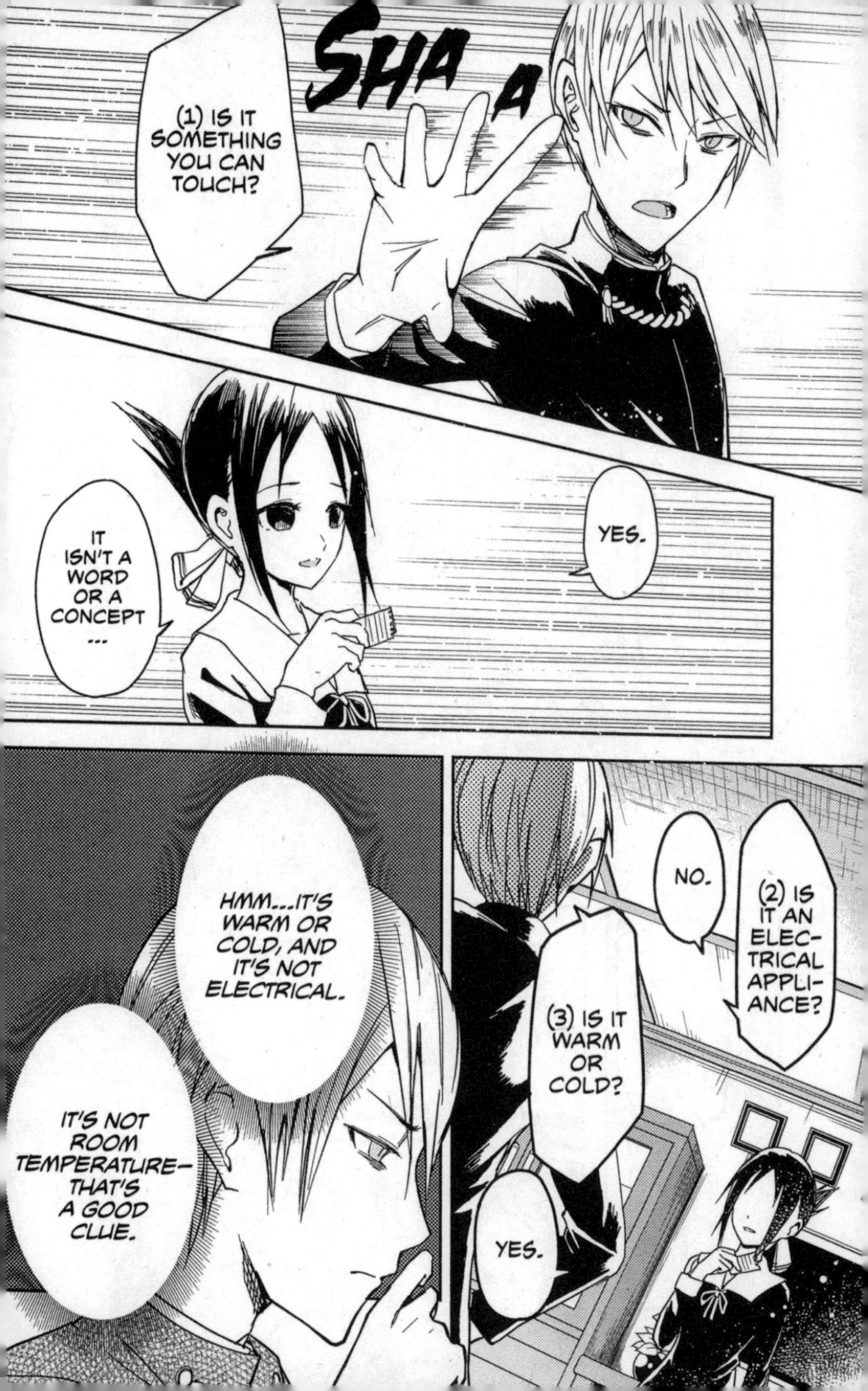
SHA A
(1) IS IT SOMETHING YOU CAN TOUCH?
YES.
IT ISN'T A WORD OR A CONCEPT ...
(2) IS IT AN ELEC-TRICAL APPLI-ANCE?
NO.
(3) IS IT WARM OR COLD?
YES.
HMM...IT'S WARM OR COLD, AND IT'S NOT ELECTRICAL.
IT'S NOT ROOM TEMPERATURE—THAT'S A GOOD CLUE.

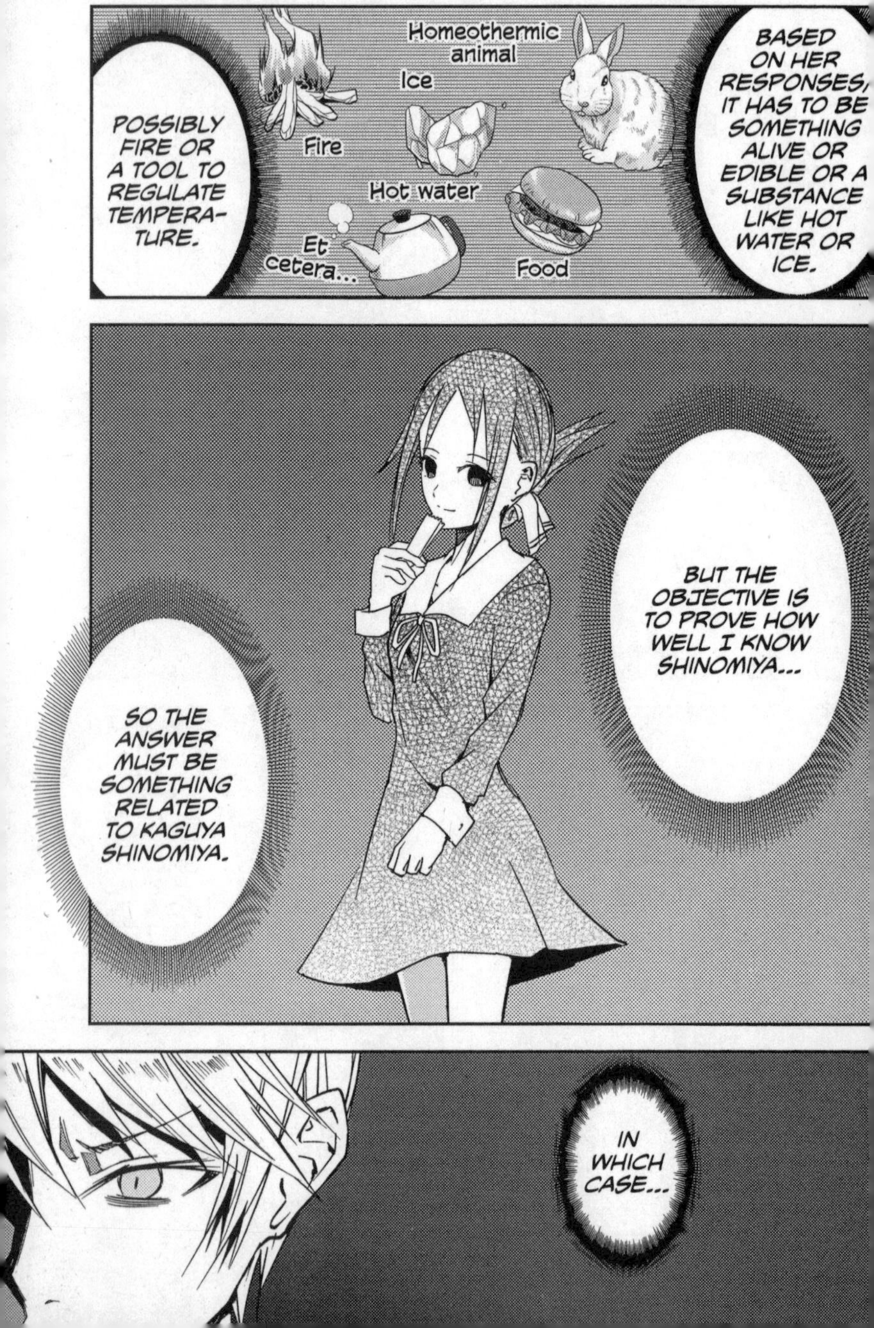
BASED ON HER RESPONSES, IT HAS TO BE SOMETHING ALIVE OR EDIBLE OR A SUBSTANCE LIKE HOT WATER OR ICE.
Homeothermic animal
Ice
Fire
Hot water
Food
Et cetera...
POSSIBLY FIRE OR A TOOL TO REGULATE TEMPERA-TURE.
BUT THE OBJECTIVE IS TO PROVE HOW WELL I KNOW SHINOMIYA...
SO THE ANSWER MUST BE SOMETHING RELATED TO KAGUYA SHINOMIYA.
IN WHICH CASE...

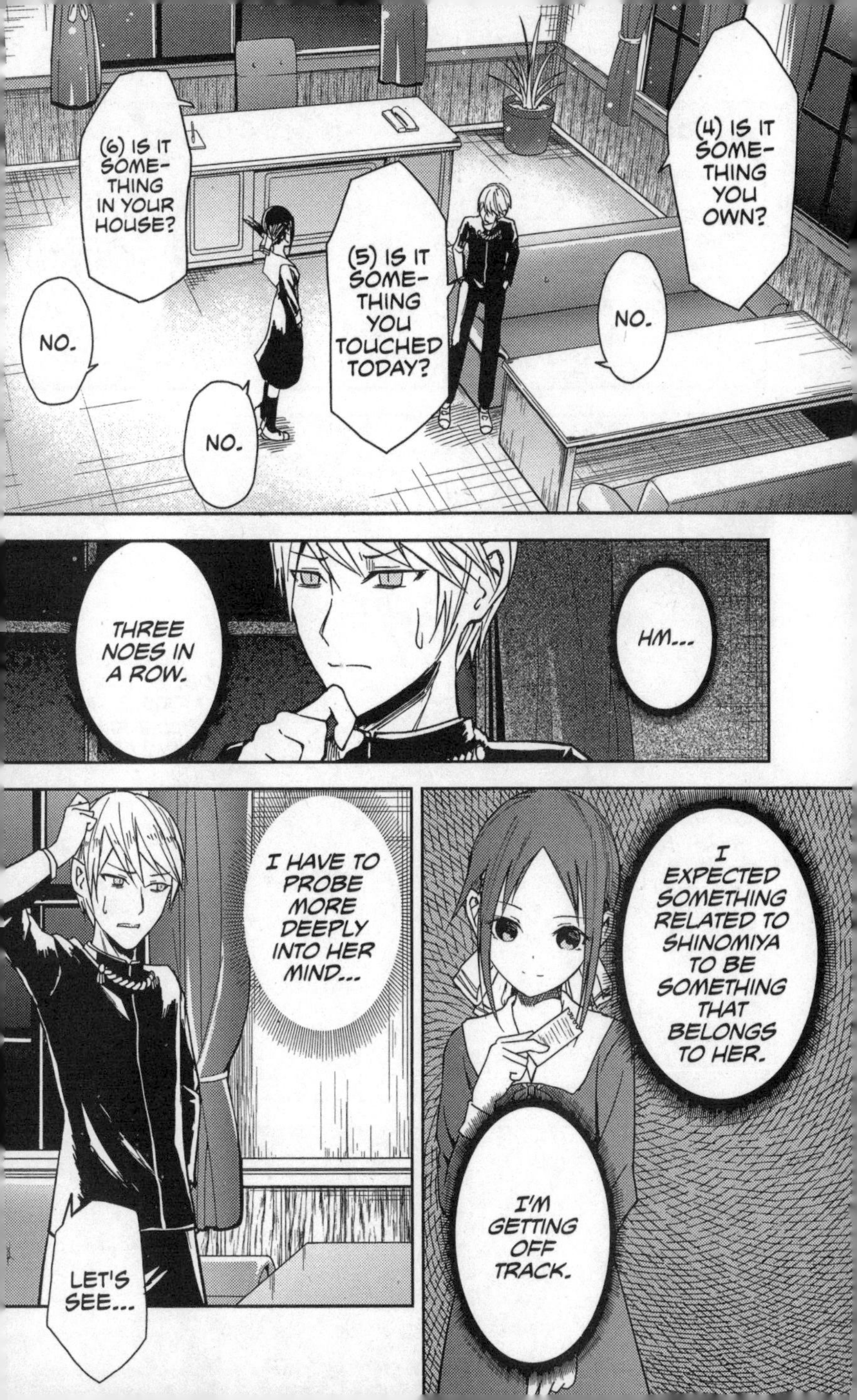
(4) IS IT SOMETHING YOU OWN?
NO.
(5) IS IT SOMETHING YOU TOUCHED TODAY?
NO.
(6) IS IT SOMETHING IN YOUR HOUSE?
NO.
HM...
THREE NOES IN A ROW.
I EXPECTED SOMETHING RELATED TO SHINOMIYA TO BE SOMETHING THAT BELONGS TO HER.
I'M GETTING OFF TRACK.
I HAVE TO PROBE MORE DEEPLY INTO HER MIND...
LET'S SEE...

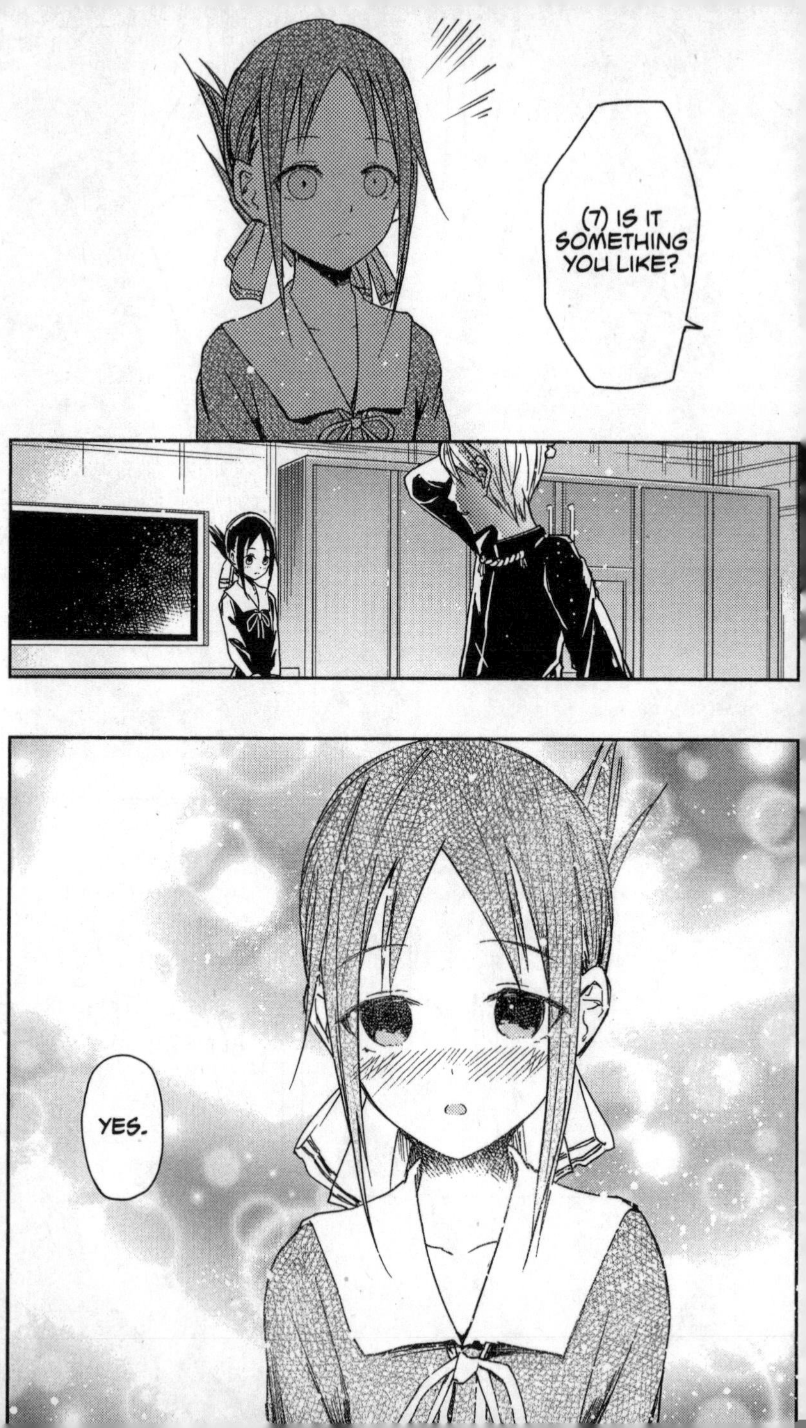
(7) IS IT SOMETHING YOU LIKE?
YES.

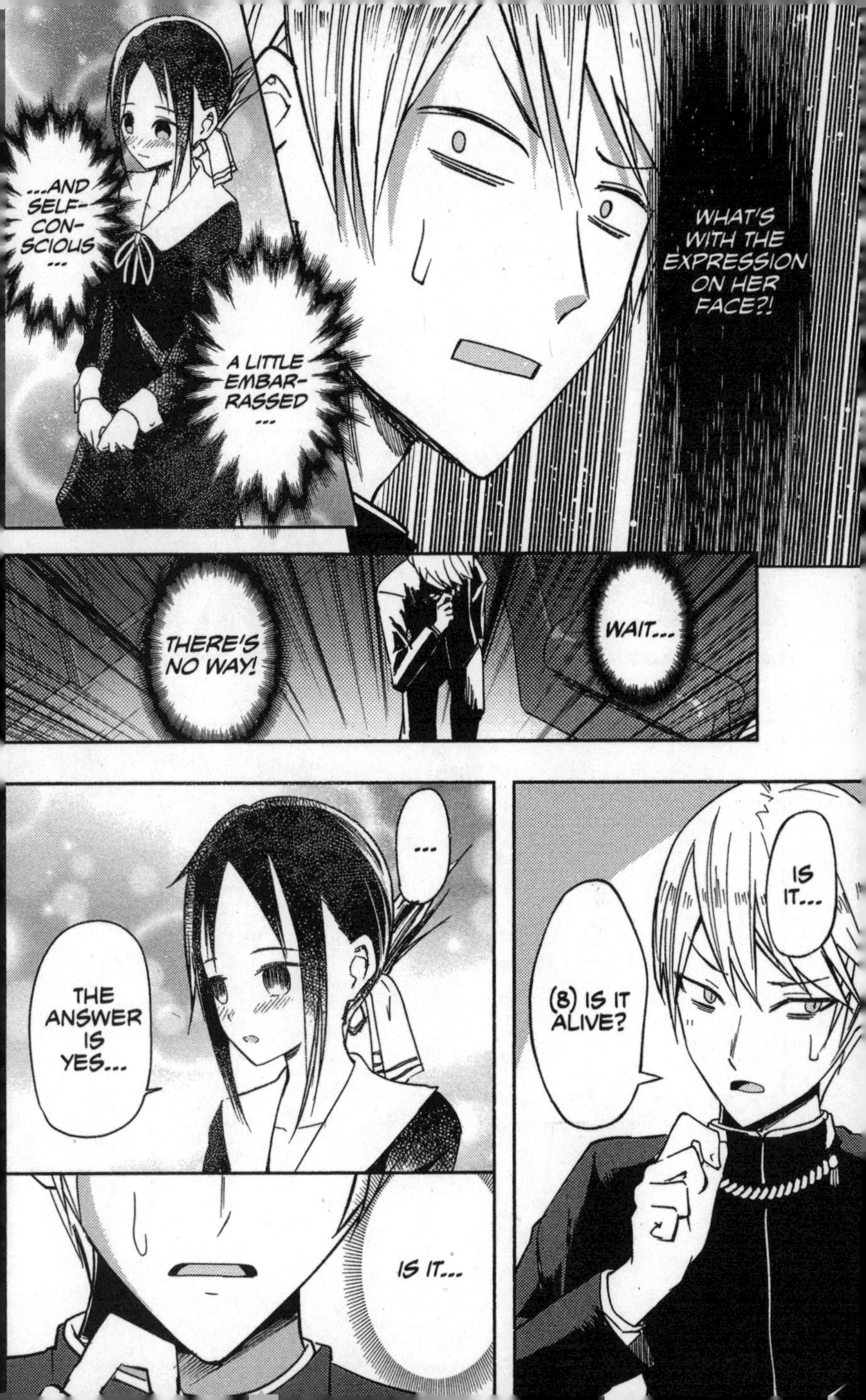
WHAT'S WITH THE EXPRESSION ON HER FACE?!
A LITTLE EMBARRASSED...
...AND SELF-CONSCIOUS...
WAIT...
THERE'S NO WAY!
IS IT...
(8) IS IT ALIVE?
...
THE ANSWER IS YES...
IS IT...

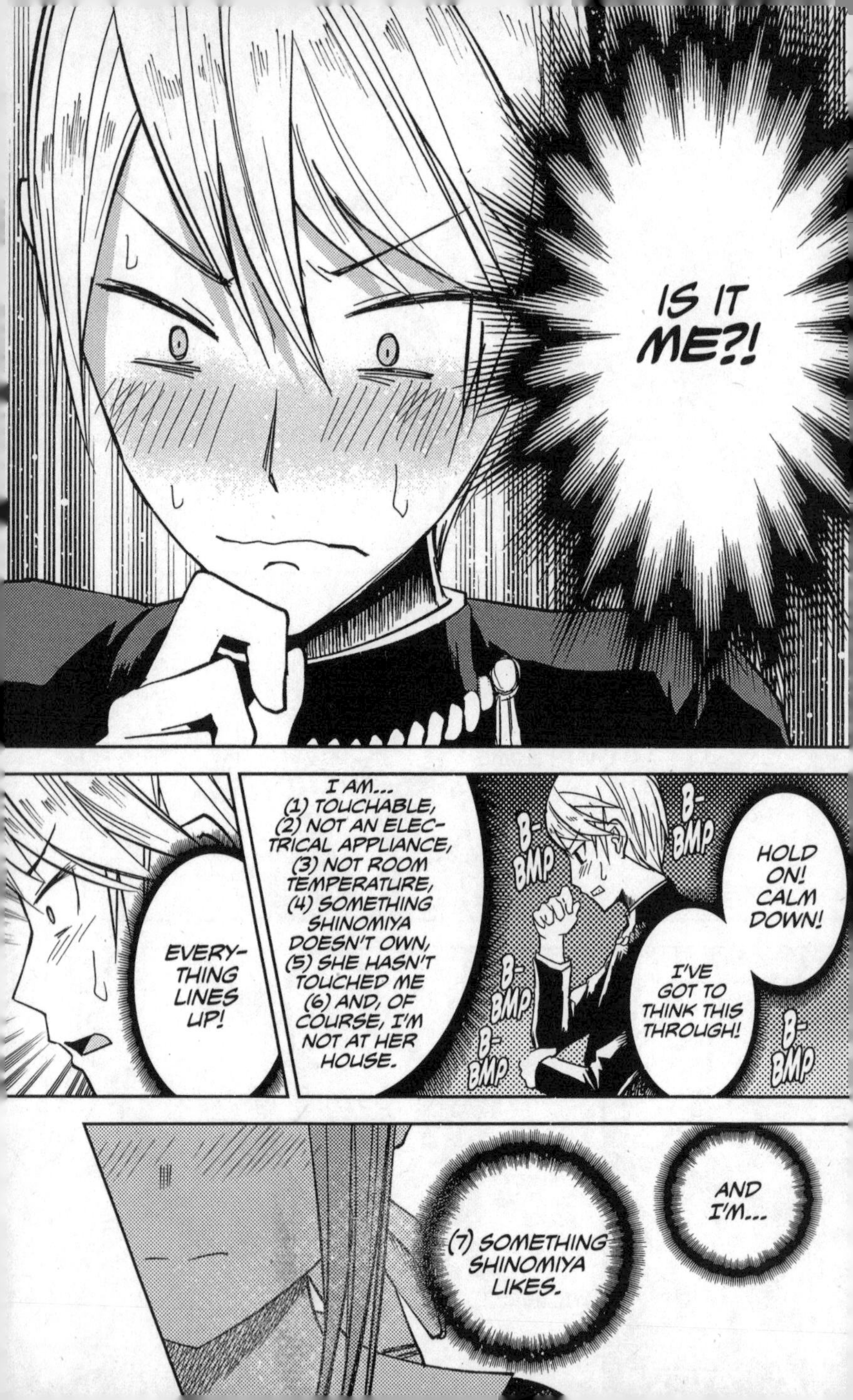
IS IT ME?!
HOLD ON! CALM DOWN!
I'VE GOT TO THINK THIS THROUGH!
B-BMP B-BMP B-BMP B-BMP B-BMP
I AM... (1) TOUCHABLE, (2) NOT AN ELECTRICAL APPLIANCE, (3) NOT ROOM TEMPERATURE, (4) SOMETHING SHINOMIYA DOESN'T OWN, (5) SHE HASN'T TOUCHED ME (6) AND, OF COURSE, I'M NOT AT HER HOUSE.
EVERYTHING LINES UP!
AND I'M...
(7) SOMETHING SHINOMIYA LIKES.

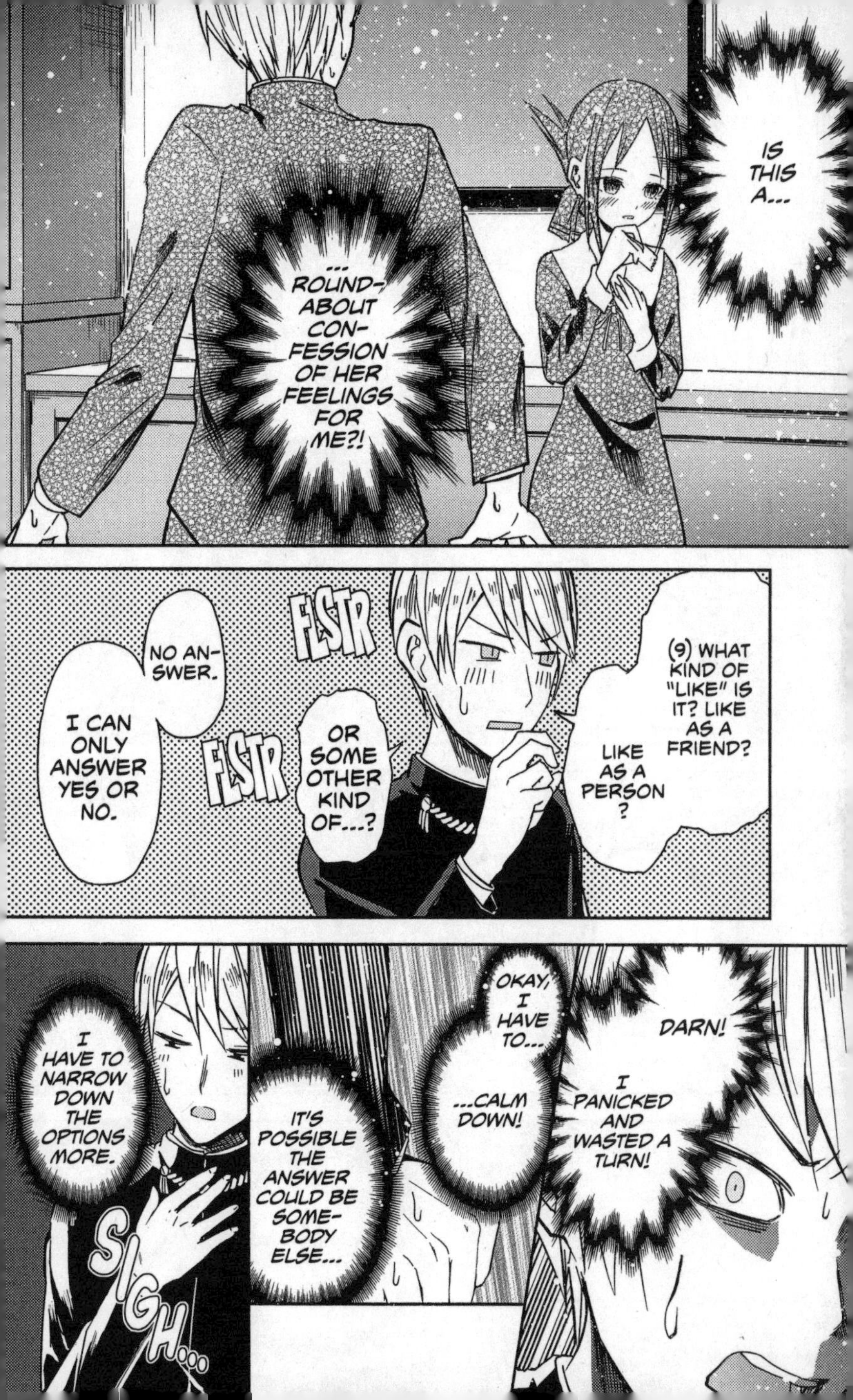
IS THIS A...
...ROUNDABOUT CONFESSION OF HER FEELINGS FOR ME?!
(9) WHAT KIND OF "LIKE" IS IT? LIKE AS A FRIEND?
LIKE AS A PERSON?
OR SOME OTHER KIND OF...?
FLSTR
FLSTR
NO ANSWER.
I CAN ONLY ANSWER YES OR NO.
DARN!
I PANICKED AND WASTED A TURN!
OKAY, I HAVE TO...
...CALM DOWN!
IT'S POSSIBLE THE ANSWER COULD BE SOMEBODY ELSE...
I HAVE TO NARROW DOWN THE OPTIONS MORE.
SIGH...

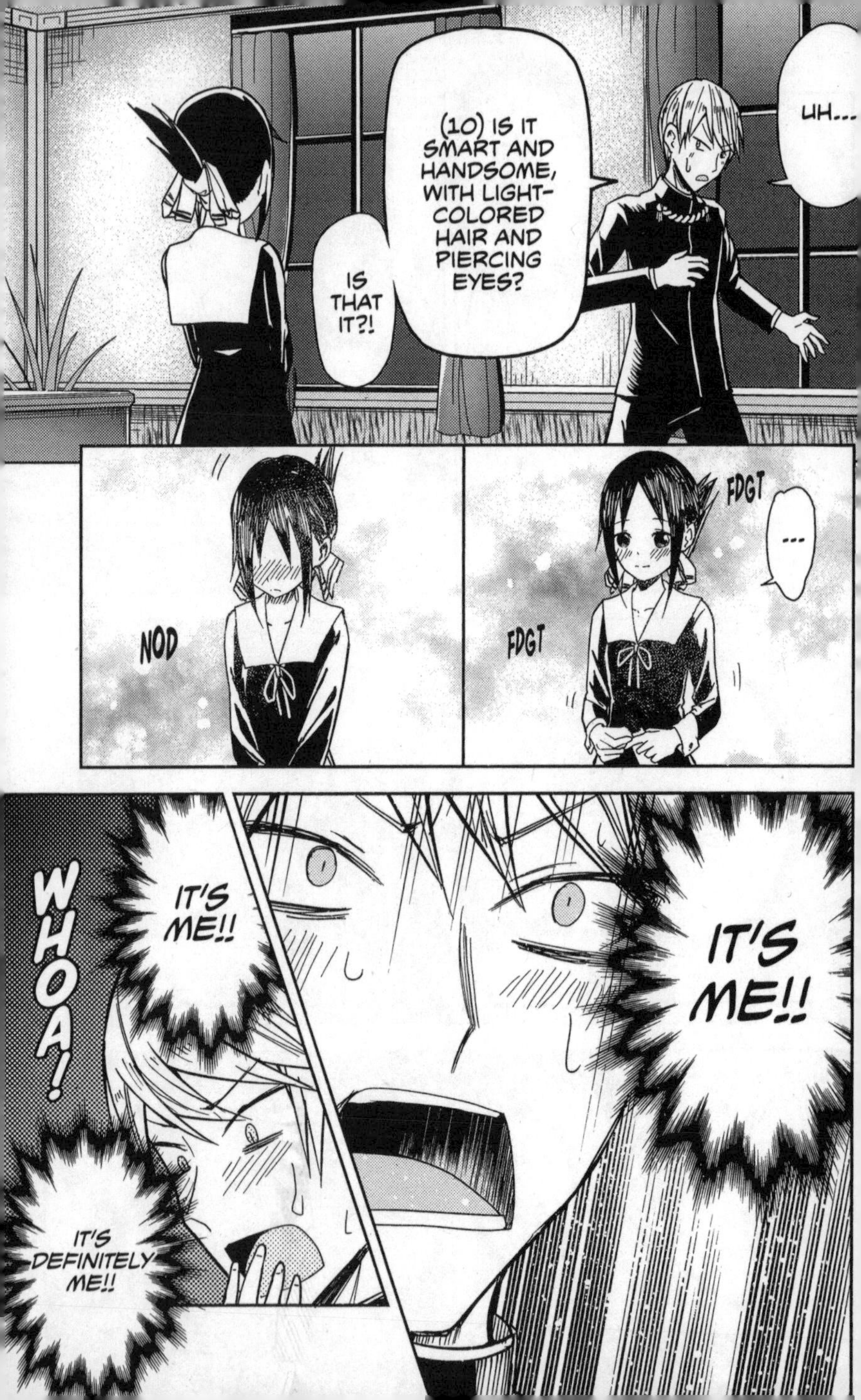
UH...
(10) IS IT SMART AND HANDSOME, WITH LIGHT-COLORED HAIR AND PIERCING EYES?
IS THAT IT?!
FDGT
...
FDGT
NOD
IT'S ME!!
IT'S ME!!
WHOA!
IT'S DEFINITELY ME!!

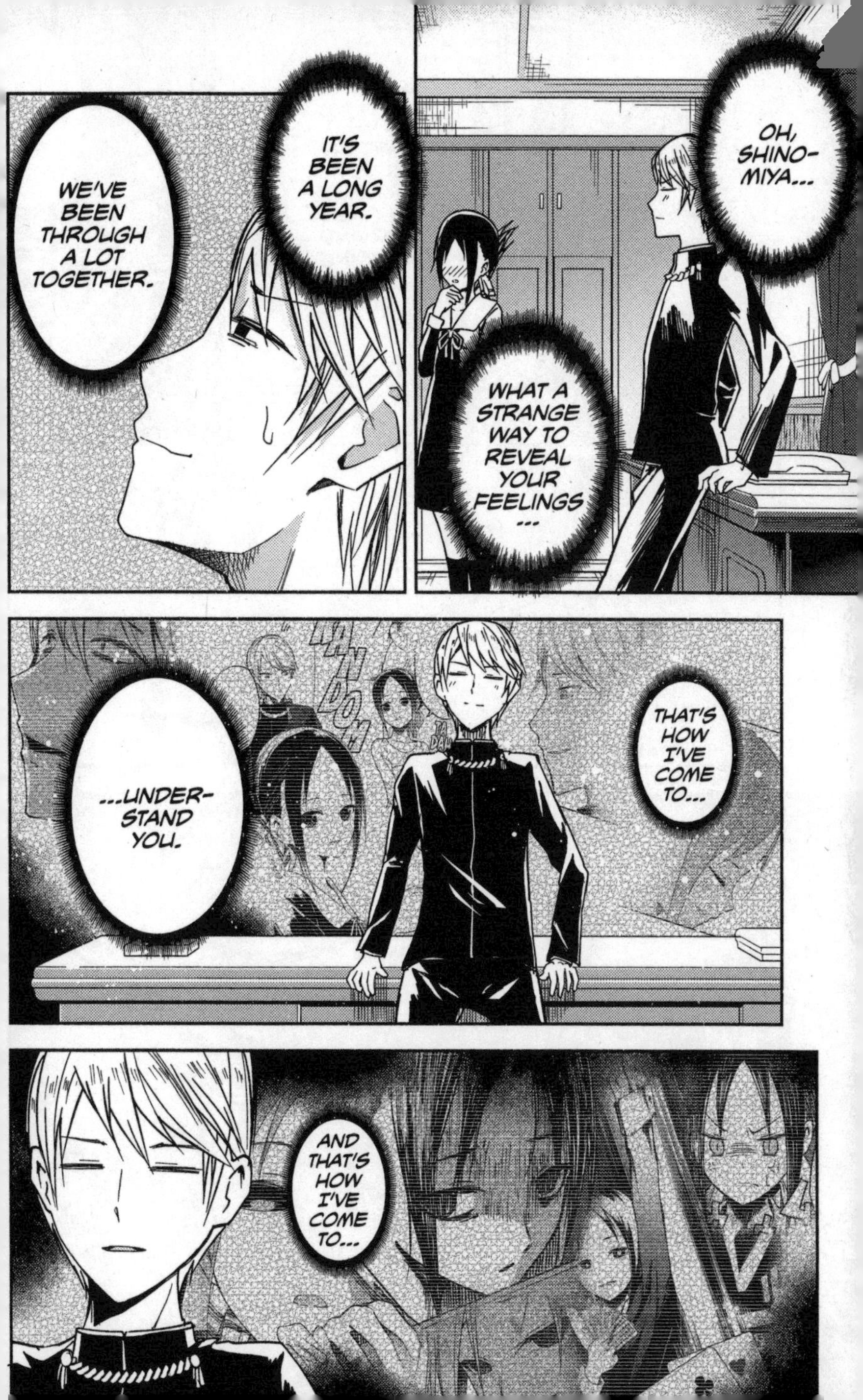
OH, SHINO-MIYA...
WHAT A STRANGE WAY TO REVEAL YOUR FEELINGS...
IT'S BEEN A LONG YEAR.
WE'VE BEEN THROUGH A LOT TOGETHER.
THAT'S HOW I'VE COME TO...
...UNDER-STAND YOU.
AND THAT'S HOW I'VE COME TO...

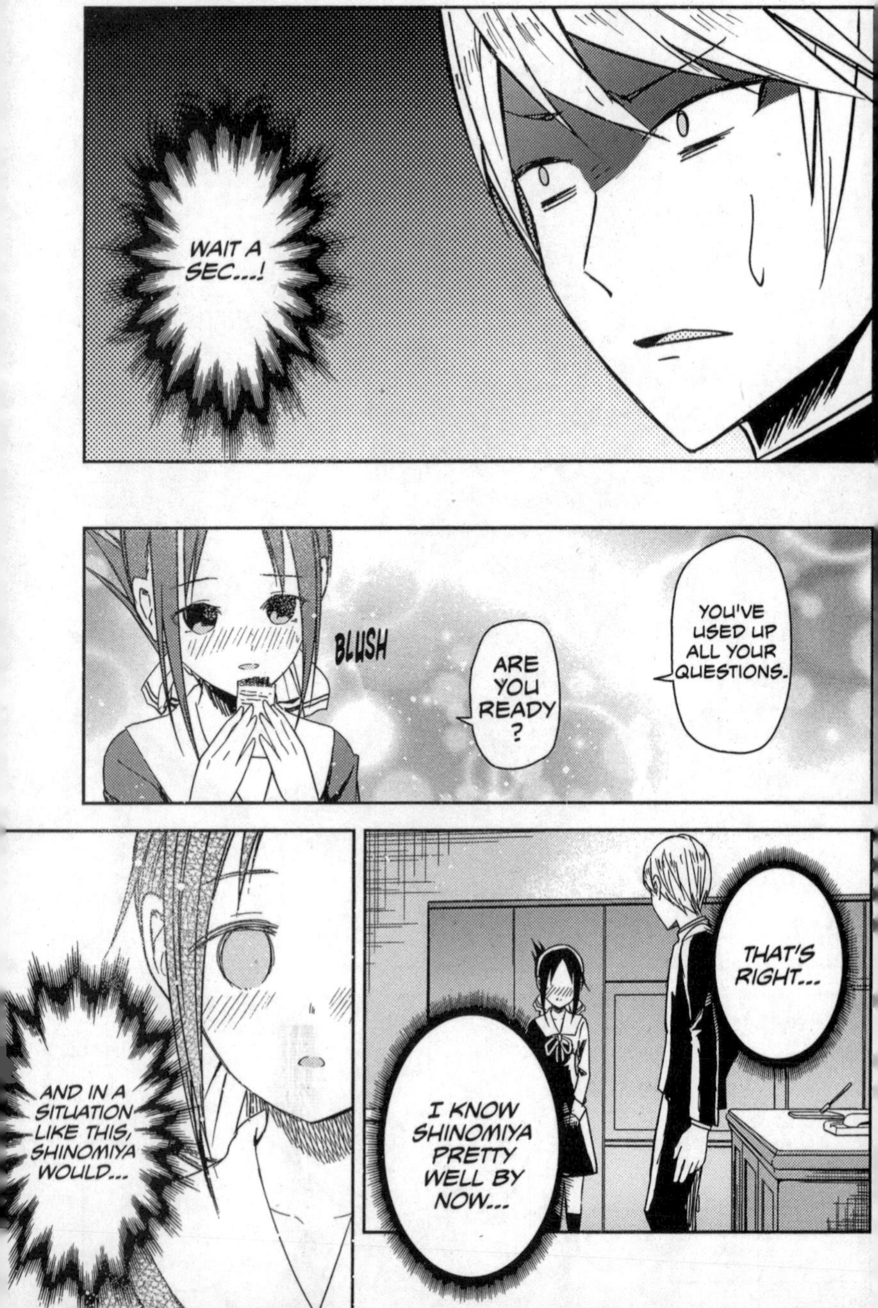
WAIT A SEC...!
YOU'VE USED UP ALL YOUR QUESTIONS.
ARE YOU READY?
BLUSH
THAT'S RIGHT...
I KNOW SHINOMIYA PRETTY WELL BY NOW...
AND IN A SITUATION LIKE THIS, SHINOMIYA WOULD...

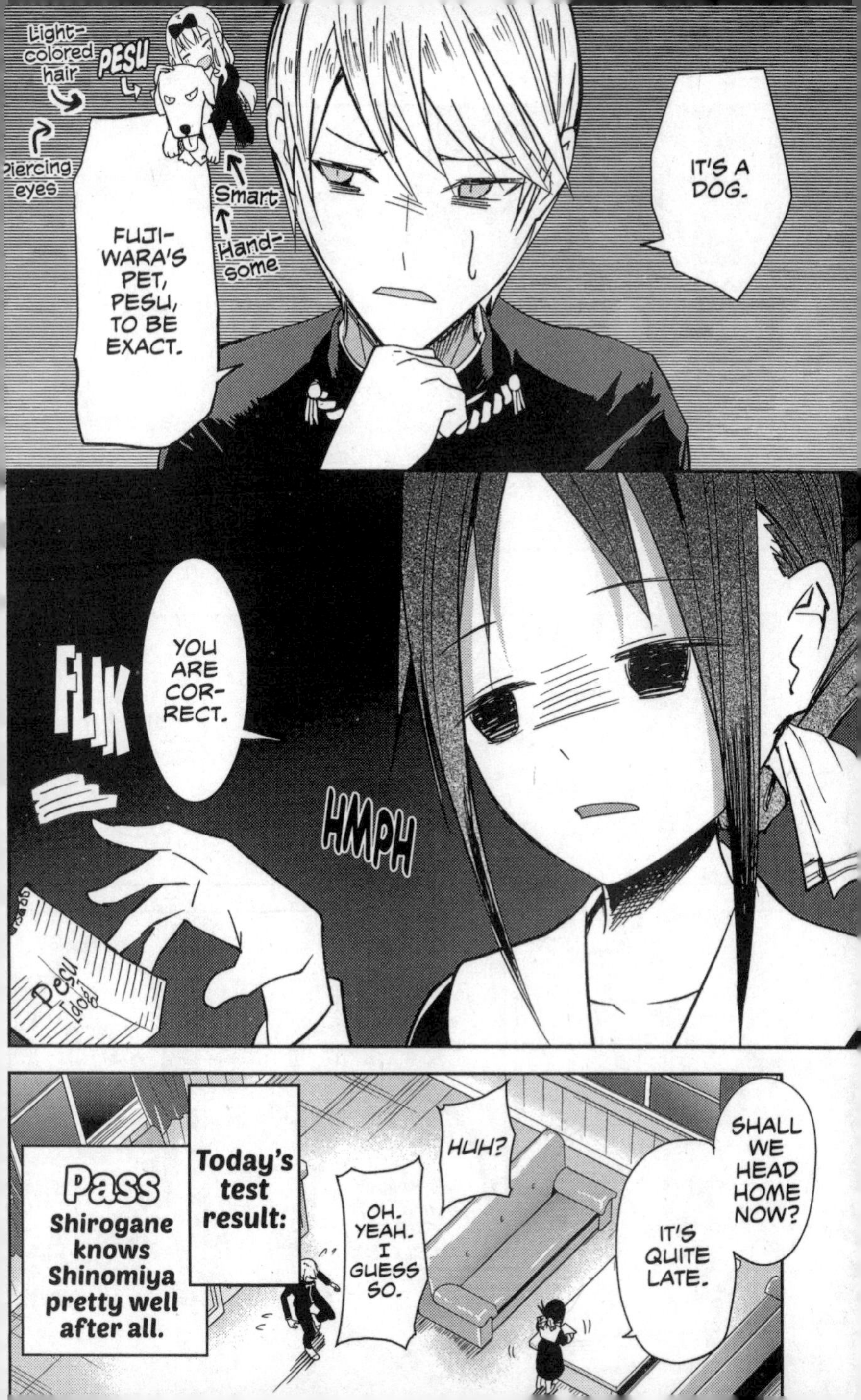

IT'S A DOG.
FUJI-WARA'S PET, PESU, TO BE EXACT.
PESU
Light-colored hair
Piercing eyes
Smart
Hand-some
YOU ARE COR-RECT.
FLIK
HMPH
Pesu [dog]
SHALL WE HEAD HOME NOW?
IT'S QUITE LATE.
HUH?
OH. YEAH. I GUESS SO.
Today's test result:
Pass
Shirogane knows Shinomiya pretty well after all.

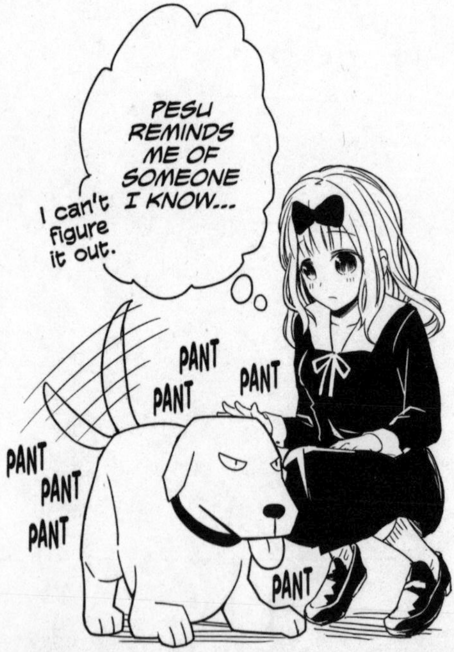
PESU REMINDS ME OF SOMEONE I KNOW...
I can't figure it out.
PANT
PANT
PANT
PANT
PANT
PANT
PANT

KAGUYA-SAMA
LOVE IS WAR

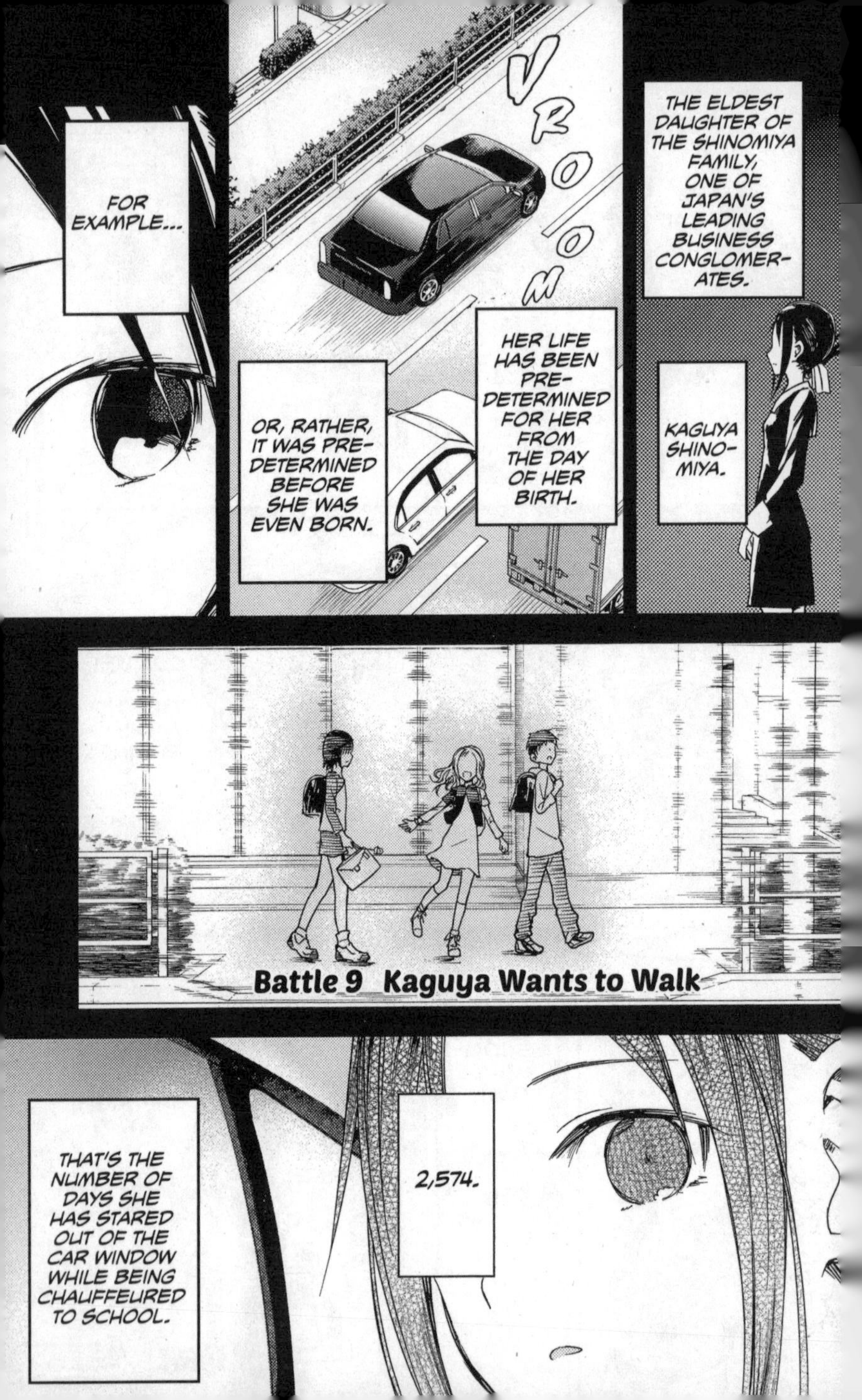
THE ELDEST DAUGHTER OF THE SHINOMIYA FAMILY, ONE OF JAPAN'S LEADING BUSINESS CONGLOMERATES.
KAGUYA SHINOMIYA.
VROOM
HER LIFE HAS BEEN PREDETERMINED FOR HER FROM THE DAY OF HER BIRTH.
OR, RATHER, IT WAS PREDETERMINED BEFORE SHE WAS EVEN BORN.
FOR EXAMPLE...
Battle 9 Kaguya Wants to Walk
2,574.
THAT'S THE NUMBER OF DAYS SHE HAS STARED OUT OF THE CAR WINDOW WHILE BEING CHAUFFEURED TO SCHOOL.

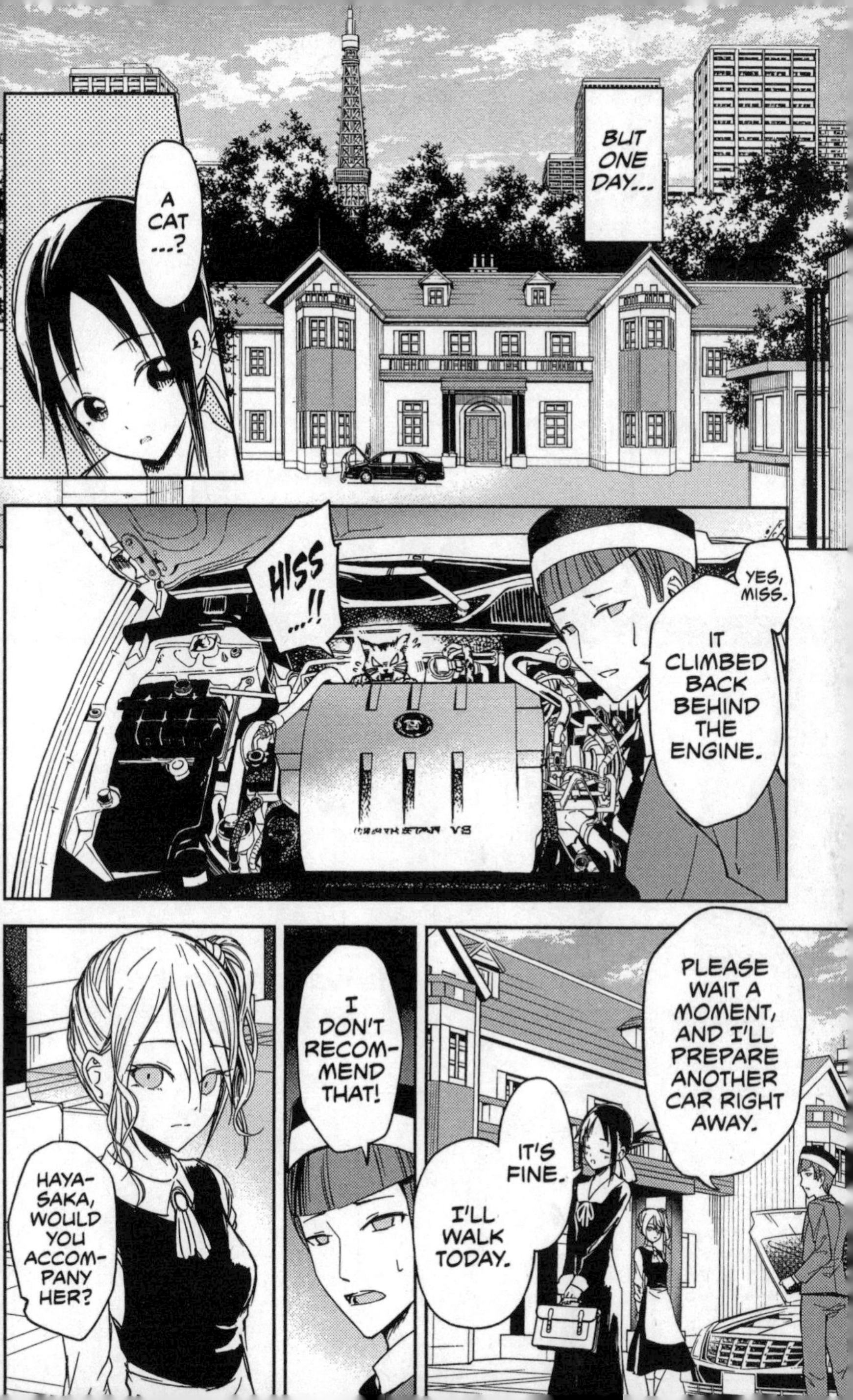
BUT ONE DAY...
A CAT ...?
YES, MISS.
IT CLIMBED BACK BEHIND THE ENGINE.
HISS ...!!
PLEASE WAIT A MOMENT, AND I'LL PREPARE ANOTHER CAR RIGHT AWAY.
IT'S FINE.
I'LL WALK TODAY.
I DON'T RECOMMEND THAT!
HAYASAKA, WOULD YOU ACCOMPANY HER?

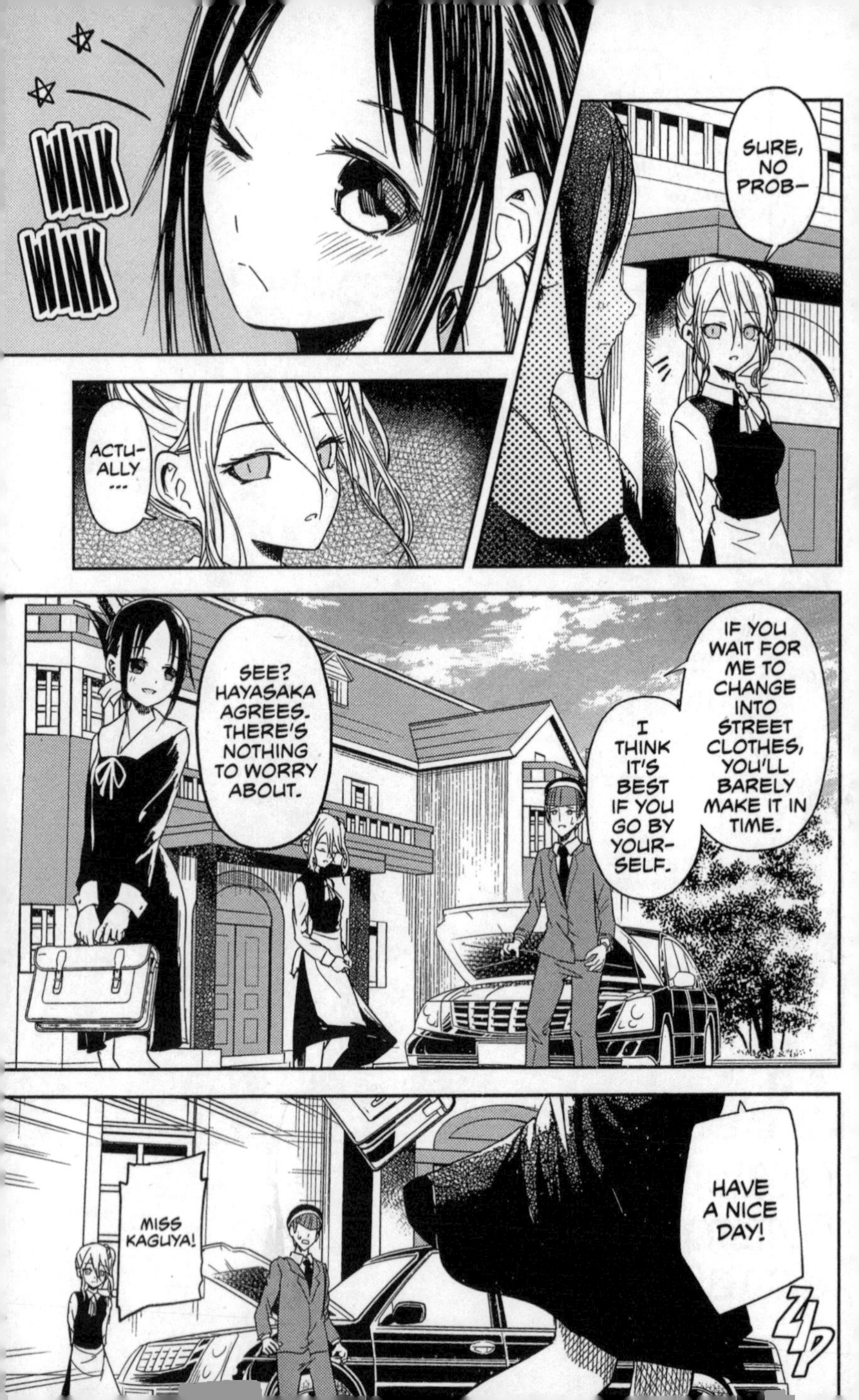
WINK WINK
SURE, NO PROB—
ACTU-ALLY ...
IF YOU WAIT FOR ME TO CHANGE INTO STREET CLOTHES, YOU'LL BARELY MAKE IT IN TIME.
I THINK IT'S BEST IF YOU GO BY YOUR-SELF.
SEE? HAYASAKA AGREES. THERE'S NOTHING TO WORRY ABOUT.
HAVE A NICE DAY!
ZIP
MISS KAGUYA!

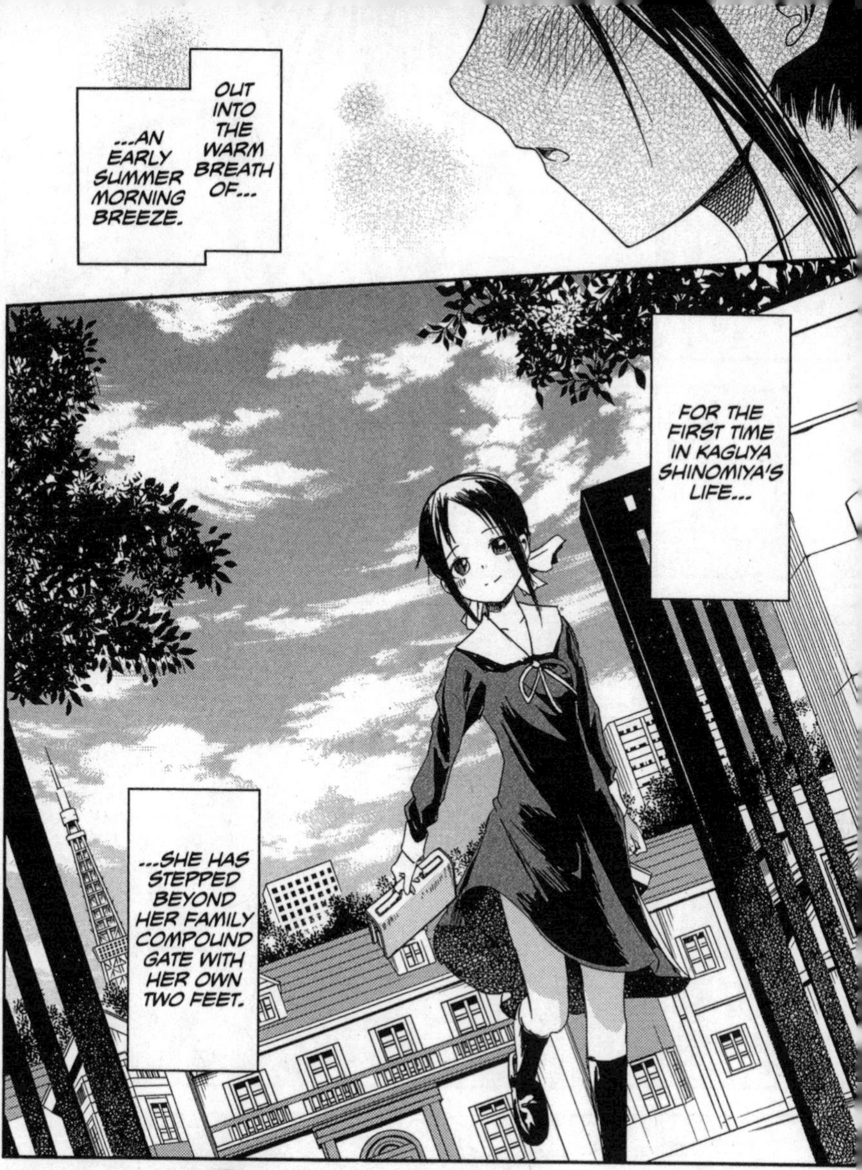
OUT INTO THE WARM BREATH OF...
...AN EARLY SUMMER MORNING BREEZE.
FOR THE FIRST TIME IN KAGUYA SHINOMIYA'S LIFE...
...SHE HAS STEPPED BEYOND HER FAMILY COMPOUND GATE WITH HER OWN TWO FEET.

Battle 9 Kaguya Wants to Walk

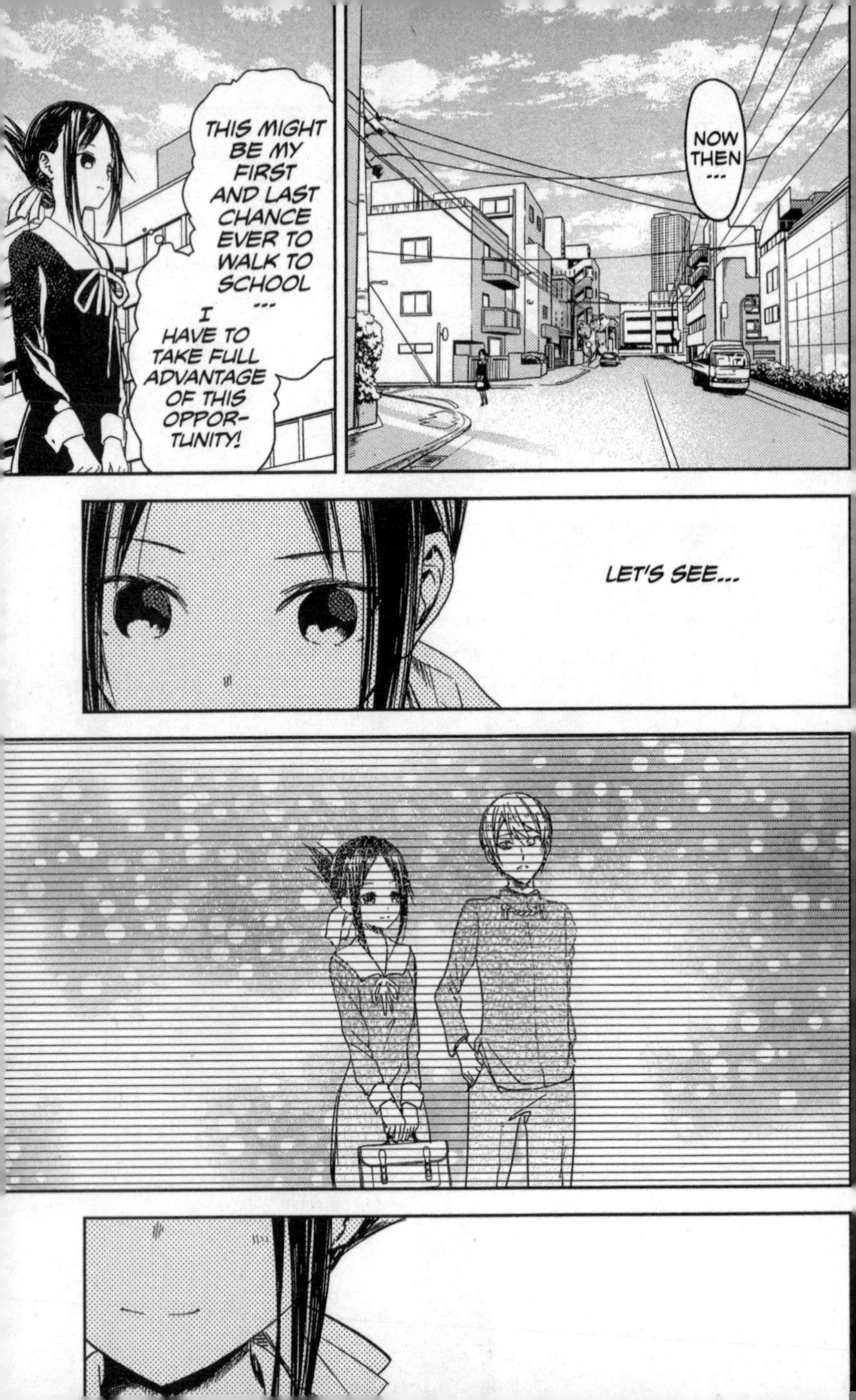
NOW THEN ---
THIS MIGHT BE MY FIRST AND LAST CHANCE EVER TO WALK TO SCHOOL ---
I HAVE TO TAKE FULL ADVANTAGE OF THIS OPPOR-TUNITY!
LET'S SEE...

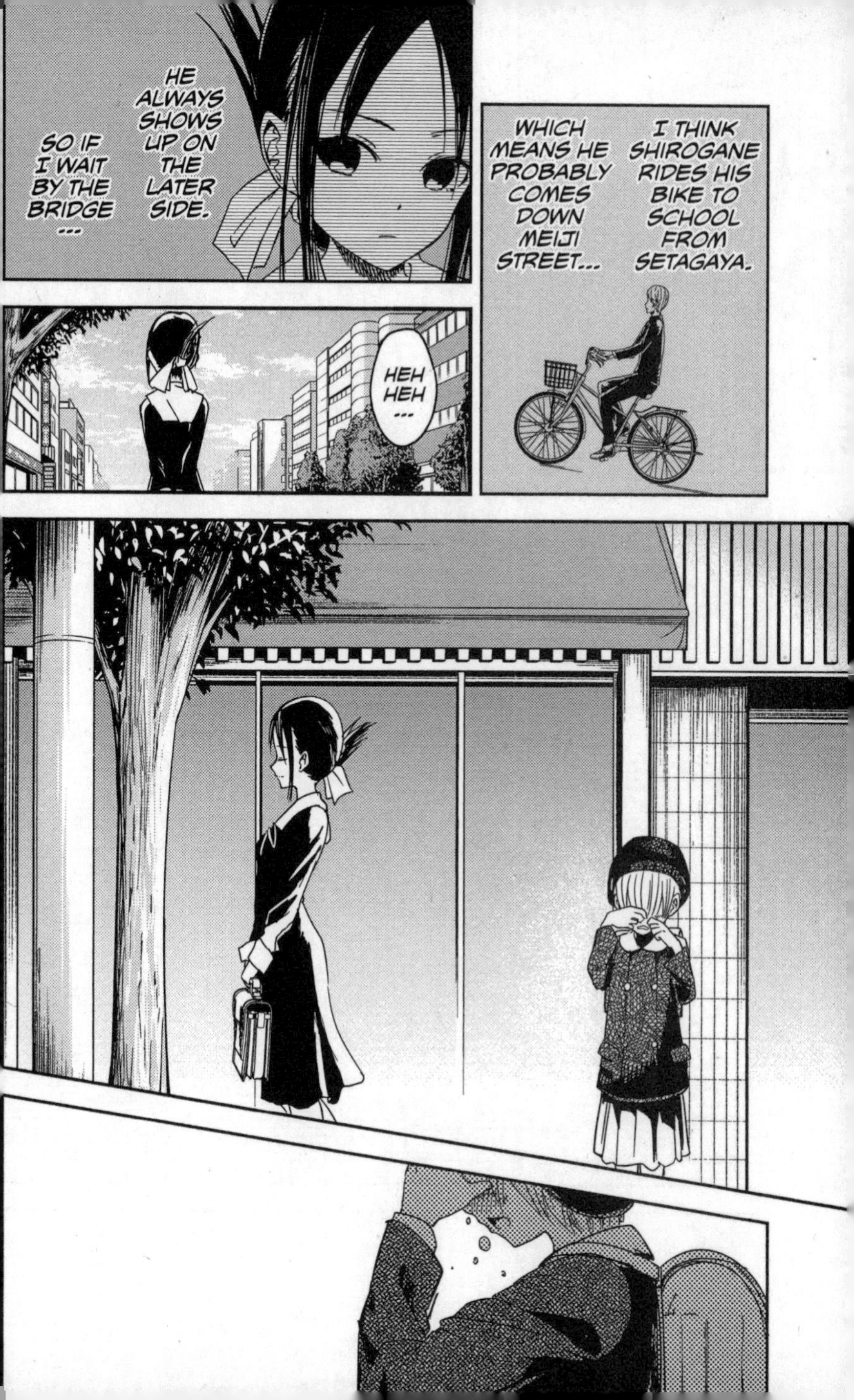
I THINK SHIROGANE RIDES HIS BIKE TO SCHOOL FROM SETAGAYA.
WHICH MEANS HE PROBABLY COMES DOWN MEIJI STREET...
HE ALWAYS SHOWS UP ON THE LATER SIDE.
SO IF I WAIT BY THE BRIDGE...
HEH HEH...

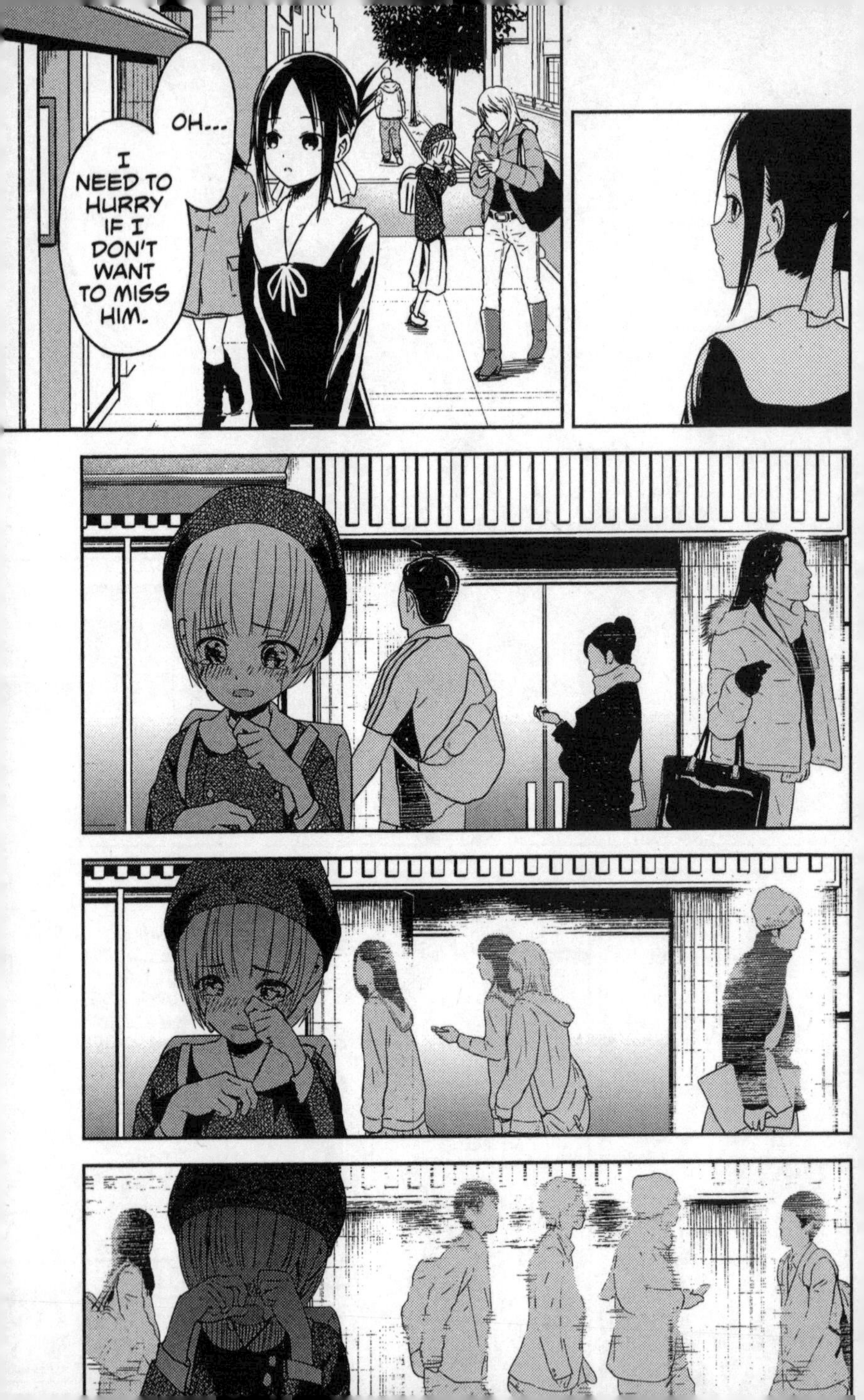
OH...
I NEED TO HURRY IF I DON'T WANT TO MISS HIM.

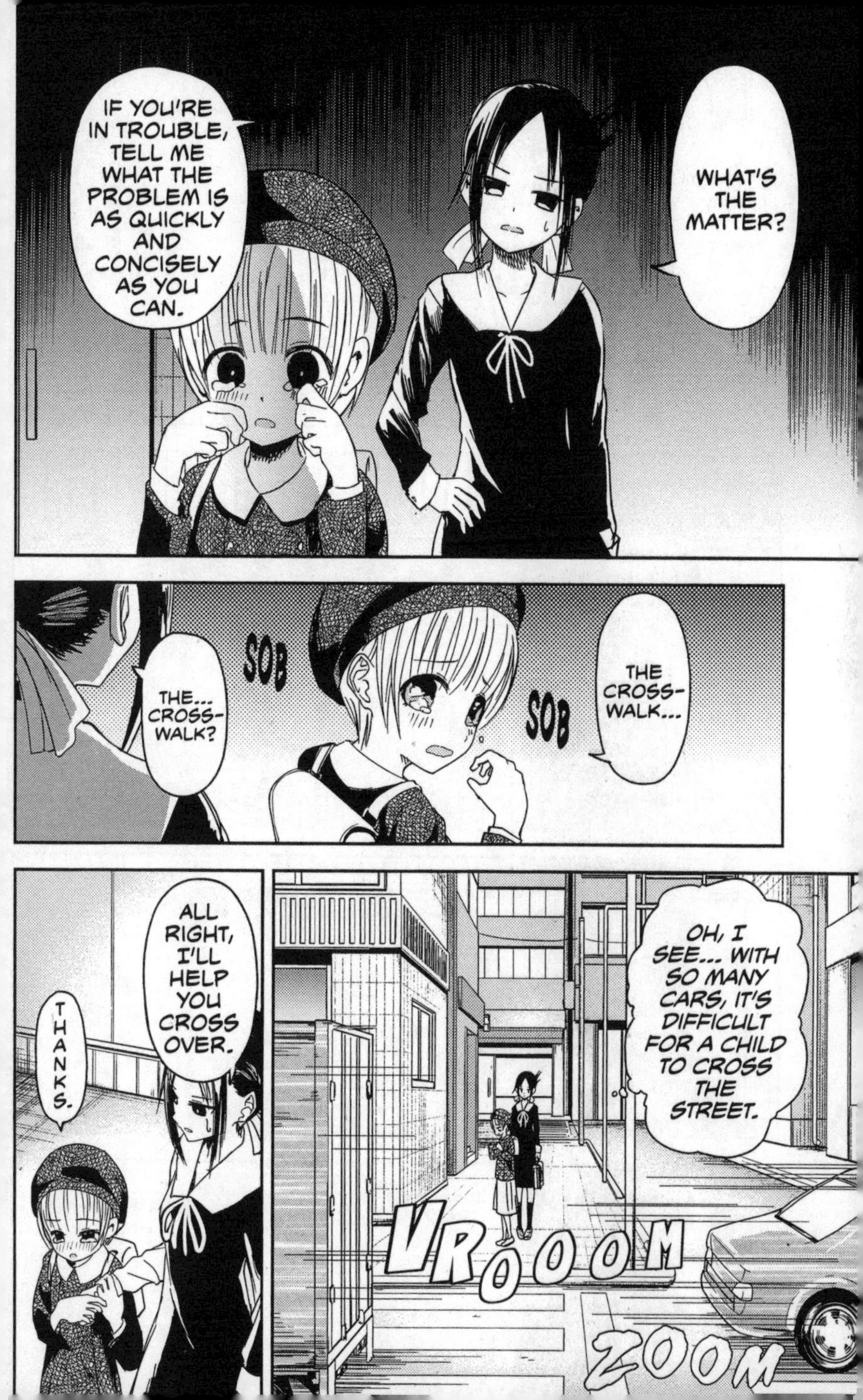
WHAT'S THE MATTER?
IF YOU'RE IN TROUBLE, TELL ME WHAT THE PROBLEM IS AS QUICKLY AND CONCISELY AS YOU CAN.
THE CROSS-WALK...
SOB
SOB
THE... CROSS-WALK?
OH, I SEE... WITH SO MANY CARS, IT'S DIFFICULT FOR A CHILD TO CROSS THE STREET.
VROOOM
ZOOM
ALL RIGHT, I'LL HELP YOU CROSS OVER.
THANKS.

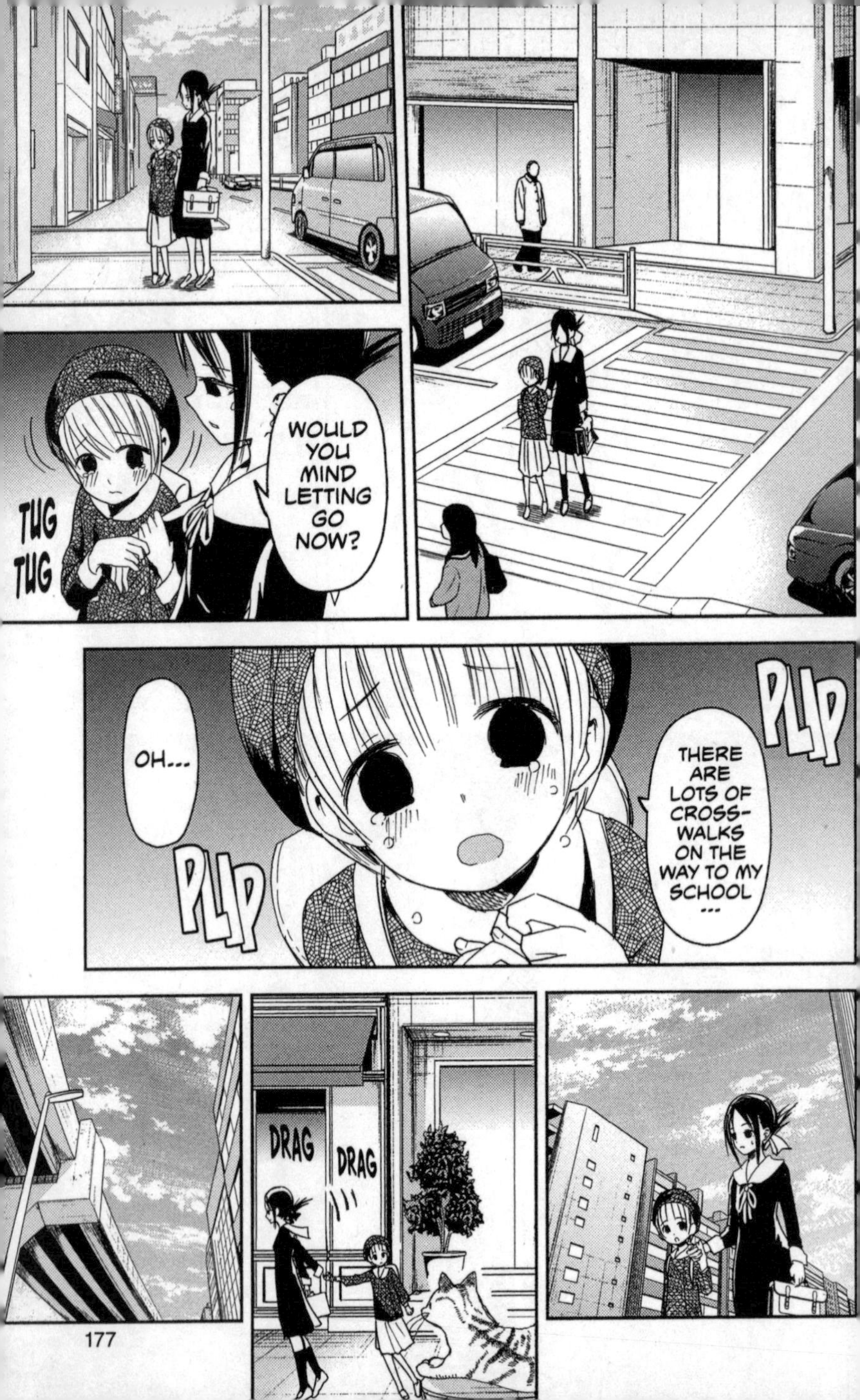
WOULD YOU MIND LETTING GO NOW?
TUG TUG
PLIP
THERE ARE LOTS OF CROSS-WALKS ON THE WAY TO MY SCHOOL ...
OH...
PLIP
DRAG
DRAG

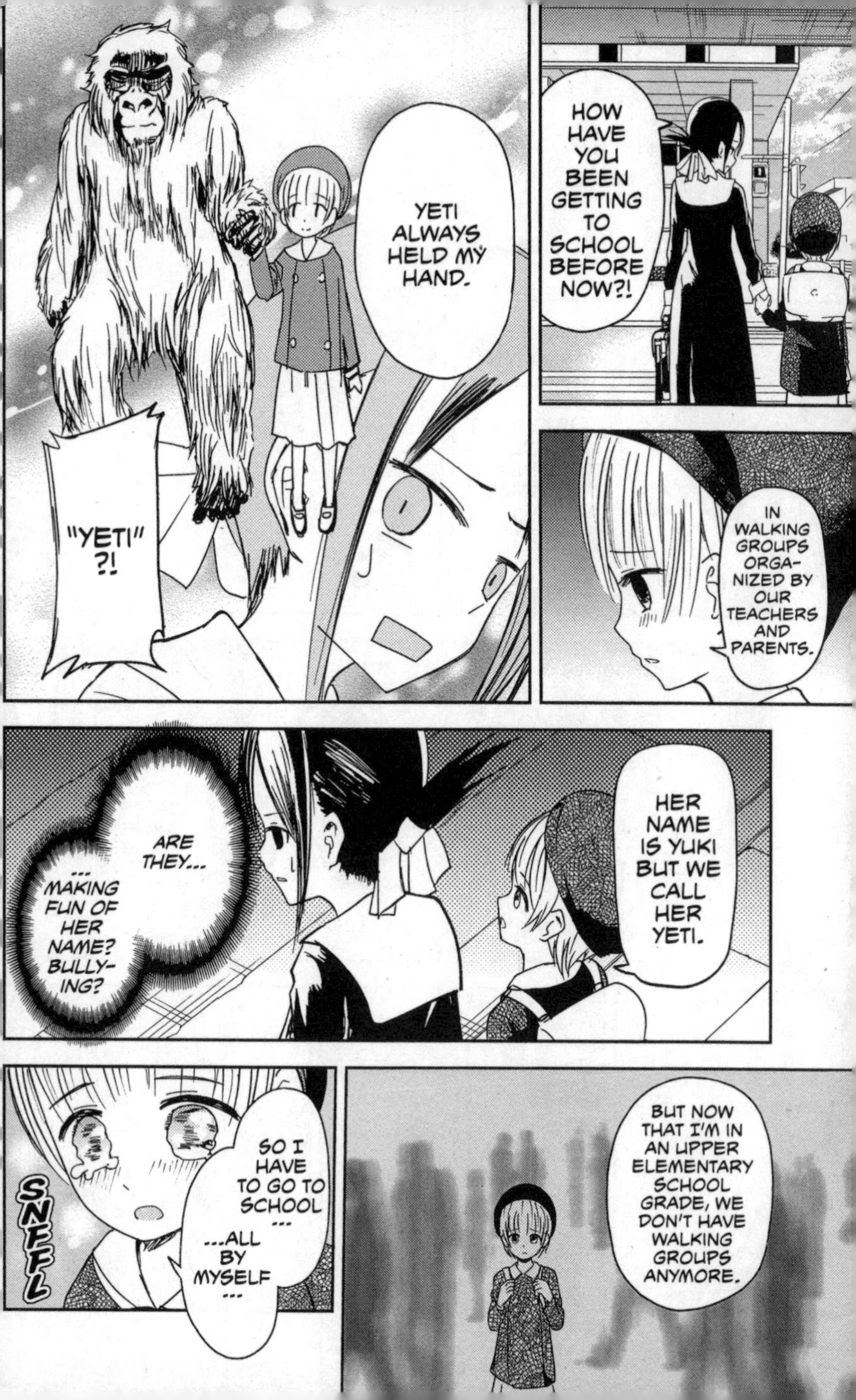
HOW HAVE YOU BEEN GETTING TO SCHOOL BEFORE NOW?!
IN WALKING GROUPS ORGA-NIZED BY OUR TEACHERS AND PARENTS.
YETI ALWAYS HELD MY HAND.
"YETI" ?!
HER NAME IS YUKI BUT WE CALL HER YETI.
ARE THEY...
...MAKING FUN OF HER NAME? BULLY-ING?
BUT NOW THAT I'M IN AN UPPER ELEMENTARY SCHOOL GRADE, WE DON'T HAVE WALKING GROUPS ANYMORE.
SO I HAVE TO GO TO SCHOOL...
...ALL BY MYSELF...
SNFFL

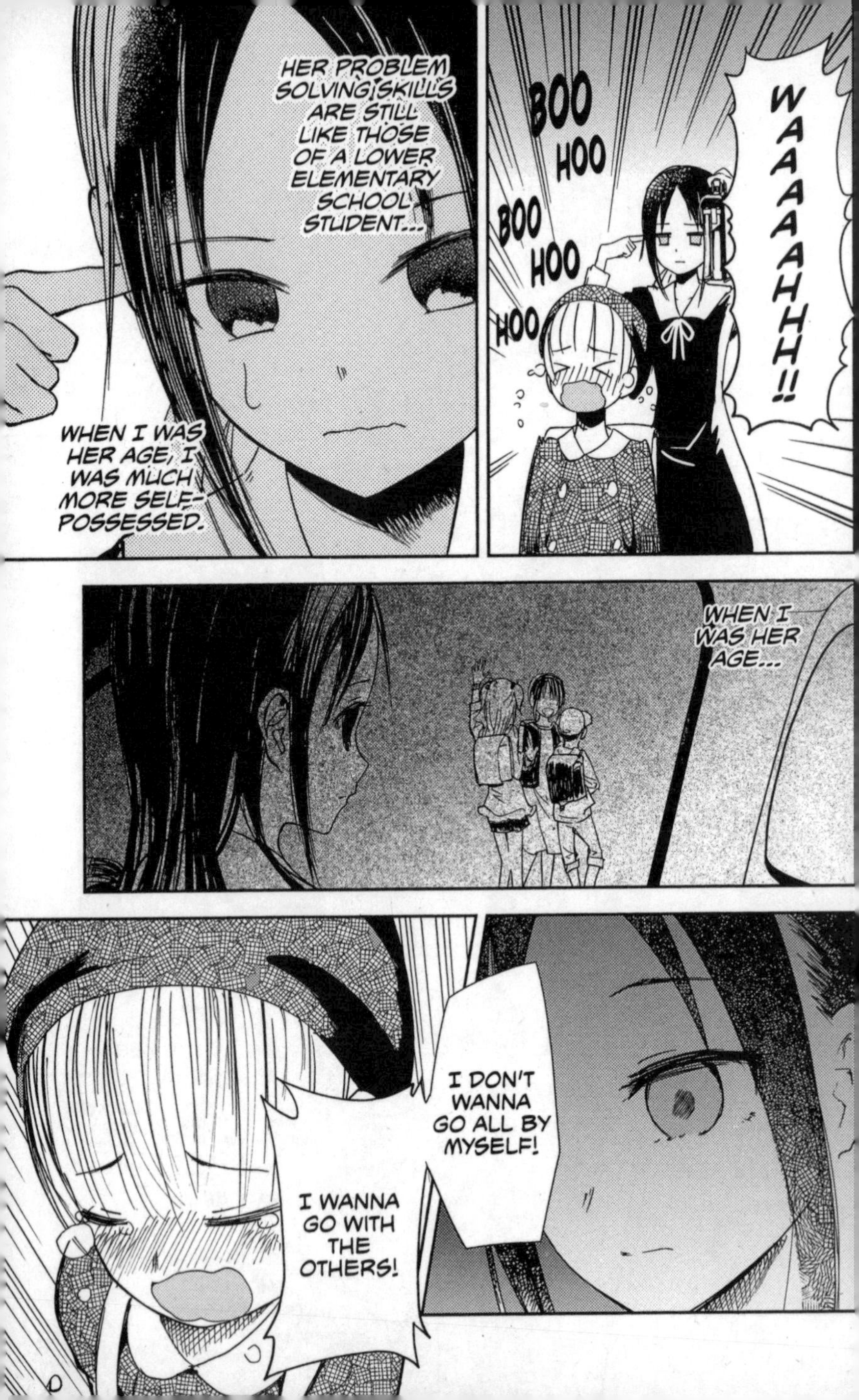
WAAAAAAHHH!!
BOO HOO BOO HOO HOO
HER PROBLEM SOLVING SKILLS ARE STILL LIKE THOSE OF A LOWER ELEMENTARY SCHOOL STUDENT...
WHEN I WAS HER AGE, I WAS MUCH MORE SELF-POSSESSED.
WHEN I WAS HER AGE...
I DON'T WANNA GO ALL BY MYSELF!
I WANNA GO WITH THE OTHERS!

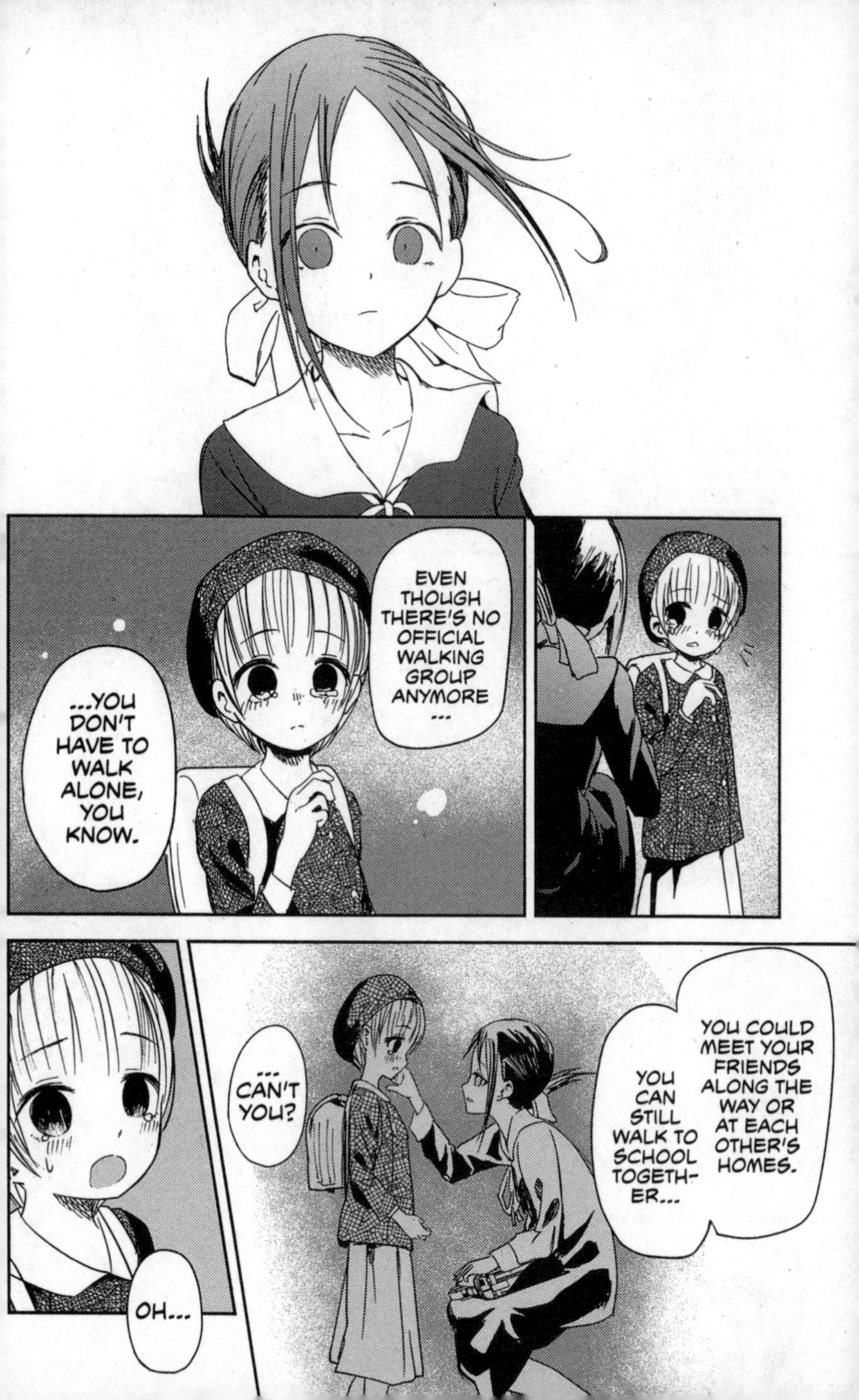
EVEN THOUGH THERE'S NO OFFICIAL WALKING GROUP ANYMORE...
...YOU DON'T HAVE TO WALK ALONE, YOU KNOW.
YOU COULD MEET YOUR FRIENDS ALONG THE WAY OR AT EACH OTHER'S HOMES.
YOU CAN STILL WALK TO SCHOOL TOGETH-ER...
...CAN'T YOU?
OH...

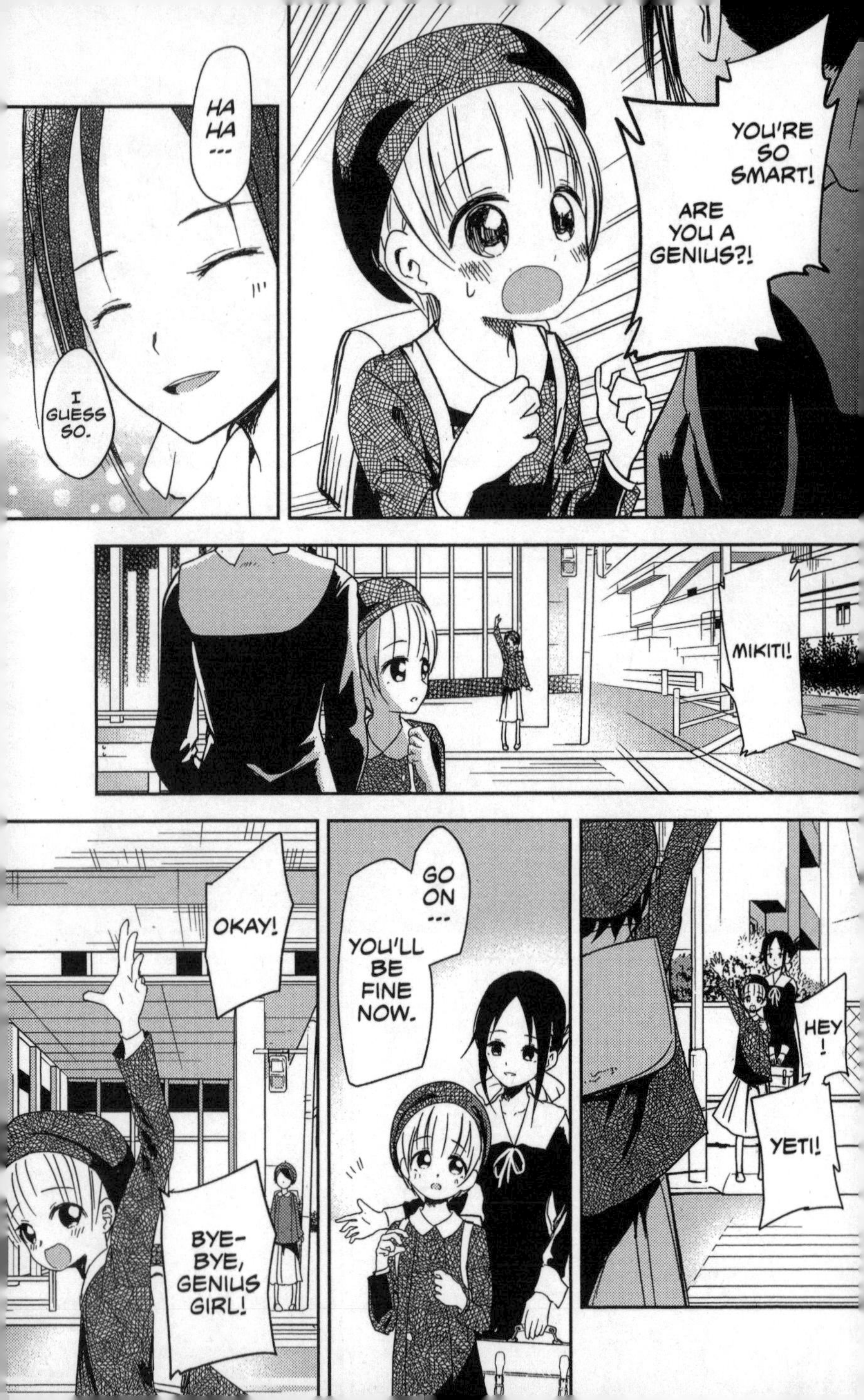
YOU'RE SO SMART!
ARE YOU A GENIUS?!
HA HA ...
I GUESS SO.
MIKITI!
HEY!
YETI!
GO ON ... YOU'LL BE FINE NOW.
OKAY!
BYE-BYE, GENIUS GIRL!

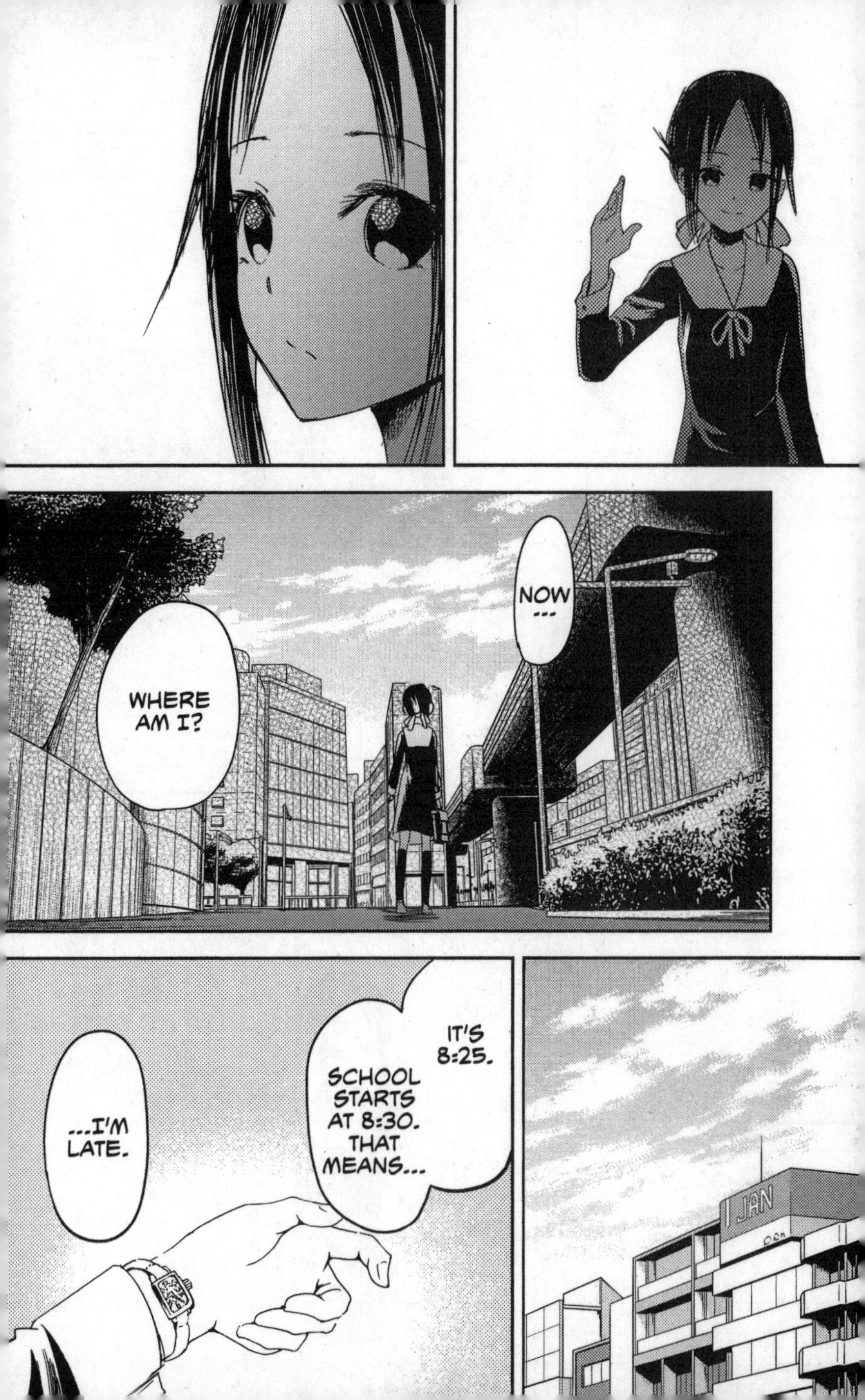
NOW...
WHERE AM I?
IT'S 8:25.
SCHOOL STARTS AT 8:30. THAT MEANS...
...I'M LATE.

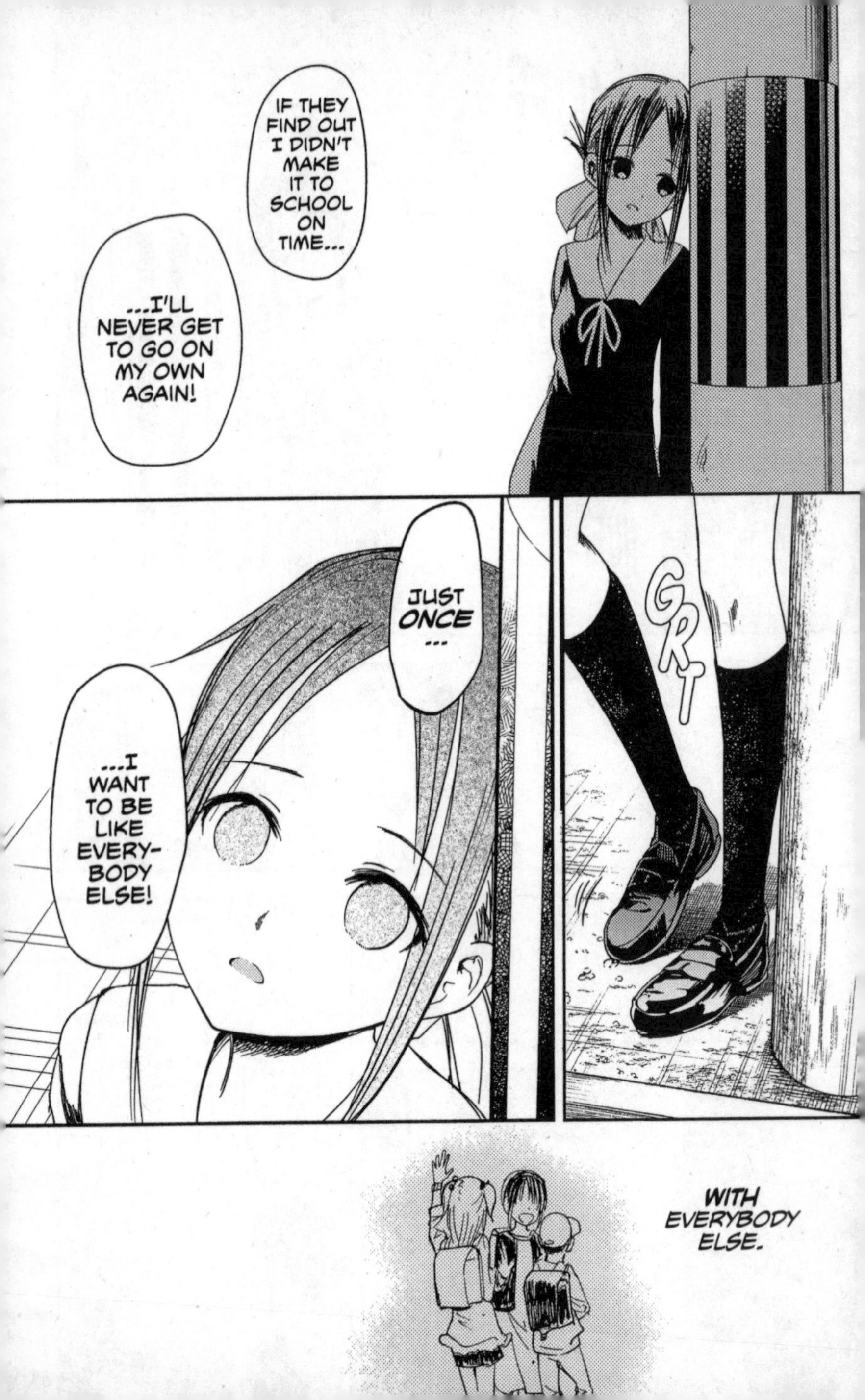
IF THEY FIND OUT I DIDN'T MAKE IT TO SCHOOL ON TIME...
...I'LL NEVER GET TO GO ON MY OWN AGAIN!
GRT
JUST ONCE...
...I WANT TO BE LIKE EVERY-BODY ELSE!
WITH EVERYBODY ELSE.

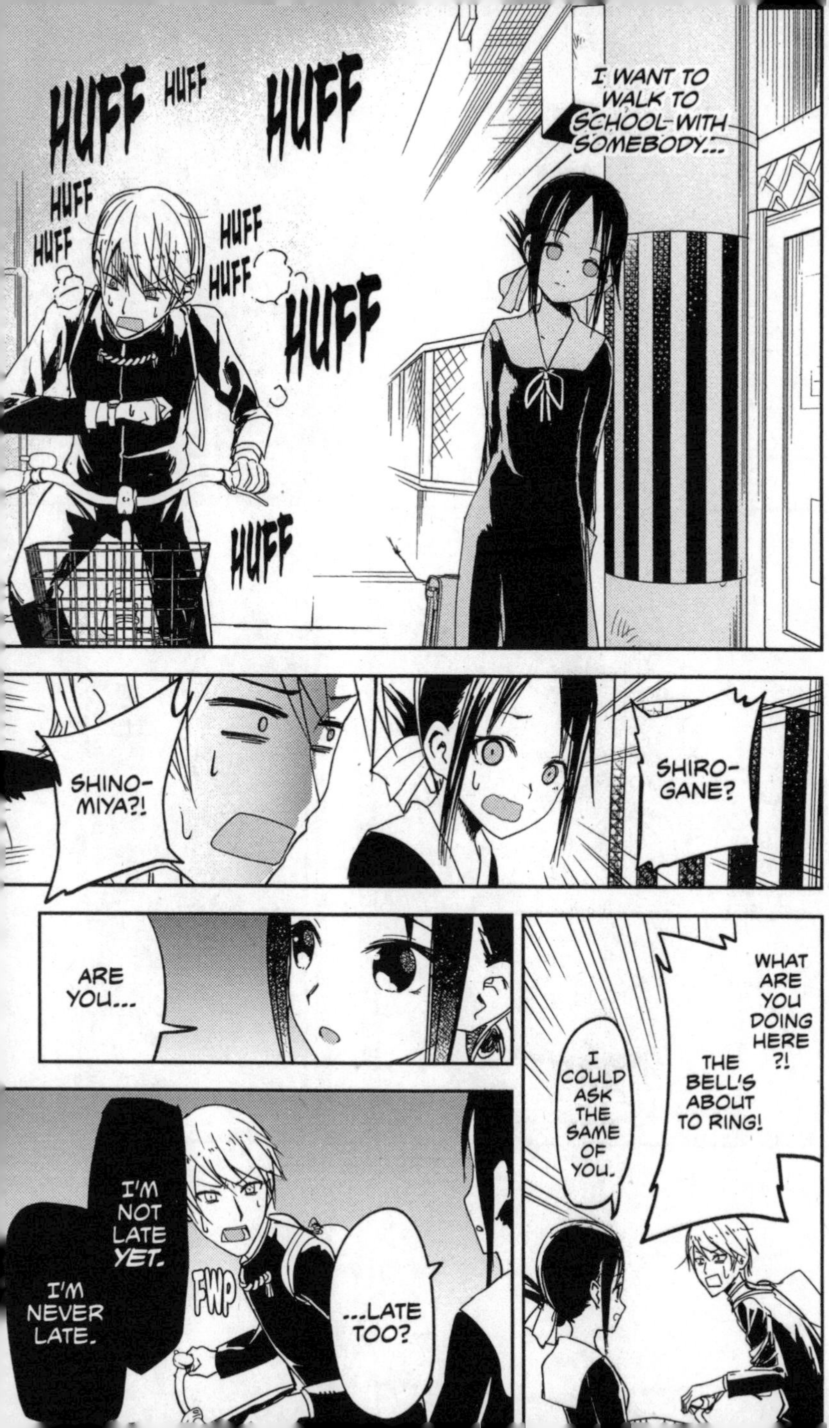
I WANT TO WALK TO SCHOOL WITH SOMEBODY...
HUFF
HUFF
HUFF
HUFF
HUFF
HUFF
HUFF
HUFF
HUFF
SHIRO-GANE?
SHINO-MIYA?!
WHAT ARE YOU DOING HERE?!
THE BELL'S ABOUT TO RING!
I COULD ASK THE SAME OF YOU.
ARE YOU...
...LATE TOO?
FWP
I'M NOT LATE *YET*.
I'M NEVER LATE.

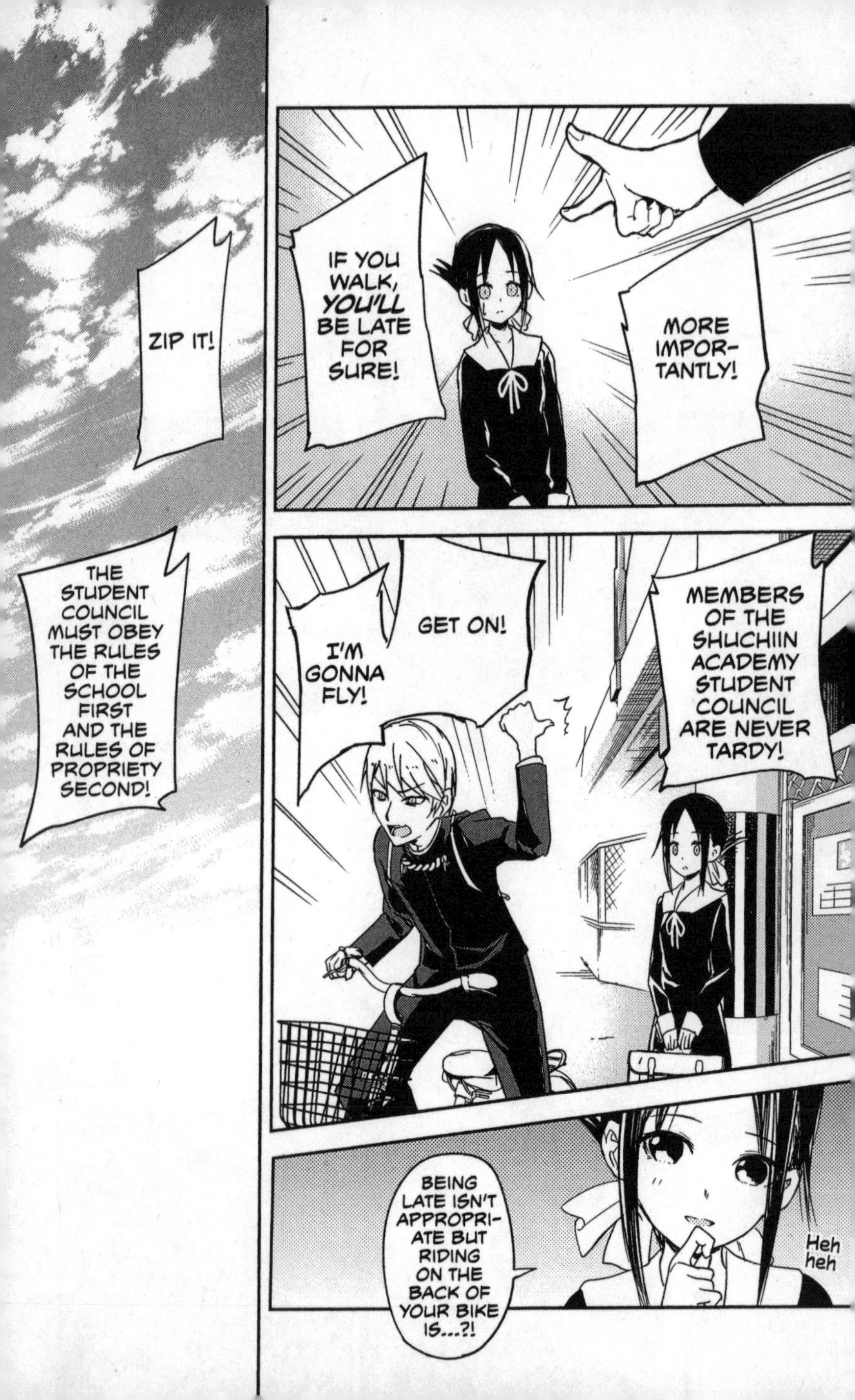
MORE IMPORTANTLY!
IF YOU WALK, *YOU'LL* BE LATE FOR SURE!
MEMBERS OF THE SHUCHIIN ACADEMY STUDENT COUNCIL ARE NEVER TARDY!
GET ON!
I'M GONNA FLY!
Heh heh
BEING LATE ISN'T APPROPRI-ATE BUT RIDING ON THE BACK OF YOUR BIKE IS...?!
ZIP IT!
THE STUDENT COUNCIL MUST OBEY THE RULES OF THE SCHOOL FIRST AND THE RULES OF PROPRIETY SECOND!

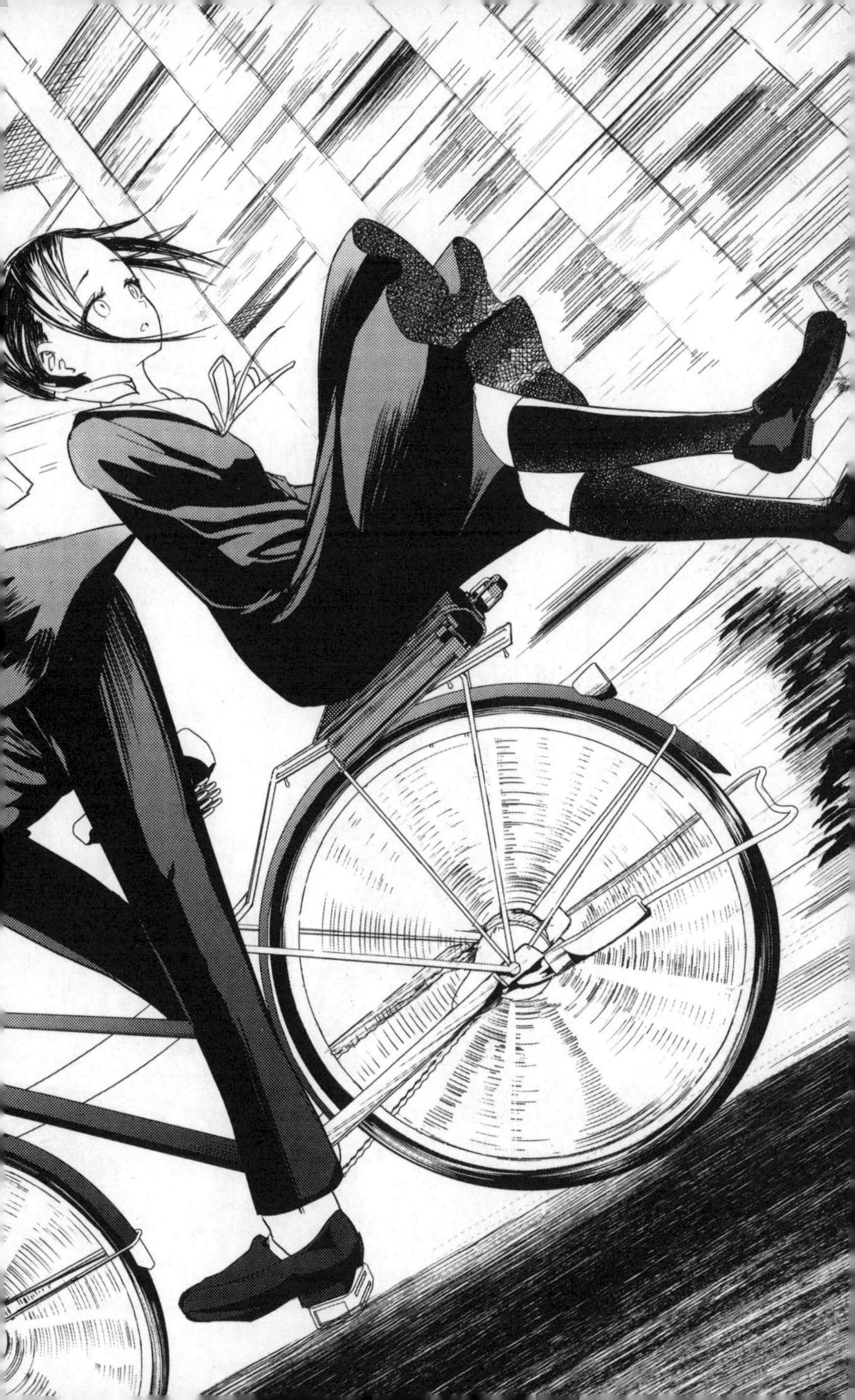

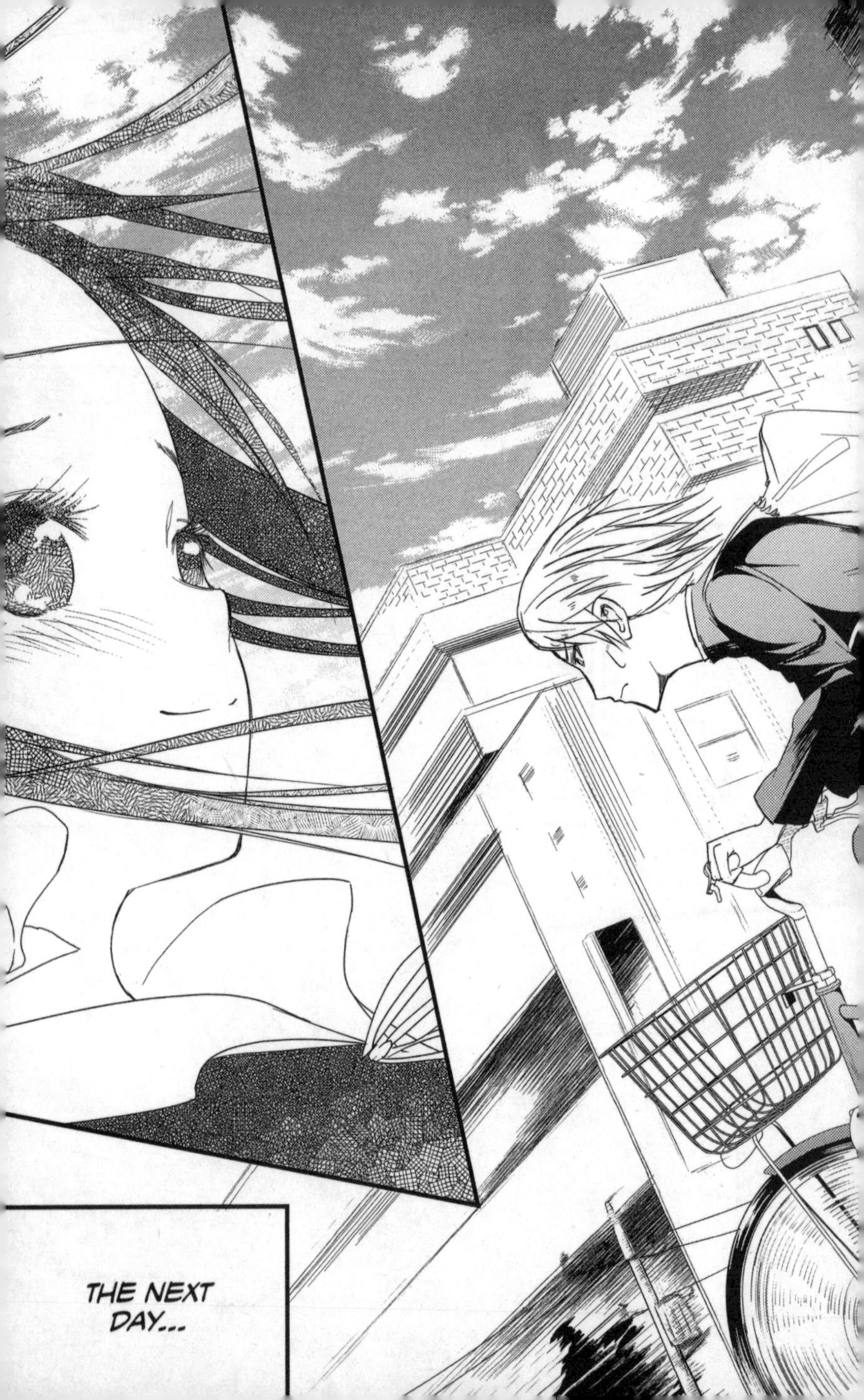
THE NEXT DAY...

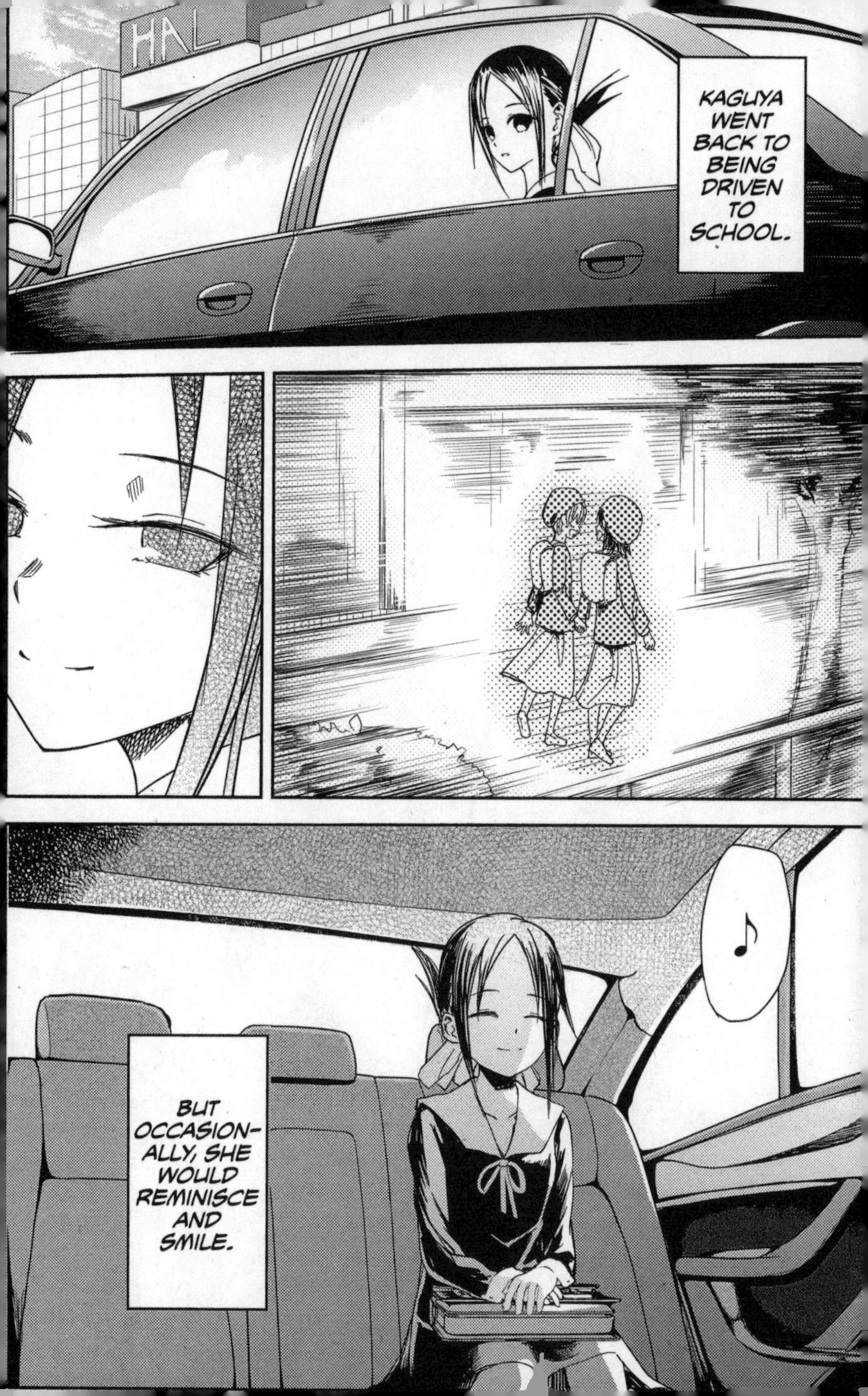
HAL
KAGUYA WENT BACK TO BEING DRIVEN TO SCHOOL.
♪
BUT OCCASION-ALLY, SHE WOULD REMINISCE AND SMILE.

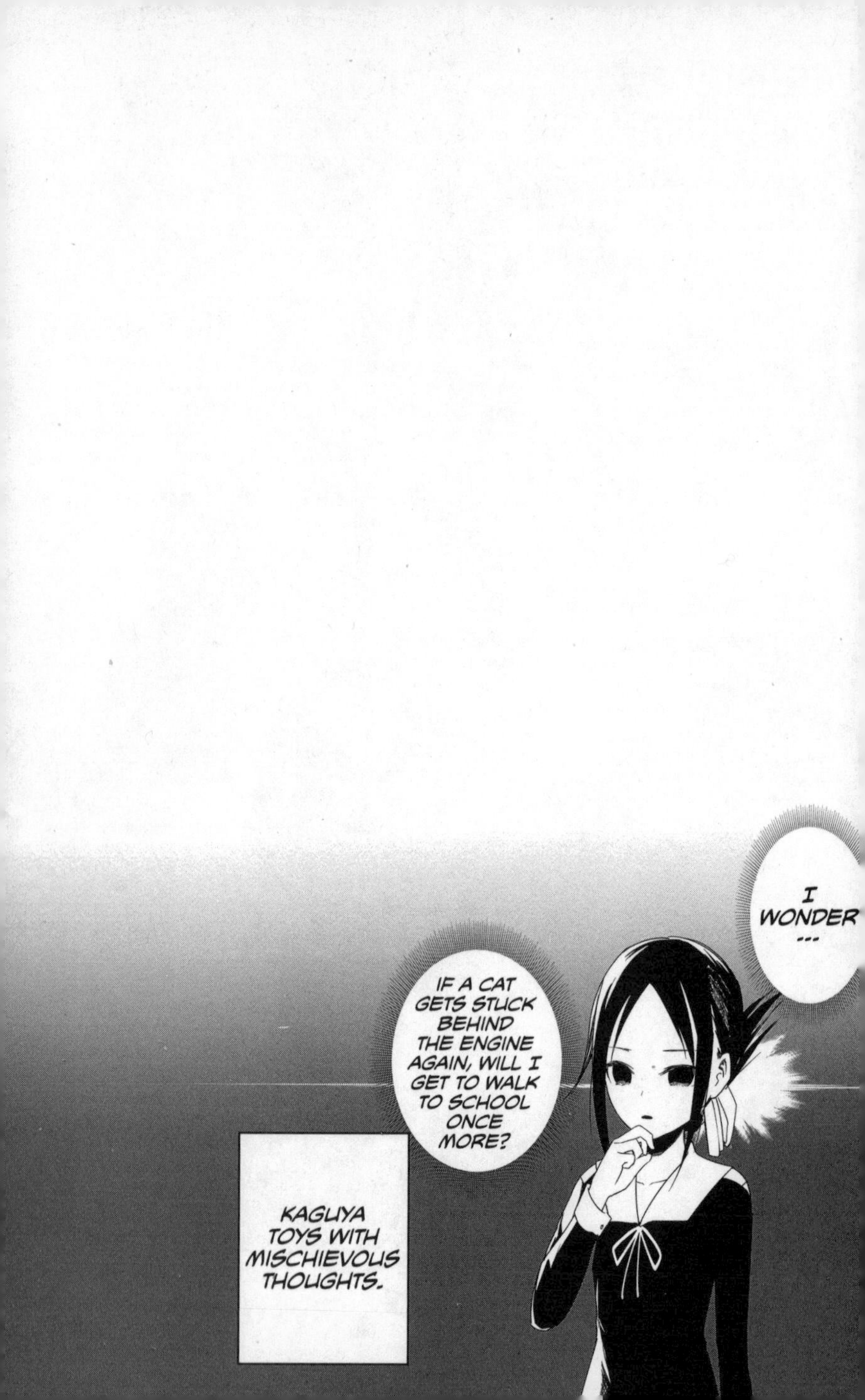
I WONDER...
IF A CAT GETS STUCK BEHIND THE ENGINE AGAIN, WILL I GET TO WALK TO SCHOOL ONCE MORE?
KAGUYA TOYS WITH MISCHIEVOUS THOUGHTS.

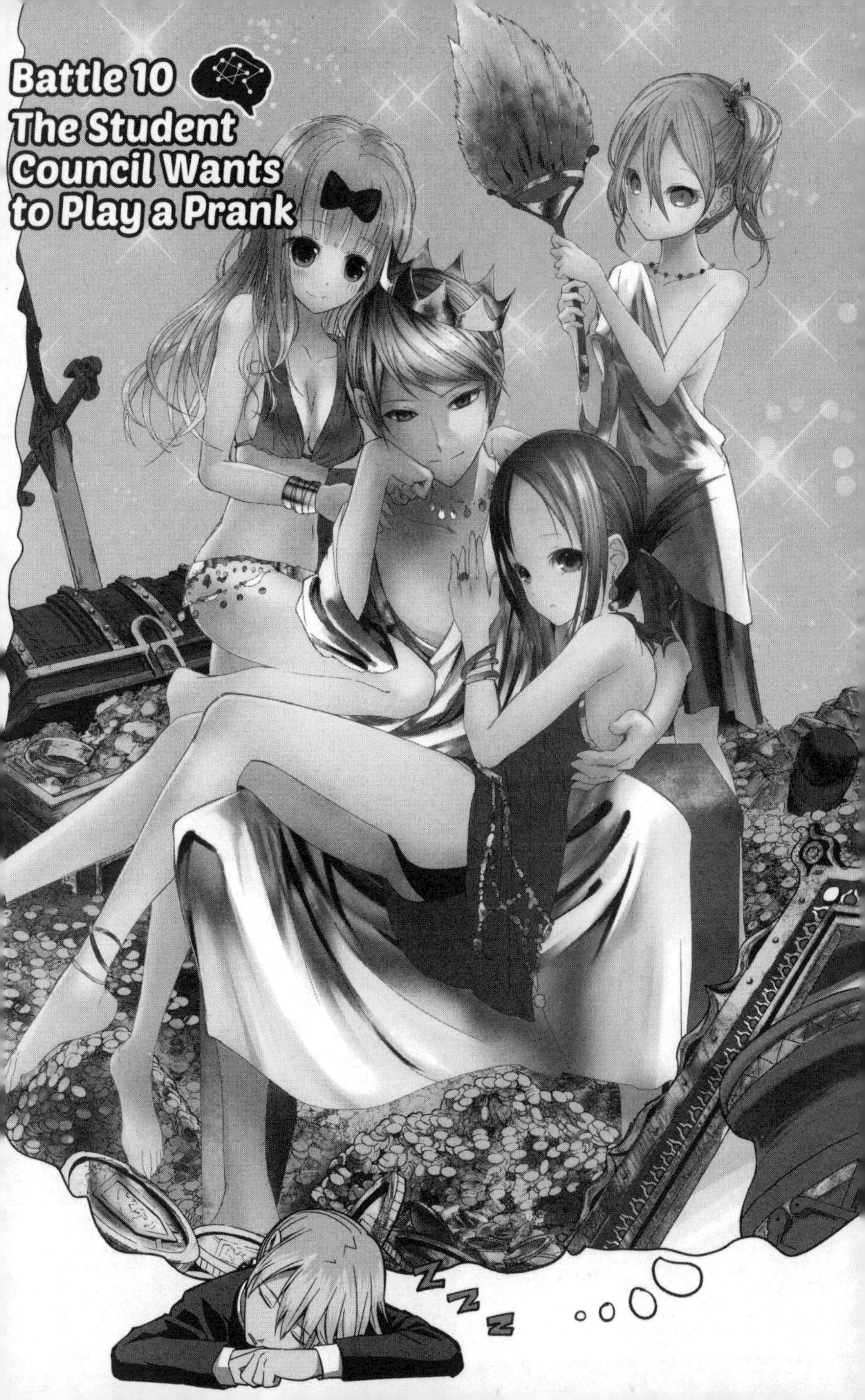
Battle 10
The Student Council Wants to Play a Prank
ZZZ

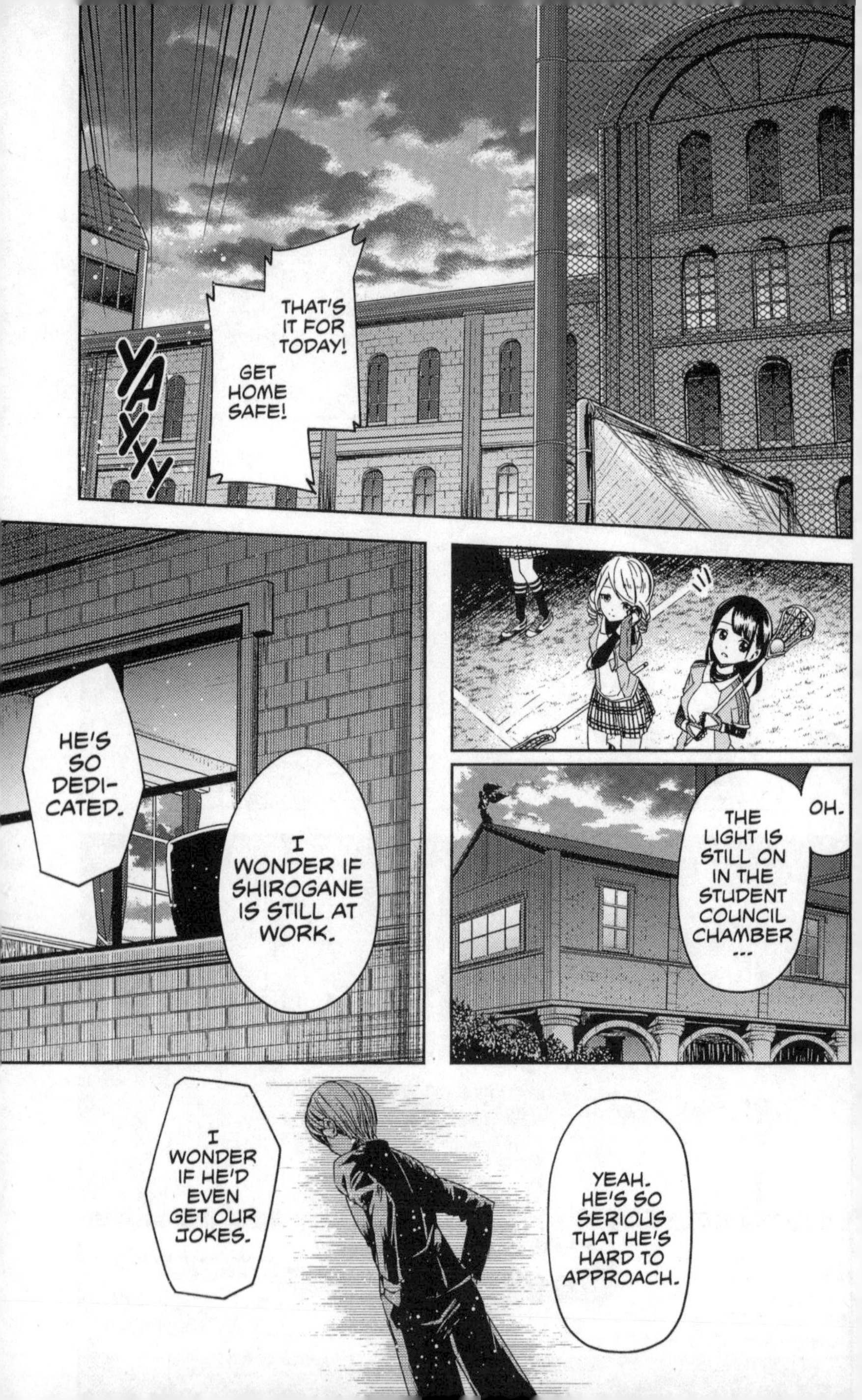
THAT'S IT FOR TODAY!
GET HOME SAFE!
YAYYY
OH.
THE LIGHT IS STILL ON IN THE STUDENT COUNCIL CHAMBER ...
I WONDER IF SHIROGANE IS STILL AT WORK.
HE'S SO DEDI-CATED.
YEAH. HE'S SO SERIOUS THAT HE'S HARD TO APPROACH.
I WONDER IF HE'D EVEN GET OUR JOKES.

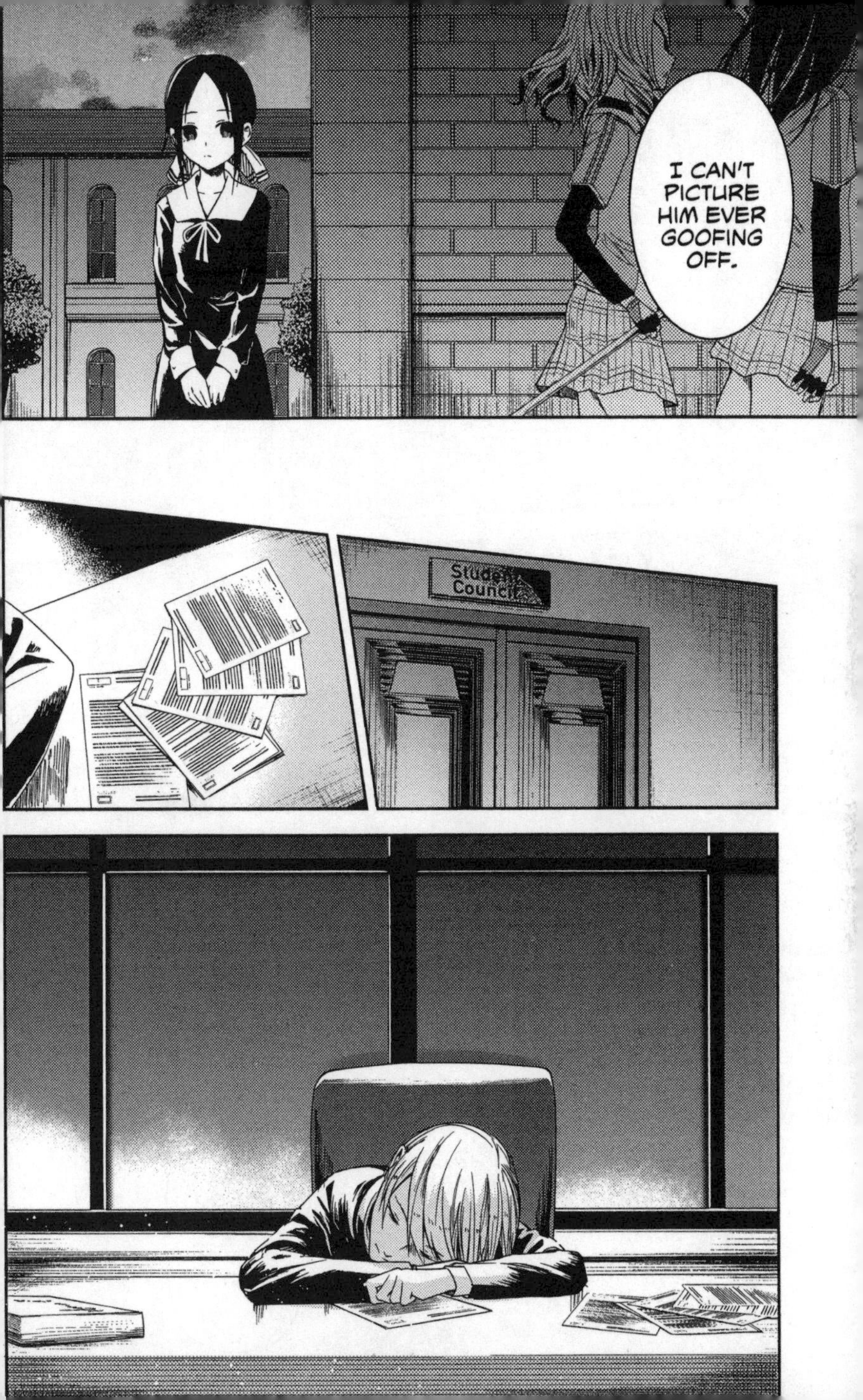
I CAN'T PICTURE HIM EVER GOOFING OFF.
Student Council

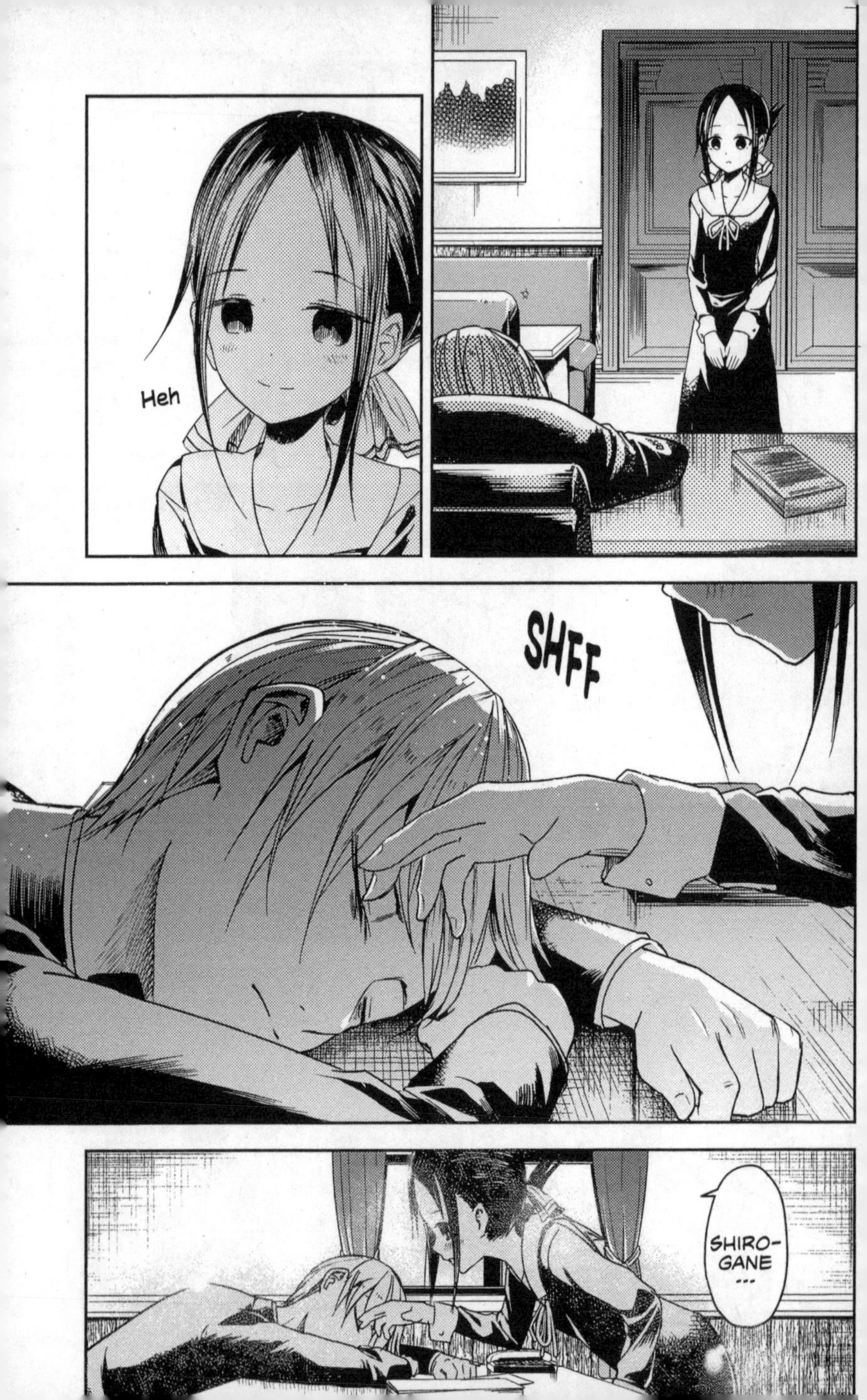
Heh
SHFF
SHIRO-GANE...

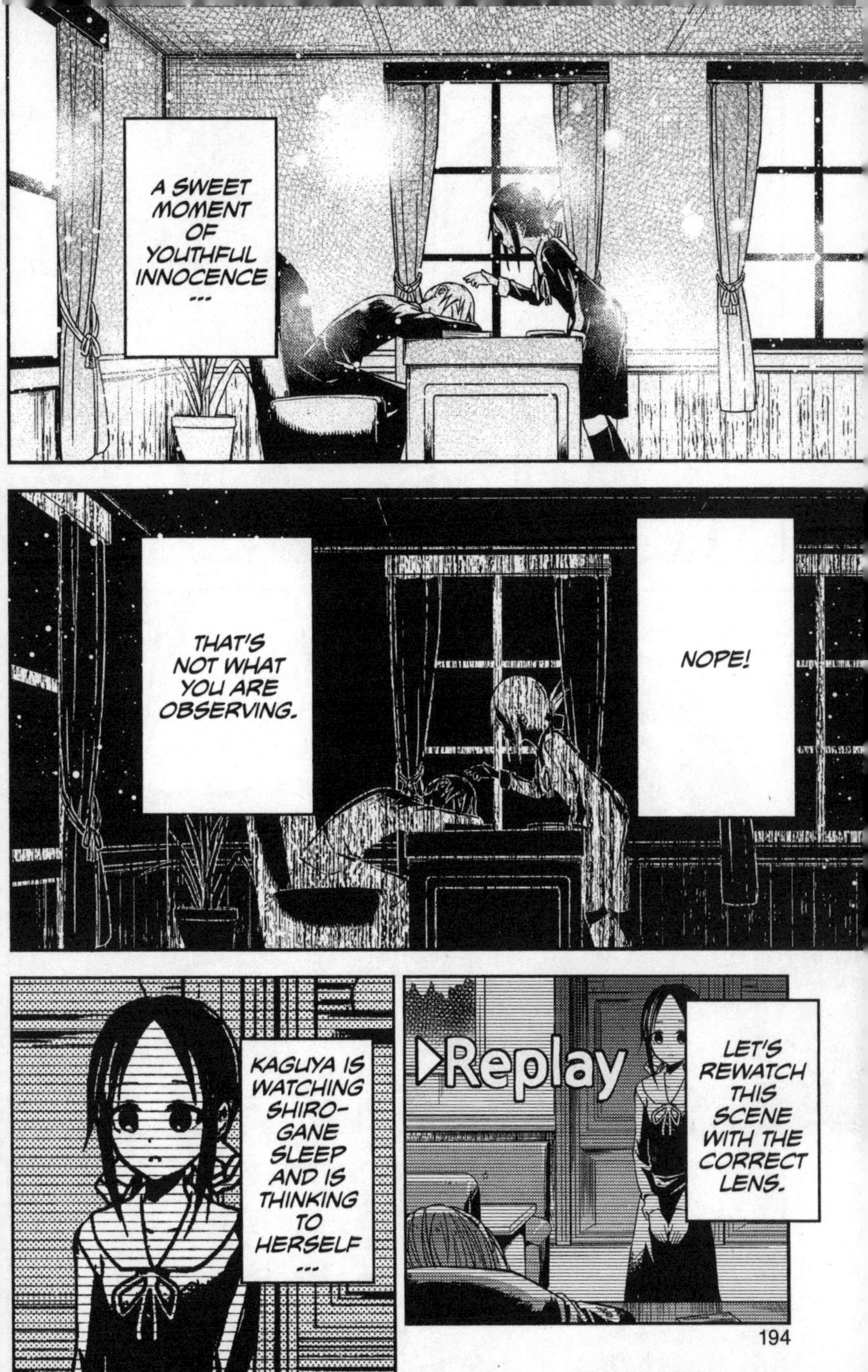
A SWEET MOMENT OF YOUTHFUL INNOCENCE ...
NOPE!
THAT'S NOT WHAT YOU ARE OBSERVING.
▷Replay
LET'S REWATCH THIS SCENE WITH THE CORRECT LENS.
KAGUYA IS WATCHING SHIRO-GANE SLEEP AND IS THINKING TO HERSELF ...

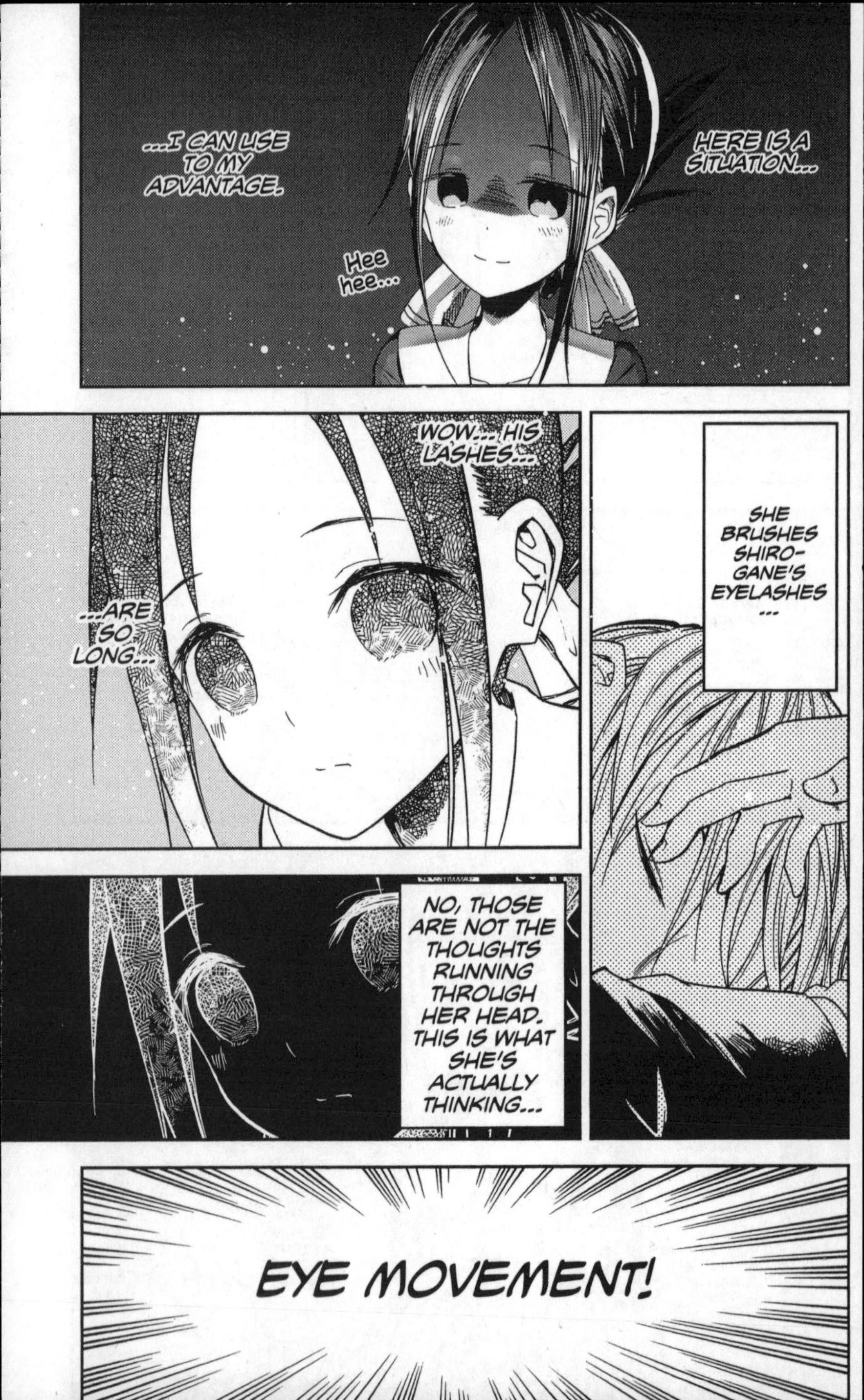
HERE IS A SITUATION...
...I CAN USE TO MY ADVANTAGE.
Hee hee...
SHE BRUSHES SHIRO-GANE'S EYELASHES...
WOW... HIS LASHES...
...ARE SO LONG...
NO, THOSE ARE NOT THE THOUGHTS RUNNING THROUGH HER HEAD. THIS IS WHAT SHE'S ACTUALLY THINKING...
EYE MOVEMENT!

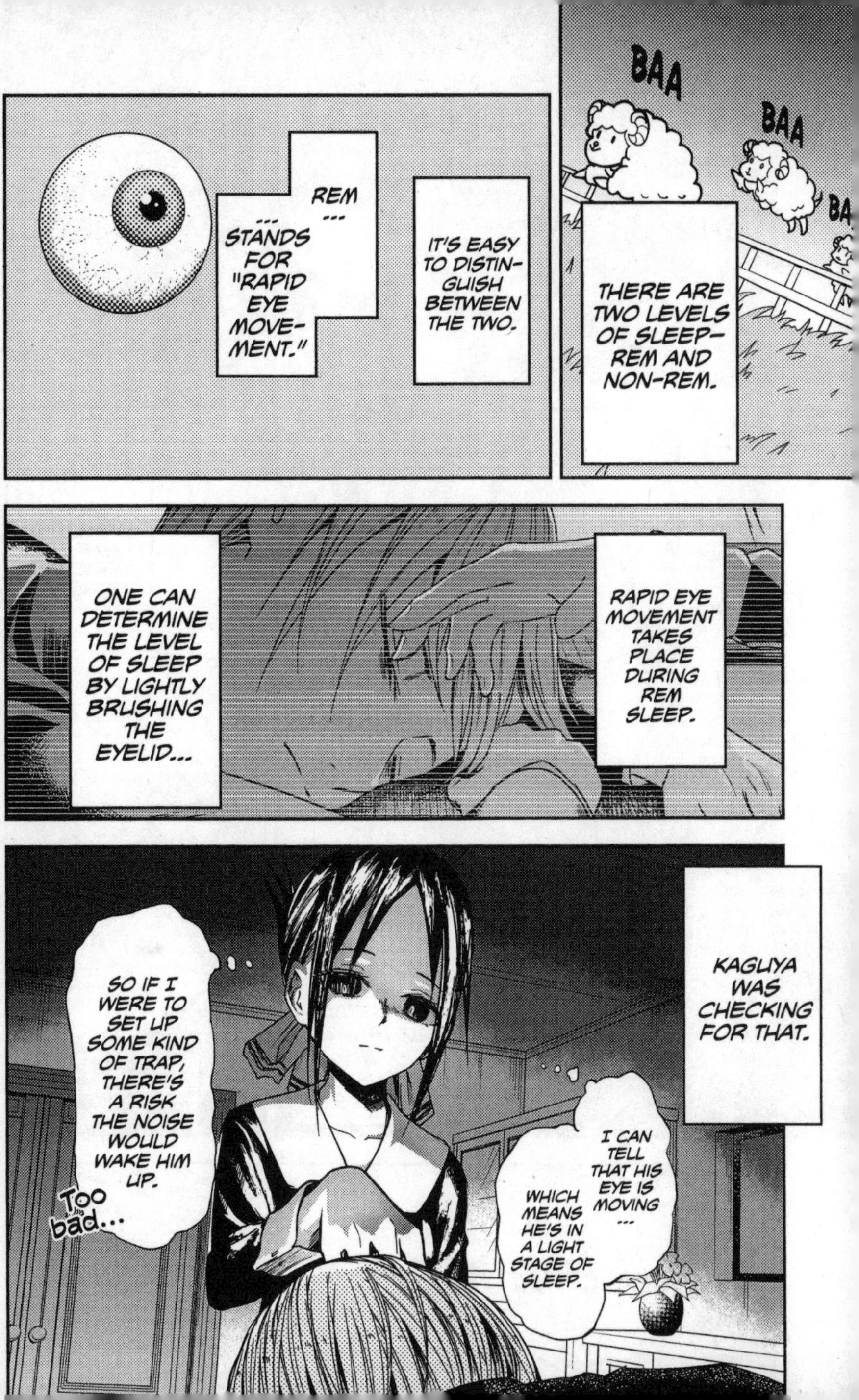
BAA
BAA
BA
THERE ARE TWO LEVELS OF SLEEP—REM AND NON-REM.
IT'S EASY TO DISTINGUISH BETWEEN THE TWO.
REM ... STANDS FOR "RAPID EYE MOVEMENT."
RAPID EYE MOVEMENT TAKES PLACE DURING REM SLEEP.
ONE CAN DETERMINE THE LEVEL OF SLEEP BY LIGHTLY BRUSHING THE EYELID...
KAGUYA WAS CHECKING FOR THAT.
I CAN TELL THAT HIS EYE IS MOVING ...
WHICH MEANS HE'S IN A LIGHT STAGE OF SLEEP.
SO IF I WERE TO SET UP SOME KIND OF TRAP, THERE'S A RISK THE NOISE WOULD WAKE HIM UP.
Too bad...

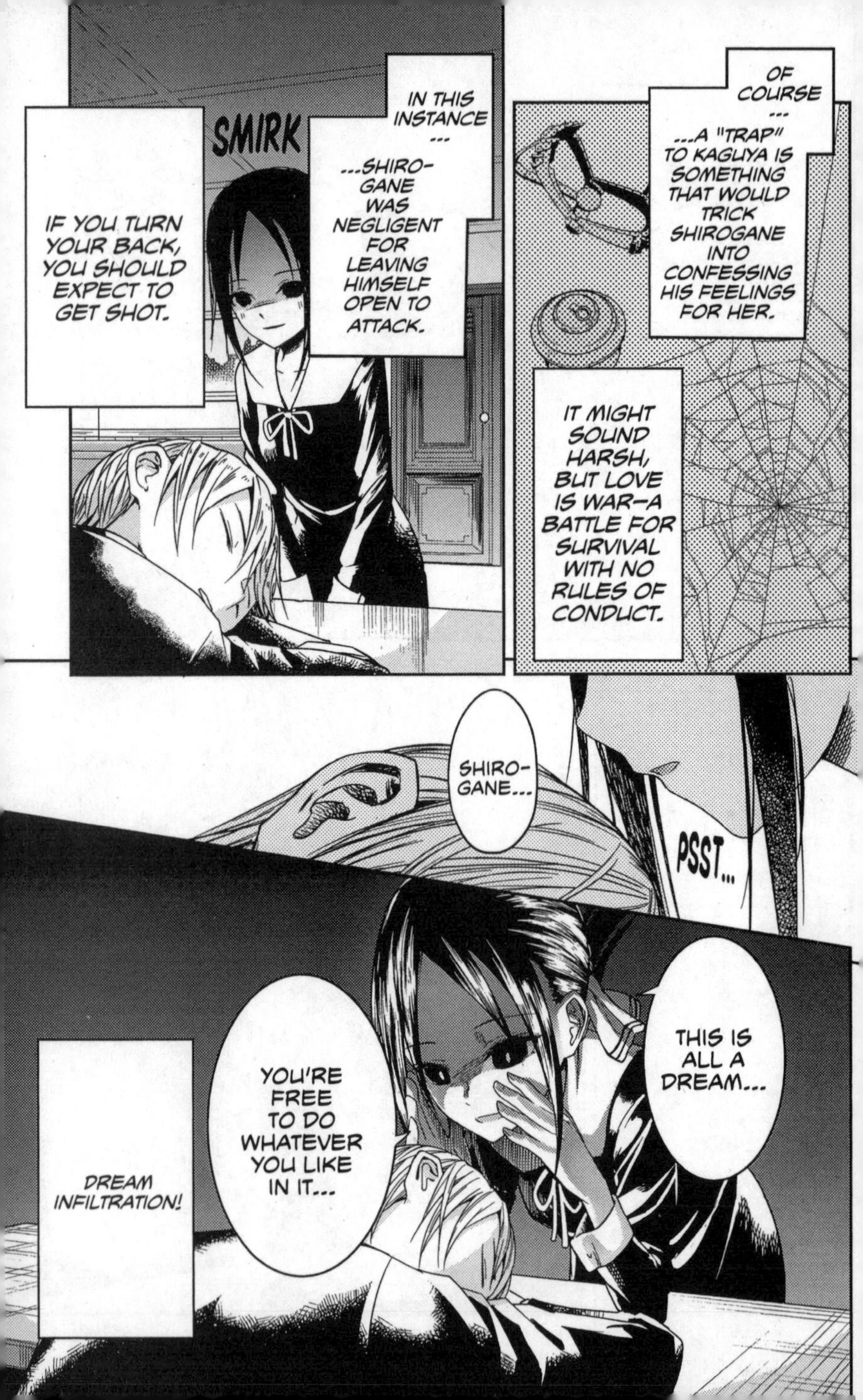
OF COURSE ... ...A "TRAP" TO KAGUYA IS SOMETHING THAT WOULD TRICK SHIROGANE INTO CONFESSING HIS FEELINGS FOR HER.
IT MIGHT SOUND HARSH, BUT LOVE IS WAR—A BATTLE FOR SURVIVAL WITH NO RULES OF CONDUCT.
IN THIS INSTANCE ... ...SHIRO-GANE WAS NEGLIGENT FOR LEAVING HIMSELF OPEN TO ATTACK.
SMIRK
IF YOU TURN YOUR BACK, YOU SHOULD EXPECT TO GET SHOT.
SHIRO-GANE...
PSST...
THIS IS ALL A DREAM...
YOU'RE FREE TO DO WHATEVER YOU LIKE IN IT...
DREAM INFILTRATION!

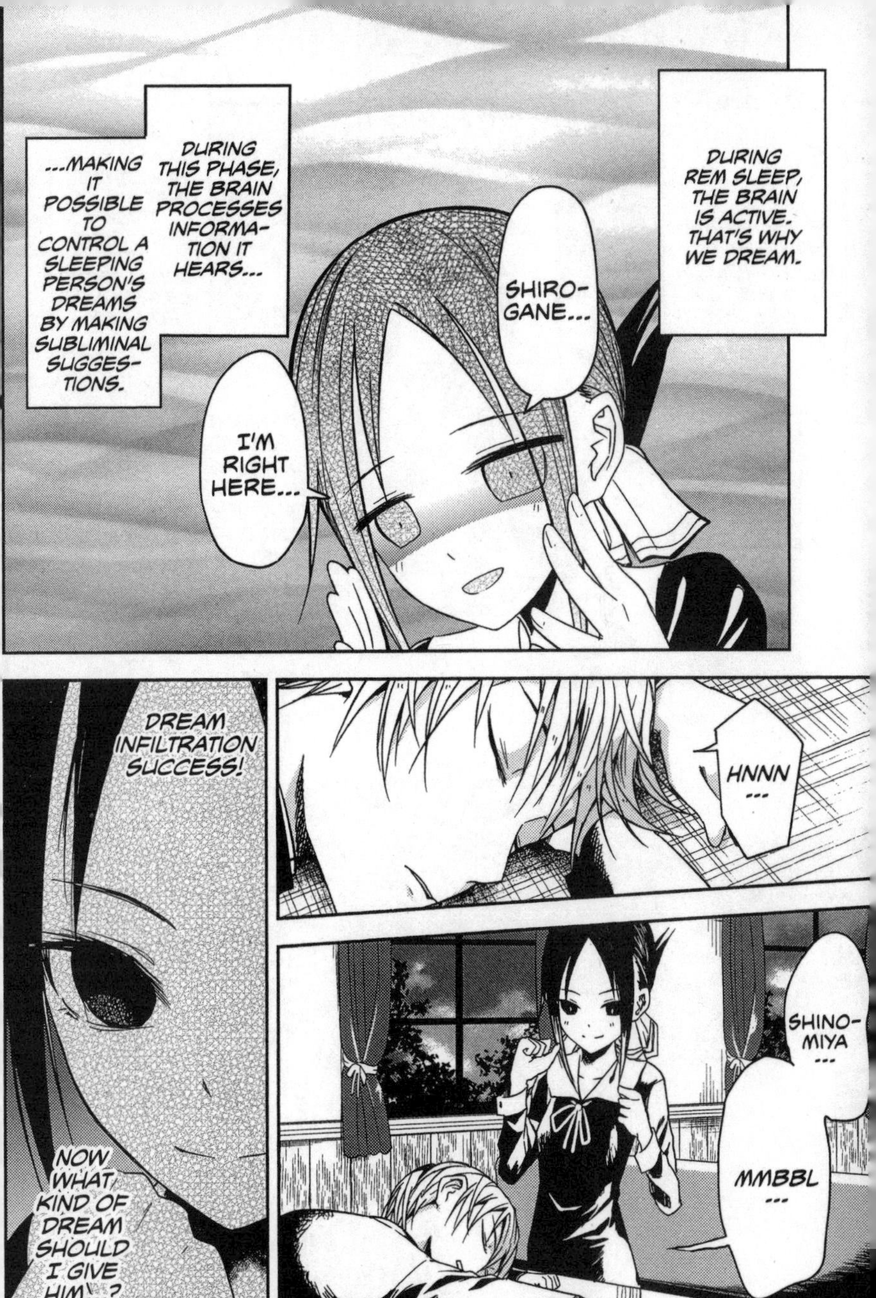
DURING REM SLEEP, THE BRAIN IS ACTIVE. THAT'S WHY WE DREAM.
SHIRO-GANE...
DURING THIS PHASE, THE BRAIN PROCESSES INFORMATION IT HEARS...
...MAKING IT POSSIBLE TO CONTROL A SLEEPING PERSON'S DREAMS BY MAKING SUBLIMINAL SUGGESTIONS.
I'M RIGHT HERE...
HNNN...
SHINO-MIYA...
MMBBL...
DREAM INFILTRATION SUCCESS!
NOW WHAT KIND OF DREAM SHOULD I GIVE HIM...?

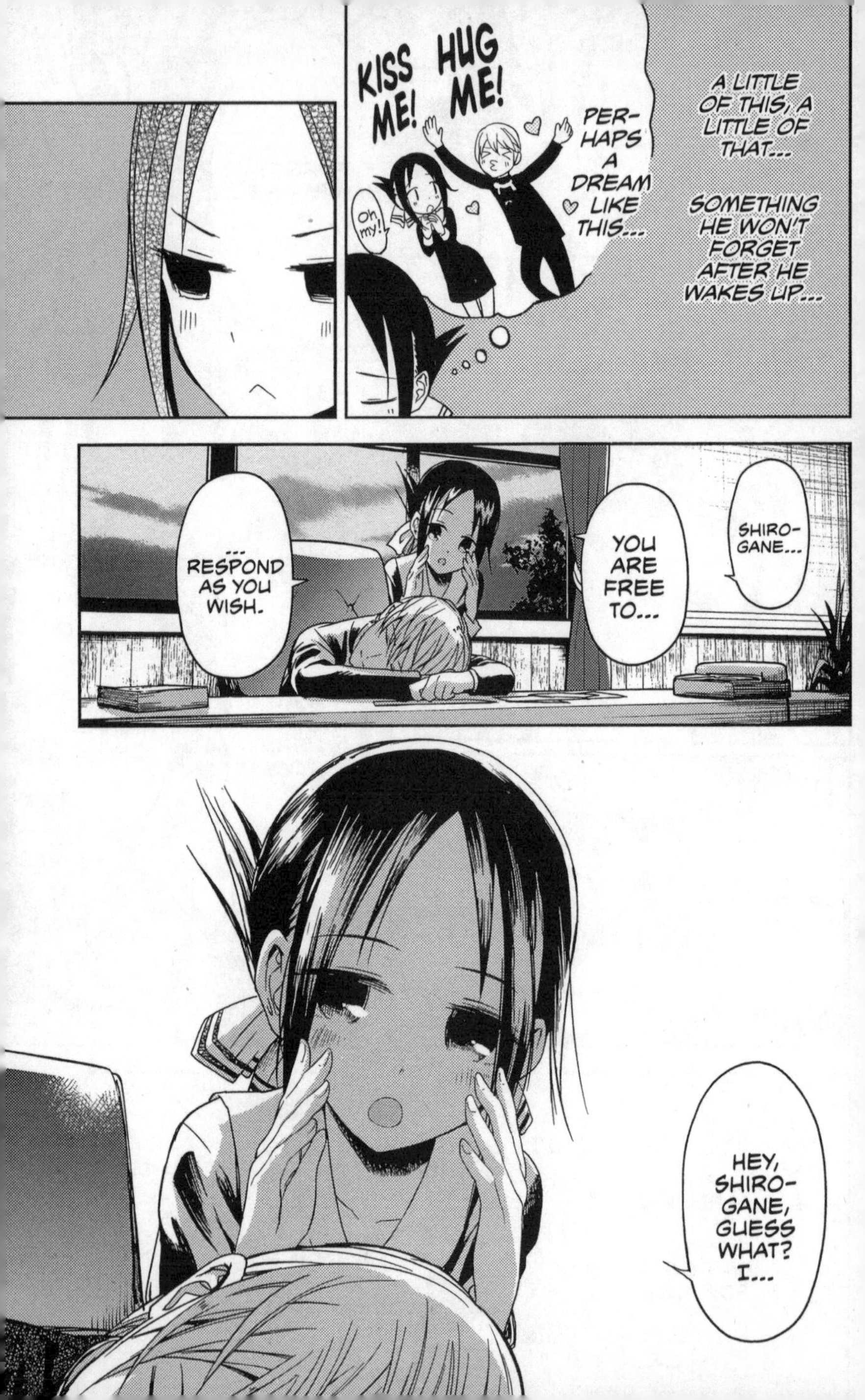
A LITTLE OF THIS, A LITTLE OF THAT...
SOMETHING HE WON'T FORGET AFTER HE WAKES UP...
PER-HAPS A DREAM LIKE THIS...
HUG ME!
KISS ME!
Oh my!
SHIRO-GANE...
YOU ARE FREE TO...
...RESPOND AS YOU WISH.
HEY, SHIRO-GANE, GUESS WHAT? I...

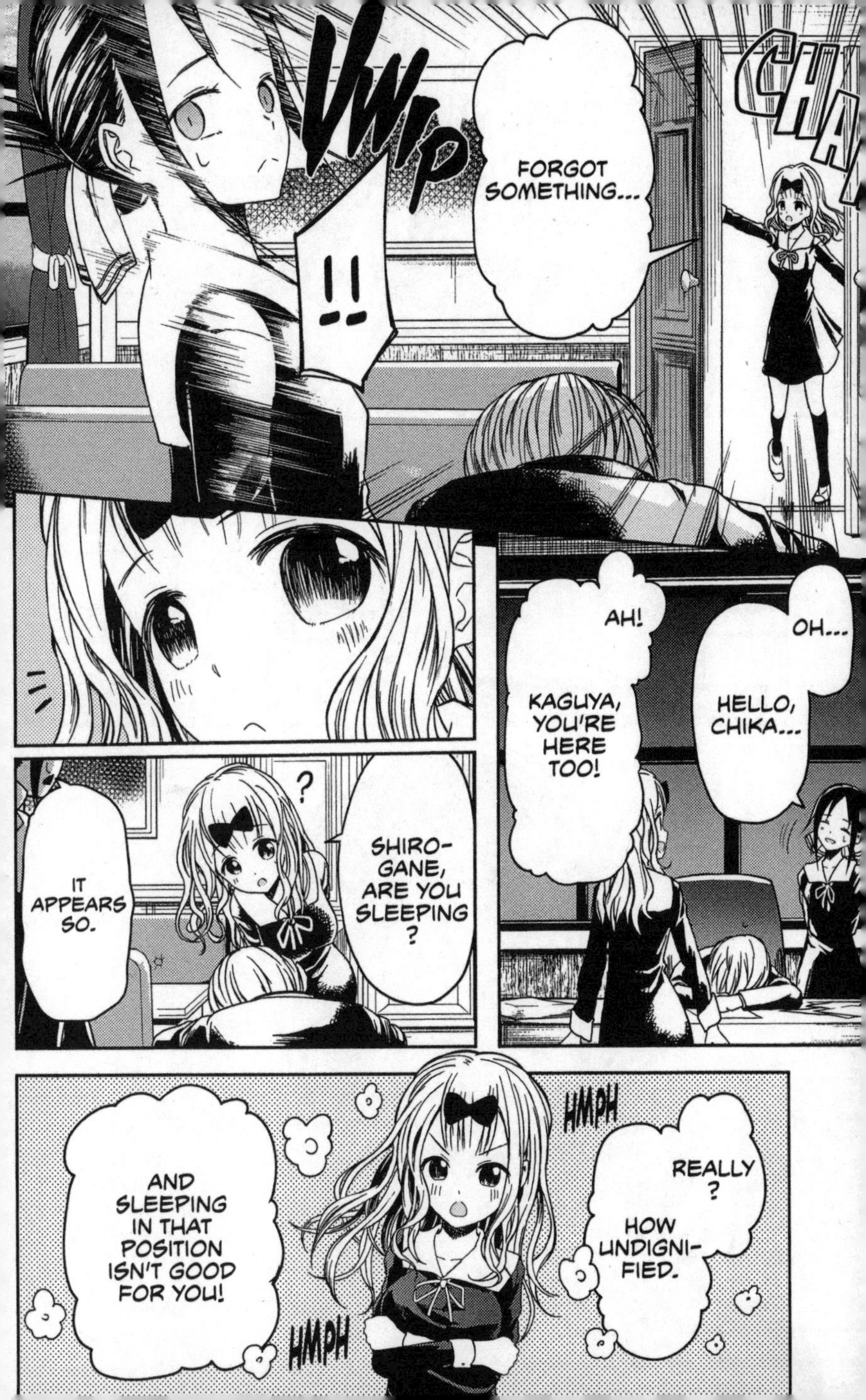
CHA
FORGOT SOMETHING...
VWIP
!!
OH... HELLO, CHIKA...
AH! KAGUYA, YOU'RE HERE TOO!
SHIRO-GANE, ARE YOU SLEEPING?
?
IT APPEARS SO.
REALLY? HOW UNDIGNI-FIED.
HMPH
AND SLEEPING IN THAT POSITION ISN'T GOOD FOR YOU!
HMPH

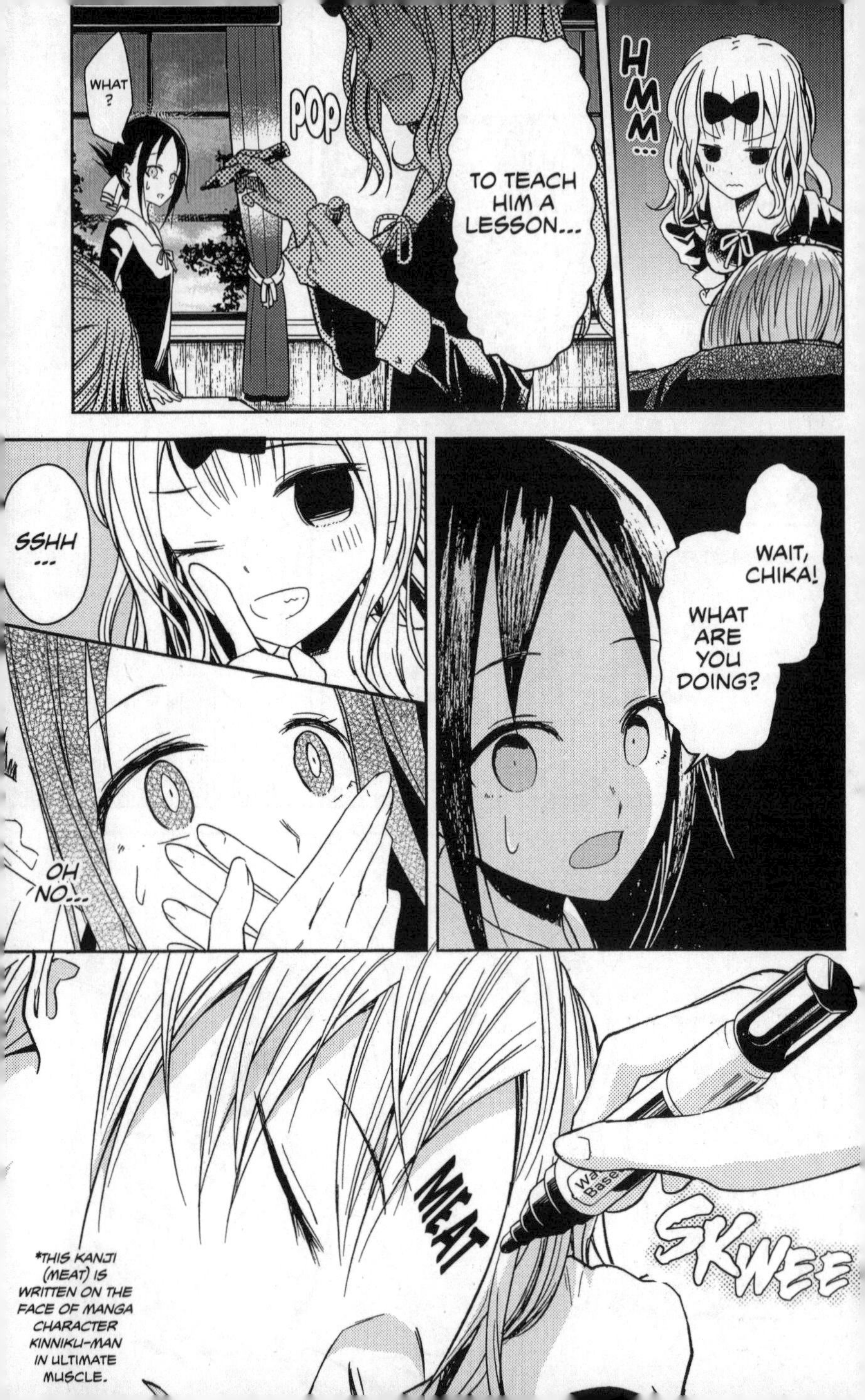
HMM...
TO TEACH HIM A LESSON...
POP
WHAT?
WAIT, CHIKA!
WHAT ARE YOU DOING?
SSHH...
OH NO...
SKWEE
MEAT

*THIS KANJI (MEAT) IS WRITTEN ON THE FACE OF MANGA CHARACTER KINNIKU-MAN IN ULTIMATE MUSCLE.

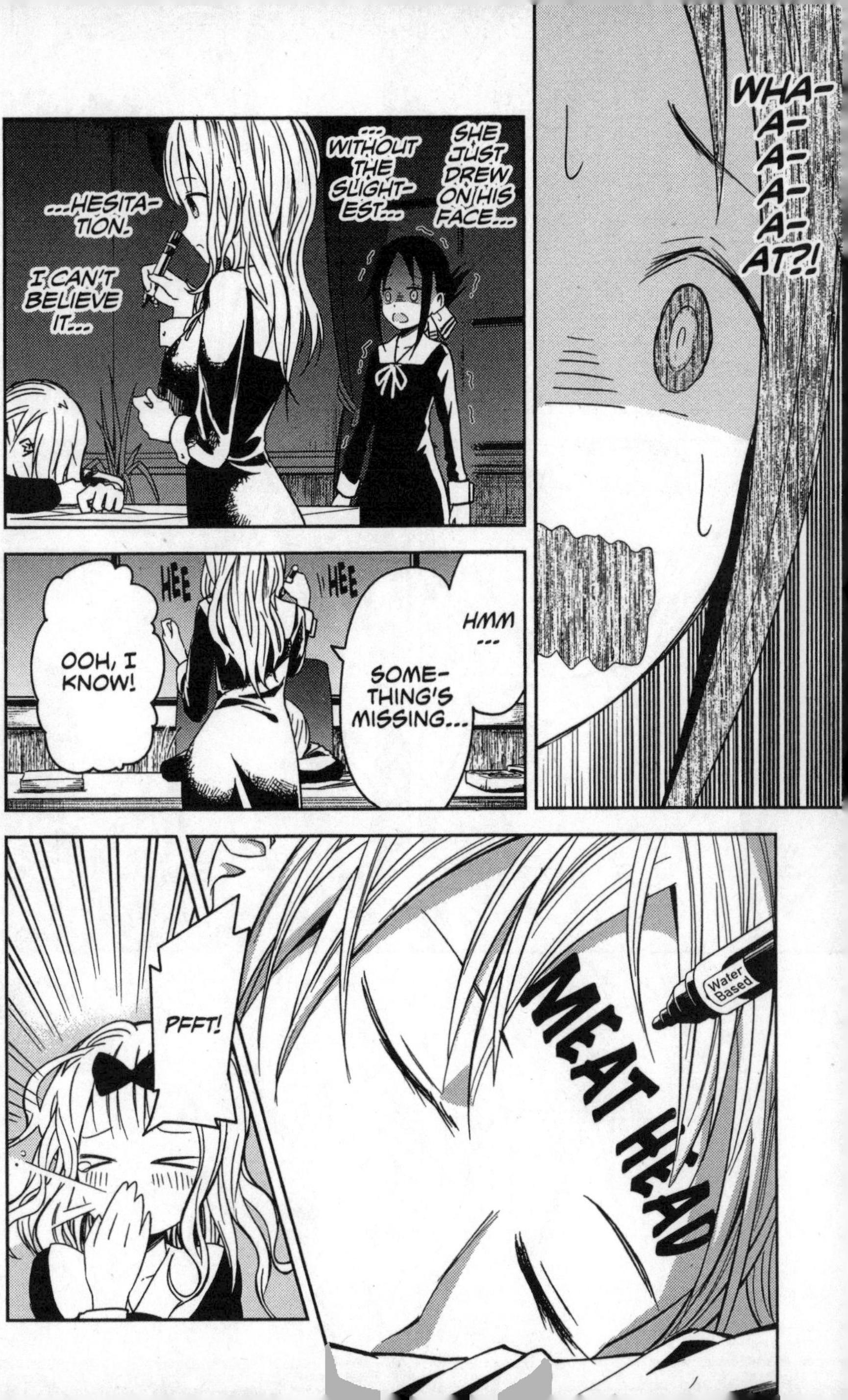
WHA-A-A-A-A-AT?!
SHE JUST DREW ON HIS FACE...
...WITHOUT THE SLIGHTEST...
...HESITATION.
I CAN'T BELIEVE IT...
HEE
HEE
HMM... SOMETHING'S MISSING...
OOH, I KNOW!
Water Based
MEAT HEAD
PFFT!

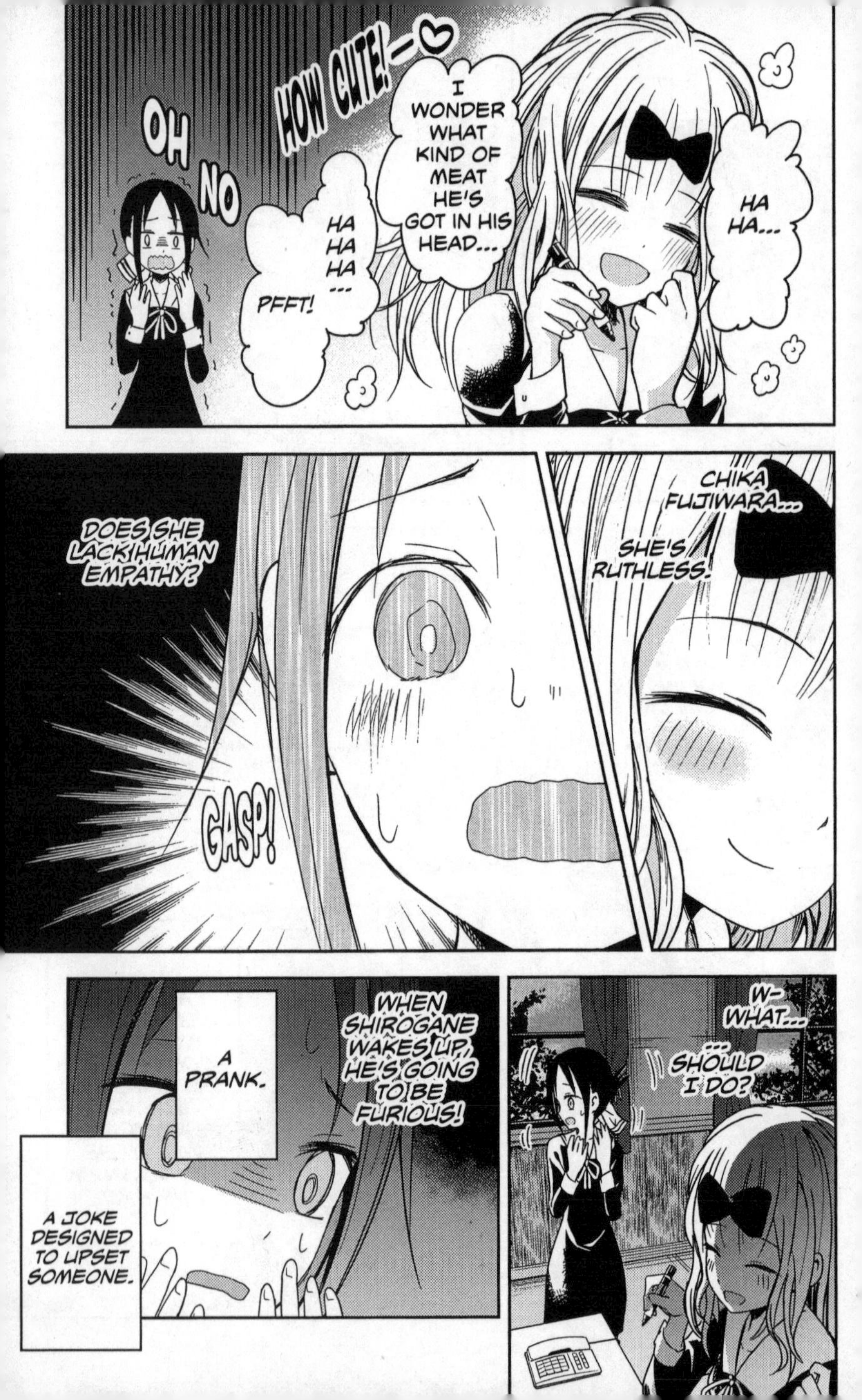
HA HA...
I WONDER WHAT KIND OF MEAT HE'S GOT IN HIS HEAD...
HOW CUTE!—♡
HA HA HA...
PFFT!
OH NO
CHIKA FUJIWARA...
SHE'S RUTHLESS.
DOES SHE LACK HUMAN EMPATHY?
GASP!
W-WHAT...
...SHOULD I DO?
WHEN SHIROGANE WAKES UP, HE'S GOING TO BE FURIOUS!
A PRANK.
A JOKE DESIGNED TO UPSET SOMEONE.

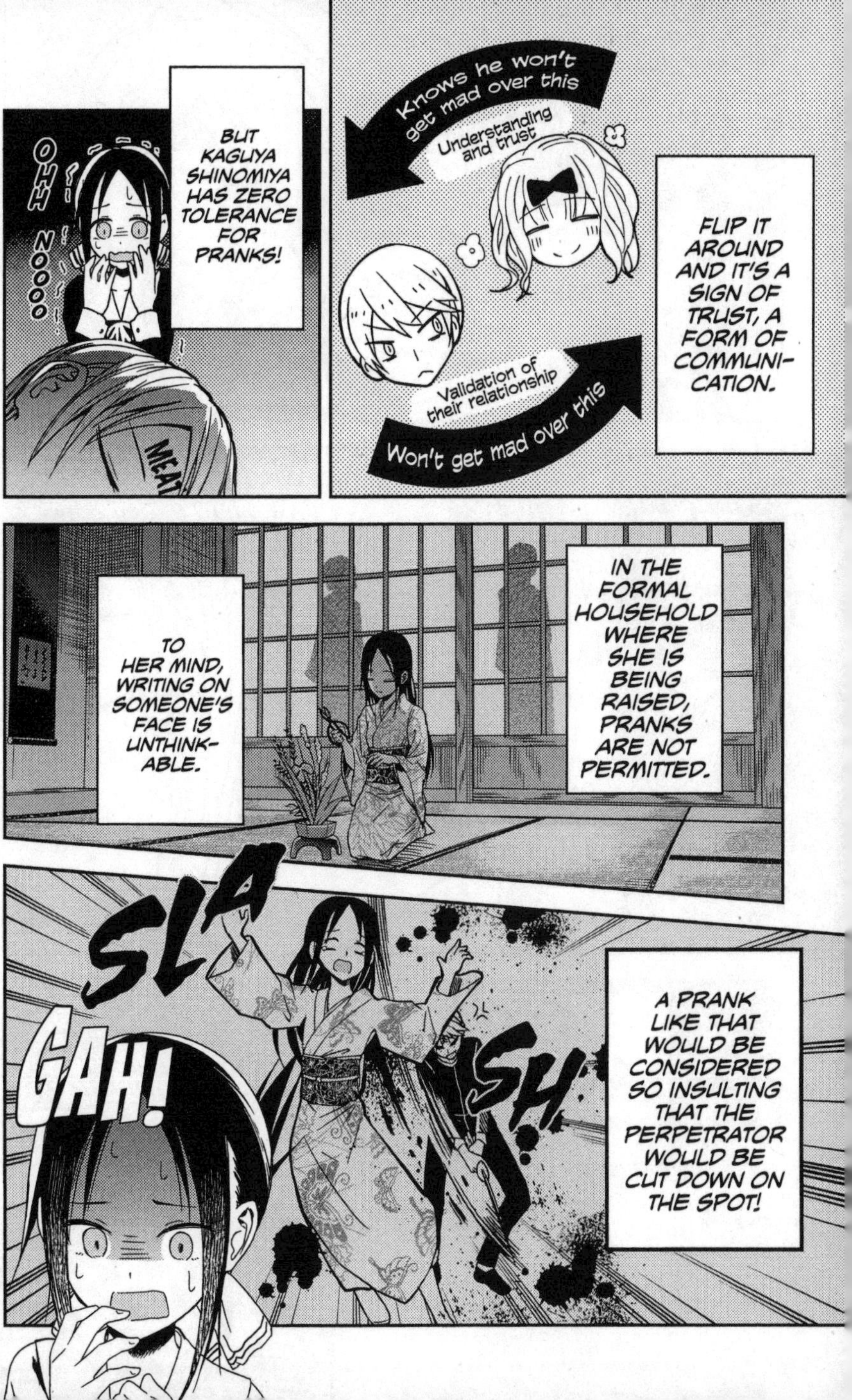
FLIP IT AROUND AND IT'S A SIGN OF TRUST, A FORM OF COMMUNICATION.
Knows he won't get mad over this
Understanding and trust
Validation of their relationship
Won't get mad over this
BUT KAGUYA SHINOMIYA HAS ZERO TOLERANCE FOR PRANKS!
OHH NOOOO
IN THE FORMAL HOUSEHOLD WHERE SHE IS BEING RAISED, PRANKS ARE NOT PERMITTED.
TO HER MIND, WRITING ON SOMEONE'S FACE IS UNTHINKABLE.
A PRANK LIKE THAT WOULD BE CONSIDERED SO INSULTING THAT THE PERPETRATOR WOULD BE CUT DOWN ON THE SPOT!
SLASH
GAH!

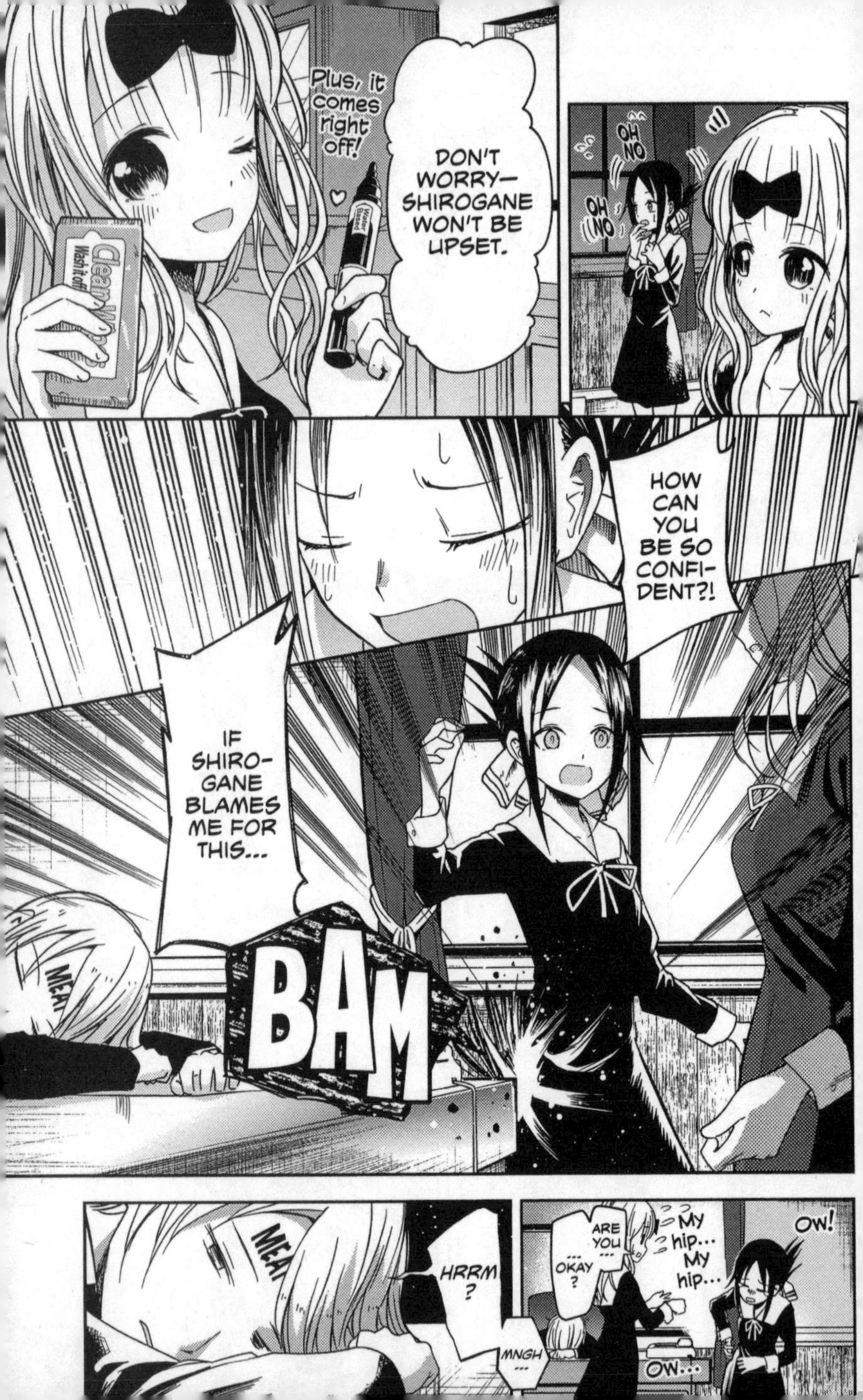
OH NO
OH NO
DON'T WORRY—SHIROGANE WON'T BE UPSET.
Plus, it comes right off!
HOW CAN YOU BE SO CONFI-DENT?!
IF SHIRO-GANE BLAMES ME FOR THIS...
BAM
MEAT
OW!
My hip... My hip...
ARE YOU ... ...OKAY?
OW...
MEAT
HRRM?
MNGH...

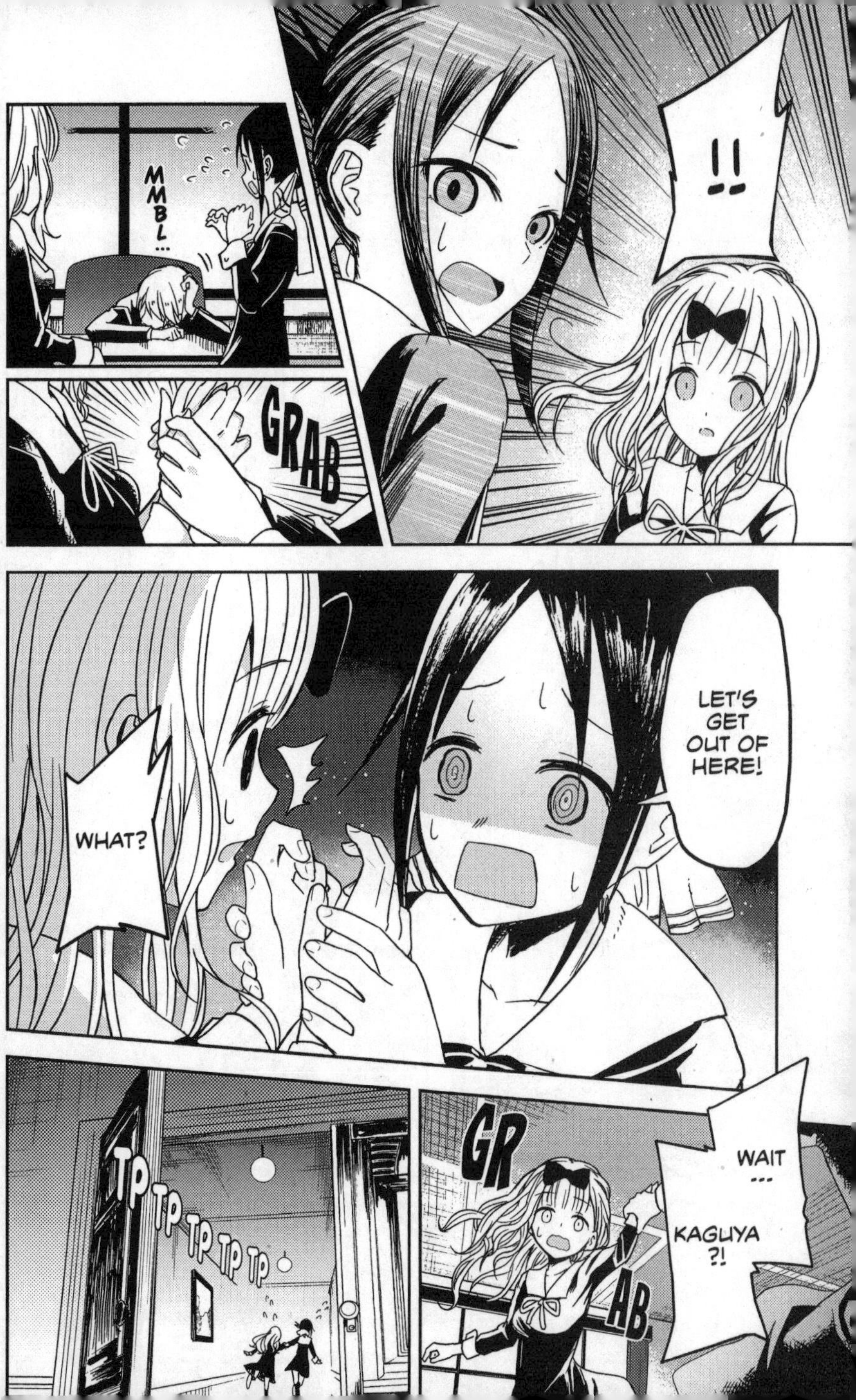
!!
MMBL...
GRAB
LET'S GET OUT OF HERE!
WHAT?
GRAB
WAIT---
KAGUYA?!
TP TP TP TP TP TP

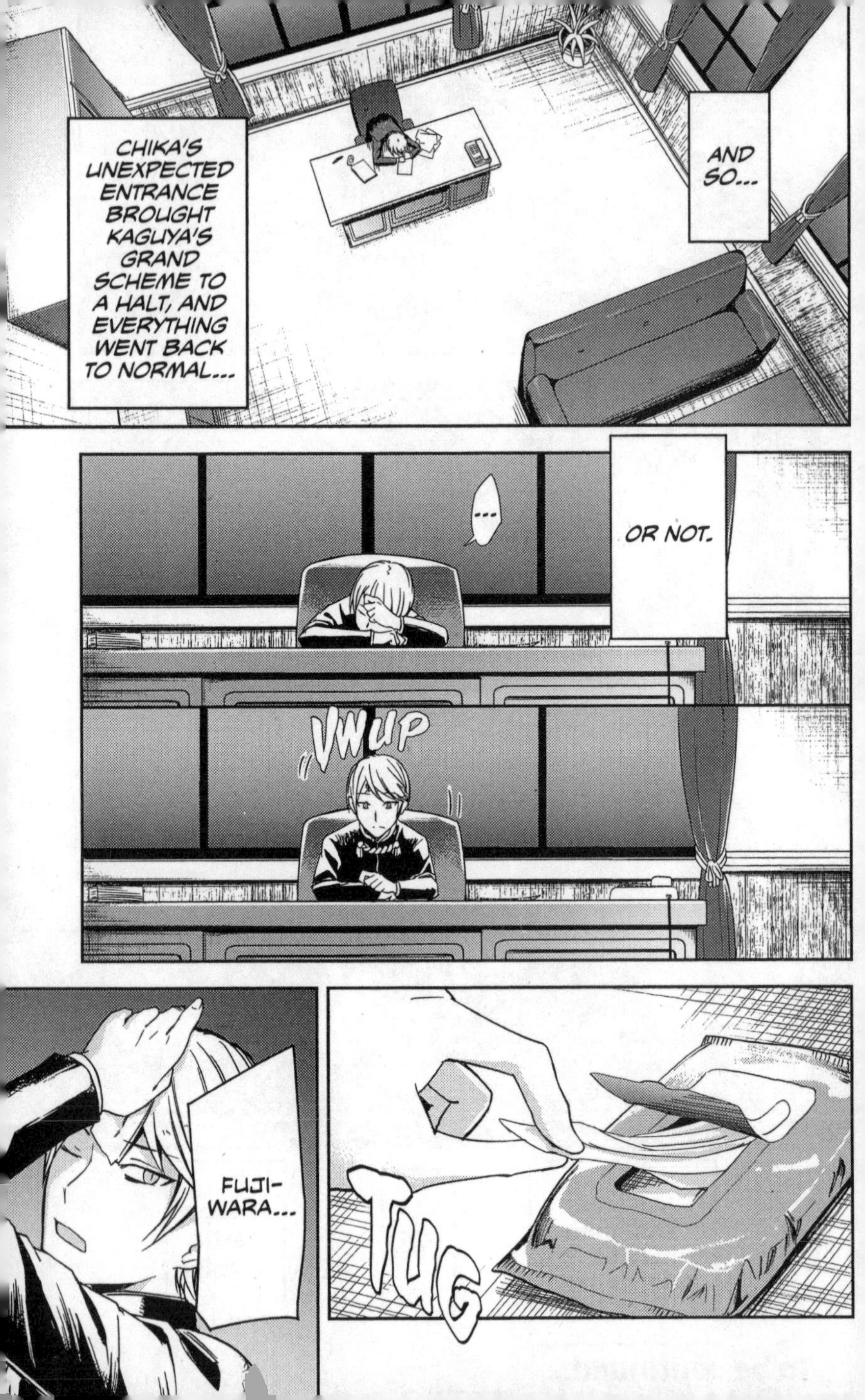
AND SO...
CHIKA'S UNEXPECTED ENTRANCE BROUGHT KAGUYA'S GRAND SCHEME TO A HALT, AND EVERYTHING WENT BACK TO NORMAL...
OR NOT.
...
VWUP
TUG
FUJI-WARA...

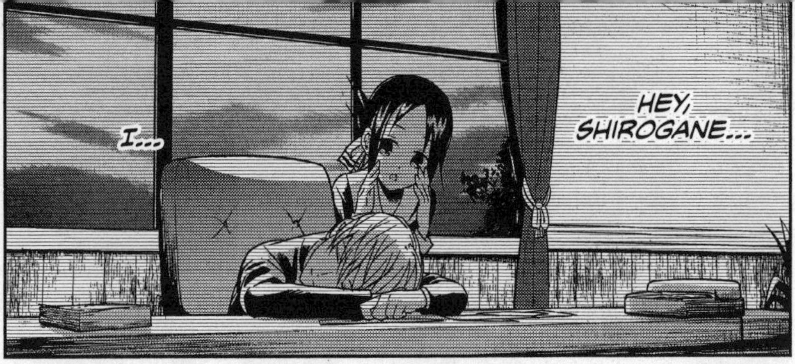
HEY, SHIROGANE...
I...

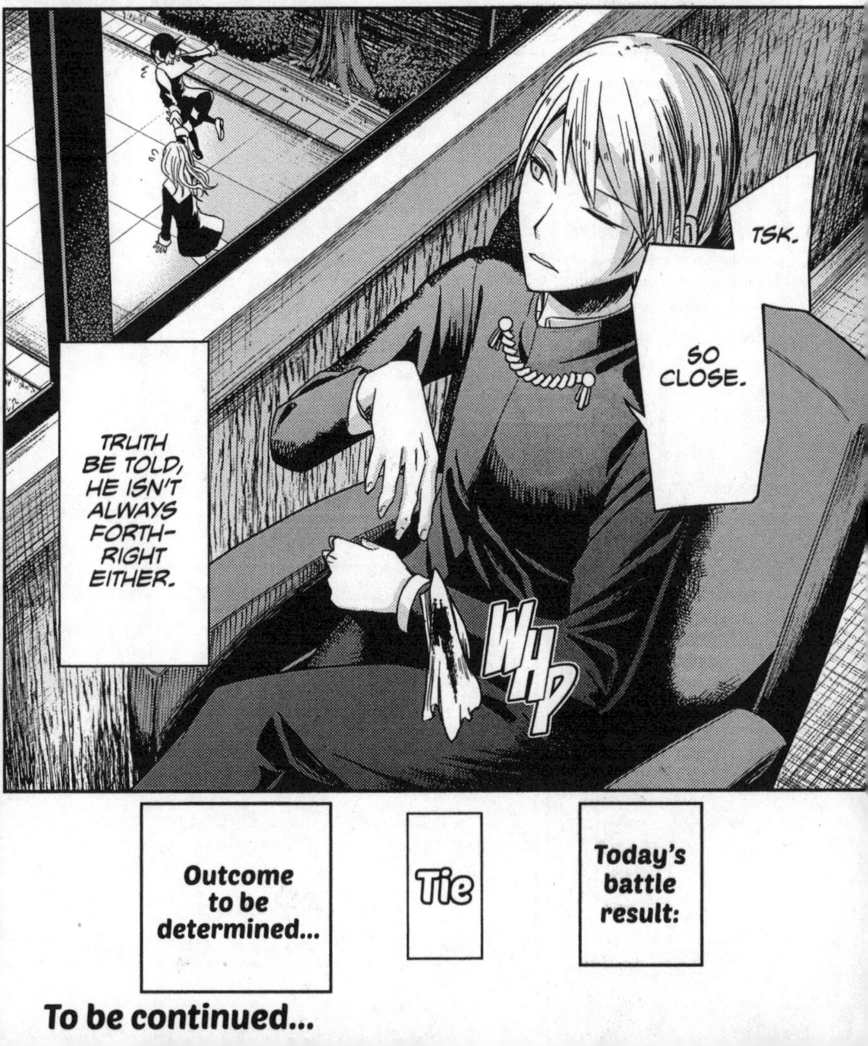
TSK.
SO CLOSE.
TRUTH BE TOLD, HE ISN'T ALWAYS FORTH-RIGHT EITHER.
WHP

Today's battle result:

Tie

Outcome to be determined...

To be continued...

Position: Student
Council Secretary →

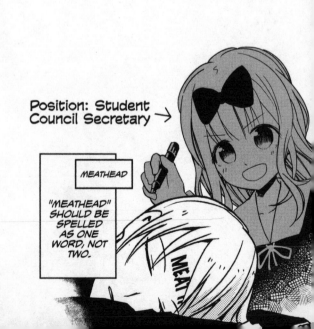

MEATHEAD

"MEATHEAD"
SHOULD BE
SPELLED
AS ONE
WORD, NOT
TWO.

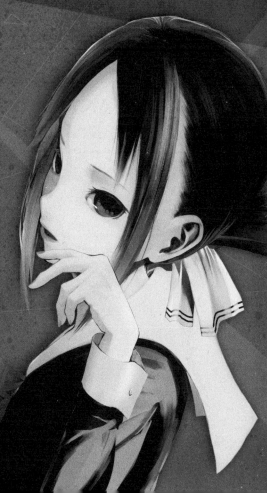

THERE'S NO SUCH THING AS UNCONDITIONAL LOVE.

AKA AKASAKA

Aka Akasaka got his start as an assistant to Jinsei Kataoka and Kazuma Kondou, the creators of *Deadman Wonderland*. His first serialized manga was an adaptation of the light novel series *Sayonara Piano Sonata*, published by Kadokawa in 2011. *Kaguya-sama: Love Is War* began serialization in *Miracle Jump* in 2015 but was later moved to *Weekly Young Jump* in 2016 due to its popularity.

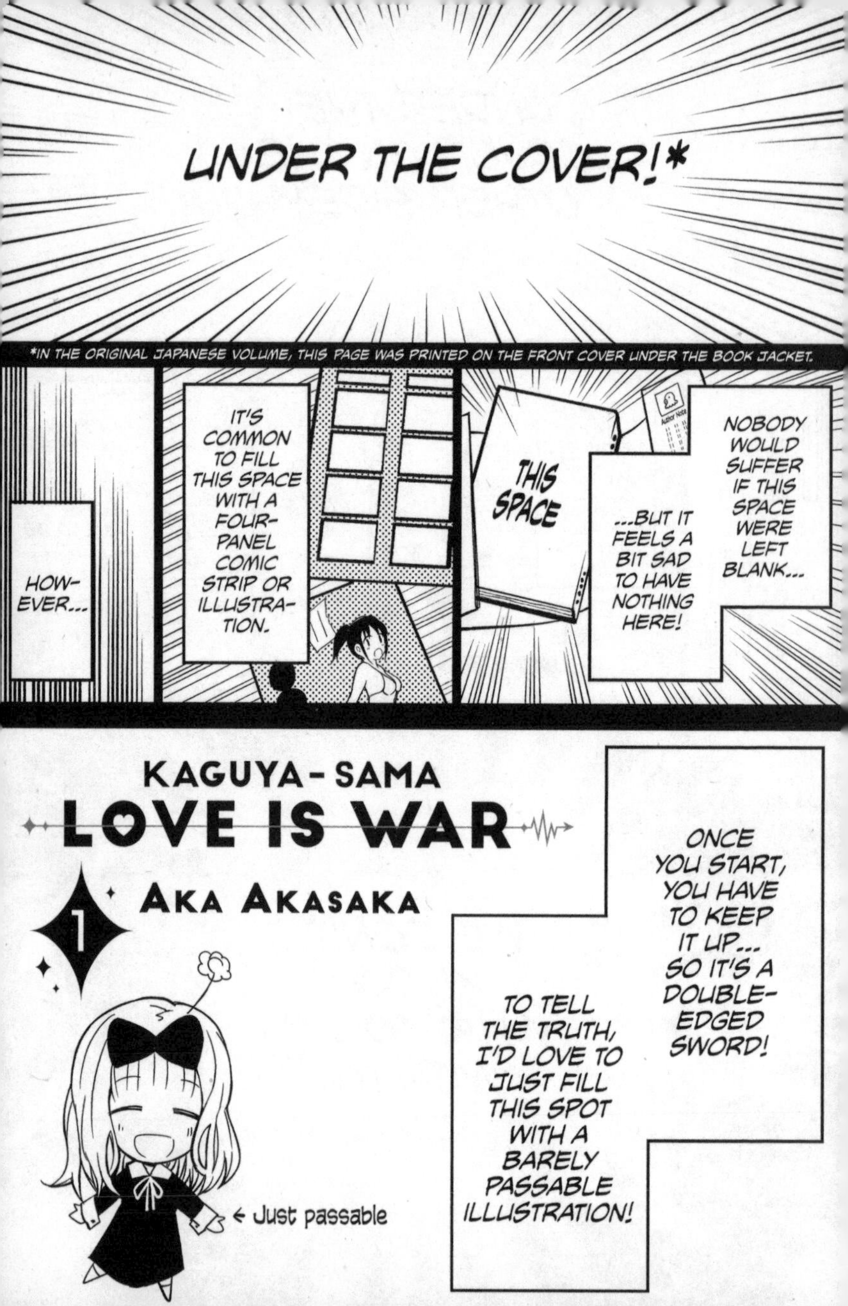
UNDER THE COVER!*
*IN THE ORIGINAL JAPANESE VOLUME, THIS PAGE WAS PRINTED ON THE FRONT COVER UNDER THE BOOK JACKET.
NOBODY WOULD SUFFER IF THIS SPACE WERE LEFT BLANK...
...BUT IT FEELS A BIT SAD TO HAVE NOTHING HERE!
THIS SPACE
Author Note
IT'S COMMON TO FILL THIS SPACE WITH A FOUR-PANEL COMIC STRIP OR ILLUSTRATION.
HOW-EVER...
ONCE YOU START, YOU HAVE TO KEEP IT UP... SO IT'S A DOUBLE-EDGED SWORD!
TO TELL THE TRUTH, I'D LOVE TO JUST FILL THIS SPOT WITH A BARELY PASSABLE ILLUSTRATION!
KAGUYA-SAMA
LOVE IS WAR
1
AKA AKASAKA
← Just passable

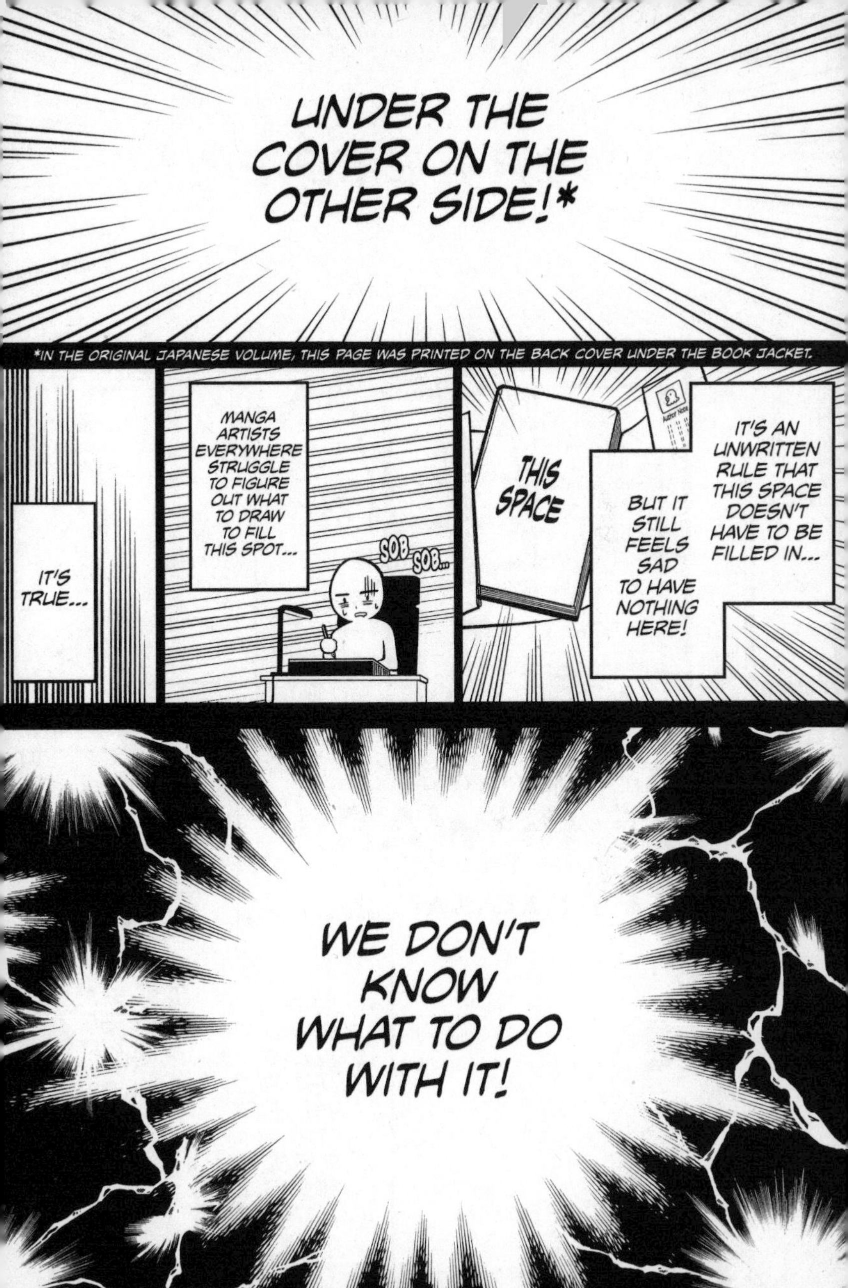
UNDER THE COVER ON THE OTHER SIDE!*
IT'S AN UNWRITTEN RULE THAT THIS SPACE DOESN'T HAVE TO BE FILLED IN...
BUT IT STILL FEELS SAD TO HAVE NOTHING HERE!
THIS SPACE
MANGA ARTISTS EVERYWHERE STRUGGLE TO FIGURE OUT WHAT TO DRAW TO FILL THIS SPOT...
SOB SOB...
IT'S TRUE...
WE DON'T KNOW WHAT TO DO WITH IT!

*IN THE ORIGINAL JAPANESE VOLUME, THIS PAGE WAS PRINTED ON THE BACK COVER UNDER THE BOOK JACKET.

KAGUYA-SAMA
LOVE IS WAR

SHONEN JUMP MANGA EDITION

1

STORY AND ART BY
Aka Akasaka

Translation/Emi Louie-Nishikawa
English Adaptation/Annette Roman
Touch-Up Art & Lettering/Stephen Dutro
Cover & Interior Design/Izumi Evers
Editor/Annette Roman

KAGUYA-SAMA WA KOKURASETAI~TENSAITACHI NO REN'AI ZUNO SEN~
© 2015 by Aka Akasaka
All rights reserved.
First published in Japan in 2015 by SHUEISHA Inc., Tokyo.
English translation rights arranged by SHUEISHA Inc.

Printed in the U.S.A.

Published by VIZ Media, LLC
P.O. Box 77010
San Francisco, CA 94107

10 9 8 7 6 5 4 3
First printing, March 2018
Third printing, February 2020

PARENTAL ADVISORY
KAGUYA-SAMA: LOVE IS WAR is rated T for Teen
and is recommended for ages 13 and up. It contains
mild language and first-love shenanigans.

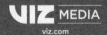

shonenjump.com

viz.com

COMING NEXT VOLUME

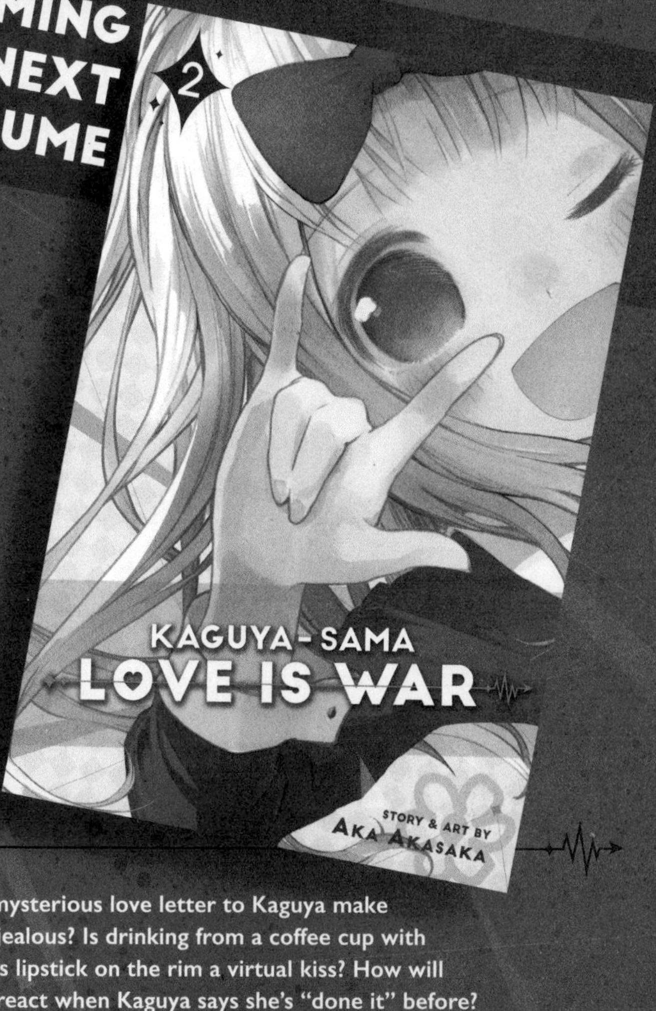
2
KAGUYA-SAMA
LOVE IS WAR
STORY & ART BY
AKA AKASAKA

2

Will a mysterious love letter to Kaguya make Miyuki jealous? Is drinking from a coffee cup with Kaguya's lipstick on the rim a virtual kiss? How will Miyuki react when Kaguya says she's "done it" before? Then, Miyuki's phobia is revealed, the VP of Shuchiin Academy's sister school in France displays epic Gallic rudeness, and the student council tries on some costumes…

Nobody can resist cat ears.

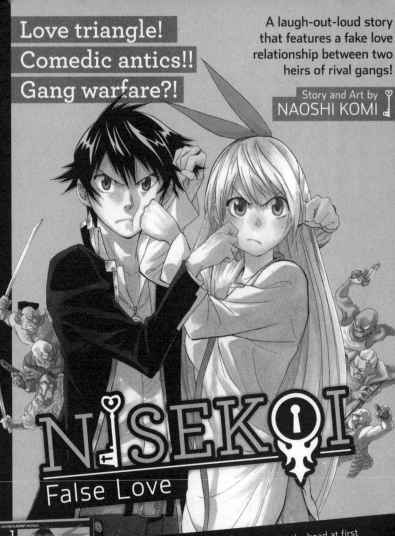
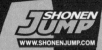

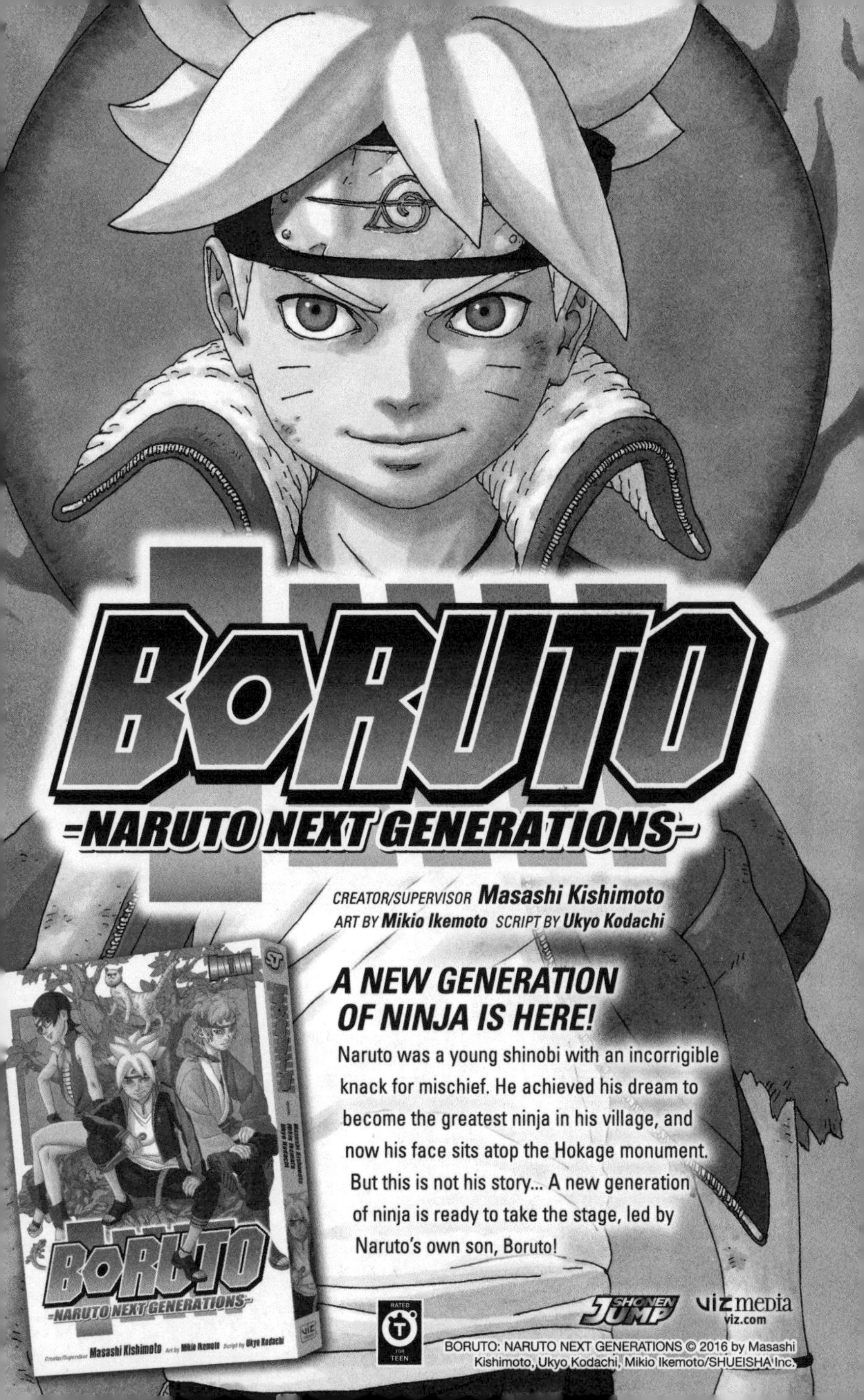
BORUTO
-NARUTO NEXT GENERATIONS-
CREATOR/SUPERVISOR Masashi Kishimoto
ART BY Mikio Ikemoto SCRIPT BY Ukyo Kodachi
A NEW GENERATION OF NINJA IS HERE!
Naruto was a young shinobi with an incorrigible knack for mischief. He achieved his dream to become the greatest ninja in his village, and now his face sits atop the Hokage monument. But this is not his story... A new generation of ninja is ready to take the stage, led by Naruto's own son, Boruto!
BORUTO
-NARUTO NEXT GENERATIONS-
Creator/Supervisor Masashi Kishimoto Art by Mikio Ikemoto Script by Ukyo Kodachi
RATED T FOR TEEN
SHONEN JUMP
VIZ media
viz.com
BORUTO: NARUTO NEXT GENERATIONS © 2016 by Masashi Kishimoto, Ukyo Kodachi, Mikio Ikemoto/SHUEISHA Inc.

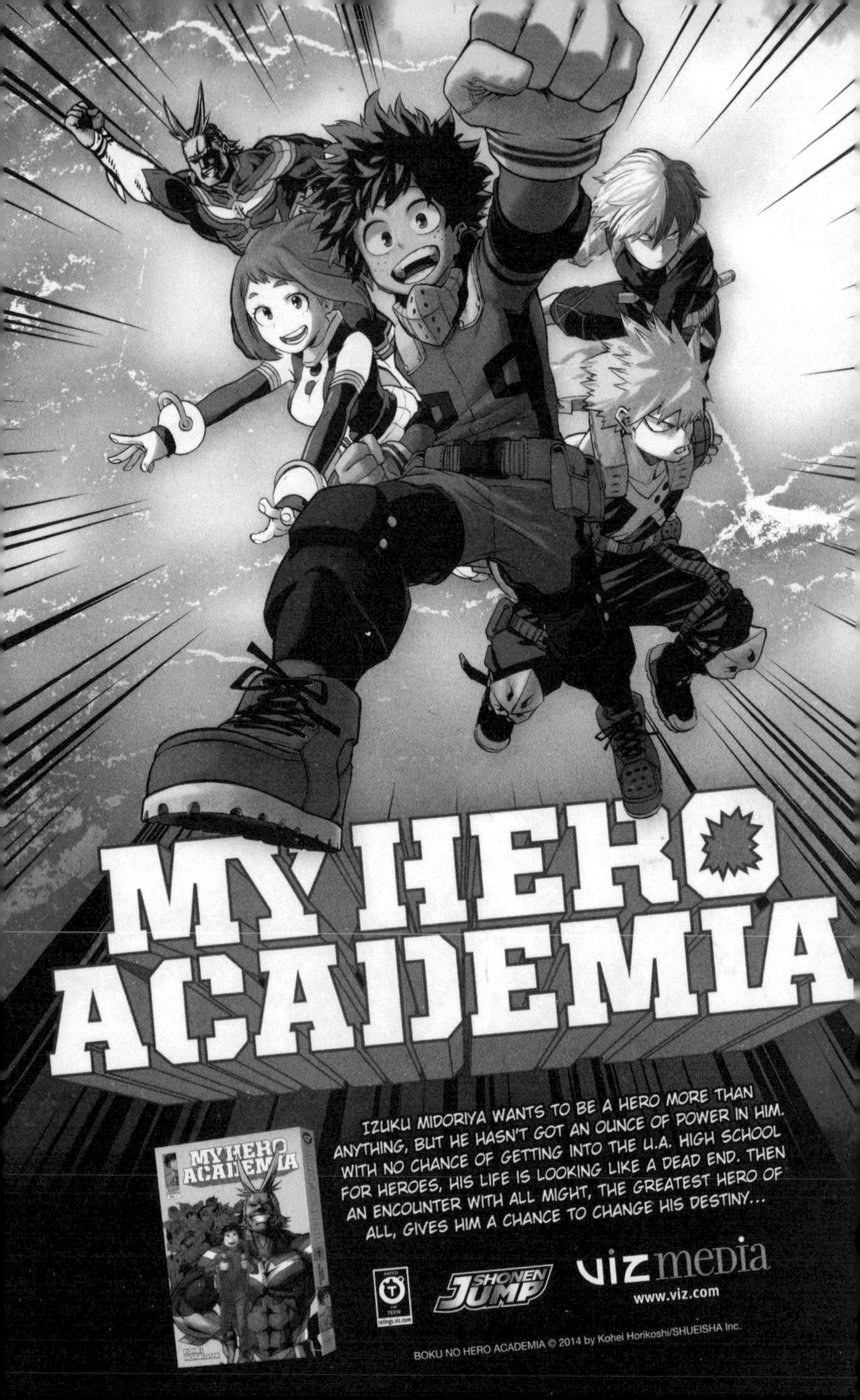
MY HERO ACADEMIA
IZUKU MIDORIYA WANTS TO BE A HERO MORE THAN ANYTHING, BUT HE HASN'T GOT AN OUNCE OF POWER IN HIM. WITH NO CHANCE OF GETTING INTO THE U.A. HIGH SCHOOL FOR HEROES, HIS LIFE IS LOOKING LIKE A DEAD END. THEN AN ENCOUNTER WITH ALL MIGHT, THE GREATEST HERO OF ALL, GIVES HIM A CHANCE TO CHANGE HIS DESTINY...
MY HERO ACADEMIA
Kohei Horikoshi
RATED T TEEN
ratings.viz.com
SHONEN JUMP
viz media
www.viz.com
BOKU NO HERO ACADEMIA © 2014 by Kohei Horikoshi/SHUEISHA Inc.

YOU'RE READING THE WRONG WAY!

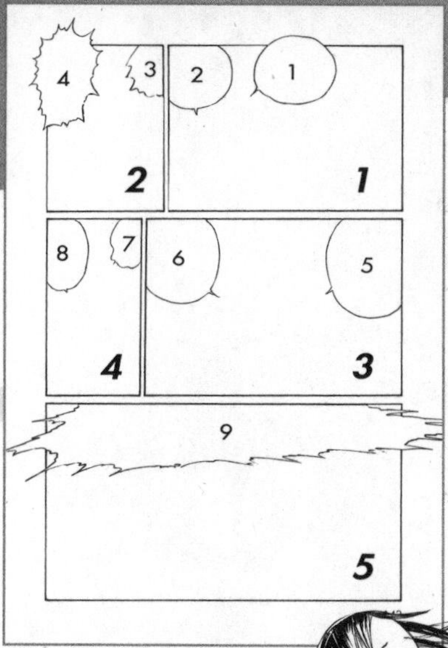
1
2
1
3
4
2
5
6
3
7
8
4
9
5

KAGUYA-SAMA: LOVE IS WAR reads from right to left, starting in the upper-right corner. Japanese is read from right to left, meaning that action, sound effects and word-balloon order are completely reversed from English order.

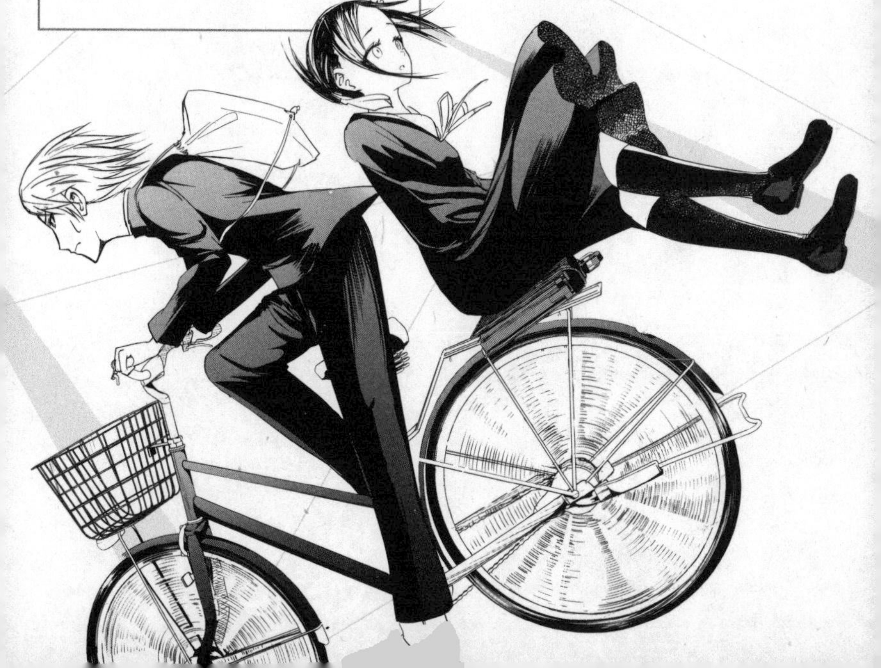

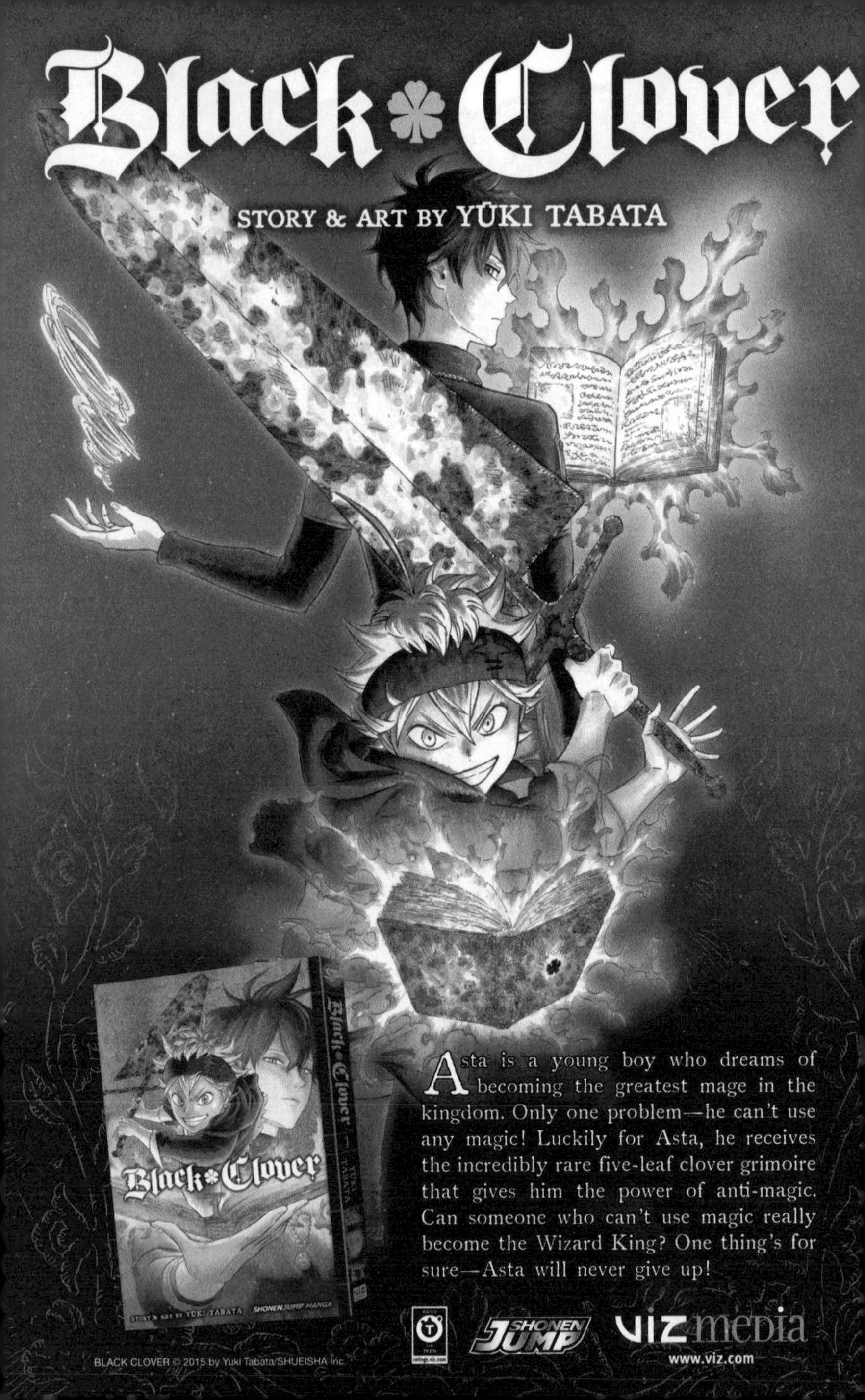
Black Clover
STORY & ART BY YŪKI TABATA
Asta is a young boy who dreams of becoming the greatest mage in the kingdom. Only one problem—he can't use any magic! Luckily for Asta, he receives the incredibly rare five-leaf clover grimoire that gives him the power of anti-magic. Can someone who can't use magic really become the Wizard King? One thing's for sure—Asta will never give up!
SHONEN JUMP
VIZ media
www.viz.com
BLACK CLOVER © 2015 by Yuki Tabata/SHUEISHA Inc.

DRAGON BALL SUPER

STORY BY **Akira Toriyama** ART BY **Toyotarou**

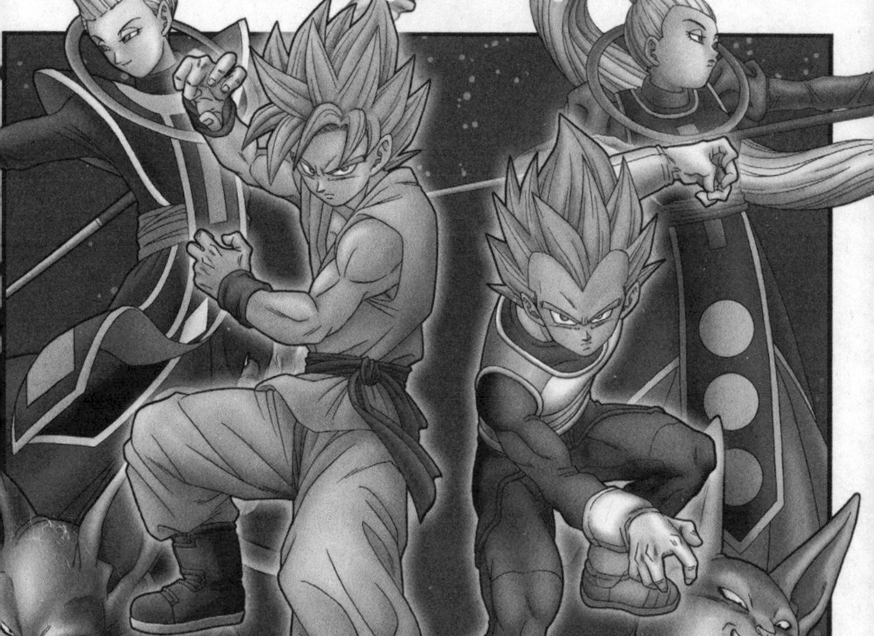

Goku's adventure from the best-selling classic manga *Dragon Ball* continues in this new series written by Akira Toriyama himself!

Ever since Goku became Earth's greatest hero and gathered the seven Dragon Balls to defeat the evil Boo, his life on Earth has grown a little dull. But new threats loom overhead, and Goku and his friends will have to defend the planet once again!

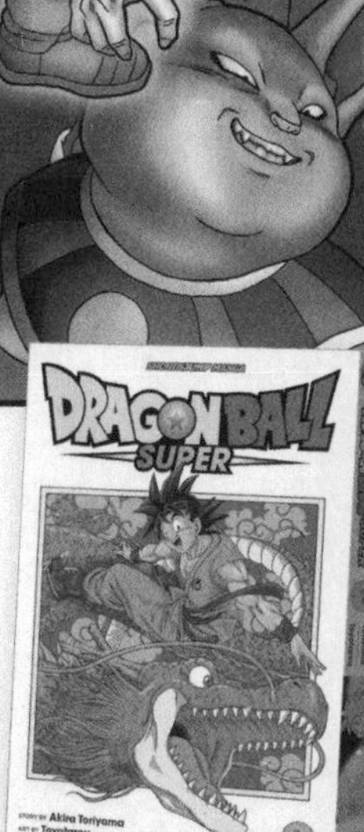
DRAGON BALL SUPER
STORY BY Akira Toriyama
ART BY Toyotarou
1

RATED T FOR TEEN

VIZ media

SHONEN JUMP

viz.com

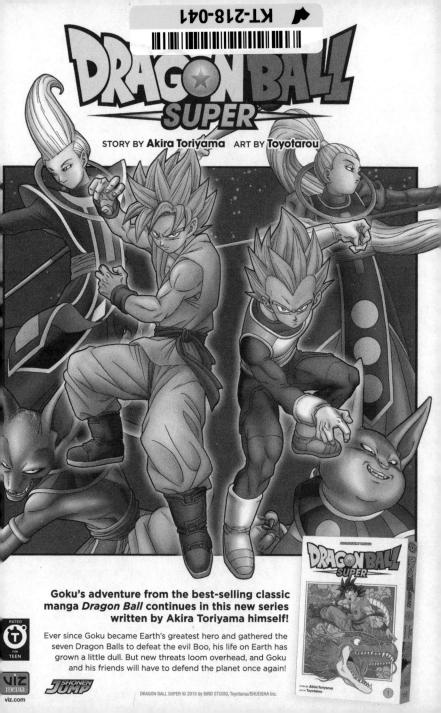